The Development of
ECONOMIC DOCTRINE
an Introductory
Survey

By the same Author

The Socialist Tradition
MOSES TO LENIN

THE DEVELOPMENT OF

Economic Doctrine

AN INTRODUCTORY
SURVEY

Sir Alexander Gray
C.B.E.

Second edition revised by
ALAN THOMPSON

London and
New York

LONGMAN GROUP LIMITED
London

*Associated companies, branches and representatives
throughout the world*

*Published in the United States of America
by Longman Inc., New York*

*First Edition 1931
Twenty-third Impression 1967
Second Edition 1980*

British Library Cataloguing in Publication Data

Gray, *Sir* Alexander
    The development of economic doctrine. – 2nd ed.
    1. Economics – History
    I. Title   II. Thompson, Alan, *b.1924*
    330.1   HB75   79–42623
    ISBN 0–582–44871–9

*Printed in Great Britain by
Richard Clay (The Chaucer Press) Ltd,
Bungay, Suffolk*

Contents

Preface

CUSTOM and convention very properly require that an author – at least of anything that looks like a text-book – should make suitable apologies for his action in accentuating the horrid and outrageous disproportion between supply and demand in the world of books, and that he should at the same time, for the benefit of reviewers and others, indicate what particular long-felt gap he imagines he is filling. The object of this book is a very modest one. The most important word in its title indicates that it is an introduction, and it is of the essence of an introduction that it should represent only a beginning of knowledge. In academic study, as in social life, an introduction is no more than the first stage in the departure from a state of complete ignorance, leaving much to be learned later, not without constant possibility of surprise.

This book is accordingly designed to be used by the beginner, along with any of the innumerable text-books on economics which may be selected for the purpose of study or instruction. My own experience is that exposition of current and accepted doctrine is always made more palatable if accompanied by a backward glance at the development of thought and opinion. If it be true that the teaching of economics requires almost constant reference to the tenets of the Mercantilists, of the Physiocrats, of Smith, Malthus, List and a great cloud of other witnesses, then even a first-year student might properly have in his hands, and by his bedside, a book containing what he wants to know with regard to the development of economic doctrine. This, with all respect to other books, is the gap which this volume is designed to fill.

For, in a sense, the available books on the history of economic doctrine are too full, too comprehensive – let us say, too good – for the ordinary student, however admirably they may serve the purpose of the student who is specializing. The beginner is merely confused if he is told something about everybody, or if it is impressed upon him that Ortes and Justi call for mention. Important as they may be, Ortes and Justi can very well afford to wait. On the other hand, when the interest of the beginner is engaged, he does want a fairly complete picture; and it is educationally better that he should have a fairly adequate idea of the landmarks, even if nothing be done to temper his dark ignorance elsewhere, than that he should have a diffused and confused knowledge of a wider field.

In this book, therefore – with my eyes on the beginner – I have endeavoured so far as practicable to mention no writer unless I could find space for something like an intelligible account of what he stood for. I have accordingly proceeded by a process of selection and concentration, ruthlessly casting overboard people of quite considerable importance. Thus in dealing with the Middle Ages, I have to all intents and purposes confined the discussion to St. Thomas Aquinas; so (apart from a slight reference to Turgot) I have placed on Quesnay the entire burden of the Physiocrats. In the later period I have likewise restricted myself to those writers whom beginners are most likely to come across.

Not always have I been ruthless without a heavy heart. McCulloch and the elder Mill I have indeed neglected with unruffled feelings. Even the German historical school has gone without causing me much misgiving; somehow the old controversy with regard to 'method' seems less important to-day than a generation ago, and, with this decline in significance, the leading figures in that controversy seem less insistently to require notice. But I should have liked to present Cantillon, who may yet come into his own when a promised reprint is more readily available; and patriotic motives made me hanker after John Law, who, as an economist, receives abroad a measure of respect withheld from him in his own country, where we tend to look upon him as a financial swashbuckler. So also I should have been glad to find a place for Cournot, the father of a long line of mathematical economists. But like other frail vessels, an introductory text-book also has a Plimsoll-line, and in deference to warnings regarding the dangers of foundering due to overloading, these and other precious bales have had to be left behind on the quay. As a consequence of this policy of rigorous exclusion in order to allow for fuller treatment of those included, I flatter myself that in no other book professing to be a history of economic doctrine are so many notable names entirely unmentioned.

There is evidence on all sides that the study of the development of economic doctrine is receiving to-day far more attention in English-speaking countries than was accorded to it by the last generation. I should like to think that this little book may encourage what I regard as a praiseworthy tendency, and that it may serve as a useful stepping stone to the more comprehensive works of Haney and of Gide and Rist.

ALEXANDER GRAY

MARISCHAL COLLEGE,
ABERDEEN,
March 1931

Author's Note to Second Impression

I take the opportunity of a reprint of this book to record three events relating to the literature of the subject. Firstly, Cantillon's *Essai sur la nature du commerce en général*, referred to in the preface above, has now been published for the Royal Economic Society by Macmillan and Co. Secondly, the work of Surányi-Unger is now available in an English translation: *Economics in the Twentieth Century* (Allen & Unwin). Thirdly, a large and detailed work on the history of economic doctrine, by H. W. C. Bordewijk, has appeared in Dutch under the title *Theoretisch-historische Inleiding tot de Economie*. It is largely devoted to the Mercantilists, the Physiocrats and the Classical School.

A.G.

April 1933

Introduction to Second Edition

'I n academic study, as in social life, an introduction is no more than the first stage in the departure from a state of complete ignorance, leaving much to be learned later.'

With these words, Sir Alexander Gray, with characteristic modesty, launched his introductory survey of the history of economic thought in 1931. In attempting to bring his book up to date, I have constantly borne in mind his objective of simplifying and summarizing economic ideas for the benefit of his student readers, while at the same time preserving as much as possible the style and the quality of thought of the economists with whom he deals. I have also followed his example by providing a brief background to the life and times of the famous economists with whom I have dealt.

Sir Alexander Gray (under whom I studied at Edinburgh University, and subsequently served as an academic colleague) was a much more erudite and analytical thinker than he liked to reveal. With his unmistakably Eastern Scottish accent (his grandfather had been a handloom weaver and a Chartist in the Angus village of Letham), his propensity for wearing a cloth cap, and a somewhat old-fashioned tweed greatcoat, for smoking an ancient bowl pipe, and for his skill at relating inimitable (and sometimes unrepeatable) Scottish dialect anecdotes in the Doric, Sir Alexander's image was firmly down-to-earth and feet-on-the-ground.

Yet behind this exterior lay decades of intense scholarship; a first-class honours degree in mathematics and subsequently in economics and periods of study at Göttingen and the Sorbonne. These achievements were followed by a distinguished career in the Civil Service, including service with Mr. Lloyd George before the First World War; a chair at Aberdeen, and subsequently at Edinburgh University, and membership or chairmanship of a number of important government committees and Royal Commissions. In addition to all this, he published a number of books of Scots poetry. Sir Alexander exemplified the Victorian belief that a man could be accomplished at a number of things without his distinction for one being called into question. The biographical background is helpful to an understanding of his book. A man who presumes to present students with a survey of economic ideas should have his own credentials examined. No economist is free from bias – whether it be social, methodological, philosophic, nationalistic or regional – and it is important that when students are being told of the bias of the great economists of the past, they should know something of the bias of the man who is telling the story.

Sir Alexander, then, was Scottish, Victorian, self-made, presbyterian in upbringing, elitist in his concept of scholarship and egalitarian in the mode of his life and social attitudes.

Gray fundamentally believed that political democracy could only prosper with the maintenance of considerable freedom in economic relationships (although he conceded the need to limit this freedom in certain circumstances by State action).

Although he preserves a commendable impartiality in his book on the relative significance of the economists with whom he deals, his lectures at Edinburgh University left students in no doubt as to who was his hero: it was Adam Smith. Smith and Gray would have enjoyed considerable *rapport*. Their regional backgrounds (East Scotland) as well as their philosophical leanings were almost identical: their cosmopolitanism (both had studied and travelled widely abroad) and dislike of totalitarian forms of government (also sharpened by their foreign travels) were passionately felt, and underlie all their writings. Neither felt any inconsistency between their internationalism (which found expression in support for *laissez-faire*) and their sense of belonging to a small, economically backward, but fiercely proud, nation – Scotland. This aspect of Gray is seen in sharp focus in his poetry (although it is always there in his economic writings) and I think he would have particularly appreciated an introduction to the history of economic thought which quoted from a volume of his poems:

' This is my country
 The land that begat me
 These windy spaces
 Are surely my own;
 And those who here toil
 In the sweat of their faces
 Are flesh of my flesh
 And bone of my bone... '[1]

Sir Alexander described himself consistently as a liberal; his political sympathies (as well as his commitments as a civil servant) were with the great social innovations of the Campbell-Bannerman (and, later, the Asquith) administrations of 1906 onwards, particularly in the field of new policies for employment exchanges, and industrial conciliation and arbitration.

His basic position, however (as revealed in his lectures and writings), always seemed to me closer to a conservative-liberal outlook. The conservative strand derived from Edmund Burke, with an emphasis on loyalty and romantic attachment to one's country allied to a responsible and

[1] 'Scotland ': *Oxford Book of Scottish Verse.*

humane approach to the under-privileged and the deprived.

The strongest strand in his liberal heritage was that of political and economic individualism. He inherited the eighteenth-century belief in spontaneity in human relationships. Spontaneity and beneficence are, in his view, intimately connected. In the eighteenth century everything spontaneous (as distinct from controlled by authority) in human activity was good and terms like 'natural', 'just', and 'advantageous' were often used as synonyms. Adam Smith had recognized that institutions, like individual citizens, had a part to play in the economy, but it was important that such institutions should be based on a spontaneous recognition of the need for them, and not be imposed without the consent of the governed. This was a view Gray shared and applied to a wide range of public economic activity. This approach has its negative aspects. Gray's chapter on Marx, although achieving a heroic simplification of the main Marxist propositions, reveals Gray's own ideological bias. In spite of the effective way in which Gray summarizes a highly difficult and complex writer, there is perhaps a lack of recognition of Marx's impact on the real world. Whatever the arguments about his technical inconsistencies (as Professor J. K. Galbraith has stated[2]) Karl Marx has had more influence on the world than anyone since Mahomet. I do know, however, from my own teaching experience, how valuable first-year economics students have found Gray's précis of Marxist doctrine, even if it has only served to stimulate them into further reading, in order to refute some of Gray's criticisms. I suspect that this was Gray's intention: the assumption of the role of *enfant terrible* was part of his pedagogic method and there is a hint of mischief and provocation in his treatment of Marx.

[2] *The Affluent Society*, p.50.

Perhaps, unconsciously, or even consciously, Gray was slip-
ping into Marx's own dialectic assumptions in order to
present a thesis to which an anti-thesis could respond.

In bringing Gray's book up-to-date, I have tried to bear in
mind his injunction that

'like other frail vessels, an introductory text-book also has
a Plimsoll-line, and ... other precious bales have had to be
left behind on the quay ...'

I have therefore continued his rigorous 'castaway' policy
towards many great names and restricted myself to four
new chapters and a new and considerably expanded bibliography. Alfred Marshall is the obvious bridge between
Gray's original chapters and my contribution to this book.
Marshall presents special difficulties in any history of economic thought. To begin with, he is perhaps under-valued and
taken for granted, because of his very achievements. Much
of the microeconomic analysis we teach today in the class-
room to first-year students is in direct descent from
Marshall, and the basic system of demand-and-supply
analysis has become an almost automatic tool for aspiring
economists. This fact blinds us to the patient dexterity and
creative originality with which Marshall originally forged
these tools. His innovatory achievements are also in danger
of being passed over because of the subsequent refinement of
his methods. The second reason is perhaps more important:
Marshall is basically eclectic. As we shall see in the chapter
on Marshall, his Victorian background and the whole tenor
of his scholarship led him to synthesize and to resolve contradictions whenever possible in pursuit of an economic
consensus.[3] This means that he does not enter the stage with
the drama and flourish of a Malthus, a Marx or a Keynes.

[3] For an interesting discussion on the possibilities of 'economic
consensus' at the present time – see Samuel Brittan, *Is there an
economic consensus?*

I suspect that Gray's omission of Marshall (apart from his argument that we should not write about our contemporaries in a history of economic thought) was based partly on the apparent lack of drama and fierce doctrinal argument in Marshall's work. Some of Gray's best passages are concerned with the astonishingly fervent battles fought between rival schools in previous ages: Adam Smith versus the Mercantilists; Malthus versus Godwin; and Marx versus almost all the rest. With Marshall comes a more patient and modest spirit of reconciliation, and his very success makes it harder to bring him to life in the way we can do with his predecessors. Yet Marshall's deep social and moral sensibilities, his superb use of language, his concern always with immaculate standards in scholarship all make him an excellent candidate for study in the hall of fame of past economists, and provide an example to modern students which some of his more flamboyant predecessors do not always provide.

In my chapter on neo-classical thought (chap. xv) I have had considerable difficulty in maintaining the Plimsoll-line and I am acutely aware of the precious bales which have had to be left behind. I can only hope that the bales which I have taken on board are representative and significant enough to compensate for the omissions.

In my final chapter, I have departed from one of Gray's criteria that a historian of thought should stop the day before yesterday, rather than attempt to deal with his contemporaries. My reason for this departure is a pedagogic one. I find that the issues raised by some recent writers have caught the imagination of many of my students, and form the basis of lively and continuous controversy, both inside and outside the classroom. I appreciate that the most recent writers have not yet passed the searching test of time to which the older economists have been subjected. Part of my reason, however, for including them is to enable their ideas to be tested and their reputations assessed against the background of scholarship and creative genius which has characterized the great economists included in this book.

I am grateful to a number of friends, colleagues and students who have encouraged my interest in the history of economic thought, and provided useful criticism. I would particularly like to mention Professor Sir Kenneth Alexander, Dr. T. L. Johnston, Dr. Gavin Kennedy, Professor Henry McKinlay, the late John Mackintosh, M.P., Professor Alan Peacock, and Mr. Thomas Taylor.

For useful material on Sir Alexander Gray's life and interests, I am indebted to his son, Mr. John Gray, and to Lord Balerno. Responsibility for errors and opinions lies, of course, solely with me.

ALAN THOMPSON

October 1979

' Political economy is perhaps the only science of which it may be said that the ignorance of it is not merely a deprivation of good, but produces great positive evil.'   REV. T. R. MALTHUS

' Political economy is . . . a science at the same time dangerous and leading to occasions of sin.'
CARDINAL NEWMAN

' Marshall was too anxious to do good.'
J. M. KEYNES

CHAPTER I

Greece and Rome

HOWEVER recent in the history of human thought may be the development of a systematic body of economic doctrine, reflection, and to a certain extent speculation, on economic phenomena must be as old as human thought itself. For if we accept the most notable of recent definitions of economic science, which in its popular and abridged version tells us that economics is the study of mankind in the ordinary business of life, it is obvious that stray reflections falling within the almighty sweep of such a department of knowledge must have passed through the mind of man ever since he was capable of reflection at all.

The industrious gleaner may therefore collect from the oldest literature chance observations and stray remarks which the enthusiast may hail as containing in embryo a doctrine of Adam Smith or the kernel of the philisophy of the Physiocrats. Moreover – apart from the *obiter dicta* of poets and philosophers – all customs, institutions and laws must contain implicitly a certain measure of economic theory, even if it be never expressly propounded. An Act which forbids usury involves a denial of the legitimacy of interest, and inferentially an affirmation of the barrenness of money; customs with regard to inheritance (or its absence) imply views with regard to private property. The Code of Hammurabi, in fixing the price of the hire of boats and goats, and the wages of tailors, stone-cutters and other artisans, implied some sort of view with regard to the just price and the standard wage; the Mosaic Law, with its elaborate provision to secure all against poverty, represents, on the economic side, an extreme example of a State founded on a Poor Law.

Two conclusions follow from this. In the first place, economic doctrine, whether it be held in solution in the laws, customs, and practices of a society, or whether it be precipitated as a more or less muddy deposit in the works of the theorist, reflects the condition of the society to which it relates. In a sense, therefore, a study of comparative politics, meaning thereby an analysis of the changing structure of society, is a presupposition of a correct understanding of the development of economic doctrine. No less important is economic history as that term is generally understood. It is no accident that Malthus wrote on population at a time when population was rapidly increasing, or that Ricardo explored the intricacies of currency problems when the currency system was disorganized. In short, Political Economy throughout has been in large measure an attempt to explain, within the existing framework and assumptions of society, how and on what theory contemporary society is operating.

The second conclusion is perhaps at first sight somewhat pessimistic. It is that any body of economic doctrine can have only limited validity. The " economic laws " proper to a society resting on tradition, status and caste may be very different from those applicable to a modern industrial competitive society. The theoretical economist might arrive at different conclusions according as chance may have assigned him to a mediaeval society with the implications of feudalism and the manorial system; to the Greek city state, where the flower of culture was rooted in slave labour, or to the State of the Incas, based on the tyranny and the orderliness of the bee-hive. Economic science, therefore, if it be a science, differs from other sciences in this, that there is no inevitable advance from less to greater certainty; there is no ruthless tracking down of truth which, once unbared, shall be truth to all times to the complete confusion of any contrary doctrine. No absurdity in the history of economic doctrine was, in its time, quite so absurd as it now appears to our complacent eyes. Moreover it is very seldom, if ever, possible to write off a heresy as having been for all time irremediably discarded, demolished and exploded. Old doctrines never die; they only fade away, with a strange power of recuperation in an appropriate environment. The dominant opinion of any age, even if it has a flavour peculiarly its own, is, on analysis, a fricassée of the thoughts of all the ages, and the latest exponent of orthodox and accepted doctrine may to a later generation appear to have added at most one further ingredient or one choice condiment before passing it on.

Greece

It is in the Greek writers that theorizing on economic matters, even if it may scarcely be termed economic theory, first explicitly emerges. But the ancient world, even as represented by Athens, was in many ways but a poor soil for any kind of economic speculation; and consequently, unless to those who are fanatically determined to find everything in antiquity, adumbration of economic theory among the Greeks will rather appear in the form of incidental observations, thrown off in the pursuit of a more worthy end. Two general considerations, which in fact involve a multiplicity of other influences, explain the relatively meagre attainments in such matters even of Greece, contrasted with her lustre in all other fields of speculation and intellectual enterprise. In the first place, the ancient State was in general a strangely comprehensive institution. The man and the citizen were identified. Religion was a part of the machinery and the mystery of the State. Ethics and politics were thus inextricably intermingled. If the subject matter of economics could not be entirely eliminated or ignored, it was viewed merely as part of the general domain of ethical inquiry, as indeed happened more than two thousand years later, when Professor Adam Smith experimented with 'The Wealth of Nations' on the Moral Philosophy Class in Glasgow. But the complete emancipation which Adam Smith conferred on economics could not be attained in Greece. Economics was not merely the attendant and the handmaiden of Ethics (as perhaps she should always be); she was crushed and blotted out by her more prosperous and pampered sister, and later excavators, in search of the origins of economic theory, can only dig out disconnected fragments and mangled remains.

The second reason for the absence of any connected system of economic theory goes even deeper. The ancient world, viewed as a whole, rested on a system of caste, and even Athens was not free from the hampering effects of such an inheritance. The city state was founded on slavery, and inevitably where a slave class exists, the work assigned to a slave falls into disrepute and becomes dishonourable. Throughout antiquity, and as markedly in Greece as any-where, the work of the craftsman was regarded as incompat-ible with a 'life of virtue.' To the Greek mind nearly all the activities of modern society would have appeared unworthy and debasing. When slaves are at hand to do the work, work becomes the mark of the slave. Agriculture almost alone, for a variety of reasons, escaped the contempt and the censure of Greek and Roman writers, and consequently classical writers made further progress in the exposition of agri-cultural economics than elsewhere. If the 'ordinary business of life' was thus despised, it is hardly reasonable to expect that its study should be regarded as a subject worthy of sustained and independent investigation.

So far as economic theory is concerned, it is in Plato that

Greek thought advances beyond the level of such wise saws as may be extracted from Hesiod and others, and arrives at some consecutiveness. Yet Plato is the supreme example of the classical tendency to regard economics as a minor sub-section of ethics and politics. It is above all in *The Republic*, and to a lesser extent in *The Laws*, where he indulges in 'an old man's game,' that Plato turns to economic questions. The former is primarily a discussion on Justice, and it is because the essential nature of Justice may perhaps be most easily discerned in the State – since for the short-sighted the larger letters may be more easily read – that the disputants turn aside in the second book to discuss the State and its origin, and are thus led to construct from the foundation an ideal polity. It is noticeable that the origin of the State is attributed wholly to economic considerations: 'A state arises out of the needs of mankind; no one is self-sufficing, but all of us have many wants,'[1] and moreover, Plato indicates that no other origin of a state can be imagined. This line of argument, after a consideration of the essential needs of mankind, leads to Plato's discussion of division of labour, which has so often been compared with the famous chapter in Adam Smith. The essential needs of mankind are food, dwelling and clothing, so that the barest notion of a state must include four or five men – a husband-man, a builder, a weaver, and perhaps a shoemaker or a representative of some other similar occupation. Each of these is, moreover, to confine himself to his own calling. The governing considerations in the application of the principle of division of labour, as conceived by Plato, are then, firstly, that there are 'diversities of natures among us which are adapted to different occupations,' and secondly, and as a consequence of this, that 'all things are produced more plentifully and easily, and of a better quality, when one man

[1] *The Republic*, Jowett's translation, p.49.

does one thing which is natural to him and does it at the right time, and leaves other things.' It is in order that this principle may be satisfied that Plato then extends his State to include a considerable diversity of other crafts – sailors, traders, retailers and others.

It is interesting to compare this passage with the corresponding section in Adam Smith, and to note how different is Plato's method of approach to this fundamental problem. The starting point here is ethical: there are diversities of natures among men, and each should do what is natural to him. Up to a certain point this may be a valid explanation of division into trades; under modern conditions, with such specialization as is presented in any large-scale system of production, it is, of course, absurd to speak of anyone's work as being 'natural' to him, or as satisfying diversity of nature. Adam Smith's explanation of division of labour begins with an absurdity which he expands into something more tenable and comprehensible. Division of labour, he says, is due to the human propensity to truck, barter and exchange one thing for another, as though men, like overgrown schoolboys, did different things for the sheer joy of subsequent 'swopping.' But the following paragraph puts a different complexion on what, at the first blush, is a rather quaint theory. Man, says Smith, in words reminiscent of Plato, has almost constant occasion for the help of his brethren; but – unplatonically – it is vain for him to expect it from their benevolence only. Division of labour is therefore, for Smith, the effective means of driving a good bargain; it is a device whereby we can count on our dinner from the butcher, relying not on his benevolence, but on his regard for his own interest.

The contrast between Plato and Adam Smith on this point is striking. In Plato, division of labour is the basis of the social organization; the city is built up on division of labour, so that it almost reads as if there could be no State where every member of a community satisfied all his own needs. In Smith it is a device for the ultimate advantage of those who practise it, operating through an increase in their bargaining power. Also, although it is not explicit in Plato, there is in *The Republic* a curious reversal of Smith's famous dictum that division of labour is limited by the extent of the market. In *The Republic* the extent of the market is imposed by the necessity of adopting division of labour. The city must be large enough to enable each to do what is natural to him. In other words, division of labour in Smith leads to diversity of occupation as its final result; in Plato it springs from diversity of endowment as its first impulse.

The point on which appeal has often been made to Plato relates to his advocacy of communism in the ideal state. To appreciate the peculiar features of Plato's communism it is necessary to consider (*a*) the scope, and (*b*) the object of these communistic institutions. These will best emerge by tracing the course of Plato's argument, leading up to the memorable passage at the close of the third book in which the principle of communism is enunciated. We have seen the city swell out to allow for the application of the principle of division of labour, so as to include merchantmen, importers and exporters, the organization of a market with a system of currency, retailers and hirelings. At this point there is a pause in the argument; we have arrived at the State matured and perfected, and a dithyrambic hymn of praise is placed in the mouth of Socrates, descriptive of the simple life which the citizens will lead therein. It is only when Glaucon objects that this is but a 'city of pigs,' devoid of the ordinary conveniences of life, that the argument acquires a new lease of life. What is now to be considered is the 'luxurious state,' and though the subsequent discussion is ordinarily accepted as a description of the ideal state, Socrates explicitly says that 'in my opinion the true and healthy constitution of the State is the one which I have described,' that is to say, Glaucon's city of pigs. What is next to be discussed is, according to Socrates, a 'state at fever-heat,' and the first result of Glaucon's desire for 'the ordinary conveniences of life' is a vast extension of the activities of the community by the addition of actors, dancers, barbers, confectioners, cooks *et hoc genus omne* – and rather satirically, more doctors. More relevant to the main line of argument is the contention that the State will now require a slice of the territory of its neighbours, who in return will be similarly covetous, since in the conditions supposed men will have exceeded the 'limit of necessity,' and have given themselves up to the 'unlimited accumulation of wealth.' This in turn leads to a further extension of the population, this time embracing a whole army.

Thus we arrive at the guardians, who practise an art which is not to be combined with any other occupation, since one man cannot practise many arts with success. The guardians require careful selection; likewise very careful education. They must combine apparently contradictory qualities, inasmuch as they must be dangerous to their enemies and gentle to their friends. We are not here concerned with the lengthy discussion of the education of the guardians, nor with the subsequent distinction between 'guardians in the fullest sense' (the real rulers) and the auxiliaries, but the words in which communism is enacted are of importance in specifying both the scope and the purpose of the communism prescribed. The guardians are to look round for a spot where they can best suppress insurrections within and defend the State from enemies without, and they are to encamp there. Further, in order to ward off the danger that they may become enemies instead of friends of the citizens, their whole mode of life is to be such that they will not be tempted to prey upon the other citizens. Consequently they are devoted to an ascetic method of life; they are to have no property beyond what is necessary; they are to receive a fixed rate of pay, sufficient to meet expenses and no more: 'Should they ever acquire homes or lands or moneys of their own, they will become housekeepers and husbandmen instead of guardians, enemies and tyrants instead of allies of the other citizens.'[2]

Firstly, as to the scope of Plato's communism, it is clear from the whole argument that it is prescribed only for the limited class of the guardians, who are indeed throughout to live a semi-military life. It is, in fact, the communism of the camp. The contrary view has been argued along lines which need not here be indicated, and one authority has contended that 'a superficial reading of *The Republic* gives the impression . . . that Plato recommends communism solely for these upper sections.'[3] It is almost sufficient to note that Aristotle himself is one of these superficial readers; it is entirely sufficient that Plato expressly describes the regulations as 'appointed by us for the guardians,' and even more conclusive is his statement that if the guardians depart from their communistic life, they will become housekeepers and husbandmen.

Then secondly, as to the purpose of the guardians' communism, it is noticeable that Plato in his motives is poles asunder from other communistic dreamers. Elsewhere the cry for communism arises from an aggrieved sense of the injustice and monstrous inequality of the world. It is not so in Plato. For his guardians, communism is an act of ascetic renunciation; it is the condition on which alone they can efficiently discharge their duties. The work they have to do is so important that they may only do it properly on condi-

[2] *Ibid.*, Book III, p.106.
[3] Beer, *Social Struggles in Antiquity*, p.97.

tion that they remain free of the snares and the entanglements of this world. In its motive therefore it is akin to the
celibacy of the Roman Catholic priesthood. The object of
Plato's communism is in no way to establish a right to equal
enjoyment; rather it is a part of the price that must be paid
by a class on whom special responsibilities have been imposed. An interesting, if trivial sidelight, illustrative of the
fact that the whole arrangements with regard to the guardians are designed to free them from the ordinary troubles
of life, is furnished by the provision that when a woman
guardian has a child, the process of suckling shall not be
protracted too long; 'the mothers will have no getting up at
night or other trouble, but will hand over all this sort of
thing to the nurses and attendants.'[4]

A slight glance at *The Laws*, as supplementing the teaching of *The Republic*, is almost essential. *The Laws* is the
work of an old man whose fire is spent, and some have
found in it the marks of the disillusionment of age. Yet here
Plato still clings to the old ideal: 'The first and highest
form of the State and of the Government and of the Law is
that in which there prevails most widely the ancient saying
that "Friends have all things in common." '[5] But that is
rather a State for gods and the sons of gods, and therefore he
now outlines the State which 'when created, will be nearest
to immortality and the only one which takes the second
place.' Such a state comprises 5,040 lots, since the city must
not be too large and the citizens should be known to each
other, and this figure is administratively convenient, as it is
divisible by all numbers up to ten. There is no longer any
question of communism, since 'community of goods goes
beyond their proposed origin, and nurture, and education.'
The regulations throughout are to aim at a middle and

---

[4] *The Republic*, Jowett's translation, p.154.
[5] *The Laws*, Jowett's translation, p.121.

contented condition of life, based on the doctrine that
poverty is to be regarded as the increase of a man's desires
and not the diminution of his property. No one is to possess
gold or silver except as coin for daily use, and the currency
of the country is to be peculiar to it and not acceptable
abroad. Inequality of condition cannot be avoided; but
undue disparity, arising from extreme poverty or excessive
wealth, is to be guarded against. For this purpose the population is to be divided into four classes, the limit of poverty
being one lot which is to be guarded unimpaired, while the
maximum possession is to be equivalent of four lots, the
surplus to be surrendered to the State.[6] No money is to be
lent at interest, and, more startling, there is to be no obligation to repay even the capital, a provision explicable on the
ground that this is to be a society of half-brothers, if not of
brothers, and that there is a definite restriction imposed on
the amount of permissible wealth.[7]

Certain of the old restrictions remain. No citizen is to be
occupied in handicraft arts; for citizenship is an 'art which
requires much study and many kinds of knowledge, and
does not admit of being made a secondary occupation.' No
one is to follow two crafts, and for the purposes of this regulation citizenship is to be regarded as a craft, and the study
of virtue as a full-time occupation.

Among other points it is perhaps worthy of mention that
the second best State is to enjoy free trade and complete
immunity from import and export duties, subject only to
the importation of unnecessary luxuries and the exportation
of what is wanted in the country being prohibited.[8] Retail
trade is forbidden, and there is also a curious desire to
preserve the virtues and the purity of the city by removing
it to a safe distance from the sea, for 'the sea is pleasant
enough as a daily companion, but has indeed also a bitter

[6] *Ibid.*, p.127.   [7] *Ibid.*, p.124.   [8] *Ibid.*, p.230.

and brackish quality; filling the streets with merchants and shopkeepers, and begetting in the souls of men uncertain and unfaithful ways.'[9] But into the rather wearisome details of the State contemplated in *The Laws*, it is unnecessary here to enter.

When we turn to Aristotle, we are confronted with a writer who, by his analytical frame of mind, went further than any other thinker in antiquity in the direction of detaching a separate science of economics. This is not the place to consider his political theories, but his starting point that man is by nature a political animal enthroned for him the science of politics, so that ethics and economics alike were viewed by him from a political angle. Two points are of peculiar interest to the economist. The first is his destructive criticism of Plato's communism in the second book of the *Politics*, and the other is his analysis of the household, leading to a discussion of the economic bases of society. On the former point, with the arguments of all the ages ringing in our ears, Aristotle's contentions may appear hackneyed. What he says about the snares inherent in community of wives need not detain us; it never has been, and is not now (it may be hoped) an urgent question. But his arguments on the general question of community of property might date from the present year of grace. It is still true that 'people pay most attention to their own private property and less to that in which they have but a part interest'[10] – as witness the carved hieroglyphics on the seats in any public park contrasted with the reverence paid to the domestic chester-field.

Aristotle's arguments, in the main, are of a highly practical character; in short, that a system of communism would not work, and that it violates natural human instincts. There

---

[9] *Ibid.*, p.87.
[10] *Politics*, Book II, chap. 3, Welldon's translation, p.43.

would be disputes between those who get less and work more, and those who get much and work little[11] – the old difficulty of distribution among frail, grudging and suspicious men. Unity built on communism is in fact a delusion; the common purse leads to quarrels arising out of trivial causes. Moreover there is an immense advantage in the sense of private property. It corresponds to natural instincts; 'the love each individual bears to himself is not purposeless,' as he remarks in a phrase in which we seem to catch the tones of Adam Smith's invisible hand. Again, in an argument which is still common, though of doubtful cogency, he urges that community of property would destroy the virtue of liberality. His own position is not, however, merely negative. As against reformers in a hurry in all ages, he contends that the evils are due, not to the institution which it is proposed to destroy (in this case private property), but to defects in human nature. Unless that is first amended, he would seem to say, there will be no advantage in abolishing something which in itself may be used for good or evil. 'The existing system, if embellished by the moral tone of those who live under it and by a code of wise laws, would be far superior.'[12] The ideal which Aristotle outlines is thus that of private possession with use in common, so far as that may be practicable – in modern language, private property mellowed by a sense of the responsibility of wealth, a position not so different from that of the Christian Socialists.

Apart from the dispute regarding communism, the main part of Aristotle's economic teaching is to be found in the first book of the *Politics*. The place which this discussion occupies in his general treatment flows from his general theory of the State. The State has in all cases a natural existence; it is the complete development of the earlier

[11] *Ibid.*, Book II, chap. 5, p.48.
[12] *Ibid.*, Book II, chap. 5, p.49.

associations, the household and the village, and Aristotle accordingly proceeds to consider, as the logical first step, the economy of the household. Here there are three fundamental relationships to be borne in mind, that of master and slave, of husband and wife, and of parent and children. The fourth and last of the parts of Domestic Economy is the art of finance, which is not to be confused with Domestic Economy, since it is the business of finance to provide and of Domestic Economy to use that which is provided.[13]

Under the section which deals with the relationship of master and slave[14] occurs Aristotle's celebrated defence of slavery, which sounds so oddly in modern ears. The principle of rule and subjection is, he says, inevitable and beneficial, and there are ' natural slaves,' persons who are as far inferior to others as the body is to the soul, or a beast to a man. In these cases a life of slavish subjection is advantageous. Aristotle is not blind to the obvious objection that, as he puts it, it may happen ' contrary to the intention of Nature that those who possess the bodies do not possess the souls of free men and vice versa ':[15] for even if there be those who are ' slaves by nature,' it calls for supreme faith to believe that the accidents of life should at any time sort out the slaves and the non-slaves, in accordance with the definition of a ' natural slave.' Hence he distinguishes between natural and legal slaves, and speaks of the law being a convention according to which all conquests in war are the property of the conqueror. The whole discussion is curious and unconvincing, and is perhaps best viewed as a reflection of the fact, not merely that many slaves were well-treated, but also that their position would have been worse but for the institution of slavery.

[13] *Ibid.*, Book I, chaps. 3 and 8.
[14] *Ibid.*, Book I, chaps. 5 and 6.
[15] *Ibid.*, Book I, chap. 6, Welldon, p.13

Coming to the question of acquisition or wealth-getting,[16] Aristotle is concerned to show how far it is or is not a part of Domestic Economy. Clearly part of wealth-getting must belong to Domestic Economy, since the household requires to be supplied with what is necessary, if this is not already provided. This leads to the rather curious distinction between true or genuine wealth to which there is a limit, and another unnatural kind of acquisition (finance in the bad sense) to which there is no limit. Nature supplies men with the means of subsistence which are gathered in various ways, so that men's lives may be classified as those of the nomad, the husbandman, the brigand, the fisherman and the hunter. Property which so arises is 'assigned by Nature,' and such property and such alone constitutes genuine wealth. Apart from the odd appearance of the brigand in this galley, this is merely, in the main, an anticipation of Physiocratic thought. Here also, so far as concerns real wealth, that is to say the acquisition of the means of subsistence, there is a definite limit assigned, since wealth in this sense must be limited by the needs and the purpose of the household and the State.

As against this, there is another kind of finance,[17] which does not have a natural existence and which is ultimately based on the distinction, familiar long afterwards as that between value in use and value in exchange. Every object has two uses; the shoe has a use as a covering for the feet; it has also a use as an article of exchange. So long as we are in the region of primitive barter, we are still concerned with what is natural, but this has ceased when we come to retail trading, where exchange is 'carried beyond the point of satisfying mere requirements.' Out of mere simple barter to satisfy a

[16] *Ibid.*, Book I, chap. 8.
[17] *Ibid.*, Book I, chap. 9.

real need, the evil art of finance – retail trading – develops as a natural consequence after the introduction of a system of currency, the successive stages of which are noted with a fair approximation to the discussion in Jevon's textbook. Finance, in the natural sense, is a part of Domestic Economy. Unnatural finance is not; it produces money merely by means of exchange, and here wealth is unlimited. The one, the healthy, might be described as the acquisition of the means of living, the securing of the 'pre-requisites which Nature ought to provide'; the other is merely money-making. The one is laudable; the other enriches one party at the expense of the other. But of all evil forms of finance, the worst is usury, since here money produces the gain itself, and is diverted from the purpose for which it was devised.

In his final classification, apart from the healthy kind of finance which belongs to Domestic Economy and comprises primarily such things as stock-farming, husbandry and bee-keeping, and the unnatural which belongs to trade and comprises commerce, usury and hired labour, Aristotle allows for a third kind of finance which is intermediate and comprises something common to each of the others. This class is concerned with the products of the earth which, however, 'do not yield fruit,' such as wood-cutting and mining – those industries, indeed, which we should now describe as extractive.

Apart from the *Politics*, there is also a passage in the *Nicomachæan Ethics* (Book V, chaps. 7 and 8) which is of some economic interest. Aristotle is there concerned with justice in private dealings. Discarding the mathematical theory of proportion in which his doctrine is embedded, the central point of his teaching is that 'when people get as the result of exchange exactly what they had at the beginning, neither more nor less, they are said to have what belongs to them and to be neither losers nor gainers.'[18] How is this principle to be carried out? That things may be exchanged, they must in some sense be comparable, and hence money is invented. It measures all things, and consequently, in the case taken, that of a cobbler and a builder, it measures the number of shoes which are equivalent to a house. 'As a builder then is to a cobbler, so must so many shoes be to a house or a meal.' It is the demand for mutual services which binds society together, and money is the recognized representative of this demand. Money, Aristotle says in this passage, has not a natural but a conventional ($\nu\acute{o}\mu\varphi$) existence, and for this reason it is called money ($\nu\acute{o}\mu\iota\sigma\mu\alpha$):[19] it is within our power to change it and make it useless, a doctrine which would seem to possess kinship with Knapp's theory that money is a creature of the law. Money, he adds, is serviceable for future exchanges; it is a guarantee that if we do not desire a thing now, we shall be able to get it when we do want it. Though the value of money is not always the same, it tends to have a more constant value than anything else. Aristotle was obviously not unfamiliar with certain orthodox views regarding the nature and the functions of money.

One last point worthy of passing mention is that Aristotle's attitude towards 'mechanics' and their share in the State is in line with that of most writers in antiquity. It is summed up in the general statement that all who are indispensable to the existence of the State cannot be regarded as citizens, and that in the best State (whatever may happen elsewhere) citizenship will not be conferred upon any mechanic.[20] There is here a striking similarity to the passage in the Book of Ecclesiasticus in praise of artificers: 'Without these

[18] *Ethics*, Book v, chap. 5, Welldon's translation, p.149.
[19] *Ibid.*, p.153.
[20] *Politics*, Book iii, chap. 5, Welldon, p.113.

cannot a city be inhabited'; yet 'they shall not be sought for in publick counsel.'[21]

Inasmuch as Aristotle comes nearest to a consistent body of doctrine it may be convenient to summarize how far he had reached. The starting point of his discussion regarding the relation of finance to Domestic Economy rests to a certain extent on a Physiocratic view of the superior place of Nature in the production of true wealth, wealth having here a somewhat ethical significance and being related to the satisfaction of needs actually felt. His condemnation of unnatural finance, or mere accumulation, is based on an acute analysis of the distinction between value-in-use and value-in-exchange. He analyses, in the main with justice, the development and the functions of money, and is commendably clear as to the distinction between money and wealth, though on the other hand money remains for him exclusively a medium of exchange, and it is to his adherence to this view that his condemnation of usury must be attributed. So, in the same way, the nature of capital escapes him; exchange in itself is barren, being ultimately and ideally merely an interchange of equivalents. Some of his observations on the unnatural kind of finance, viewed as the manifestation of an impulse to accumulation, are not without a certain suggestiveness of Marxian criticisms of the hunger

[21] Ecclesiasticus xxxviii. v. 32, 33. The corresponding passage on the same subject in Xenophon (*Œconomicus* IV, 2, 3) is interesting, inasmuch as the writer assigns reasons for the contempt of the illiberal arts: ' They utterly ruin the bodies of workers and managers alike, compelling men, as they do, to lead sedentary lives and huddle indoors, or in some cases to spend the day before a fire. Then as men's bodies become enervated, so their souls grow sicklier. And these vulgar crafts involve complete absence of leisure and hinder men from social and civic life; consequently men such as these are bad friends and indifferent defenders of their country. Moreover, in some states, particularly in those accounted warlike, no full citizen is permitted to practise the vulgar arts.' (As translated in Laistner's *Greek Economics*, pp.39, 40. See also Loeb edition, p.391.)

of capital for surplus value. On the subject of value itself, Aristotle definitely ranges himself with those who seek a subjective explanation. It is in the demand for mutual services that value is rooted, and it is this principle of demand which binds society together. Such, summarily, are the main features of the Aristotelian approach to a body of economic doctrine.

The third Greek writer to contribute certain embryonic elements to an economic science is Xenophon, who approaches matters throughout in an entirely practical spirit. His achievement is perhaps greater than has generally been admitted, and even where his speculation is confused, it may at least be pleaded on his behalf that the man who gives a wrong answer to a question has at least made some progress, insofar as he realizes that a question exists. The pleasantly innocuous dialogue *Œconomicus*, devoted to a discussion of the principles of estate management, opens with an analysis of wealth in the manner of Ruskin. Wealth is only wealth to him who can use it, or, more epigrammatically, useful things are those things which one knows how to use; so also, even money is not wealth to him who does not know how to use it.[22] Further, wealth is to be interpreted in relation to needs: the man of simple tastes and little substance is wealthy in comparison with the man of great possessions on whom excessive claims rest. All this is the stuff of which proverbial philosophy and the home-spun poetry of contentment are woven. Primarily, Xenophon is an agricultural writer, and it is of interest to note that he furnishes the motto to Quesnay and the Physiocratic school many centuries later: 'When husbandry flourishes, all the other arts are in good fettle; but whenever the land is compelled to lie waste, the other arts of landsmen and mariners alike wellnigh perish.'[23] His praise of agriculture is indeed

[22] Loeb translation, pp.367, 409.   [23] *Ibid.*, p.405.

of Physiocratic excess. It is the easiest of all things to learn; none gives quicker returns (to a careful man); it is the giver of all things; no art is 'dearer to servants, or pleasanter to a wife, or more delightful to children, or more agreeable to friends.'[24] Moreover, on Xenophon has been fathered an approach to the familiar agents of production, two – land and labour – being recognized; for though agriculture or the land supplies good things in abundance, 'she suffers them not to be won without toil.'[25] So also in a fumbling way he approaches, or seems to approach, the Law of Diminishing Returns: 'the landowners could all tell you how many teams and how many labourers are required for their estates. If anyone employs hands in excess of requirements, it is reckoned as a loss.'[26]

It is, however, in the short essay on *The Ways and Means to Increase the Revenues of Athens*[27] that Xenophon is most interesting, most enlightened and perhaps also most confused. Here he is concerned with finding a 'remedy for the poverty of our citizens,' and the tract therefore resolves itself into an elementary discussion of public finance. Throughout, a more liberal view than customary is manifested. The foreign residents are seen as a source of revenue, and Xenophon argues for the abolition of all regulations that inflict disabilities on this class. He is indeed anxious to attract 'more and better class foreigners to settle at Athens,' and in pursuance of this policy he would show favour to merchants – by free seats at festivals and invitations to banquets. No less significant is his suggestion to raise a capital sum to provide accommodation for merchants and shops and houses for retail dealers. Equally enlightened is his contention that it is the cities which have been longest at

[24] *Ibid.*, p.517.
[25] *Ibid.*, p.401.
[26] Laistner, *Greek Economics*, p.16; *Ways and Means, etc.*
[27] Printed in Laistner, *Greek Economics.*

peace that have been most prosperous; despite the booty of war, it is in peace that wealth is accumulated; it is in war-time that it is spent.

More curious are the views expressed by Xenophon with regard to silver-mining. Here, with grotesque over-state-ment, is an industry following the Law of Increasing Returns; the greater the number of people employed, the more prolific becomes the ore. Elsewhere excess of entrepre-neurs leads to their bankruptcy; excess of commodities leads to cheapness. But there is no limit to the demand for silver: 'Silver ore will never give out, and silver will never lose its value.' Gold does not have this marvellous property; for 'when an abundance of gold makes its appearance its value depreciates, and it sends up the price of silver.' Conse-quently the city should acquire slaves to be let out to work in the silver-mines, and in order to overcome the risks in-herent in opening new cuttings, he suggests something ap-proaching to a joint stock method of operation.

Even a brief survey of Xenophon would be incomplete without reference to a passage in the *Cyropædia* which, being quoted by Marx and others, has become one of the curiosities of economic literature. It represents division of labour as applied to the kitchen, run mad, with one man to boil fish and another to bake them. Here, surely, the cen-turies have shown retrogression.[28]

[28] 'For just as all other arts are developed to superior excellence in large cities, in that same way the food at the king's palace is also elaborately prepared with superior excellence. For in small towns the same workman makes chairs and doors and ploughs and tables, and often this same artisan builds houses, and even so he is thankful if he can only find employment to support him. And it is, of course, impossible for a man of many trades to be proficient in all of them. In large cities, on the other hand, inasmuch as many people have demands to make upon each branch of industry, one trade alone, and very often even less than a whole trade, is enough to support a man: one man, for instance, makes shoes for men, and another for women; and there are places even where one man earns a living by only

Apart from these three main representatives of Greek thought, a passing reference is perhaps due to the dialogue called *Eryxias*, which is of interest as being devoted wholly to an analysis of wealth, and which clearly distinguishes between material and immaterial wealth, so that ' in exchange for their art' men may obtain the necessaries of life;[29] and to Aristophanes' wholly diverting play *Ecclesiazusæ*, a skit on communism (not neglecting votes for women) which is full of the most modern thrusts.

Rome

Economic doctrine in Rome may be more summarily discussed. As a record of social struggle, the history of Rome is of the highest importance, but the specific contribution which Rome made to theory is meagre to the extent of being negligible. Moreover, such as it is, it is largely an echo of Greece. It is indeed in accordance with the genius of the Roman people that their theory should be implicit in their actions, their laws and their jurisprudence, rather than explicit in the works of professed theorists. It is a wise observation of Roscher's that in Rome it was the most prac-

---

stitching shoes, another by cutting them out, another by sewing the uppers together, while there is another who performs none of these operations but only assembles the parts. It follows, therefore, as a matter of course, that he who devotes himself to a very specialized line of work is bound to do it in the best possible manner. Exactly the same thing holds true in reference to the kitchen; in any establishment where one and the same man arranges the dining couches, lays the table, bakes the bread, prepares now one sort of dish and now another, he must necessarily have things go as they may; but where it is all one man can do to stew meats and another to roast them, for one man to boil fish and another to bake them, for another to bake bread and not every sort at that, but where it suffices if he makes one kind that has a high reputation – everything that is prepared in such a kitchen will, I think, necessarily be worked out with superior excellence.' (*Cyropædia*, Book VIII, ii, 5-6; Loeb translation, pp.333-335.)

[29] Laistner, *op. cit.*, p.41.

tical men who concerned themselves most with economic matters; and their most influential thought on economic questions, being in effect the economics of the Civil Service and the Law Courts, was never formally propounded.

Another characteristic of such economic fragments as Rome offers is that much of it dates from a time when the splendour was dimmed, and when the more far-sighted could see the hastening approach of the day of ruin. It is therefore mixed up with a good deal of head-shaking over evil times, and lamentations, doubtless sincere, over the departure of the days of primitive simplicity. It thus becomes on one side a criticism of the weaknesses of the times; and the praise of agriculture – a common feature of ancient thought – is in part also a sigh for a vanished simplicity and a censure of prevailing ostentation and greed.

The contribution of Rome to the discussion of economic topics – even if it may not amount to a theory – falls conveniently and traditionally under three groups: the philosophers, the agricultural writers and the jurists. A few points may be noted under each heading.

Of the philosophers (of whom Cicero, Seneca and Pliny may be taken as typical) it may be suggested that in so far as they merely censure luxury, or emphasize the beauty of simplicity and the right uses of wealth, they are primarily moral rather than economic teachers. To a considerable extent this exhausts their content. On other questions there is little that is new. One of the most illuminating passages in Cicero's *De Officiis* is that in praise of agriculture, which is also and even more emphatically in dispraise of all other occupations.[30] In itself this passage indicates why the spirit

[30] ' Now in regard to trades and other means of livelihood, which ones are to be considered becoming to a gentleman and which ones are vulgar, we have been taught, in general, as follows: First, those means of livelihood are rejected as undesirable which incur people's ill-will, as those of tax-gatherers and usurers. Unbecoming to a

of antiquity could scarcely be expected to evolve a body of
economic doctrine. As has been properly observed, Cicero is
here concerned with the respectability of various occupations, not with their productiveness. Notable is his comparative tolerance towards wholesale trade, especially if it leads
to a country estate. Usury naturally is condemned, in this
passage on the feeble ground that it incurs people's ill-will;
but it is also to Cicero that we owe Cato's terse comment:
'How about murder?' to one who inquired: 'How about
money-lending?'[31]

---

gentleman, too, and vulgar, are the means of livelihood of all hired
workmen whom we pay for mere manual labour, not for artistic skill;
for in their case the very wages they receive is a pledge of their
slavery. Vulgar we must consider those also who buy from wholesale merchants to retail immediately; for they would get no profits
without a great deal of downright lying; and verily there is no
action that is meaner than misrepresentation. And all mechanics are
engaged in vulgar trades; for no workshop can have anything liberal
about it. Least respectable of all are those trades which cater to
sensual pleasures:

> "Fishmongers, butchers, cooks, and poulterers,
>   And fishermen,"

as Terence says. Add to these, if you please, the perfumers, dancers,
and the whole *corps de ballet*.

But the professions in which either a higher degree of intelligence
is required or from which no small benefit to society is derived –
medicine and architecture, for example, and teaching – these are
proper for those whose social position they become. Trade, if it is on a
small scale, is to be considered vulgar; but if wholesale and on a
large scale, importing large quantities from all parts of the world
and distributing to many without misrepresentation, it is not to be
greatly disparaged. Nay, it even seems to deserve the highest respect,
if those who are engaged in it, satiated, or rather, I should say, satisfied with the fortunes they have made, make their way from the port
to a country estate, as they have often made it from the sea into port.
But of all the occupations by which gain is secured, none is better
than agriculture, none more profitable, none more delightful, none
more becoming to a freeman.' (*De Officiis*, Book I, xlii; Loeb translation, pp.153-155.

[31] 'Et cum ille, qui quæsierat, dixisset: "Quid fænerari?", tum
Cato: "Quid hominem," inquit, "occidere".' (*De Officiis*, Book II,
xxv; Loeb, p.266.)

Seneca's views on economic matters are not in the main of great interest. Money (and not merely the love of money) is emphatically the root of most evils. Envy and greed are the sources of all injustice.[32] But in the midst of much in this train of thought which, even if true and well-expressed, has ill-founded claims to originality, there is one thought that is significant, namely that the various quarters of the earth have been differently endowed in such a manner that the peoples of the world would appear to have been called to enter into intercourse with each other for the mutual satisfaction of their needs.[33]

In the tangled mass of Pliny's *Natural History* there are certain interesting passages relating to money. There is more than a touch of Rousseau in his assertion that the worst crime against mankind was committed by him who was the first to put a ring (of gold) upon his finger.[34] There is much vitriolic denunciation of gold 'discovered only for the ruin of mankind.' How much more happy the age when things were bartered for one another! Yet despite this, he explains, not unreasonably, the causes which led to the pre-eminence of gold, as that it suffers no damage through fire, that it wears the least of all the metals by use, that no material is more malleable, that it is not subject to rust and so on.[35] The other passage in Pliny which has been so frequently quoted is that which relates to the extent of the farm. He refers with approval to Vergil's maxim 'to praise a large farm, but cultivate a small one,' and adds in a celebrated and ominous phrase that the widespread domains had been the ruin of Italy: '*latifundia Italiam perdidere.*'[36]

The agricultural writers have but a slender claim to

[32] *De Ira*, III, 32, 33.
[33] *Ad Helviam Matrem de Consolatione*, chap. 9.
[34] Pliny, Book XXXIII, chaps. 3, 4.
[35] Pliny, Book XXXIII, chap. 19.
[36] Pliny, Book XVIII, chap. 7.

appear here. Their works are a striking testimony to the regard in which agriculture was held in antiquity, and at the same time it is here alone that we have a careful analysis of an industry. Yet these writers, of whom Cato, Varro and Columella are most noteworthy – with, of course, Pliny, who neglects nothing – are concerned above all with the technique of agriculture and only incidentally with the economics of agriculture. Moreover, it is in nearly all cases the management of an estate, self-contained and self-sufficing, that is the problem considered; in other words, agriculture here is viewed not as an industry run for profit; the problem, in Aristotelian phraseology, is one of Domestic Economy rather than of 'chrematistics.' Lastly, it is difficult to resist the impression that the more important writers, in their praises of agriculture, were obliquely pointing to what they regarded as the salvation of Rome in degenerate times; and with a certain amount of force, an analogy has been drawn with the Physiocrats, who many centuries later also emphasized the importance of agriculture under the shadow of approaching evil.

Apart from dithyrambic praise of agriculture, as, for instance, when Columella says that husbandry is next to and near akin to wisdom, it is notable that the writers of this group condemn slave-labour as inefficient. Pliny may be taken as typical: 'It is the very worst plan of all to have land tilled by slaves let loose from the house of correction, as indeed is the case with all work entrusted to men who live without hope.'[37] Certain sayings of Cato, as on the superiority of an agricultural population, and his dictum that he has been a useful member of society who leaves more at his death than he inherited, passed into current wisdom. But in the main these writers are concerned with tips for the landowner (and his wife): hints on the pruning of trees,

[37] Pliny, Book XVIII, chap. 7.

where to buy tunics, the medicinal effects of cabbage, the salting of gammon and the like.

To the third contributory stream derived from Rome, represented by the jurists, it is possible to make merely a vague reference, though indeed their influence on the world at large, and on the subsequent method of approach to economic questions, has been of the profoundest. It might indeed be argued that Roman Law represents the greatest legacy of Rome to the civilized world, inasmuch as a large portion of the daily transactions of the world are still regulated in accordance with the principles laid down by the Roman jurists and embodied in Roman Law. For our present purpose, influence along two different lines is notable. The progress of Rome from its earliest self-contained beginnings to its widest expansion was marked, on the one hand, by increasing contact with other nations and peoples, which were found to have laws of their own, and, on the other hand, by an advance to a state of considerable economic, financial and commercial complexity, in which men made contracts, and in which the art of banking and the mysteries of credit were not unknown. In response to the first of these lines of development, the Roman lawyers evolved the idea of a 'jus gentium,' an idea not in itself of economic importance, though later it impinges on the development of economic ideas. The 'jus gentium,' the body of law common to different nations, readily passes into the idea of natural law, that is to say, the idea of a body of law, which, being common to all peoples, is 'natural' to them, and can therefore claim a higher sanction than that of any earthly legislature. It is an idea which, in the varying shades of meaning of which it is susceptible, never wholly faded out. In the eighteenth century it colours the doctrine that certain things are 'natural,' which is so large a part of Smith, and which even more emphatically is the foundation-stone of the Physiocrats.

The other development led, not indeed to economic doctrine, but to a careful analysis of certain economic conceptions, above all those relating to contract and the nature of property. Here the influence of Roman Law was in the direction of a rigid, and indeed a somewhat harsh individualism. To the influence of the Roman jurists must in large measure be attributed the prevailing tendency to consider that each one, in the common phrase, has a right to do what he likes with his own, that the conception of private property necessarily includes the right not merely to enjoy, but also arbitrarily to abuse and destroy, and logically likewise an untrammelled right of bequest. Here, in the two great principles of private property and complete freedom of contract, Rome left a bias towards unfettered and irresponsible individualism as against the possible claims of the family, the sept, or the nation.

CHAPTER II

The Middle Ages. St. Thomas Aquinas. Oresme

St. Thomas Aquinas

A N Y O N E who would essay to present in a few pages what purports to be a statement of the economic doctrines current in the Middle Ages must be conscious, if he has a conscience, that he is postulating a simplicity that does not exist. It may be left to the historians to decide what period should be assigned to the 'Middle Ages,' and to specify the limits of that yawning gulf of time which must be allowed to have begun somewhere, and which certainly came to an end with the fall of Constantinople and the discovery of America, if indeed it had not ended a century earlier. Viewing the twelfth and the thirteenth centuries from afar, it is now dangerously easy to consider that the condition of Europe was relatively static for a vast period of time, and to speak as though Europe, like a sleeping princess, slumbered through many centuries until the elfin horns of the Renaissance heralded a new and a rosy morning.

Yet though the tendency to look upon the Middle Ages as static is deceptive, there is a certain convenience for our purpose in looking comprehensively at the economic doctrines of the Middle Ages, especially if that vague period be left undelimited. Indubitably, opinion on economic matters developed; but there was certainly a point of view which was dominant for a lengthy period of time, and which, though subject to modification, reached its highest expression in the twelfth and thirteenth centuries, above all in the writings of St. Thomas Aquinas (1225-1274). Without attempting to notice its development or modifications, this chapter will be devoted to a consideration of what may be fairly called the mediaeval point of view, above all as that is represented in St. Thomas Aquinas, whose thought governed an epoch.

Here, as elsewhere, the theory reflects the conditions and the circumstances of men's lives. For an understanding of the mediaeval point of view – for ' theory ' is here hardly the fitting word – it is necessary to bear in mind the dominant characteristics of the structure of society at the time with which we are concerned, both on the secular and religious side. On the secular side, the Middle Ages are for many people more or less synonymous with the feudal system. It is unnecessary to consider how feudalism worked in practice; it is equally unnecessary to idealize it, as Müller (and many others) have done in an attempt to escape from the nine-teenth or the twentieth century, forgetting that the past will always win a glory from its being far. Yet, without doubt, the theory of feudalism in its essence implied a system in which society was held together by mutual obligations and services, so that each one had his place assigned to him, and his tenure of that place involved the giving and receiving mutually of support and assistance. The same was true of the guilds and crafts when these began to develop. There rested on the crafts the obligation to render good service to the public; so also, as in the regulations governing the rela-tionship of the members of the same body to each other, it is evident that the accepted code of honour required the members to share opportunities and to play the game honestly by one another. On the whole, then, the accepted theory was that the members of society held their places in society on condition that they rendered certain specified services to their fellows. There was thus a considerable element of status. Rank, or whatsoever kind, imposed obli-gations, but it also conferred privileges. Each one should not merely discharge the obligations resting on him; he should also live as his position in life required – '*convenienter,*' as the mediaeval Latinist expressed it. To complete the picture on the secular side, the Middle Ages inevitably lived to a large extent in a 'natural economy.' Though there is much talk of trade, the actual volume of trade must have been relatively small; men lived in small units, which to a large extent must have been virtually self-supporting. Nor was it merely the difficulties of transport that stood in the way of exchange on any large scale. Until the discovery of the silver-mines in America – that is, until after the passing of the Middle Ages – there was something of the nature of a dearth of money throughout Europe, and money transactions were perforce naturally limited. Enterprise, as we understand it to-day, presented few openings. It was consequently a society in which the members were expected to maintain themselves by rendering service to the community, and in which to a large extent the possibility of making gains, or laying up treasure on earth, was excluded.

On the religious side the great all-dominating fact was the Church. The effect of its teaching is a matter for more detailed consideration later. Here it is sufficient to observe, firstly, that the Church sought to regulate all human relationships, on the postulate that this earthly life is but a preparation for another, and that the only reality is eternal salvation; and secondly, that the Church was, in its very nature, a cosmopolitan organization. The curiously non-national atmosphere of the Middle Ages, in so violent contrast to the presuppositions of the later mercantile period, is in part the gift of the Church, which thus conferred a certain unity on Europe before centralized nations found satisfaction in the misfortunes of their neighbours. In these days Latin was still a universal language for those who were sufficiently clerkly to read. All Europe could join in the

Crusades, and wandering scholars were equally at home in Oxford or Paris, in Padua or Cologne.

These conditions are in themselves almost sufficient to explain the point of view of the Middle Ages on economic questions. If we turn to the exponents of mediaeval thought, we find above all two dominant influences. The one is the authority of Aristotle; the other is seen in the transformations of values effected by Christianity, as found expounded not only in the orginal sources of the Christian religion, but also in the writings of the early Christian Fathers. The Bible, Aristotle, and the Christian Fathers are the authorities to whom St. Thomas turns with equal reverence, and there is much to be said for the old view that what the angelic doctor aimed at was a synthesis of Christianity and Aristotelian doctrine. Aristotle is chiefly influential in moulding the views of the Middle Ages with regard to the nature and functions of money, the iniquity of usury, the principles which should govern exchange and the nature of justice. On much of these, indeed, St. Thomas merely repeats Aristotle, with an added buttress drawn from Christian sources.

Much more important is the influence of Christianity on those points in which the Christian view was directly opposed to certain aspects of the Greek and classical tradition; and even though nothing is easier than to point to certain phases of mediaeval life in which the implications of Christianity were not fully accepted, nevertheless these continued to work as a leaven, modifying increasingly the views held on certain fundamental economic aspects of life.

Firstly, and most comprehensively of all, there was the view derived from Judaism, but generalized by Christianity beyond the limits of one race, that all men were the children of a common father; if the children of a common father, then brothers. Here was a principle ultimately destructive of class distinctions, ultimately destructive likewise of national distinctions. It was a principle which made it impossible permanently to defend such an institution as slavery, even though on this question St. Thomas is surprisingly prepared to swallow what Aristotle had said. The other side of the question is no less significant. Each individual represents an immortal soul, so that each in the light of eternity is of equal value. Here at the outset is implied an emphatic affirmation of human dignity, of the equality of all men in the sight of God, and of the brotherhood of all peoples. As an immediate practical inference from this implied brotherhood of all, it is necessary to note, even though there be no space for comment, on the emphasis laid on almsgiving, both as an act of charity and as a means of salvation.

Secondly, there is implied in Christianity a further point of view which, curiously, prevented some of these conclusions from being drawn or applied, or at least made their application relatively a matter of indifference. This world is but a preparation, and all that is is transitory. If the only thing of substance for each individual is to work out his salvation with fear and trembling, then every other mundane consideration sinks into insignificance, except in so far as it is a means to that higher end. Viewed from the altitude of the next world, there is so little that really matters in this. Here, fundamentally, is the explanation of St. Thomas Aquinas's attitude on slavery. Even a slave may enter the Kingdom of Heaven. Anyone to whom eternity is as real as the present (and vastly more enduring) must arrive at an attitude of detachment with regard to the things of this life; and an air of detachment leads to an attitude of tolerance with regard to things doubtless indefensible in themselves. Thus, though the initial assumptions of mediaeval Christianity ought to have led to an extreme equality, nevertheless it accepted inequality as part of the arrangement ordained by the Almighty for this present state of preparation, in which all things ought to be seen, illumined by the burning light of eternity, in their true proportion and in their true insignificance.

On a third point Christianity represented an even more complete reversal of the traditional Greek view. It insisted on the dignity of work in a manner which would have been repugnant in a State resting on slave labour, where work was consequently the mark of a slave. The New Testament, on the other hand, is a prolonged incitement to 'work with your own hands.' St. Paul, who was somewhat boastful that he had laboured night and day that he 'might not be chargeable to any of you,' laid down the rule that if any man would not work, neither should he eat. With few exceptions the Apostles were mean workers. Work, indeed, had been prescribed by God; and even if it were part of the curse resting on mankind, it was also part of the way of salvation. Christ continually spoke of Himself as working; and indeed to go back to the Book of Genesis, God Himself worked, and rested from His work on the seventh day. It need therefore occasion no surprise that Christianity brought with it a new conception, not merely of the dignity and the nobility of work, but also of its inevitability.

In the nature of things, one need not expect to find a specifically economic literature in the Middle Ages, for it was of the essence of the mediaeval point of view that the economic factor should be rigorously subordinated to more important considerations. Just as in Greek thought economic speculation was at most a by-product (and a minor by-product) of ethical and political thought, so in the Middle Ages, when economic questions are touched on, they are considered strictly in relation to private morality. Moreover the Church, which from the secular point of view was also a large and efficient administrative machine intent on the enforcement of the Church's point of view, took into its

control the whole moral life of the community. It is not
infrequently said that the two cardinal economic doctrines
of the Middle Ages are found in the notion of the 'just
price' and in the prohibition of usury. Certainly round
these two points most controversy raged. But this is to
view matters too superficially. These two principles are
neither independent nor are they fundamental. They are
but two aspects of a deeper and more comprehensive conception. If one word were sought to cover all phases of
mediaeval economic teaching, it would probably be found in
the idea of 'justice,' which has unfortunately tended to
become associated primarily with the notion of 'price.' We
are brothers and should behave as brothers, respecting each
other's rights and position in life. Each should receive that
to which he is entitled. Justice, as the mediaevalist understood it, should be done. No one, under any circumstances,
should take advantage of his neighbour. This is the sum and
substance of mediaeval economic teaching.

The relationship in which the two most familiar of mediaeval economic doctrines stand to the sum total of mediaeval
teaching in these matters is most conveniently seen in the
writings of St. Thomas Aquinas. The best method of
approach is perhaps to consider in the first place his teaching on the vexed question of the permissibility of private
property, and the allied question of the theoretical desirability of a system of communism. Here, however, the position is confused by the fact that there had been so much
previous history, and there has indeed been endless discussion of the extent to which the early Christian Church at
Jerusalem and the Christian Fathers had left a tradition in
favour of some communistic form of life. Certainly the
Gospels had underlined the truth that wealth might be a
snare; for is it not easier for a camel to go through the eye
of a needle than for a rich man to enter the Kingdom of

God? In one case also the way of perfection was said to lie in selling all and giving to the poor. Yet it is equally certain that no words of Christ can be invoked directly in aid of an argument for a communistic mode of life. More importance is attached to the early position of the Church at Jerusalem, where 'they had all things common' (Acts iv. 32), yet a careful perusal of the relevant passage appears to point to a condition of, at most, unrestrained liberality, which nevertheless remained voluntary.[1] There remain the Christian Fathers, from whom it would be easy to cull a nosegay of explosive aphorisms which might make it appear that Moscow was their spiritual home. Yet if they denounce wealth and roundly call the rich man a thief, it is equally true that passages may be cited in support of the legitimate use of private property. Probably, like less wise people, they were not always guarded in their expressions: on a survey of all the passages commonly cited, it is probable that the Fathers in the main were concerned merely to condemn the improper use of wealth, and to underline the deceitfulness of riches. That the early Fathers were communists might equally appear from selected passages chosen for the purpose. Certainly the state in which all things are held in common is their professed ideal, and evokes a wealth of glowing language. Yet again it is doubtful how far any of the passages usually cited can be regarded as a precept for the introduction of a communistic system, or as an argument for its practicability under existing circumstances. That men do not hold all things in common may be a mark of the depravity of man; but the depravity of man has to be accepted along with the fall of man. Praise of communism is indeed, in the Christian Fathers, largely praise of the

[1] Otherwise it is difficult to give any meaning to Peter's question to Ananias: 'Whiles it remained, was it not thine own?' Ananias was not a martyr in the cause of individualism; popular sentiment rightly regards Ananias and Sapphira as being primarily liars.

blessed state which man by his sins has forfeited. This probably is the true significance of the communism of the Christian Fathers.[2]

If this interpretation be right, there is not, in fact, on this question of private property, that contradiction between St. Thomas Aquinas and the Christian Fathers that is sometimes assumed. Fundamentally, his view of external things rests on their subordination to the ends of men: always the more imperfect exists on account of that which is more perfect.[3] But, having regard to the use of external things, St. Thomas holds, following Aristotle, that possession is ' natural to man.' The argument that seeks in natural law a sanction for community of possessions he counters by contending that natural law does not indeed require that all things should be held in common; all that can be derived from the argument is negative in its nature, namely, that under natural law there can be no justification for distinction of possessions. This, however, rests on human agreements, which is a matter of positive law. Thus private property is not contrary to natural law; rather it is added to natural law by a further creation of human reason.[4]

Possession being thus justified, as in accordance with human nature, St. Thomas distinguishes the two kinds of right which men may have in things. The first is the power of acquisition and administration (*potestas procurandi et dispensandi*), and here the full right of private property is allowed on lines which are similar to the Aristotelian argument. Greater care, greater order, greater satisfaction result when each has his own, and the disputes which spring from the common purse are avoided. But the second right in

---

[2] On all this see O'Brien, *Essay on Mediaeval Economic Teaching.*
[3] *Sum. Theol.*, II/II, quæstio 66, art. 1.
[4] ' Unde proprietas possessionum non est contra jus naturale, sed juri naturali superadditur per adinventionem rationis humanæ.' (II/II, quæstio 66, art. 2.)

things, that of use (*usus ipsarum*), is in a different case. Here things are to be regarded as common, ready to be shared with others in need. It is the old Aristotelian solution, that property should be private in possession but common in use.

Thus, while the right of property remains, the harshness of the Roman conception of the *jus utendi et abutendi* has gone. The owner is, in fact, the adminstrator of his possessions in the general interest, even though the administration of the property is left to the judgment of each individual. How far St. Thomas is prepared to carry this doctrine may be seen in his argument, that theft is permisssible in the case of extreme necessity.[5] For human law cannot abrogate from natural law or divine law, and it is part of the divine providence that inferior things are ordained that men may be aided in their necessities. Consequently that which is held in superfluity belongs by natural law to the maintenance of the poor. Here we are not concerned with what constitutes 'necessity,' nor with what is to be understood by 'superfluity'; but it is significant of the mediaeval respect paid to the rights of status that St. Thomas should expressly stipulate that almsgiving should be restricted so as to leave such a residue as will enable man to live as his status in life requires, *convenienter, secundum proprium statum.*[6]

St. Thomas's view of the value of earthly goods is in accordance with these general principles. The life that men live here leads to the life of blessedness in heaven as its final goal, and the good things of this life are to be judged in respect of their efficiency from this point of view.[7] Wealth is, or may be, good, but a good of a lower order, as a means to an end. It is good if it helps to a life of virtue. So also poverty may be good, if it frees men from the burdens in

[5] ii/ii, quæstio 66, art. 7.
[6] ii/ii, quæstio, 32, art. 6.
[7] *De Regimine Principum*, Book i, chap. 15.

which many are entangled by wealth. But poverty in itself is not good; it is only good in so far as it frees a man from what may hinder his spiritual life. Neither poverty nor wealth nor any other external thing ('any other creature,' St. Paul would have said) is good in itself; nor is anything evil apart from its evil use. Here, surely, is the supreme indifference of the Middle Ages.[8]

Granted the existence of private property, there arises the question of the principles which should regulate exchange. Human relations should be governed by 'justice,' and hence the central conception is that of the 'just price.' Into that large field which is concerned with the mediaeval analysis of justice and with the two kinds of justice as derived from Aristotle (commutativa and distributiva) it is unnecessary to enter here. Of the two aspects of justice – one governing the relations of the part to the part, and the other that of the part to the whole – it is essentially commutative justice, or justice in exchange, which governs the conception of the just price. Cutting down to the roots of things, justice consists in rendering to each one what belongs to him. Justice implies equality, and there should therefore be equality in exchange. In effecting exchanges, therefore, a measure is necessary, and it is for this purpose that money has been invented. Money is thus primarily, and almost merely, a measure of values. If the price exceeds the value of a thing, or conversely if the value of a thing exceeds the price, justice is violated; and therefore to sell a thing at a higher price or buy it a lower price than it is worth is unjust and impermissible.[9]

[8] *Summa Contra Gentiles*, Book III, in particular chap. 133, 'Quomodo paupertas sit bona.'

[9] The statement is so fundamental that perhaps the Latin of St. Thomas Aquinas may be forgiven: '. . . et ideo debet secundum æqualitatem rei inter eos contractus institui. Quantitas autem rei, quæ in usum hominis venit, mensuratur secundum pretium datum; ad quod est inventum numisma, ut dicitur. Et ideo si vel pretium

Carius vendere quam valeat – here indeed is a very fine
hare which, with no obvious asthmatic symptoms, is still
gallantly breasting the uplands, pursued from afar by a
great company of short-winded metaphysicians and economists. But St. Thomas at least did not join in the chase, nor
indeed was the hare of his starting. On the contrary, the
idea of value, lurking behind the just price, receives singularly little analysis from St. Thomas. It might be inferred
that it is an objective quality inherent in each thing, but he
seems to assume that we know what it is, rather than
explains how in any given case we may determine it. Probably a comparison of many passages would suggest that at
the back of his mind he had a cost-of-production theory,
linked up with his views as to the remuneration of labour.
Yet the idea of need and of use also figures in mediaeval
theory; but it is not the need of any individual, rather is there
everywhere the idea of a ' common estimate,' of the common
usefulness. In sum, the just price is largely the customary
price – a concept natural in a customary age. Perhaps one
cannot get nearer the truth than by recalling Mr. Gonnard's
felicitous phrase that the just price is determined, less by
positive elements than in accordance with the conscience of
the honest producer – the ' reputable employer ' of Austra-
lian wage-fixing legislation.

Yet the just price, though apparently objective in
character, was not exempt from modification by external
circumstances. To take one instance cited, in the case of the
exchange of a commodity of great use to the original owner,
regard should be had not only to the thing itself (and what
one might call its normal ' just price ') but also to the loss

---

excedat quantitatem valoris rei, vel e converso res excedat pretium,
tolletur justitiæ æqualitas. Et ideo carius vendere vel vilius emere rem
quam valeat, est secundum se injustum et illicitum.' (*Sum. Theol.*,
(ii/ii, quæstio 77, art. i.)

which the seller would incur in parting with it.[10] But it is characteristic of the mediaeval view that the contrary case of excessive urgency of need on the side of the buyer, accompanied by no special detriment to the seller, affords no justification for advancing the just price. These and other considerations indicate that there must be a certain margin allowed with regard to the just price. It cannot, as St. Thomas says, be fixed with complete accuracy, but must depend on a certain process of estimation; therefore within limits, a certain slight variation up or down need not be regarded as impairing the equality which justice demands.[11] The discussion of the obligation resting on the seller to reveal to the purchaser defects in the thing sold indicates more clearly than much argument that the fundamental idea of the Middle Ages was that no one should take advantage of another, and that in this life of trial brothers should observe towards each other the golden rule that 'as ye would that men should do to you, do ye also to them likewise.'

It is almost self-evident that the principle of the 'just price' includes the idea of the 'just wage' – indeed the example which St. Thomas takes in illustration of the equality which is inherent in justice is the payment of the due wage for services rendered. Elsewhere he places the payment of wages on exactly the same footing as the obligation of the just price.[12] It might even be said that the doctrine of the just price was built up on that of the just wage; for that

---

[10] 'Et in tali casu justum pretium erit ut non solum respiciatur ad rem quæ venditur, sed ad damnum quod venditor ex venditione incurrit.' (II/II, quæstio 77, art. 1.)

[11] 'Quod ideo dico, quia justum pretium rerum non est punctualiter determinatum, sed magis in quadam æstimatione consistit; ita quod modica additio vel minutio non videtur tollero æqualitatem justitiæ.' (II/II, quæstio 77, art. 1.)

[12] 'Unde sicut reddere justum pretium pro re accepta ab aliquo, est actus justitiæ; ita etiam recompensare mercedem operis vel laboris, est actus justitiæ. (I/II, quæstio 144, art. 1.)

the labourer was worthy of his hire was a living principle in the Middle Ages. In so far as the idea of the just price represented vaguely a cost-of-production theory, then the labourer's hire was a dominant, if not exclusive, factor in the determination of prices. By the just wage was meant that rate of remuneration which was required to enable the worker to live decently in the station of life in which he was placed; and thus, if one may so express it, such a wage, representing reasonable decency, was made a first charge on industry. The mediaeval doctrines of the just price and the just wage should appear less strange to a generation which has become familiar with trade boards and with various attempts to devise price-fixing machinery.

The other main feature of economic doctrine, the prohibition of usury, appears on analysis to be likewise merely a particular case of the just price. Usury, for the mediaevalist, was not merely what the modern economist would call 'pure interest'; it covered likewise any injustice in trade, any violation of the just price. Nevertheless, as Aristotle had exalted usury to an evil eminence among the various kinds of bad finance, so usury, although frequently used in a wider sense, was more specifically indentified with the making of profits out of loans as a particularly heinous example of the sin of avarice. Here was a subject on which the natural authorities of the Middle Ages seemed to be in agreement. Usury had been condemned by Aristotle on the grounds of the barrenness of money; to use money which was properly merely a means of exchange as a device for making more money, was unnatural, and therefore to be condemned. In the Bible there were the various prohibitions of usury in Leviticus and Deuteronomy, though how far these prohibitions related to the taking of usury from a 'brother' need not detain us. The Psalmist had indicated, as one of the qualities of a citizen of Zion, that he should not put his money to usury (Ps. xv. 5). There was above all the passage in the Gospels which was more frequently cited than any other authority, to the effect that the Christian should lend, hoping for nothing again (Luke vi. 35).[13]

Two points call for notice before considering what is more specifically the canonical view of the offence of usury. The first is that, despite the passage in St. Luke and certain *obiter dicta* of the Christian Fathers, the attitude of the Church was not at first so rigid as it became later. When the question first emerged, usury was forbidden only to clerics; it was not till relatively late that the prohibition was made general and usury became an offence in the laity. Secondly, it is impossible to appreciate the mediaeval attitude towards usury unless it be remembered that in an age of little enterprise and industry, loans were made mostly to those who for one reason or another were in distress. The typical loan, therefore, was probably advanced to someone who had suffered the scourge of fire or of flood, who had been ruined by bad seasons, whether occasioned by blight, by pestilence, or by the inclemency of the heavens. Moreover, in a community undeveloped financially, loans were to a large extent made as between people who were known to each other apart from their relationship of borrower and lender. Doubtless there were transactions of various types, but probably the characteristic loan was one, not designed for productive purposes, springing out of a misfortune and designed to tide the sufferer over the consequences of that misfortune, and

---

[13] *Mutuum date nihil inde sperantes.* Or should the correct reading be: *Mutuum date nihil desperantes*? Should loans be made ' hoping for nothing therefrom,' or ' without worrying about them '? Even on the former reading, does the *nihil* imply that the lender is not merely to hope for no interest, but that he is equally not to look for the return of the capital? It is curious that so many doubts should subsequently be raised with regard to the interpretation of a verse which was so authoritative in the Middle Ages. See O'Brien, *op. cit.*, on this.

advanced moreover by someone purporting to be a friend of the victim. That the taking of usury should be discouraged under these circumstances is but natural, for it assumes the appearance (to fall back on one of the Fathers) of 'trafficking in the miseries of others.' Even the Merchant of Venice recognizes this point of view when he asks: 'When did friendship take a breed of barren metal of his friend?'

The early condemnation of usury rested in part on the authority of the Bible and Aristotle, being compounded of the Aristotelian doctrine of sterility and the view that usury represents a grinding of the faces of the poor in their distress. In the hands of St. Thomas Aquinas, however, the objection to usury becomes more deeply grounded, and by reasoning of some subtlety it is demonstrated that usury involves an offence against justice. The argument rests on the distinction between those things in which use and consumption are identical, and those in which they can be separated (*res fungibles* and *res non fungibles*, to use a legal expression). In the case of wine and bread, for instance, there cannot be use without consumption. When the use is granted, the thing itself is granted. You cannot give a man the use of a loaf without, by that very act, giving him the loaf itself; and if he uses the loaf, it is idle to expect its return. On the other hand, there are things in which the use and consumption are not identical. A man may have the use of a house without destroying it. He may therefore be given the use of a house, and at the end of the period he may properly be expected to return the house in its original condition. Putting it in a manner more germane to the controversy, it is possible to sell a house, and it is possible to sell the use of a house, since they are distinct; but it is not possible to sell bread and the use of bread, since the sole purpose of bread is to be consumed. Come now to money, and invoke Aristotle's definition of money. Money exists for the purpose of effecting exchanges. It is the function of money to part company with its possessor; its proper use lies in its consumption or alienation. It is therefore pre-eminently a fungible commodity: use and consumption are inseparable.[14]

In a sense St. Thomas's argument is that what purports to be a loan of a fungible is in fact bound to be a sale. As it is inadmissible to sell a loaf to a man and simultaneously charge him for the use of it, so it is inadmissible to sell money and charge also for its use. The proper price, on mediaeval doctrine, is the return of the same money; the additional charge for its use is of the nature of a swindle. What, then, is the offence of the usurer? Bearing in mind the foregoing analysis, it may be variously expressed. Either he is selling something that does not exist (the use, apart from the consumption, when the two are identical), or he is charging for the same thing twice, or, if the lapse of time be invoked, he is selling time, which belongs to God, and which no man may appropriate.

It is not infrequently said that the mediaeval view of usury rests essentially on the Aristotelian view of money, as being merely a medium of exchange, and as being consequently inherently barren. It would perhaps be truer to say that they regarded a loan of money (being a fungible) as essentially involving a change of ownership; that while they realized that money could be productively used, it could only be so used when brought into conjunction with labour. The productivity, in fact, springs primarily from the labour of the borrower, to whom also the full use of the money has been granted. The usurer, therefore, from this angle, is levying a toll on the labour of another. The just price for the money

[14] 'Ita proprius et principalis pecuniæ usus est ipsius consumptio, sive distractio.' (*Sum. Theol.*, II/II, quæstio 78.)

advanced is the return of the money; anything more is injustice.

The development and gradual refinement of the doctrine with regard to usury constitute one of the most interesting chapters in economic thought and practice; but it can only be glanced at here. It was in accordance with the mediaeval conception of justice and equality that the lender, by lending, should not suffer. In such a case the restoration of the original capital would not be sufficient; the borrower should also make good such losses as the lender had suffered on his behalf. Thus arose a number of modifications which in practice tended to break down the prohibition of usury, though in theory they were merely variations necessary for the fuller attainment of the idea of justice. The two which figure most largely in discussion were the payments permissible in the case of *damnum emergens* and *lucrum cessans*. If the lender could prove that, arising out of the loan, he had suffered a definite loss, or that alternately a source of gain had dried up, then it was but equitable that the borrower should indemnify him. Somewhat different was the *poena conventionalis*, which stipulated for the return of the money on a certain date, under penalty of a further payment in respect of the inconvenience alleged to result from the lender being prevented from receiving his money when, as anticipated, he should have occasion for its use. A fourth exception was the *periculum sortis*, a payment to cover the risk inherent in the possibility of the money not being repaid. In the light of this discussion, two conclusions are evident. Firstly, in practice these various modifications were in time sufficient to break down the prohibition of usury, especially with the development of industry and of financial technique. For implicitly the exceptions assume that the lender could not normally himself make use of his money. In an economy offering unlimited scope for investment and enterprise, it would be increasingly possible for a lender to plead either a *damnum emergens* or a *lucrum cessans*. Secondly, these exceptions are no exceptions in principle. Taking interest where there is no risk, no loss incurred, no inconvenience suffered, still remained evil in the eyes of the mediaevalist. The emphasis on the permissibility of payment in respect of those elements which in modern language constitute the difference between gross interest and economic interest, merely underlines the fact that economic interest, the payment for the use of money pure and simple, continued to be regarded as illegitimate.

To guard against misapprehension it should, however, be added that the mediaeval doctrine did not condemn investment when investment took the form of a partnership, provided the partner did in fact share the risks of the business. The *commenda*, the original form of partnership, had always been regarded as entirely legitimate, and here one party might advance money to another and share in his profits, while refraining from taking any direct part in the enterprise. It was essential, however, that he should not be absolutely entitled to receive his money back in full, for such a position would clearly involve usury. But if he merely ' entrusts ' his money by a kind of partnership, the money remains his; ' so that the merchant trades with it, or the craftsman uses it at the owner's risk.' The original owner may therefore claim a portion of the profit which has sprung from the use of the money, which has never in fact left his possession, although entrusted to another.[15] As Mr Tawney has well put it, the person whom mediaeval doctrine

---

[15] ' Sed ille qui committit pecuniam suam vel mercatori vel artifici per modum societatis cujusdam, non transfert dominium pecuniæ suæ in illum, sed remanet ejus; ita quod cum periculo ipsius mercator de ea negotiatur, vel artifex operatur; et ideo sic licite potest partem lucri inde provenientis expetere, tanquam de re sua.' (*Sum. Theol.*, II/II, quæstio 78, art. 2.)

condemns is the debenture-holder, the man who eschews all risk, whose money is safe and who yet looks for a reward.

One last point in mediaeval doctrine, above all as exemplified in St. Thomas Aquinas. The Middle Ages had their theory of division of labour, based on the Aristotelian doctrine of the essentially social nature of man. But if people live in society they must aid each other by doing different things. (Hence, indeed, the peculiar human property of speech, so that men may communicate regarding their diverse needs and attainments).[16] Different occupations are necessary, but are all equally honourable? Only one aspect of this need detain us here, namely, the attitude towards trade. The test of the reputability of any occupation lay in the extent to which it was serviceable to the community; private gain was, in a sense, the antithesis of public service, and therefore those occupations which offered opportunities of private gain were, to say the least, dangerous – and perhaps something worse. Originally the view had been that a merchant could hardly be pleasing to God. In St. Thomas Aquinas we have advanced to the view that trading is not necessarily sinful, but he clearly regards the calling of the trader as so beset with the opportunities of sin that a man mindful of his immortal soul will shun it. First of all, what is a trader? Only he who buys a thing with the express intention of selling it at a higher price. If a man buys an article, having no such intention, he may subsequently re-sell it (and at a higher price) without thereby becoming a trader. And the causes which are enumerated as justifying a higher price are interesting as revealing the considerable degree of haziness in which the just price shrouded itself. A higher price might be justified either because the buyer had improved the article in some respect, or because the price had varied through changes in time or place, or

[16] *De Regimine Principum*, Book 1, chap. 1.

because of the danger involved in its transport.[17] But on the main question St. Thomas repeats ominously the distinction drawn by Aristotle between natural and unnatural exchange, the latter being designed not to meet the needs of life, but to acquire gain. As such it is regarded as somewhat dishonourable. Nevertheless, even if gain does not involve anything honourable, it does not logically involve anything sinful. Thus the centre of the argument is rather moved from the gains to the use made of these gains; and St. Thomas contemplates the case where a man may devote himself to trade for the public welfare, seeking gain not as an end but as a reward for his efforts. Gains, if reasonable, may thus be regarded as a kind of wage.

More interesting because less negative is a passage in *De Regimine Principum*, wherein St. Thomas discusses the two methods whereby a State may obtain what it requires. These are, firstly, by its own natural fruitfulness; and secondly, by trade. The argument is all in favour of the self-sufficient State, partly on mercantilist grounds of the beauty of self-sufficiency; but partly also because of the corrupting influence of the trading class. The conclusion, however, is that merchants are a necessity, if only owing to the difficulty of obtaining for the State a situation which has potentially a prospect of complete self-sufficiency. Hence the perfect state will make use of merchants – but in moderation.[18]

Oresme

No survey of the economic views of the Middle Ages would be adequate without a reference, if only by way of a

---

[17] 'Vel quia in aliquo rem melioravit, vel quia pretium rei est mutatum secundum diversitatem loci, vel temporis, vel propter periculum, cui se exponit, transferendo rem de loco ad locum.' (11/11, quæstio 78, art. 4.)

[18] 'Unde oportet quod perfecta civitas moderate mercatoribus utatur.' (*De Regimine Principum*, Book 11, chap. 3.)

corrective, to the remarkable treatise written by Nicholas Oresme, Bishop of Lisieux (?1320-1382), entitled *De Origine, Natura, Jure et Mutationibus Monetarum*.[19] This treatise of twenty-six short chapters, although scarcely deserving the wild praise bestowed upon it by Roscher as a theory of money which is still perfectly valid to-day, is nevertheless a sufficiently remarkable performance. In its spirit it antici-pates the scientific, objective frame of mind of writers of a much later age. In truth, however, it is less a treatise on money than a sustained and emphatic refutation of the rights of the Prince to tamper with the currency. He begins on orthodox lines, dealing with primitive barter and its diffi-culties, which led *les hommes subtilz* to resort to money and thus devise a more suitable method of exchange. Money is thus artificial wealth merely; a man may be possessed of much money and yet die of hunger, as witness the often cited example of Crœsus. It is merely an instrument for circu-lating wealth, an *instrumentum permutandi divitias naturales*, a medium of exchange, as we should say to-day.

Two points perhaps are specially notable in Oresme. As a medium of exchange, in the modern tag, money must have certain properties, but the problem of finding any one sub-stance convenient both for large and small exchanges, leads Oresme to the principle of bimetallism. He is remarkably clear as to the difficulties that may arise from a divergence between the mint ratio and the market ratio, and is definite that the mint ratio should follow the market ratio: ' Cette proportion,' as he says, ' doit ensuivir le naturel habitude ou valeur de l'or à l'argent.' Further, it is evident that he is familiar with Gresham's law that the over-valued metal will drive the under-valued metal out of circulation; the Prince therefore must not arbitrarily fix or alter the ratio, as this

[19] In addition to the Latin original, there is a French translation by Oresme himself.

would open the door to all kinds of hanky-panky – as in buying silver with gold at one ratio, altering the ratio, and thereafter buying gold with silver.

The second point of importance is his strict delimitation of the powers of the Sovereign with regard to the currency and the inferences he draws therefrom. Currency may not be issued by everyone, but only by a public person, acting on behalf of the community. Naturally, therefore, it falls to the Prince to issue currency, but he does so purely in a representative capacity: 'convenienter est quod ipse pro communitate faciat fabricare monetam et eam congrua impressione signare.' This act is merely done on behalf of the community, and it follows therefore that the mere fact of issue by the Prince does not make him the owner and the proprietor of the money so issued.

This principle is of importance when Oresme comes to discuss the various ways in which money may be altered, changed or debased. It is unnecessary to differentiate these various *mutationes*, as of appellation, weight, substance, etc. What is important is the vigour, one might almost say the rudeness, with which Oresme denounces all debasements of the currency. A prince who does these things is a liar; he commits perjury; he bears false witness; for it is clearly a shame for a king to certify that a thing is gold when it is not gold, or that it weighs a pound when it does not do so. The gain which flows from such practices is not merely dishonest, it is also unnatural. Money-changing, usury, debasement of the currency are all alike, in the Aristotelian and Thomist sense, unnatural methods of making a profit out of money; but they represent an ascending scale of turpitude. Towards the close, Oresme's treatise almost becomes a political tract in its denunciation of debasement of the currency as an engine to create a tyranny. Once the path of rectitude has been abandoned, he sees the possibility,

almost the inevitability of repeated debasements, transferring by degrees the whole wealth of the people to the Prince,
and thus reducing them to a state of servitude.[20] Oresme
clearly sees the evils of a debased currency, and records its
natural manifestations in a general impoverishment of the
community, in the flight of money elsewhere, in the cessa-
tion of foreign trade, and in the general disorganization of
life. Even if the enthusiastic critics lead one to expect too
much of Oresme, his is nevertheless an extraordinarily
realistic and practical voice to hear in the fourteenth
century.

[20] ' Car nature humaine est toujours encline et preste à augmenter
Richesses à elle, quant legièrement les peut acquerir, que en fin le
prince pourroit attraire à luy comme la pécune et les Richesses de
tous les subjectz et par ce ramener en servitude.'

CHAPTER III

Mercantilism

I. THE HISTORICAL BACKGROUND

I t has become an accepted phrase to speak of 'mercantilist doctrine' and 'mercantilist theory,' yet Mercantilism is a misleading and deceitful word, if it is interpreted as implying that at any time there was a group of writers who consciously advanced a body of mercantilist thought to which any canon of orthodoxy could be applied. A mere indication of the spatial and temporal frontiers of Mercantilism is a sufficient warning against the old vulgar error implicit in the view (which perhaps still survives) that Mercantilism was the current orthodoxy before it was attacked by the Physiocrats and that both schools were subsequently superseded by Adam Smith. For if there be such a thing as Mercantilism, it had a three hundred years' run, and it coloured the thought (and still more the action) of every country in Europe. Certain views indeed, bearing a strong similarity to each other, began to appear throughout Europe consequent on the portentous changes which marked the close of the Middle Ages. These views, based on certain common assumptions, were in marked contrast to the non-national, moral and other-worldly point of view which had charac-terized such a writer as St. Thomas Aquinas. These views emerged, at first in a crude form, about the end of the four-teenth or the beginning of the fifteenth centuries; despite refinements, variations and modifications, the family resem-blance in the views currently held continued until the second half of the eighteenth century. Mercantilism indeed is still with us, and shows signs of a healthy and glorious resurrection. But it is clear that no general body of doctrine could have maintained itself unchanged for three centuries, especially when it is recalled that Mercantilism, so-called, prevailed not merely in France, England and Italy, but was likewise rampant in Scotland, Spain and Russia.

Mercantilism, therefore, varied, adapting itself to the changing conditions of time and to the circumstances of its local habitation. Yet if one can nowhere pick out the wholly complete and orthodox mercantilist, the common usage of the term has a certain convenience. Economic doctrine is everywhere the expression of the conditions of the time in which it emerges, and Europe from the end of the fifteenth century onwards was a very different place from the Europe of the twelfth and thirteenth centuries. Mercantilist writers may, and do, differ; but to a large extent they start from common postulates, and these postulates were imposed on them by the altered conditions of the Europe in the period which superseded the Middle Ages.

That Europe changed mightily as a result of the Renaissance, the Reformation, the invention of printing and the discovery of America, is a very familiar theme among those who prescribe essays and devise examination questions. A very brief survey of some of the changes which marked the age of transition will reveal the intimate connection between Mercantilism and the general tendencies of the time in the world of politics and of thought. First, and most fundamental, was the political change. It is not for us here to concern ourselves unduly with history, or the cause and course of events. It is sufficient to observe that in the countries of most importance, the mediaeval warring of turbulent barons, with a king doubtfully stronger than his leading subjects, gave way to the reality of a strong centralized State with an effective, and in some cases even an efficient, government. In English history the change is represented by the Tudors. The power of the King became not merely predominant; it became comprehensive. In short, England, France and Spain became definite entities, and not merely geographical expressions. Feudalism, linking society together by a chain of privileges and obligations, had emphasized loyalty to the overlord as the first obligation, and in doing so had stymied the possibility of national unity. With the barons put in their proper place, the King became, in theory, the 'father of his people.' England and all who lived in England were realized to have common interests, and it was the duty of the King and of the Government to watch over and to further these interests. It followed also from this emergence of 'England,' and of 'France,' each as a definite entity with interests of its own, that the nations and states which had so emerged were at least in potential rivalry, if not in conflict with each other. The cosmopolitanism implicit in the non-national sentiment of the Middle Ages was gone. Unified states had come into being; these lived in rivalry in peace, and might at any time be pitted against each other in war. Wars doubtless there had been in the past, but it is significant to note in how large a proportion of instances these had arisen out of the complexities of the feudal system. If the King of England was at variance with the King of France, it was as likely as not that he went to war in his capacity of Duke of Normandy; from the English point of view the Scottish War of Independence was largely a matter of disciplining a feudal inferior. But in the new conditions the conflict of interests was definitely between states and nations.

Moreover, political thought, partly inspiring and in part interpreting development, tended in the same direction. For their relationship to the fundamentals of Mercantilism, two writers are indirectly of supreme importance. Machiavelli (1469-1527) in *The Prince*, with an admirable air of detachment and a scientific aloofness from moral considerations, discussed how in the Italy of his day a 'principality' could be established and maintained. A book written with a specific purpose, its lessons were found applicable far beyond Italy. Machiavelli postulated that the times called for a strong prince, and in effect his book is an analysis of what must be done to create the strong state – conscience being hushed and all scruples ignored. Machiavelli thus became the unscrupulous despot's guide to power. His significance lies in the facts, firstly that he freed – perhaps offensively freed – politics from all moral and ethical considerations; and secondly, that though originally and of design applicable to the Italian city state, his work served as an incentive to despotism everywhere. The other writer is Jean Bodin (1520-1596), who, analysing political conceptions, presented to the world the fruitful idea of sovereignty, which though now creaking, has dominated all political thought until the present generation. The essence of the doctrine of sovereignty in its various forms is that there is, in every state a supreme power, subject to no other power within the state itself, but to which all else is subject. The conception of sovereignty, unless handled with gingerly care and subtle refinement of statement, is thus apt to underline the importance of a strong centralized state; inevitably, also, it entails an element of irresponsibility in the sovereign power. Moreover, it irreconcilably confronts sovereignty with sovereignty in the international anarchy.

Mercantilism may not inappropriately be viewed as the economic equivalent of Machiavelli and Bodin. Bodin deduced that of necessity there was a supreme power in each state. Machiavelli in effect said: 'If you want a strong state, you must do this, and avoid doing that.' Strong states were in demand, and the mercantilists, practical men confronted with practical problems, were concerned with the means whereby the State could be made strong. In the somewhat hackneyed phrase of Schmoller, Mercantilism is merely ' state-making ' – although it should be added that it is state-making on the economic side. From this analysis there follows further a consideration of the highest importance in explaining the varying shades of mercantilist doctrine. Mercantilism was never more than a means. The true end was political in its character – the creation of a strong state; Mercantilism was the sum total of the means on the economic side, appropriate to the attainment of this end. But while an end may be absolute, it is of the essence of means that they should be variable according to time and circumstance; and Mercantilism, in its various phases, reveals such variety.

These considerations explain the essential kernel of Mercantilism; they do not explain the particular form which mercantilist doctrines assumed. To carry the analysis to this further point, two further elements in the problem must be invoked. The first centres in the perpetual neediness and indigence of the prince; the second lies in the reactions, immediate and more remote, on European financial conditions occasioned by the discoveries of the precious metals in the New World. These two causes, mingling together, give Mercantilism its most characteristic outer features.

The King in his capacity of father of his people, the responsible custodian of the national interests, had perforce to incur heavy and onerous expenses. So long as there still remained in the air vague memories of the pleasing tradition that ' the King should live of his own,' taxation inevitably lagged behind the needs of the situation. That the King should live of his own implied that he should live as other barons did, on the revenues of his private estates. It was indeed a relic of the time when he did not differ materially from other barons; but the doctrine was incompatible with the new conditions when the King was the defender of the safety and the welfare of his country. In short, taxation, which in an earlier age had spasmodically supplemented the King's private revenue, had of necessity to be regularized and become permanent. Old wars might have been waged by retainers, as part of the universal system of payment in kind; the new age of standing armies was at hand, and this required money. Indeed *pecunia nervus belli* became one of the accepted maxims of the age. For all the purposes of government, the King required a revenue, thought of in terms of money, a steady and calculable revenue, unfortunately also an increasing revenue. How to increase this revenue became the first thought of those concerned with public policy.

The possibility of securing a revenue by taxation was itself, however, one of the indirect consequences of the geographical discoveries, and in particular of the discovery of America. What first commended the New World to the European was its promised store of precious metals. The influx of silver rapidly revolutionized the trade, commerce, and the finance of Europe. The consequence of the new discoveries of silver on the European price-level is one of the most familiar exemplifications of that dowdy platitude, the quantity theory of money. But more important than the nominal rise in the price of hens and sheep is the fact that the influx of the precious metals over a large part of the field resulted in the transition from a natural economy, based to a considerable extent on barter and the feudal ideal of services in kind, to a money economy. Taxation is no easy matter in a natural economy; when all things are thought of in terms of money, and when money is effectively used in all transactions, the possibilities of taxation are enormously facilitated. In an age when the engine of regular taxation was thus newly fashioned, the administration of the King's, or the State's, affairs became more akin to a merchant's business. There was expenditure and there was income, both thought of in terms of money. Increased power rested on the attainment of a balance of revenue over expenditure, and thus inevitably the possibilities of increasing the sources of revenue were assiduously explored.

Wealth, as the source of a nation's power, above all visualized as money – that form of wealth which endures, which is adaptable to all ends, which can be made to fetch and carry at command – had thus come into respect. But the picture would not be complete without some reference to the correspondingly changed view of the individual. Not merely was the State directed to the pursuit of wealth and the discovery of the sources of wealth, leading among other things to colonial acquisitions and colonial rivalries, the individual likewise was liberated from the restraining abstemiousness and asceticism which had marked the finest thought of the Middle Ages. Not so long ago it had been sinful, or at least perilous, to accumulate wealth – perhaps because in what was so largely a natural economy it had been so difficult and indeed ' unnatural ' to do so. In a money economy, the accumulation of wealth became meritorious and to some inevitable. Hitherto it had been held that a merchant could hardly be pleasing to God; now the proof of the pudding was in the eating thereof, and if merchandise yielded a profit, it was *ipso facto* justifiable and justified. On this side also deeper causes were operative. The Renaissance on one side was a frank bubbling up of delight in the enjoyment of life. Rabelais, perhaps more than any other, sums up the spirit of the Renaissance. Waiving his philosophy, his name recalls vast uproarious laughter, unashamed delight in eating and drinking and whatever else may minister to a sense of satisfaction that it is a good thing to be alive. It is a far cry from St. Thomas Aquinas to that Rabelaisian Abbey of the Thelemites, living joyfully under the motto: '*Fais ce que vouldras.*' Here indeed is the ideal of reckless individualism, so markedly at variance with the mediaeval ideal of an individual swallowed up in his class, with duties and obligations imposed upon him by his status in life.

The Reformation in certain of its aspects doubtless encouraged a spirit of asceticism, but it was an asceticism which no longer viewed with horror the accumulation of wealth. Max Weber indeed has familiarized us with the idea that modern capitalism has its roots in Calvinistic theology. Protestantism, particularly in its Canvinistic form, is essentially individualistic in its outlook. Salvation is a matter between each individual and his Creator, even though the ultimate decision may be rather a one-sided affair. But Calvin, or so Weber would have us believe, laid down in the economic sphere two cardinal injunctions; firstly the duty of working assiduously in one's calling, and secondly the duty of refraining from pleasurable consumption of wealth. The only possible outcome of unrestrained activity, combined with a self-denying refusal to enjoy the fruits of that activity, is an accumulation of wealth. Indeed increased substance came to be regarded as a special sign of divine favour, and thus it was possible to grow rich to the greater glory of God. It is impossible here to consider the element of truth in Weber's thesis; it is sufficient to note that Protestant asceticism, unlike mediaeval asceticism, so far from being hostile to the accumulation of wealth, tended rather to look upon it with favour.

These last considerations are perhaps on the fringe of our subject. But enough has been said to indicate that in the transition from the Middle Ages to the modern period, a multiplicity of causes tended to re-create Europe as a family of centralized states, living in uneasy rivalry, each struggling to be strong against possible competitors; that the conditions of the time attached a new importance to wealth, and that as the individual could now unashamedly pursue wealth, so also the State saw in wealth the secret of strength. Out of these conditions Mercantilism arose.

II. GENERAL OUTLINE OF MERCANTILIST DOCTRINE AND DEVICES

It has been wisely noticed as worthy of remark that none of the mercantilist theoreticians approved   all the expedients which are ordinarily embraced under the designation of Mercantilism. The complete mercantilist, in fact, never existed. Even if, for this reason, any general statement of mercantilist views is apt to mislead, it may nevertheless be convenient to attempt something of the nature of a composite photograph of the mercantilist mind, it being clearly premised that this represents the views not of any individual mercantilist, or of the mercantilists of any particular country, but rather the general type to which mercantilists everywhere in greater or less degree tended to conform. One other caveat is necessary. Mercantilism was pre-eminently rooted in practice. Although, particularly in England, the movement is reasonably prolific in theoretical exponents, it is noticeable that these came rather late in the day. In its origins and by its very nature, Mercantilism was anything but a 'system'; it was primarily the product of the minds of statesmen, civil servants, and of the financial and business leaders of the day. It follows also that in its earlier and cruder manifestations, Mercantilism is frequently best discovered as an inference from the terms of an Act of Parliament, in an *obiter dictum* inserted by a garrulous Parliamentary draftsman in the preamble of an Act, or in a memorandum or State paper, dealing with a specific administrative problem. Any attempt to state generally the essence of Mercantilism must be read in the light of these reservations.

Fundamental for the mercantilist was the strength of his country. This was the end to which all means were subservient. Moreover, in considering the prosperity and the strength of his country, the true mercantilist had always at the back of his mind a comparative standard. His country was engaged in a race with other countries, and in this race it must not be a loser. When the mercantilist came to look for a test of strength, he found it in the wealth of his country – above all in that portion of wealth which consisted of the precious metals. Herein, in a sense, they transferred to the State an idea which is entirely appropriate when applied to the individual citizen. The difference between a man of straw and a man of substance, between the man who can do and get what he wants and the man who cannot, can best be ascertained by consulting the banker who keeps their accounts. So also by a transference of ideas more permissible then than now, the king who could support a large army and maintain a powerful navy was the king who had behind him the treasure necessary for the purpose, that *pecunia nervus belli*. Hence the mercantilist attached preponderating importance to treasure and bullion as the most enduring, the most useful because the most generally acceptable, form of wealth. Adam Smith, who rather made the mercantilists a classical example of clotted economic nonsense, is responsible for the view so long prevalent that they confused money and wealth. Here Adam Smith was less than just. Despite incautious statements, it would probably be truer to say that they regarded money and bullion as the sign of wealth; and also, at least among the more enlightened, that they regarded the precious metals as beneficial because of their power to stimulate the economic activity of the country.

Assuming that bullion is in some sense wealth *par excel-*

lence, how is a country to get it? If it has mines, or can acquire plantations with mines, well and good. Its task, then, is merely to prevent the silver and gold from flowing to other countries – if need be by 'sanguinary laws,' to use Adam Smith's phrase. But if a country has no mines, the desired silver and gold can only be obtained as the result of trade, and the whole trade of the country must accordingly be so ordered and conducted that as a result of its operations gold may come into the country. It is familiar doctrine that in respect of its exports – what a country sells to others – a country must receive payment, which will ultimately be in the form of silver or gold; on the other hand, what it buys in the form of imports will have to be paid for. In a most rudimentary form of the equation of indebtedness, exports represent money coming into the country; imports represent money going out. In order that the supply of bullion in the country may increase, it is therefore necessary that there be a 'favourable balance of trade,' represented by an excess of exports over imports, leading in its consequence to a balance of payment being due to the country. It is an easy further step to consider that the trade with any country should be cherished or discouraged, according as that trade, viewed in isolation, tends to render the balance favourable or unfavourable; and it is likewise easy to conclude that all exports are, in the nature of things, good and desirable, whereas all imports are evil and damnable. It was thus a primary principle of the typical mercantilist to maximize exports while minimizing imports.

While the conception of the balance of trade has become popularly almost synonymous with Mercantilism, the consequences of the doctrine were no less important than the doctrine itself. For if exports are to be increased, then every lawful industry which produces goods meet for exportation calls for encouragement. So also, if imports are to be restricted, then we must make shift to do without foreign wares, or alternatively we must, out of our existing resources, contrive to supply ourselves with what would otherwise have come from abroad. The country must be a hive of industry, primarily with an eye on the needs of other countries. There must be no waste; preferably there ought to be a certain austerity of life, so that there may be more for export. Complete use should be made of all the resources of the country. In a sense the nation's life should, in current jargon, be 'rationalized,' so that no economy may be missed, no opportunity for gain neglected.

A further consequence of the importance attached to the balance of trade lies in the fact that it naturally led in the mercantilist doctrine to a hierarchy of occupations. Least important was agriculture. Agriculture, it is true, might feed the population; intensive tillage of every waste strip, especially if exotic crops like tobacco were raised, might render certain imports unnecessary. But in itself agriculture, as is indeed true of all domestic trade and industry, brought no money into the country, and therefore on the cruder mercantilist theories did not increase the country's wealth. More important were industry and manufactures, where a definite excess could be created for the satisfaction of the needs of other countries, and the sale of which, therefore, was pure gain for the country. Most important of all, however, was trade. If a former age had doubted the accept-ability of a merchant in the sight of the Almighty, the merchant had now come into his own, and was become the head-stone of the corner.

Such was the mercantilist programme and the mercantilist point of view; equally significant was the machinery whereby that programme was to be carried into effect. For in all their schemes the mercantilists looked to a benevolently paternal government, assumed wise enough to interfere everywhere.

Mercantilism was a policy of ubiquitous and perpetual government activity. There was nothing the Government might not do; there was nothing it ought not to do, if thereby its activity was calculated to promote the general well-being. In regard to the primary matter of restraining imports and encouraging exports, the machinery was obviously at hand in the form of import duties to keep out foreign goods, and bounties to encourage exports. But when it comes to the remoter stage of encouraging enterprises which in their consequences will lead to a healthier balance of trade, no limit can be assigned to the list of expedients devised or prescribed. The issue of patents of monopoly in respect of the introduction of new processes, the direct importation of foreign workers in order to establish a new industry, the fixation of prices and wages (partly in the interests of production), the whole series of devices to encourage shipping and the Navy, of which the Navigation Acts are the most familiar and the prescription of fish days the most curious, the creation of privileged trading companies, the foundation of plantations in order to secure supplies of raw material as well as a market for the finished commodities – such are only some of the more outstanding examples of Mercantilism in practice, of devices tending to the greater glory of the King and the increased strength of the Realm. So, too, in certain of its phases, Mercantilism tended to incorporate a definite policy with regard to population. For increased population does, or should, mean both an increase in the potential number of soldiers and sailors and an increase in the number of productive workers; and consequently encouragements to increased population can almost claim to be an essential part of Mercantilism.

In its view regarding the functions of government activity there is an obvious kinship between Mercantilism and State Socialism. The mercantilist regarded the State as the appropriate instrument for promoting the well-being of his country. Moreover, in his view the country was regarded as a unit; there were national interests to be promoted, quite irrespective of the interests of particular sections or individuals. Indeed, the interest of the State might be in conflict with that of the individual, and in such a case obviously the interest of the whole was to be preferred. Mercantilism thus endeavoured to take a comprehensive view of the needs of society, and looked upon the State as the appropriate administrative machine to secure the satisfaction of these needs.

Until recently the mercantilists have suffered from the cloud cast over them by Adam Smith. Lately there has been a disposition to treat them with greater respect. They were certainly not such consummate fools as was apt to be assumed in the middle of the nineteenth century. The rather harsh traditional judgement rests on two misinterpretations, firstly that the balance of trade theory represented substantially the whole of their aims and doctrines, whereas in fact this was but one aspect of a larger and more comprehensive policy; and secondly, that they were guilty of the folly of Crœsus in thinking that wealth consisted in gold and silver instead of the things that gold and silver could bring. A fair interpretation would probably be that they valued gold and silver as the avenues by which power and strength were to be attained, and a final judgement, moreover, should take into consideration how far their views were justified by the circumstances of the time. Yet, even so, they can scarcely be entirely acquitted of the suspicion that at times they confused the means and the end, and wrote as if bullion were possessed of some magic quality which made its acquisition the only worthy end of national policy. On two other grounds also criticism is permissible. In witnessing their intense desire to increase the national productivity, their zeal to make the best use of everything, one sometimes gets the impression that they regarded wealth, and labour that results in wealth, as the end to which man's existence is subservient. In bustling too much, one forgets that the purpose of labour is rest, that wealth exists to be consumed, that man's chief end is to glorify God and enjoy Him for ever. The second obvious line of criticism is that the mercantilists never thought out their theories to a logical conclussion. It was of the essence of their view that what one country gained, another lost; the idea of a mutually advantageous trade eluded them. The device of the favourable balance of trade was intended to ensure that it should be the other country that should lose. But clearly all countries could not have, in the mercantilist sense, a favourable balance of trade simultaneously. It was a device which all sought to practice, but which nevertheless could not be generalized. So also it is doubtful whether they ever asked themselves what would happen in a country which, in the delectable phrase of the Scottish Parliament, should find itself 'stuffed with bullion' as a result of the application of mercantilist expedients, or what measures could effectively be taken to prevent the stuffing from coming out. But this is merely to say once again that the mercantilists were practical men and not a school of economists.

III. FOUR REPRESENTATIVE MERCANTILISTS'

The previous section has perhaps been concerned with an attempt to define unreality, to wit, the complete mercantilist who can only be imagined as resulting from the fusion, into one personality, of many mercantilists, each stressing different aspects of the problems of his age. It may be convenient to supplement this general composite representation by a brief reference to four typical mercantilist writers, representing four different nations. The authors so cited are not, however, to be regarded as necessarily the leading mercantilists; others with equal appropriateness might have been hailed for the purpose. They are merely examples from a cloud of witnesses, summoned to give precision to the foregoing account.

Montchrétien

From France a convenient representative may be found in Antoine de Montchrétien[1] (1576-1621), who in 1615 dedicated his *Traicté de l'Œconomie Politique* to the King and the Queen Mother. This work derives a slight additional interest from the fact that it represents, so it is said, the earliest use of the phrase 'Political Economy.' But let no one, beguiled by the title, imagine that he will here encounter a treatise on Political Economy in the modern sense. It is really a survey of the industries of France, inspired by an exuberant and ebullient patriotism, and interwoven with much advice to the King on how matters may be improved. The book is divided into four parts, in which successively the author deals with the manufactures, the commerce and the navigation of France, and lastly of the 'principal cares' of the Prince. Of the industries surveyed it is remarkable, and not wholly characteristic of mercantilist thought, that agriculture appears first. Indeed he writes here with something of Physiocratic enthusiasm. Agriculture – and he appeals to Aristotle and Cato – is to be regarded as the beginning of all wealth;[2] if agriculture is depressed, it is not due to the infertility of the soil (a suggestion which would imply disloyalty to France) but to the poverty of the labourers. But, despite

[1] Born at Fallaise about 1576; led an adventurous life, punctuated by duels. A tragic poet and a manufacturer of hardware. Shot in a kind of battle in 1621.

[2] Reprint of 1889, edited by Funck-Brentano, p.41.

this, it is clear that Montchrétien's real interests are engaged elsewhere in the other industries which he discusses.

The first point of general interest in Montchrétien – and here he is in the true mercantilist tradition – lies in the importance which he attaches to the principle that every-one should work, and in his antipathy to all kinds of idle-ness. Man, he says, is born to live in continual exercise and occupation; the policy of the State should be to secure that no section of the population remains idle.[3] As a result of Eve's remote offence, labour is imposed on us by a right of succession, so that life and labour are inseparably united. He never fails to react to the word *l'oysivité* with constant varying phrases of moral indignation. Men reduced to doing nothing are easily induced to do evil; idleness corrupts the vigour of men and the chastity of women. Idleness is a fatal pest to rich and flourishing states; it is the mother of all vices and the cause of all sins.[4] Thus for Montchrétien, prosperity and morality alike demand the intensity of the bee-hive. If the happiness of man consists in wealth, then wealth consists in labour.

The second general characteristic of Montchrétien is, on the lyrical side, a glowing enthusiasm for France, which, when Monchrétien forgets that he is also a poet, becomes tainted with a rather rigid and chauvinistic exclusiveness. The object of the rulers of France, dowered as France is, should be to make the country rightly regarded as 'incom-parable.'[5] A proud self-sufficiency is his ultimate aim. For France is a world in itself. 'En un mot, la France est un monde; qui l'a toute veue, a tout veu ce qui se peut voir;'[6] and it follows from this proud boast that it can dispense with what it receives from neighbouring countries; but neigh-

[3] *Ibid.*, pp.21-22.
[4] See, e.g., *Ibid.*, pp.65, 74, 101.
[5] *Ibid.*, p.23.
[6] *Ibid.*, p.147.

bouring countries can in no wise do without her; it has
infinite wealth, known and to be known.[7]

A country which is thus a world in itself ought to be in a
position to maintain her children; 'being born in France, it
is right that they should live there,' but this they cannot do,
if they lose their means of subsistence.[8] Much of Montchrétien's volume tends to be a dirge on the familiar theme of
trade lost to the foreigner, who is represented as in process of
strangling the industries of France. He enlarges on the unrestrained liberties which foreigners enjoy in France, compared with the restrictions imposed in the contrary case. His
ideal, indeed, approaches the *geschlossene Handelsstaat*,
except in so far as France may be able to export out of her
pure superfluity. The arguments are on the usual lines –
the folly of having made by another that which one's self
can produce, the evil economy of spending one's substance
on what can be obtained by one's efforts. The argument,
though not peculiar to Montchrétien, is put by him with
unusual vigour:

'Premierement, je represente à vos Majestez que toute la
quinquaillerie, à la fabrique de laquelle sont occupez, tant
dedans que dehors le royaume, non des villes seules, mais
des provinces entières, se peut faire abondamment et à prix
très raisonnable dans le pays de vos Seigneuries, que d'y en
admettre et recevoir d'estrangere c'est oter la vie à plusieurs
milliers de vos subjects dont ceste industrie est l'heritage et
ce travail le fonds de leur revenue; c'est diminuer d'autant
vostre propre richesse, laquelle se fait et s'augmente de celle
de vos peuples.'[9]

On this he accordingly exhorts the King: 'Faites-nous donc
jouissance du fruict de nostre industrie; c'est à dire, rendez
nous à nous mesmes.' Such is the ideal of proud national
self-sufficiency, and Montchrétien in his appeal does not

[7] *Ibid.*, p.24.   [8] *Ibid.*, p.73.   [9] *Ibid.*, pp.51-52.

disdain what would now be called sob-stuff, by invoking 'the tender sighs of the women and the pitiable cries of the children of those whose labours have suffered from foreign competition.'[10]

For Montchrétien, the foreigner is in the main a person given to fraud and guile. Specifically 'whatever is foreign corrupts us.'[11] In particular, foreign books 'poison our spirits and corrupt our manners,' and therefore their importation should be prohibited.[12] Indeed Montchrétien approves of a vigorous all-round national exclusiveness hinting at a divine ordinance which has assigned to the inhabitants of any area the use of the elements and the goods which it produces. Further, he cites with admiration the example of Lyons, which acted on the principle that 'each town should have something particular and in reserve for its own children, in order that it may help them.'[13] Montchrétien is thus a stout defender of the maxim which enjoins upon us the expediency of rendering to our own sea-maws their ancient and prescriptive dues.

On some other questions Montchrétien shows a departure from the mercantilist norm. His scheme of things would be almost destructive of international trade, and there is therefore little, if anything, of the doctrine of the balance of trade in Montchrétien. Likewise he appreciates the importance of internal trade, and in one place he argues, and doubtless with truth, that no country could excel France in happiness and wealth and glory, if it could only keep the whole of its internal trade to itself, and restrict its foreign trade to the export of what it produced in superabundance.[14] He approves of the doctrine 'que l'un ne perd jamais que l'autre n'y gagne.'[15] but draws from the maxim the inference that in domestic trade between citizen and citizen, there can be

[10] *Ibid.*, p.73.   [11] *Ibid.*, p.241.   [12] *Ibid.*, p.92.
[13] *Ibid.*, pp.114-115.   [14] *Ibid.*, p.146.   [15] *Ibid.*, p.161.

no loss for the public such as he fears may result from foreign trade. Varying the familiar analogy which finds in a national debt a transfer from the right trouser pocket to the left, domestic trade is like a man with a jar in each hand, pouring a liquid from one to the other. Foreign trade is thus for Montchrétien something of a snare and a gamble; it may lead to loss, and from this danger domestic trade at least is free.

From all this it naturally follows that the bullionist aspect of Mercantilism is less prominent in Montchrétien. He approves, it is true, of the old dictum that money is the 'nerve of war,' and adds on his own account that gold has often been shown to be more powerful than iron.[16] But he never loses his head on this aspect of the question, and there is one remarkable passage – it is true a somewhat isolated passage – in which he seems to fly in the face of all mercantilist orthodoxy: 'It is not the abundance of gold and silver, the quantities of pearls and diamonds which make states rich and opulent; it is the conveniency (accomodement) of things necessary to life, and fit for wearing; he who has more of these has more of wealth.' Then after contrasting the position in the time of Charles VI, when, if money was scarcer, prices were lower, he adds: 'It is true we have become more abundant in gold and silver than our fathers were; but we are not therefore more comfortable and more rich.'[17] It is such a passage as this that reveals the fatuity of endeavouring to make the mercantilists conform to a type. Montchrétien, in short, is the rather repellently patriotic patriot, contemptuous of other peoples. His vision is that of the isolated state, with France in acknowledged supremacy, supplying all her needs, and having in addition something left over for export, so that trade represents a system of one-way traffic. Domestically all are to work, and work inces-

---

[16] *Ibid.*, pp.141-142.   [17] *Ibid.*, p.241.

santly; idleness is to be banished to foreign parts – where presumably it will do no harm.

Thomas Mun

Of the innumerable company of English mercantilist writers and pamphleteers, one has, by common consent, a pre-eminent claim to be chosen as spokesman of the somewhat heterogeneous group. It is not merely that Thomas Mun[18] (1571-1641) approaches most nearly to a systematic statement of mercantilist principles; of no less importance is the fact that he wrote at a time when Mercantilism was yet scarcely exposed to the disintegrating forces which made the mercantilist of the middle and later periods in some respects anticipators of a more liberal policy. Mun is perhaps the nearest approach to the perfect mercantilist; yet even he was unnecessarily conscious of heterodoxy, and is at times involved in those contradictions which are inevitable in a school, one of whose characteristics it was to refuse to push their thoughts to their logical conclusions.

Mun's book was written for the better upbringing and instruction of his son, and it only appeared posthumously in 1664. Its very title is a condensed summary of Mercantilism: *England's Treasure by Forraign Trade, or, The Ballance of Our Forraign Trade is the Rule of our Treasure*. His opening statement, after he settles down to business, gives a precise statement of the theory of the balance of trade in its least compromising form. To increase our wealth and treasure we must ever observe this rule: ' to sell more to strangers yearly than we consume of theirs in value.'[19] This rule, moreover, will give us a precise index of the amount of

[18] Born in London, 1571; engaged for most of his life in mercantile affairs in connection with Italy and the Levant. A member of the Committee of the East India Company. Died 1641.
[19] *England's Treasure*, chap. 2.

precious metals entering or leaving the country. If exports are £2,200,000 and imports £2,000,000,

'we may rest assured that the Kingdom shall be enriched yearly two hundred thousand pounds, which must be brought to us in so much Treasure; because that part of our stock which is not returned to us in wares must necessarily be brought home in treasure.'[20]

Such being the situation, the secret of accumulation lies in choking off the imports and in the encouragement of exports, and the most valuable chapter in Mun is that in which he proceeds to enumerate twelve methods whereby these so desirable ends may be attained. This chapter (No. 3) is really a complete catalogue of mercantilist devices, as these were apprehended at the time when Mun wrote, and the programme he outlines gives so luminous an account of Mercantilism in its robuster days that it may be permissible to reproduce the main points of his programme.

Firstly, Mun recommends the cultivation of waste grounds (which he rashly says are infinite) in such a way as will not interfere with the revenues derived from already cultivated lands. Thus hemp, flax, cordage and tobacco could be grown and the corresponding imports cut off.

Secondly, we should 'soberly refrain from excessive consumption of foreign wares in our diet and rayment'; also from unnecessary change of fashion, 'which vices at this present are more notorious amongst us than in former ages.'

Thirdly, with regard to exports, 'we must consider our neighbour's necessities.' Where they cannot get elsewhere the wares they require, we must sell them as dear as possible; but if they can supply their wants elsewhere, 'we must in this case strive to sell as cheap as possible we can, rather than to lose the utterance of such wares.'

[20] *Ibid.*, chap. 2.

Fourthly, the value of exports could be increased by confining these to our own ships, as then we should gain not merely the price of our wares, but also the merchants' gains – the invisible exports of modern theory.

Fifthly, by frugally expending our natural wealth, we might have more left for export. If we insist on being prodigal, it should be with the manufactures of our own country, so that the poor may be employed. This, however, Mun clearly regards as only a second-best; it would be still better if the poor were employed for the use of strangers.

Sixthly, the fishing in the adjacent seas should be developed, instead of allowing the Dutch to serve many places in Christendom with our fish.

Seventhly, a Staple, for the encouragement of the entrepôt trade, should be established, making England a distributing centre, thus increasing shipping, trade, and the King's customs.

Eighthly, Mun recommends, in curious contrast to Smith later, that we should especially cherish trade with far countries. The reasoning is curious and fallacious; if pepper is 2s. the pound in London, it may be 20d. at Amsterdam, but the merchant may get it in the East Indies at 3d. 'which is a mighty advantage.'

The *ninth* device Mun regards as a heresy in himself, and therefore postpones it for further consideration; it is that in certain cases it would be beneficial to allow the export of money itself.

The *tenth* and *eleventh* points are akin. Mun recommends that manufactures of foreign materials (velvets, silks, etc.) should be allowed to be exported free. This would furnish employment, increase exports, and by encouragement of imports with a view to manufacture, would increase His Majesty's Customs. So also native commodities should not be burdened with too great customs, lest their enhanced price diminish their sale abroad. Logically, of course, this would lead to a system of bounties to encourage exports.

The *twelfth* and last injunction is vague and comprehensive; it is that ' we must endeavour to make the most we can of our own.' Such is Mun's programme, and it will be seen that taken in its entirely, it represents a policy of abstemious frugality, shunning all waste, and despising no opportunity of gain; leaving it to the foreigner to enjoy life, provided we enjoy the turnover.

All of this, except the ninth point, is of the mercantilist scheme of things. On the question of the exportation of money, Mun recognizes that his view is contrary to the common opinion; his argument in favour of allowing money to go is, briefly, that 'money begets trade and trade encreaseth money.'[21] He argues – and here true Mercantilism begins to crumble – that merely keeping the money in the kingdom will not make a quick and ample trade; that depends on the need other countries have for our wares. Indeed, he realizes that abundance of money raises prices, and 'dear wares decline their use and consumption,' thus leading to a diminution in the volume of trade. It is therefore necessary to have faith that our moneys sent out in trade will come back again in treasure.

Like all mercantilists of yesterday and to-day, Mun is scathing in his condemnation of the idleness of his countrymen, contrasted with the industry of the foreigner. For him, the Dutch were, morally, the good boys of Europe. In contrast with them

' we leave our wonted exercises and studies, following our pleasures, and of late years besotting ourselves with pipe and pot, in a beastly manner, sucking smoak, and drinking healths, until death stares many in the face.'[22]

[21] *Ibid.*, chap. 4.　　　[22] *Ibid.*, chap. 19.

Not the least interesting point in Mun is that even here, in the citadel of Mercantilism, there are signs of dismemberment. Thus in contradistinction to the rigour of the programme outlined in the third chapter, later on he will not allow all kinds of bounty and pomp to be avoided. If we use few or no foreign wares,

'how shall we then vent our own commodities? what will become of our Ships, Mariners, Munitions, our poor Artificers and many others? doe we hope that other Countreys will afford us money for All our wares without buying or bartering for Some of theirs?'[23]

These are indeed searching questions!

And on another equally fundamental point he says this:

'For although Treasure is said to be the sinews of the War, yet this is so because it doth provide, unite and move the power of men, victuals, and munition where and when the cause doth require; but if these things be wanting in due time, what shall we then do with our money?'[24]

'What shall we do with our money?' What indeed? This, some would suggest, is precisely the question which the mercantilists refused to answer, and which they could not have faced without devastating effects on their scheme of thought. On the other hand, that such a person as Mun gets so far as to ask the question may also indicate that the mercantilists were not quite so muddle-headed as has frequently been assumed.

It is not possible here to consider representatives of later English Mercantilism; but even at the risk of repetition, it should be again emphasized that, increasingly, although the postulate of national power remains, there are doubts and divergencies from the original mercantilist system of

[23] *Ibid.*, chap. 15.   [24] *Ibid.*, chap. 18.

thought. Thus Josiah Child (1630-1699), after correctly defin-
ing the mercantilist conception of the balance of trade, refers
to the practical difficulties of ascertaining what that balance
may be, and concludes that the whole conception is 'too
doubtful and uncertain as to our general trade, and in
reference to particular trades fallible and erroneous.' For
him the best test is to be found in the volume of trade as
revealed in the increase of shipping, and the greatest stimu-
lator lies in an abatement of the rate of interest.

Serra

To spread the net wider, one earlier mercantilist from
Italy may be glanced at. Like Mun, Antonio Serra epito-
mizes the mercantilist creed in the title of his short
pamphlet, published in 1613 under the title: *A Brief Treatise
on the Causes which can make Gold and Silver Abound in
Kingdoms where there are no Mines.*[25] Serra begins by
assuming as a proved proposition the importance of a kingdom abounding in gold and silver, the contrary belief being
indeed an indication of doubtful sanity. Apart from those
blessed countries which possess gold and silver ' naturally,' the
presence of the precious metals is due to collateral causes.
Certain causes may be peculiar to a given country, such as
its situation; otherwise Serra finds four main factors to which
the presence of gold and silver may be attributed. These are
the quantity of industry, the quality of the population, extensive trading operations and the regulations of the sovereign. With regard to the first point Serra gives reasons for
the mercantilist's preference of industry to agriculture.

[25] A selection is given in Monroe's *Early Economic Thought.* The
whole pamphlet will be found in the *Economisti del Cinque et Sei-
cento,* edited by Graziani. The only fact that appears to be known
with regard to Serra is that his celebrated tract on how to secure
an abundance of money was written in prison (in 1613) while Serra
was undergoing sentence for coining. Or is this addition to the legend
merely the happy invention of a later humorist?

Firstly, it is safer; the artisan is more sure of a profit than is the peasant. The peasant depends on the weather, and his efforts may therefore result in a loss. 'But in industry there is always a certainty of gain, provided labour is expended.' To-day this sounds rather naïve. Secondly, although of course he does not use the phrase, industry is subject to increasing returns, whereas agriculture is not. Industry can always be multiplied two-fold or two-hundredfold, and with proportionately less expense (*con minor proporzione di spesa*). The third reason is that industry has a sure market. Produce is difficult to keep; but the fruits of industry can be preserved for a long time. They can therefore be held up for a better market, or exported. (Serra was not familiar with the canning industry.) Lastly, there is more profit in industry than in 'produce.' The other causes leading to abundance of gold and silver may be disposed of summarily. The inhabitants must be diligent, eager to build up trade, without as well as within the country. The country should possess a great trade preferably in the produce of other places rather than its own. On the fourth cause, the regulations to be made by the sovereign – the essential point of Mercantilism in operation – Serra is feeble. It may be honest, but it is not helpful to say that 'it is not easy to know how to arrange this factor well,' or that it is necessary to attend to more than one cause, since the same cause may produce different effects in different cases (as a light whistle rouses dogs and quiets horses). Such instructions are hardly calculated to produce the great civil servant. When the Chancellor of the Exchequer whistles lightly, who are the dogs and who are the horses?

Much of the remainder of Serra's pamphlet is occupied with a consideration of the reasons which make gold and silver abound at Venice, and why, on the other hand, Naples is poor; also – a characteristic of Italian Mercantilism – with questions relating to rates of exchange. It is perhaps note-worthy that, like Mun, Serra disapproves of the prohibition of the export of money. If money is exported, it must be with an object, and therefore 'if money is exported for any purpose whatever, it must return with a profit into the kingdom from which it was sent' – perhaps a rather large assumption, which incidentally would rather tend to make Mercantilism as a whole much talk about nothing.

Von Hornick

To preserve the balance a fourth and last mercantilist, this time from Austria, may be cited. Philipp W. von Hornick[26] (1638-1712), the author of *Oesterreich über alles wann es nur will,* is amusing by reason of his uncompromis-ing vigour and a certain quaint *naïveté.* His definition of policy rests on what is regarded as an axiomatic truism, which is in itself an interesting statement of mercantilist faith. It is to the effect that the might and eminence of a country consists in its surplus of gold and silver, and all other things necessary or convenient for its subsistence, derived from its own resources without dependence on other countries. For the attainment of this end Hornick lays down, after the manner of Mun, a sequence of rules which are 'especially serviceable.' These rules are nine in number, and naturally present a considerable degree of similarity to Mun's points, though there are interesting variations in emphasis. Briefly, Hornick's programme of Mercantilism comprises the following points: (1) The most is to be made of the country's soil; not a clod of earth is to be uncon-sidered; every form of plant is to be experimented with; above all, if possible, gold and silver are to be discovered. (2) Commodities are to be worked up in the country. (3)

---

[26] Born at Mainz, 1638; studied law and practised at Vienna; later in the service of the Cardinal of Passau.

Population is to be encouraged, and people turned from idleness (the populationist element, it may be observed, is a peculiar characteristic of German Mercantilism. (4) Gold and silver, once in the country, are under no circumstances to be taken out for any purpose; equally, however, they are not to be hoarded, but are to remain in circulation. (5) The inhabitants are to get along with their own domestic products, and do without foreign products as far as possible. (6) When absolutely essential to obtain goods from the foreigner, these should be obtained in exchange for other wares, and not by the payment of gold and silver. (7) In the event of the unavoidable importation of foreign goods, they should be imported in unfinished form, and worked up in the country. (8) *Per contra*, opportunity is to be sought night and day to sell superfluous goods to the foreigner, but these should be sold in a finished form, and for gold and silver. (9) No imports should be allowed whenever there is a sufficient supply of the relevant commodity in the country, and this even if the home article is of inferior quality and of higher price.

The condensed reproduction of this programme will not be merely vain repetition if the juxtaposition of the 8th point alongside the 6th and 7th serves to bring out the one-sided character of Mercantilism, and the failure of the mercantilists to realize that in the international clash, a State inspired by a Hornick might encounter a rival inspired by a Mun. For the rest, Hornick is a mercantilist of pronounced justquauboutist tendencies. His essential maxim from which all others flow is the fifth in this enumeration, and as a first step to the realization of the ideal of self-sufficiency he recommends the prohibition of the four chief groups of foreign imports – silk, woollen, linen and French wares. In respect of these alone, the Austrians throw away to the foreigner every year at least ten million thalers. Think how the lifeless body of Austria would revive if this sum were saved even for one year! If it were saved for twenty years, what country in Europe would equal Austria? His fundamental doctrine is that it is better to pay for an article two thalers which remain in the country than only one which goes out. As he dolefully and fatalistically says: 'What once goes out, stays out.' Moreover, it is surprising to note how the other precepts will be automatically observed if this first measure is adopted. Take, for instance, population. Prohibition of these imports will throw many foreigners out of work; artisans go where they can get a living; they will therefore be compelled to come to Austria, and the population problem is solved. On other questions, Hornick speaks with the authentic voice of Mercantilism. Will there be any danger that, in the absence of foreign competition, prices will be unduly raised? Not if the Government supervises things as it should, and checks wantonness; further, the philosophically minded may reflect that it is better to be a victim to one's own countrymen than to a stranger. Then again, what about Dame Fashion, for surely we must dress like other nations? 'It would be a good thing,' quoth Hornick, 'if we sent Dame Fashion to the Devil, her father.' An excellent sentiment with which to conclude a chapter.

CHAPTER IV

The Physiocrats: Quesnay and Turgot

Quesnay

T H E position of François Quesnay[1] (1694-1774) in the history of economic doctrine is in many ways remarkable. The man himself is an interesting and engaging personality. A successful medical practitioner attached to the Court, with a record of medical dissertations on such subjects as suppuration, gangrene and fevers, he burgeoned as an economist at the age of sixty-two. Yet despite this tardy blossoming, he lived to be the acknowledged head of the most compact of any of the schools of economists, and he died, at the age of eighty, the revered master of a large band of disciples, whose panegyrics sound extravagant even for an age when the art of eulogy was assiduously cultivated. It naturally follows also from Quesnay's late absorption in economics that his literary labours were unusual. It is not true, as has sometimes been said, that he wrote little, but it is true that all he wrote has the appearance of disconnected efforts, contributions to encyclopædias, periodicals, and what not; and moreover hardly any of it was published under his own name.

It is a further consequence that Quesnay tends to merge into his school, that body of men who called themselves 'economists,' and whom posterity has agreed to designate as 'Physiocrats.' It is true, of course, that there were differences of view, different shades of emphasis among the Physiocrats,

---

[1] Born at Méré (Seine et Oise), 1694; brought up in the country and largely self-taught. After a distinguished medical career, became physician to Madame de Pompadour in 1749, and to the King in 1755.

but it is a remarkable tribute to the cohesion of the school that common usage lumps them comprehensively under the name of the 'Physiocrats,' and seldom thinks of the units concealed behind the collective phrase. It is, however, from Quesnay that the entire impulse comes, and all that is characteristic of Physiocratic doctrine is to be found in his writings. This section will therefore be confined almost exclusively to Quesnay, as representative of the whole body of physiocratic theory.

Three points of a general character can hardly fail to strike any reader who approaches Quesnay. In the first place the economic doctrine, such as it is, is really only a corollary to something much larger. For Quesnay, as for all the Physiocrats, his economics was but part of a *Weltanschauung* – it is difficult to avoid the German word. He is a moralist; primarily perhaps the foundation of the whole structure is to be found in his view of natural and positive law, a conception indeed (that of the 'rule of nature') to which the school owes the title by which it is now universally known. Consequently it is necessary to disentangle, somewhat gingerly, the economic aspects of the Physiocratic structure. The second point is that, despite the immingling of relatively alien elements, Quesnay has substantial claims to be regarded as the real founder of Political Economy in the modern sense. With him the empirical element has gone; whether he is right or wrong, Quesnay realizes that the problem of the nature of wealth, the conditions of its production and the laws of its distribution are matters to which scientific and precise reasoning may be applied with the object of arriving at universal truths. The third point is perhaps rather a comment on, or an illustration of this; it is the extent to which Quesnay anticipates Adam Smith. The differences are obvious, and have indeed been excessively underlined by Smith himself, but the similarities are still more remarkable. The exact relationship between Quesnay and Smith has been much discussed, and for a time there was a tendency to suggest that Smith may have been influenced by Quesnay, with whom he was familiar during his visit to France. It is now clear, however, that the main outlines of Adam Smith's thought had been evolved while he was still professing in Glasgow, at a time when Quesnay could not have influenced him. Almost certainly the similarities of Quesnay and Smith merely exemplify once more the wholly natural fact that independent inquirers do frequently, about the same time, arrive at substantially the same conclusions.

Firstly, and warily, as to the fundamental point of natural law. For Quesnay there is a 'law' which governs human actions, no less than the rest of the field of nature, and the problem is to find the structure of society which will accord with this natural law. What is this 'droit naturel,' most elusive of conceptions? It differs from the 'droit légitime,' the mere act of a legislature, in that it is recognized by the light of reason, and by that evidence alone. It is binding apart from any constraint, whereas a 'droit légitime' is obligatory by reason of the penalty attached. Thus the 'droit naturel' is superior to the laws of man's making, as is abundantly proved by the multitude of contradictory and absurd laws which have been enacted.[2]

But to change the ground and come to a point of more direct economic substance, to what does man have a 'natural right'? Vaguely, these are comprehended in the right he has to the things which are 'propres à sa jouissance.'[3] But this must be defined. The theoretical right of everyone to everything is illusory; it must be limited to the right of everyone

[2] *Le Droit Naturel*, chap. 2, pp.365-366, in Oncken's complete edition, to which subsequent references relate.
[3] *Le Droit Naturel*, chap. 1, p.359.

to that portion of things which he can obtain by his own labour. The swallow might be said to have a right to all the flies that dance in the air; in fact, the swallow's rights are limited to those he can catch. (The rights of the fly are not discussed.)[4] When men come to enter into society, they will increase this natural right, and guarantee its enjoyment, 'if the constitution of the society is in agreement with the order which is evidently the most advantageous to men relatively to the fundamental laws of their natural right.'[5] One further natural right calls for emphasis; each one has the right to make use of the faculties given him by nature on condition that he hurts neither himself nor others – though why, at this stage, he should not be allowed to hurt himself is not clear.[6] It will be obvious how far, on the economic side, these propositions take Quesnay. He has consecrated private property on the basis of labour; he has established the principle of freedom of contract, and he has made it a primary function of the State to guarantee these rights. Indeed, so fundamental is this, that where property and liberty are not guaranteed, there is no government but merely anarchy.[7]

We come then to human society, which is subject to two kinds of laws, the *lois naturelles* and the *lois positives*, the former, despite their high authority and the praises bestowed upon them – are they not 'immuables, et irréfragables et les meilleures lois possibles'?[8] – remaining somewhat nebulous, the latter being of human origin, and therefore strictly subordinate. Indeed the primary function of the positive

[4] *Ibid.*, chap. 2, pp.366-367.
[5] *Ibid.*, chap. 3, p.368.
[6] *Ibid.*, chap. 3, p.371.
[7] *Ibid.*, chap. 5, p.374. The two fundamental principles of security of property and freedom of contract are expressed with perhaps even greater emphasis in the *Maximes Générales*. See Maxime 4 and 13, pp. 331, 333.
[8] *Ibid.*, chap. 5, p.375.

laws is to 'declare' the natural laws.[9] The first positive law, underlying all other positive laws, consists in the institution of public and private instruction in the laws of the natural order.[10] although, regrettably, the syllabus of the course is not provided. Positive laws are merely deductions from, or comments on, the primitive natural laws. The fundamental laws of society are imprinted on the hearts of man; they form the light which illumines his conscience. In relation thereto, the sphere of positive law is little more than that of interpretation. Positive laws are thus essentially subordinate, and should only be introduced in so far as they are in conformity with, and rigorously subject to, these other essential laws. They are therefore not of arbitrary institution, and 'the legislator cannot render them just by his authority, except in so far as they are just in their essence.'[11]

Further discussion of the subtleties of 'natural law' may be left to the political philosopher, to whom the subject properly belongs. Here we are only concerned with the economic implications of Quesnay's generalizations. And it is clear in what direction he is heading. The art of the legislator is to interpret for this confused world certain natural laws (though it is as well not to be too curious as to their contents). The test of good legislation is found in the extent to which positive laws are a faithful reflection of their shadowy prototypes. Clearly there must be no contradiction; but clearly, also, embroidery should be reduced to a minimum. In short, having caught the reflection of these eternal immutable laws, the less legislation the better. Thus, on high abstract grounds, we arrive at the great principle of non-intervention, the doctrine of *laissez-faire, laissez passer,* to use the tag which the Physiocratic school has bequeathed

[9] *Ibid.*, chap. 5, p.376.
[10] *Ibid.*, chap. 5, p.375.
[11] See *Le Despotisme de la Chine*, chap. 8, and especially sections 6 and 19, pp.642, 650.

to the world. It is the duty of the Government to see to the defence of society. Since prosperity (apparently a simple matter) depends merely on cultivating the soil and keeping down thieves and blackguards, positive law will be necessary to restrain the evil-doers.[12] But if positive law fussily goes beyond the point of protection against invasion, restraint of the wicked, and of routine administration, can it lay any claim to be but a reflex of eternal law? The blessedness of Free Trade and of Goverment inactivity is knocking at the door.

The search for the natural order leads, on the economic side, to the adoration of agriculture, the most familiar of Physiocratic doctrines. It was not merely, as Quesnay emphasized – and perhaps he was right – that agricultural nations alone can form empires which are fixed and durable,[13] but agriculture is itself the only source of wealth. The Physiocratic accentuation of the importance of agriculture was doubtless in origin but a reflection of the needs of France at the time, and a reaction against that phase of Mercantilism which stressed the importance of manufactures, and which, being sponsored by Colbert, has made 'Colbertism' almost a French synonym for Mercantilism. Yet the Physiocrats devised for their instinctive preferences a theoretical basis which led to inextricable entanglements. For they sought to prove that agriculture alone produced the wealth of the community, and that, in contrast to this 'productive' activity, all other occupations, however laudable and necessary, were 'unproductive' and 'sterile.' 'Agriculture,' says Quesnay, 'is the source of all the wealth of the State and of the wealth of all the citizens.'[14] Again, 'every-

---

[12] *Le Droit Naturel*, chap. 5, p.375: *Despotisme de la Chine*, chap. 8, sec. 6, p.642.
[13] *Despotisme de la Chine*, chap. 8, sec. 12, p.647.
[14] *Maximes Generales*, No. 1, p.331.

thing that is disadvantageous to agriculture is prejudicial to
the State and the nation, and everything that favours agriculture is profitable to the State and the nation.'[15] Nor is
this merely an echo of the vague generalities of Xenophon
and Cicero. The exaltation of agriculture over other
economic activities rests on a subordination of these which is
theoretically demonstrable. In Quesnay's earliest articles on
Fermes and *Grains*, this position is already emphatically
stated:

'Agriculture and commerce are constantly regarded as
the two sources of our wealth. Commerce, like industry, is
merely a branch of agriculture. These two states exist only
by virtue of agriculture. It is agriculture which furnishes
the material of industry and commerce and which pays
both; but these two branches give back their gain to agriculture, which renews the wealth which is spent and consumed each year' (*Grains*; p. 216).

Indeed Quesnay at times speaks as if the commercial classes
were scarcely a part of the nation at all. A mixed agricultural and commercial kingdom, he says, unites two nations
which are distinct one from the other. The agricultural is
'the constitutive part of the society.' The other is an
extrinsic addition which forms a part of the general republic
of external commerce.[16] He returns to the idea that the
commercial classes are a race apart from all other nations,
forming in a sense a sect among themselves: 'Nos commerçants sont aussi les commerçants des autres nations; les
commerçants des autres nations sont aussi nos commerçants.'[17] As is natural in the light of this contrast, Quesnay

---

[15] *Analyse du Tableau Économique*, p.319; but one might say
passim.
[16] *Analyse du Tableau Économique*, p.321.
[17] *Ibid.*, p.328.

regards it as a mistaken policy to show favour to the inhabitants of the towns, as by cheap grain, at the expense of the country. In this way 'on desole les campagnes, qui sont la source des vraies richesses de l'Etat.'[18]

The distinction between agriculture on the one hand and industry and commerce on the other, is further revealed by the fact that in the former there is a surplus, while the others merely pay their way. This surplus is the famous 'produit net,' the token of Nature's superior bounty in agricultural operations. On Quesnay's theory, agriculture is carried on by advances of various kinds (*avances foncières, avances primitives, avances annuelles*), some of these falling on the proprietor and some on the cultivator. But when all expenses have been met, and the cultivators have taken all that is required to maintain themselves and reimburse them in respect of their annual advances, there still remains something over, a 'produit net'[19] (a rent) which is payable to the proprietor. This 'produit net' is in fact the real revenue of the nation, and it is this which, in one form or another, supports the manufacturing and commercial classes. Thus we get the triple division of classes, so dear to the Physiocrats. There is, firstly, the class of proprietors, to whom the 'produit net' is paid, whose services consist in making the *avances foncières*, and also in the more general and social duties which fall upon them; there is, secondly, the productive class, who cultivate the soil; and thirdly, there are all those who are lumped together under a title, which, despite all apologetics, has in it something wounding and depreciatory, the 'unproductive' or sterile class. Strictly speaking, there is a fourth class, the wage-earners, but they do not occupy a large place in Physiocratic classification.

The 'sterility' of these unproductive sections of the com-

---

[18] *Fermiers,* p.180.
[19] *Analyse du Tableau Économique,* pp.304-309.

munity may require a further word of explanation. So far as concerns commerce, there need be little difficulty; the view corresponds to what is in some ways an instinctive reaction of the unsophisticated human mind. The man who merely exchanges does not ' produce '; and Quesnay pushes to its logical conclusion the view that the purchases represented by commerce are merely ' exchanges of value for equal value, without loss or gain on one side or the other.'[20] The trader merely brings about a transference of wealth from one hand to the other. Whereas the cultivators can pay with what they have received from the hand of Nature, rendered productive by their labours, the traders can only pay out what they have been paid: ' ils sont payés pour payer.' The difference is between *les salariants* and *les salariés*; or in another phrase of which frequent use is made, the unproductive class is the *classe stipendée*: it is kept and maintained by the other.[21]

With regard to the industrial and manufacturing classes the argument is similar, though inevitably it seems more forced and unnatural. The common value of a commodity is merely the value of the original material and of the cost of maintenance of the worker during the time he has been engaged.[22] If the work of the artisan were ' productive,' it would be desirable to increase the amount of work necessary for a job.[23] In fact, however, such labour cannot increase the wealth which the nation spends annually, because the labour is limited by the amount of this wealth, and this can only be increased by agriculture, and in no way by the expense involved in the work of the artisans (a question-begging argument; but he means for what it is worth, that to increase the number of cobblers, e.g., there must first be

[20] *Du Commerce,* p.458.
[21] *Ibid.,* p.471.
[22] *Sur les Travaux des Artisans,* p.537.
[23] *Ibid.,* p.532.

an increase in the number of cow hides).[24] The product of the artisan then is merely worth the expense involved; he merely acquires a right to share in the consumption of wealth produced by the cultivator. But in contradistinction to agriculture, there is no surplus. In his own language, which happens to be correct, the worker speaks of 'earning his keep'; he does not say that he produces it: 'il dit qu'il *gagne* sa subsistance, et ne dit pas qu'il la produit.'[25] Thus by arguments which appear thin and unconvincing, as is inevitable in the defender of a confused cause, Quesnay demonstrated that the artisan, the industrial worker, is an unproductive labourer.[26]

The distinction between productive and unproductive labour was the most tiresome of the legacies which the Physiocrats bequeathed to the economic world. For at least two generations every writer on these matters felt it incumbent upon him to return to the point and to attempt to give some sense to a distinction which in truth had none. As expressed by the Physiocrats, the position is clearly untenable. There is no such sharp distinction between agricultural labour and all other occupations as would justify us in classifying the former as productive labourers and all others as unproductive. It is a useful, if trite, maxim that production is not completed until the commodity, whatever it be, is in the hands (or on the table) of the consumer; and if we ask for bread, the ploughman, the miller, the baker, and the

[24] *Ibid.*, p.533. As this is of the essence of the argument the exact words may be given: 'Ces travaux ne peuvent donc accroître les richesses que la nation dépense annuellement, puisqu'ils sont eux-mêmes limités par la mesure de ces richesses, qui ne peuvent s'accroître que par les travaux de l'agriculture et non par les dépenses des travaux des artisans.'
[25] *Réponse au Memoire de M.H.*, p.390.
[26] The reader who is beclouded by this brief summary should refer to the *Réponse au Memoire de M.H.*, pp.384-395, and the dialogue *Sur les Travaux des Artisans*, p.256 et seq., where this point is discussed with much Physiocratic subtlety.

baker's van-boy (if he be indispensable) all alike minister to our needs. What is wanted in this life is the right thing in the right place at the right time, and all who contribute to this so desirable end are economically, on this point at least, doing the same kind of thing. Further, the argument that agriculture produces in rent a 'produit net,' whereas elsewhere there is no surplus, is of course entirely fallacious. But that is a matter for Mr. Ricardo to deal with.

This may be the place for such notice as is unavoidable of the 'Tableau Economique,' in its time the crowning achievement of Quesnay and the Physiocratic school, now perhaps better reduced to an embarrassed footnote. Despite Dupont's assurance that the Tableau Economique is obscure only to those who are lacking in the power of comprehension, it may be doubted whether it will ever be anything but a vast mystification, a subject to be treated gingerly by commentators, rendered uneasy by the feeling that they do not quite understand what they are talking about. The attitude of the Physiocrats towards Quesnay's masterpiece was one of extravagant adoration. In the eyes of Mirabeau (the elder) there had been since the world began three great discoveries – the invention of writing, the invention of money and the Tableau Economique; and though Mirabeau reached the top-notch in adulation, others were not far behind in prophesying that posterity would derive incalculable advantages from Quesnay's supreme discovery.

It is easier to say what are the ideas behind the Tableau Economique than to explain how it gives expression to these ideas. Firstly, as Dupont remarks, whereas Economics had hitherto been a conjectural science, subject to inductive reasoning, the Tableau Economique attempted to make Economics an exact science (or rather suggested the possibility of such an attempt being made). More important, the Tableau Economique endeavoured to trace the flow of wealth through a community in terms of Physiocratic doctrine, with the practical end of ascertaining the health of the community. It was thus to be a tool in the hands of the Government, 'la boussole du gouvernement des états.' Assuming that the 'produit net' is 100 per cent. of the *avances annuelles*, i.e. that 2,000 livres disbursed by the productive classes will yield 2,000 livres to the proprietors after all expenses are met, the problem is to trace the subsequent history of these 2,000 livres. Half (Quesnay assumes) will go back to the productive classes, and this sum of 1,000 livres will again yield a 'produit net' of 1,000 livres; the other half will go to the sterile classes, who, however, will pay back a half (500 livres) to the producers; and so we proceed by what Quesnay calls the 'ziczac,' dividing by two as we go along.

In the case postulated by Quesnay there is equilibrium at the end of the proceedings; here we have a state in which there is neither increase nor decay. If an undue proportion of the national revenue is diverted to the right (i.e. to the unproductive classes) an unhealthy condition arises and the State is threatened with decline. Though recognizing that the Tableau would vary according to the different data and assumptions, and that 'a different case would lead to a different result,'[27] no attempt seems to have been made (and probably none could be made) to apply the Tableau to the special circumstances of any community. If the Tableau was an *outil*, as the Physiocrats were given to declaring, it was one which the Physiocrats made no attempt to use. The idea that wealth flowed through a community, and that the health of the community depended on how it flowed, and might be imperilled by an undue diversion in one direction, was however, a useful conception. Here alone is the signifi-

[27] *Analyse du Tableau Économique*, pp.311, 316.

cance of the Tableau Économique; otherwise, apart from its interest to the economic antiquarian, a detailed study of the 'ziczac' is but an example of unproductive labour.

On this general view of the relation between different classes of society, the encouragement of agriculture becomes the chief article of policy of the Physiocrats. For agriculture to be profitably pursued, it is essential, in Quesnay's eyes, that it be conducted on a large scale. This is the constantly recurring theme of his first two articles on *Fermiers* and *Grains*. Indeed it is not too much to say that he aims at giving agriculture something of an industrial form. He constantly emphasizes the need of capital in agriculture, the importance of the rich 'fermier.' The 'fermier' is not to be a labourer who himself tills the ground; he is to be an 'entrepreneur qui gouverne.'[28] So, negatively, manufactures are not to be encouraged at the expense of agriculture. Above all, there is for Quesnay a wisdom in high agricultural prices; it is fatal to seek to encourage manufactures through lowering the price of the means of subsistence.[29] His detailed observations regarding agriculture are, however, of his time, and hardly concern us here.

It is, however, when Quesnay advocates Free Trade and analyses the assumptions of the mercantilists, that he most clearly speaks with the voice of Adam Smith. Money is supposed to be wealth, because with money one can buy what one has need of. But money is not obtained for nothing; it also costs as much as it is worth to the buyer, and nations will always be able to obtain as much money as

[28] *Grains*, p.219.
[29] See *Maximes du Gouvernement Économique* (No. 9), attached to the article on *Grains*, p.327; also *Fermiers*, p.180. Quesnay epigrammatically sums up his position in the eighteenth of the *Maximes Générales*: 'Abondance et non-valeur n'est pas richesse. Disette et cherté est misère. Abondance et cherté est opulence,' p.335.

they require, if they have things to give in exchange for it. Wealth consists in the sum total of things necessary for life and in the annual reproduction of these things, and the quantity of money may diminish without these things being affected, since in a rich country, with freedom of commerce, there are means of supplying the place of money. The opulence of a state must not therefore be judged by the greater or less supply of money it possesses. Money is therefore but a *richesse sterile*, the only utility of which consists in its employment in effecting purchases and sales.[30] Further, buying and selling are but two aspects of the same operation; every purchase is a sale, and every sale is a purchase. It follows that the central idea of the mercantilists, that of a nation selling more than it buys, is not merely erroneous but absurd: ' Instead of saying that you wish our sales to exceed our purchases, which is physically impossible, you ought merely to say that you wish to purchase money with your productions.'[31] In an effective phrase, selling more than is bought is merely a ' commerce commencé,'[32] an incomplete transaction. The argument resting on the greater durability of metal is admirably disposed of by a *reductio ad absurdum*, that if the contention be valid, then in logic it leads to the conclusion that any quantity of the metals, however small (being durable), is worth more than any quantity of commodities however large (being perishable).[33] The doctrine of the balance of trade is thus reduced to ' nothing and perhaps less than nothing.'[34] Commerce is not to be regarded as a state of war against an enemy; the only interest a nation has is to leave trade entirely free, in order that the greatest possible competition of buyers and sellers

[30] See in particular the seventh observation on the *Analyse*, p.324; and the note on the thirteenth of the *Maximes Générales*, pp.347-348.
[31] *Du Commerce*, pp.478, 479.
[32] *Ibid.*, p.473.   [33] *Ibid.*, p.479.   [34] *Ibid.*, p.482.

may guarantee the highest possible price for the sale of its products and the lowest price for the purchase of what may be necessary.[35] Commerce cannot be conducted at the expense of other nations, for a good and a just God has decreed that commerce shall always be 'le fruit d'un avantage évidement réciproque.'[36] All this and much more may strike the retentive student as strangely familiar, and as an echo of certain classic passages in the fourth book of Adam Smith.

It would, however, be a mistake to consider that the Physiocratic advocacy of Free Trade was rooted in any importance attached to foreign trade as such. On the contrary, foreign trade, like all trade, is for the Physiocrats essentially unproductive. As Quesnay specifically puts it, it is only possible to buy from the foreigner as much as one sells to him; and the consequence is that in a state of free competition in foreign trade, there can only be an exchange of value for equal value, without gain or loss on one side or the other.[37] Reverting to Quesnay's distinction between the two nations – agricultural and commercial – combined in a mixed kingdom, the expenses of the second, even if necessary, are to be regarded as an 'onerous expense,' laid on the revenues of the landed proprietor.[38] Foreign trade is thus primarily a liability rather than an asset. The whole tendency of Physiocratic thought is to depreciate the importance of foreign trade. It is above all by the condition of internal commerce that the wealth of a country must be judged; a nation that is making the best use of its soil and its men has no occasion to be envious of the commerce of its neighbours.[39] It is curious that the first school in modern

[35] *Ibid.*, p.477.
[36] *Ibid.*, p.484.
[37] Fifth observation on the *Analyse*, p.321.
[38] *Ibid.*, p.321.
[39] Nos. 12 and 13 of the *Maximes*, attached to *Grains*, p.239.

times to proclaim Free Trade did so, not from any belief in the advantages of foreign trade, but on general principles of a quasi-philosophical and religious nature.

Quesnay's peculiar views with regard to agriculture as the only productive activity and the only source of the national revenue lead to certain important conclusions in the field of taxation. Taxation also is subject to laws and immovable rules, capable of rigorous demonstration.[40] Here it is only possible to note two of Quesnay's fundamental points. The first (a counsel of perfection) is that the State should avoid loans; the statesman should hope for resources in special emergencies from the prosperity of the nation, and not from the credit of the financiers. The objection to loans is primarily that they create a 'traffic in finances,' from which spring 'fortunes pécuniaires' and 'rentes financières.' Sterile fortunes, withdrawing money from agriculture, are thus created (the corresponding Tableau Economique would show a drain to the right to the unproductive classes). Moreover such 'pecuniary fortunes' knows no king nor country. In more modern language, loans lead to a rentier class operating in an international field of investment.[41]

The second point is more fundamental. Since there is only one source of national wealth, all taxation must ultimately fall there, and therefore all taxation should be imposed at once where the burden will ultimately fall. Quesnay, in short, advocates a single direct tax falling on the 'produit net.' In this he is wholly logical on Physiocratic assumptions. Sooner or later a tax is bound to be shifted on to the 'produit net,' if the 'produit net' is what Quesnay considers he has shown it to be; and therefore the simplest and least onerous way of raising a revenue is to divert directly to the State a part of what is the only real national revenue. Quesnay in

[40] *Despotisme de la Chine*, chap. 8, sec. 7, p.645.
[41] Nos. 28, 29, 30 of the *Maximes Générales*, p.337.

various places devotes considerable attention to proving the inconvenience and loss, and the detriment to the State which would result from any other method of taxation; and in particular, in *The Second Economic Problem*, he proves (at least to his own satisfaction) that though the landowner might imagine that he would be advantaged by some other form of taxation, yet in the end, owing to the shifting of the tax, the burden – and moreover an increased burden, owing to the inevitable incidental frictions and losses – will fall upon him. It is interesting to note, in passing, that in the course of his discussion of the incidence of taxation, Quesnay enunciates what a later generation has come to know as the Iron Law of Wages: 'Wages, and in consequence the enjoyments which wage-earners can obtain, are fixed and reduced to the lowest level by the extreme competition which is among them.'[42]

Turgot

Of the other members of the Physiocratic school, one only requires mention in such an elementary discussion as this, partly because in some respects he stood slightly apart from the main body of Physiocrats, partly because the lustre of his great name has given dignity to the school from which he drew his inspiration. Moreover, his high office in the State, held for too brief a period, gave him an opportunity of revealing Physiocracy in action. This is not the place to discuss the life and achievement of Ann-Robert-Jacques Turgot[43] (1727-1781), who, as Intendant of Limoges and

---

[42] *Second Problème Économique*, p.706.
[43] Born at Paris in 1727; prior of the Sorbonne in 1749. Giving up the career in the Church for which he had prepared, entered the magistracy and rose to be Intendant of Limoges. Called to Paris by Louis XVI in 1774 and made Secretary of State for the Navy, and soon afterwards Comptroller-General and Minister of Finance. His reforms aroused opposition, and he was dismissed in 1776.

later Comptroller-General (August 1774 – May 1776), did what he might to put things in order. His achievements were indeed reversed on his fall from office, but his admirers may and do, claim that though in his life his greatest works were nullified, he triumphed at the Revolution and dominated the nineteenth century.

Turgot's doctrine is to be found primarily in two small tracts, the *Éloge de Gourney* and the *Réflexions sur la Formation et la Distribution des Richesses*; in addition Turgot had the pleasant habit of infusing statements of economic doctrine into his official and state documents, and from this point of view such edicts as those suppressing the *corvées* and the *jurandes* have an economic as well as an historic interest. The *Éloge de Gournay* is a pious appreciation of one of the earliest of the Physiocrats wno, perhaps even more than Quesnay, influenced Turgot's development. While purporting to be a statement of Gournay's views, it is clear that Turgot is also expressing his own. The *Éloge*, in fact, is a rather extreme statement of *laissez-faire*, along lines which later developed into an orthodoxy. Government restraints and interference, whereby towns come to regard each other as mutual enemies, are treated as 'remnants of Gothic barbarism.' The new system of M. Gournay had rested on the maxim that 'in general every man knows his own interest better than another man to whom that interest is entirely indifferent.' The State is interested in commerce in two ways: (1) it is interested in seeing that no one can do to another any considerable wrong, against which the sufferer cannot guarantee himself; and (2) it is interested in the mass of the wealth of the State being as large as possible. The first of these objects requires that the Government should protect the natural liberty which the buyer has to buy and the seller has to sell. Freedom of competition among buyers and sellers is a sufficient guarantee against any abuse;

complete liberty in this respect can alone assure the seller a price capable of encouraging production, and give the buyer the best wares at the lowest price. To go beyond this and to seek to prevent anyone from ever being defrauded is to assume the obligation of providing pads for all the children who might fall (*de fournir des bourrelets à tous les enfants qui pourraient tomber*); it is (since all regulations are onerous in execution) to impose on commerce and on the nation a heavy tax in order to dispense a small number of lazy people from the trouble of learning how not to be cheated.

A consideration of the second point leads to the same conclusion. On familiar Smithian lines, the wealth of the nation, being but the produce of the soil and the industry of its inhabitants, will be greatest when the produce of each acre of land and of the industry of each individual is carried to the highest possible point. But indeed it requires no proof that each individual is the only capable judge of the employment of his resources; he alone has the necessary local knowledge and experience. It follows, therefore, on all grounds, that the interest of the individual, who is left free to pursue that interest, ' will more surely produce the general good than the operations of the Government, which are always at fault and necessarily directed by a vague and uncertain theory.'

This is sturdy and uncompromising *laissez-faire* doctrine, and even the words 'in general,' in the fundamental formula regarding enlightened self-interest, leave but a small opening for retreat. For the rest, the *Éloge* contains familiar Physiocratic doctrine to the effect that ' l'agriculture, animée par le commerce ' (the modification is significant), is the source of all revenues and that all taxes are paid by the proprietor. Interesting also, in view of Turgot's later edicts, is the statement that what Gourney most condemned in the system which he attacked was that 'it always favoured the rich and the idle section of society to the prejudice of the poor and labouring sections.'

The *Réflexions* are arranged in a hundred short paragraphs, and may be taken as a summarized statement of economic doctrine, as apprehended by one Physiocrat. In this brief treatise – written, it is said, for the instruction of two Chinese students – there are many acute and ingenious observations embedded in a dogmatic statement of the more untenable portions of Physiocratic theory. The superiority of agriculture is here in its full glory, and the iron law of wages, as applied to the worker who has only his arms and his industry, is one of the consequences of this superiority. The simple labourer is beaten down in his negotiations with a master who has a choice among many workers.[44] It is different with the worker on the soil: 'Nature does not bargain with him to oblige him to be content with the absolutely necessary.'[45] The happy position of the agriculturist is that he receives, over and above his subsistence, a 'richesse independente et disponible' which he has not bought and which he sells. The land is therefore the unique source of all wealth, and that part which it gives as a pure gift (*en pur don*) is the net product. There is something excessively naïve in this touching faith in the bounty of Nature which few farmers – at least in Buchan – could share. Of other points in the *Réflexions*, it must suffice to note Turgot's zealous plea for the abolition of all restraints on the fixing of the rate of interest; the payment of interest, being to the advantage of both parties concerned, should be

[44] Turgot's statement is not infrequently quoted, and is almost classical: 'En tout genre de travail il doit arriver et il arrive en effet que le salaire de l'ouvrier se borne à ce qui lui est nécessaire pour lui procurer sa subsistance.' *Réflexions*, section 6.
[45] *Ibid.*, section 7.

determined solely by the course of trade.[46] On this point, which Turgot also discusses elsewhere, he reveals the logic of *laissez-faire* in its most cogent form.

Reference has been made to the importance, economically, of some of the State documents for which Turgot was responsible. The edict for the suppression of the *Jurandes* (i.e., for the abolition of all restraints on the freedom of work) may be taken as an example of Turgot's reforming zeal, and of the high grounds of economic policy on which his action was based. 'Le droit de travailler' which his edict established is an awkward phrase to translate, if one would avoid ambiguity. Louis Blanc criticized Turgot because in proclaiming 'le droit de travailler,' he had in no wise recognized 'le droit au travail.' What the edict did was to abolish the privilege which conferred on some a monopoly of certain kinds of work, so that the right to engage in such work was preserved for a favoured section of the community. Here also what was aimed at was an enlargement of the liberty of enterprise, so that all the avenues of life should be open to everyone. This liberty, as indeed it ought to be on *laissez-faire* principles, is for Turgot the most fundamental of all rights:

'Dieu, en donnant à l'homme des besoins, en lui rendant nécessaire la ressource du travail, a fait du droit de travailler la propriété de tout homme, et cette propriété est la première, la plus sacrée et la plus imprescriptible de toutes.'

The object of this step was indeed to assure to commerce and industry 'the entire liberty and the full competition which they ought to enjoy.' It is perhaps worthy of notice, in view of criticisms much later, when another age had brought other problems, that the fourteenth article of the edict forbade all and sundry, 'maîtres, compagnons, ouvriers et

[46] *Ibid.*, sections 71-75.

apprentis' to form any manner of association or assembly on any pretext whatever. Here, if one chooses, expression is given to the view that the maintenance of full freedom requires the denial of the right of association. But it is rather unfair to entangle Turgot in the controversies of the nineteenth and the twentieth centuries; he might with reason plead that he wasn't there.

'This system, with all its imperfections, is perhaps the nearest approximation to the truth that has yet been published upon the subject of political economy.' Thus Adam Smith on his immediate forerunners. The achievement of the Physiocrats was indeed remarkable. Even in these days when *laissez-faire* no longer commands the reverence it once did, it may be agreed that in reaction against the mercantilists the doctrine of *laissez-faire* had to be stated. On all this side of the question the Physiocrats were courageous champions of freedom, and expressed the central truths of Adam Smith's doctrine with an enthusiasm, a vigour and a logic unexcelled even by the economist of Kirkcaldy. This is their imperishable memorial. Their 'imperfections' are too obvious to require disentanglement and comment. They were right, particularly in the circumstances of their time, in emphasizing the importance of agriculture; they were wrong in seeking to prove the superiority of agriculture by abstract reasoning, based on an untenable distinction between productive and unproductive labour. From this all their errors flowed. The whole doctrine of the net product, which makes rent a token of the bounty of nature, an extra douceur or tip given to those who work the soil, is tinged with eccentricity, and the consequent advocacy of the single tax is not so much a serious contribution to the science of finance as an exercise in logic, being indeed a perfectly valid inference from Physiocratic assumptions. These embroideries, with the fantastic Tableau Économique, add a piquant interest to the Physiocrats, and have been a godsend to countless examiners; but that which is fundamental is their anticipation of Adam Smith. Even an admirer of Smith may have no scruple in finding in the Physiocratic group the real beginnings of modern economics.

CHAPTER V

Adam Smith

Hume

O N the way to Adam Smith, it is only decent to salute one whose great distinction in other fields seems to be the chief justification for the rather meagre treatment which he generally receives when discussed as an economist. Had David Hume[1] (1711-1776) not been a pre-eminent philosopher, he would have ranked as an eminent economist. A perusal of his essays underlines, even more emphatically than a plunge into the Physiocratic morass, the extent to which Adam Smith was indebted to his forerunners. That adequate justice has seldom been done to Hume is perhaps also in part due to the fact that he never ventures on a comprehensive treatment of any economic topic; rather is he a gentlemanly essayist who, with a dignity only attainable in the eighteenth century, combines grace, learning and profundity in discoursing of many subjects, among which (on a liberal estimate) some ten may be deemed to be economic in character. Of these, the Essays *Of Commerce, Of Money, Of the Balance of Trade, Of the Jealousy of Trade* are specially noticeable as embodying on many points the essentials of Smith's criticism of the mercantilists. To a large extent his argument is directed to proving, as against the mercantilists, the relative unimportance of gold and silver in the national economy. Taking any kingdom by itself, 'the greater or less plenty of money is of no conse-

---

[1] Born in Edinburgh in 1711. In the main a student, with visits to the Continent as a tutor after the manner of the times. Later (1752) Librarian to the Faculty of Advocates, Edinburgh.

quence.' Primarily, money is a method of rating or estimating labour and commodities; if in greater plenty, a greater quantity will be required to represent the same quantity of goods; the consequent change is analogous to the change springing from the adoption of a new method of notation. The increasing quantity of gold and silver can only be favourable to industry in the interval between the acquisition of money and the subsequent rise of prices. The secret of prosperity lies elsewhere: 'the want of money can never injure any state within itself; for men and commodities are the real strength of any community.'[2]

In the essay *Of the Balance of Trade*, the same ideas are applied to the central doctrine of the mercantilists. The fear that a country may lose its supply of precious metals is a groundless apprehension. 'I should as soon dread,' says Hume, 'that all our springs and rivers should be exhausted, as that money should abandon a kingdom where there are people and industry.' Assuming a people adequately supplied with industry, they will get the money they require, and he tests this doctrine by two extreme hypotheses. Imagine four-fifths of the country's money annihilated in one night, what would be the consequence? The price of all labour and of all commodities would at once sink to a mediaeval level. What nation would then dispute with us in any foreign market? Consequently in how short a time would we not get back the money which we had lost? Prices would rise once more to the level prevailing in neighbouring countries, and we should lose the advantage of cheapness of labour and of commodities. Take the converse hypothesis and suppose that our supply of gold and silver had increased five-fold over night. Prices would rise to so exorbitant a height that no neighbouring country could afford to buy from us, and in spite of all laws to the contrary, their commodities 'would

[2] *Of Money.*

be run in upon us, and our money flow out.' And the conclusion of the argument is that

' a government has great reason to preserve with care its people and its manufactures. Its money, it may safely trust to the course of human affairs, without fear or jealousy.'

A further consequence is that no nation has any reason to be envious of the prosperity of another; on the contrary, it is only if our neighbours are prosperous that we can expect them to be good customers and so contribute to our own prosperity. If we succeeded in reducing our neighbours to a condition of sloth and ignorance, we should ourselves suffer and should soon fall into the same abject condition. Hume's protest on this point is characteristic, and has frequently been quoted:

' I shall therefore venture to acknowledge, that, not only as a man, but as a British subject, I pray for the flourishing commerce of Germany, Spain, Italy and even France itself.'[3]

Of Smith's immediate predecessors, Hume is the most considerable. He is introduced here, however, not that he may be adequately discussed, but because no account of Smith can claim to be fair or proportioned if it fails to disclose Hume in the background.

Adam Smith

Adam Smith[4] (1723-1790), especially for us in this country, occupies so central a place in the history of Political

---

[3] *Of the Jealousy of Trade.*

[4] Born at Kirkcaldy, 1723. Educated at Glasgow and Oxford. Professor of Logic and later of Moral Philosophy in Glasgow, 1751-1763. Thereafter travelling tutor to the Duke of Buccleuch. Returned to Kirkcaldy 1767. *Wealth of Nations* published 1776. Commissioner of Customs in Edinburgh from 1778 until his death in 1790. On the philosophic side of his activities, wrote *The Theory of Moral Sentiments.*

Economy, and has become popularly so much of a legend, that the prudent mariner hesitates to embark on so vast an ocean. Here, if anywhere, discussion in a few pages is bound to be inadequate, for the influence of Smith and the reactions against Smith, extend throughout the whole subsequent history of economic doctrine. There is at least this excuse for the lingering tendency to regard 'Adam Smith' and 'Political Economy' as terms which mutually exhaust each other. Yet both aspects of the legend are wholly fallacious. Adam Smith was not the founder, the inventor, or the discoverer of Political Economy. That he did so much was entirely due to the fact that so much had been done before him. In no sense was he a pioneer. The mercantilists, doubtless with practical obsessions, had discussed all manner of economic problems. The Physiocrats had jointly come very near to giving a systematic account of the economic process, though they had embellished it with strange frills. Quite apart from Adam Smith it was an age of much economic speculation, and doubtless out of the Physiocrats, David Hume and some others, the enterprising student could reconstruct a large part of *The Wealth of Nations*. Smith throughout, in short, was discussing problems which had already been the subject of discussion. The other aspect of the legend which assumes that Adam Smith found Political Economy brick (if so far advanced) and left it marble, is equally wide of the mark. *The Wealth of Nations*, to speak candidly of the achievement of the greatest of Scotsmen, is a work which singularly abounds in obvious defects. Those who, like Say, speak of it as a 'vast chaos' may be harsh in their judgment; but it is certainly a disorderly book, in which the sequence of thought is successfully concealed behind lengthy digressions. Moreover, on essential points, Adam Smith, for all his acuteness, is sometimes singularly confused, and on rare occasions – as in the discussion of value – the reader may even suspect that Smith is not clear in his own mind as to which of two subjects he is discussing. In the same way, though this defect is sometimes a merit, he develops in one and the same chapter contradictory lines of thought, so that he hints at alternative doctrines without ever resolving, or apparently even being conscious of, the inherent contradictions. Political Economy, as it left the hands of Adam Smith, was by no means a complete and rounded system of doctrine. Like all the other works of frail man, it has its errors, its gaps, its ambiguities and its bias.

Yet, having said so much to placate the devil, it remains true that Adam Smith's name is incomparably the greatest in the history of economic thought. Himself a groper, he at least marked out the ground. He looked at things comprehensively, as none of his predecessors had done; and defective as his own arrangement may be, it is nevertheless true that his analysis, refined and made systematic by his followers, has to a large extent furnished the plan according to which all later economic thought has proceeded. Before Adam Smith there had been much economic discussion; with him we reach the stage of discussing economics.

Unfortunately Adam Smith is difficult to apprehend in his totality, for the perverse reason that he is in part so regrettably well known. Bits of Adam Smith, in isolation, are known even to those who make no profession of economic knowledge. His chapters on division of labour (above all as represented in the manufacture of pins), his discussion of the causes of different rates of remuneration in different employments, his canons of taxation and the more purple passages in his polemic against the mercantilists – these are tit-bits which are not to be escaped even by those who foreswear economic study. But precisely this familiarity with Adam Smith's teaching on certain specific points makes it more difficult to grasp the sum and substance of his doc-

trines viewed as a whole, and the nature and extent of
his influence on the development of economic doctrine.
Instead of discussing airily certain aspects of Adam Smith,
this chapter will therefore in the main endeavour to obtain
a compendious view of *The Wealth of Nations* as a whole,
so that the more familiar portions may be seen in their
proper relationship to the whole structure.

But before attempting to assess his doctrine, a few sentences may be devoted to his more general standpoint. The
influences producing Adam Smith were many, and need not
detain us here. Something may be allowed to his teacher,
Hutcheson, in his emphasis on what is 'natural'; something
– since all the critics agree and it is therefore the correct
thing to say – to Mandeville and his paradoxical contention
that private 'vices' (private 'interests' would be a saner
word) may tend to the public good; something may be
allowed to his familiar intercourse with the Physiocrats,
although it is now certain that the main scheme of his
thought was developed before he met the leaders of that
school. It is enough that Adam Smith shared with the
Physiocrats, and with other aspects of eighteenth century
thought, the belief in a natural order. This belief, in Adam
Smith's case, was founded in ideas which were partly philosophical and partly religious. The natural order implied the
removal of restrictions of all kinds, and Smith is therefore
a passionate (though not a dogmatic or doctrinaire) advocate
of liberty. But the removal of restrictions will not in his
view, lead to an economic chaos; on the contrary, only then
will the natural order be able to function. In such a natural
state the divinely appointed impulse which keeps the
machine going is a psychological instinct, in short the
interest which each man has in himself and in his own.
Herein lies the *a priori* element in Adam Smith; there is an
order, appointed by a wise Providence in which self-interest

will supply the necessary drive to make the machine go, and will also so act as to produce equilibrium between contending forces. This leads to what is in the main a wholly optimistic view of a world in which a beneficent deity has arranged that progress and harmony shall result from the free-play of instincts which are, frankly, self-centred and self-concerned. But alongside this *a priori* element, there is another aspect of Adam Smith, in virtue of which he is a hard realist, at times indeed a realist with a dash of cynicism. With whatever philosophic bias Adam Smith approached his problems, his feet were always firmly planted on the ground. He was no amateur in mundane affairs, and consequently his philosophical preconceptions never blind him to the possible expediency of waiving the application of those inferences which would seem to be implicit in his starting point. So also, though Adam Smith is undoubtedly optimistic in his general outlook, he is far from thinking that all's right with the world when it comes to particular cases.

For the eighteenth century one method of stating the economic problem was to discover and lay bare the source of wealth. The mercantilists, speaking broadly, had attributed the increase of the nation's wealth to a favourable balance of trade; the Physiocrats had found that all wealth comes from agriculture, and that all other occupations are 'unproductive.' Adam Smith's opening sentence is significant of his whole position: 'The annual labour of every nation is the fund which originally supplies it with all the necessaries and conveniences of life which it annually consumes.'[5] The source of all wealth is thus found in labour, and to this is due the rather misleading practice, current on the Continent, of referring to Smith's system (or Smithianismus) as the industrial system. It is misleading because

[5] *The Wealth of Nations*, Introduction and plan.

Adam Smith in fact wrote before the Industrial Revolution and is therefore in no wise its exponent or apologist, as is sometimes assumed; he is, moreover, much more favourable to agriculture and much more critical of the industrial and commercial interests than is frequently realized. Increase of wealth, on Smith's initial assumption, will therefore depend on the skill, dexterity and judgment with which labour is applied. It is thus that Smith is led directly in the first chapter of the first book to expound the principle of division of labour. The principle of division of labour is clearly in no sense new. It lay at the root of Plato's ideal state; Xenophon, as we have seen, knew all about it, and the proverbial wisdom of all nations has rendered homage to the essential part of the doctrine. Yet popular opinion is right in attaching peculiar importance to Smith's exposition. For here, division of labour is placed in the forefront as the cardinal fact of economic life. The reaction of this on Smith's doctrine is enormous. The influence of this fundamental conception in two directions may be indicated. In the first place, division of labour postulates exchange later; and in fact Smith, from his starting point, is led at the next stage to consider money and value. It has been said that the weakness of the Physiocrats is that they had no theory of value; Smith's point of departure inevitably impelled him to a consideration of this problem. In the second place, the emphasis laid on division of labour and its inevitable concomitant, the subsequent exchange of products, led Smith to look on society as a vast concourse of people held together by the exchanges effected between them, and also to regard wealth as increased by anything tending to increase these exchangeable values. Here lies the root of much German criticism of Smith's thought.

The significance of the opening chapters therefore lies not so much in what Adam Smith says with regard to division of labour as in the central and dominating place which it occupies in his theory. That division of labour leads to increased output; that its advantages spring from increased dexterity, from economy of time, from the encouragement it gives to inventions are not, in themselves, epoch-making discoveries.[6] Even the further celebrated dictum, that division of labour is limited by the extent of the market,[7] is, properly viewed, little more than a truism; for the extent to which labour can be divided will clearly depend on the amount of work to be done or, otherwise expressed, the extent of the market. His explanation of the effects of division of labour is more satisfactory than his account of the principle which gives occasion to it. It is not, he says, the result of human wisdom, aiming at increased opulence. It springs from a natural tendency to truck or barter, as though the mere act of exchange was in itself one of the joys of life.[8] But having made this lapse into the comparatively absurd, Smith at once and more reasonably makes division of labour the expression of man's continual need for the co-operation and assistance of his fellows. 'Man has almost constant occasion for the help of his brethren, and it is in vain for him to expect it from their benevolence only.' And the true Smith further adds: 'It is not from the benevolence of the butcher, the brewer, or the baker, that we expect our dinner, but from their regard to their own interest.' On this view each one, labouring to satisfy the needs of others, secures at the same time that others will supply his wants. Society is held together by exchanges which are prompted by self-interest, and which are founded on division of labour.

Having thus disposed of division of labour in the first three chapters, Smith proceeds, in the fourth, to discuss the

[6] *Ibid.*, Book I, chap. I.
[7] *Ibid.*, Book I, chap. 3.
[8] *Ibid.*, Book I, chap. 2.

origins of money, the need for which he makes one of the consequences of the rise of different occupations among men. 'Every man . . . becomes in some measure a merchant,' and therefore, in effect, a currency is required to serve as 'the universal instrument of commerce.' Thus emerges the idea of 'relative or exchangeable value of goods,' and we arrive at that celebrated, almost notorious, paragraph in which Smith says that value has two different meanings, sometimes expressing the utility of a particular object, and sometimes its power of purchasing other commodities – the former being 'value-in-use,' the latter 'value-in-exchange.' He correctly notes the paradox of value, citing the instances of water and diamonds to show that a high value in use may be combined with little or no value in exchange, and conversely. Here is the fruitful source of much discussion, above all when the Austrians take the boards. But as for Adam Smith, in the immortal words of Mr. Hubert Phillips,

> The wily bird
> Had never heard
> Of marginal utility.

Enough at this stage to note that Smith, having stared 'value-in-use' in the face, proceeds to consider value-in-exchange.

The next three chapters, so far as subject matter is concerned, logically develop the conception of exchangeable value thus arrived at. In the first place, Adam Smith is concerned (in chap. 5) to consider what is the 'real measure' of this exchangeable value. This is one of the most obscure chapters in Smith, and it is difficult to resist the impression that in Smith's mind two entirely different questions were confused. At times he seems to be discussing what is the determinant of value; again he seems to be considering what, in this wayward, changeable world, is the best, because the most stable, measure of value. Conceivably the value of my fountain pen may be determined by the amount of labour that went to its making, and if it costs 10s., that may be because 10s. worth of labour, however calculated, is incorporated in it. That is one question; but witnessing the oscillation in the value of 10s. calculated in 1800, 1890, 1920, to go no further, I may feel that I am not very much further on when I say that my pen is worth 10s. But if to-day a charwoman will work for 5s. a day, I may say that my pen is worth two days' work of a charwoman. In that case I should be regarding labour as a better measure of the value of my pen than its gold price. To consider what is the determinant of value, and what is the ideal measure of value are indeed two questions, and in the main it is the latter which Smith is after. Without descending into minute points of textual criticism, the main conclusions in this important chapter may be indicated. Perhaps the most fundamental passage is in the opening statement:

'The value of any commodity, therefore, to the person who possesses it, and who means not to use or consume it himself, but to exchange it for other commodities, is equal to the quantity of labour which it enables him to purchase or command. Labour, therefore, is the real measure of the exchangeable value of all commodities.'

In short, the value of anything to a possessor who wants to exchange it, is best measured by the quantity of labour which its selling price will secure.

But though labour in this sense is the real measure of the exchangeable value of commodities, their value is in general otherwise estimated; from motives of convenience and custom they are in fact estimated in money. But whereas gold and silver vary in value, 'equal quantities of labour, at all times and places, may be said to be of equal value to the labourer.' Presumably he means that an aching back to Adam, after his expulsion from the garden of Eden, is equivalent to the aching back of a navvy taking up Regent Street. With one other possible standard Smith toys for a moment. Equal quantities of corn, representing the subsistence of the labourer, will answer the purpose, probably better than any other commodity; and indeed, if we assume a generally operative subsistence law of wages and a uniformity in the requirements of life, this comes to pretty much the same standard as labour. The final conclusion is that 'labour, therefore, it appears evidently, is the only universal, as well as the only accurate, measure of value, or the only standard by which we can compare the values of different commodities, at all times, and at all places.' From century to century, corn is a better standard than silver; from year to year, silver is a better measure than corn. The whole discussion is befogging, involving not merely wholly unwarranted assumptions about the stability of the value of labour, but also a semblance of circular reasoning. The important point, however, is that Smith's conclusion primarily relates to labour regarded as the best measure of value, and that, apart from certain ambiguities of expression, the argument is not directed, here at least, to proving that labour is the determinant of value.

In the following chapter (Book I, chap. 6) Smith proceeds to consider the component parts of the price of commodities. In an 'early and rude state of society,' before the accumulation of stock (capital) and the appropriation of land, he clearly now makes labour both the determinant and the measure of value. At this stage the whole produce of labour belongs to the labourer; and (a different order of idea) 'the quantity of labour commonly employed in acquiring or producing any commodity is the only circumstance which can regulate the quantity of labour which it ought commonly to . . . exchange for.' This, however, is only in the early and rude state of society. When capital accumulates, over and above the price of materials and the wages of the workmen, there must be something for the profits of the undertaker. Although Adam Smith regards the profit of stock as merely wages for a particular form of labour, they are, he contends, regulated on wholly different principles from ordinary wages. At this stage neither does the whole produce belong to labour, nor is labour any longer specifically the determinant of value. Lastly, a third element arises with the appropriation of land. 'The landlords, like all other men, love to reap where they never sowed, and demand a rent even for its natural produce.' Smith, whose views on rent were never clear, here regards it, it will be observed, as mere extortion. Thus we have the very familiar tripartite division whereby in all prices there is an element of rent, of wages and of profits, corresponding to the great trinity, Land, Labour and Capital.

But how does this work out in practice? The following chapter (No. 7) 'Of the Natural and Market Prices of Commodities,' contains Smith's answers. He postulates (it is largely an assumption) in each society an ordinary or average rate of wages, of profit and of rent. These ordinary or average rates he calls the 'natural rates' (a horrible queston begging-phrase) at the time and place in which they prevail. Corresponding to this is the 'natural price' of a commodity, which is arrived at when it yields the natural rates of wages, profit and rent. In that case the commodity is sold 'precisely for what it is worth,' an expression which seems to imply that value is an objective reality, capable of being determined. In short the natural (or shall we say say 'normal'?) price represents in its essence a 'cost-of-production' theory of value. The natural price is in its nature an ideal; opposed to it, is the actual or market price which is arrived at by conditions of demand and supply and the competition among buyers and sellers. As a result of this competition, the natural price will be the central price to which prices will continually gravitate; but in certain exceptional cases the market price may for a long period of time be above the natural price. Of such cases he notes what we should now call quasi-rents, as represented by increased demand where 'secrets in manufactures' are for a time successfully kept; cases where conditions of production are limited, but the demand is great, as in the case of wines requiring a peculiar soil and situation, and also the cases of monopoly, where the price is 'the highest that can be got.' Such then, is Smith's theory of value. In short, the ideal measure of value is labour: at any given moment value is determined by conditions of demand and supply, but under the influence of competition it constantly tends towards the cost of production, apart from exceptional cases where the seller is favourably situated.

Having thus deduced the contributory factors of Labour, Capital and Land, Smith in the remaining chapters of the first book proceeds to consider how the corresponding revenues, that is to say wages, profits and rent, are determined. The eighth chapter, dealing with wages, is an excellent example both of the strength and (if one so chooses) the weakness of Smith. It may be suggested that his arguments lead to no definite conclusion with regard to a tenable theory of wages; on the other hand he suggests many trains of thought, and there are indeed few subsequent theories of wages which cannot appeal for support to some passage in this chapter.

The chapter opens with the doctrine that 'the produce of labour constitutes the natural recompense or wages of labour' – a phrase again embodying the unfortunate word 'natural.' In the original state of society, Smith says, 'the

whole produce of labour belongs to the labourer.' Here at
the outset, if one cares, is high sanction for the doctrine of
the 'right to the whole produce of labour,' which distinguishes a large part of nineteenth century Socialist theory.
Such a position, however, cannot survive the appropriation
of land and the accumulation of capital. Somewhat shifting
his ground, Smith next outlines a theory of wages resting on
the bargaining strength of employers and workers – in effect
demand and supply as applied to labour. Wages depend
upon a contract betwen workmen who desire to get as much,
and masters who desire to give as little as possible. Hence
there will be a tendency to combine on both sides, but Smith
has no doubts on which side the advantage will lie. Masters
are few and can combine easily, whereas combinations of
workmen are prohibited. Masters can hold out longer.
Despite appearances, ' masters are always and everywhere in
a sort of tacit, but constant and uniform, combination, not to
raise the wages of labour above their actual rate.' In every
sense the master is in a strong position, while the workmen
seldom derive any advantage from their 'tumultuous combinations.' Wages, then, depend on a bargain, but all the
bargaining strength is on one side. There is, however, a
lower limit below which it is impossible to reduce wages for
any considerable time. The labourer's wage must be sufficient to support himself and to enable him to bring up a
family, if the race of workmen is to be maintained. Here is
foreshadowed the Iron Law of Wages, arrived at as the
natural outcome of a bargain in which the pull is all on one
side.

Proceeding to consider cases where the labourer has an
advantage (as in the ' scarcity of hands '), we find ourselves
quivering on the brink of the wages fund theory: 'The
demand for those who live by wages, it is evident, cannot
increase but in proportion to the increase of the funds

which are destined to the payment of wages.' While the fund for the payment of wages is thus dependent on national wealth, it is not the actual greatness of national wealth that is decisive, so far as wages are concerned, but its 'continual increase.' It is therefore not necessarily in the richest countries, but in the most thriving, that wages of labour will be highest. Here we seem for a moment to be approaching the later produce theories of wages: 'The liberal reward of labour, therefore, as it is the necessary effect, so it is the natural symptom of increasing national wealth.' Contrariwise, in a stationary state wages may be low.

The chapter concludes with an extraordinary anticipation of the essence of Malthusianism in its relation to wages:

'Every species of animal naturally multiplies in proportion to the means of their subsistence, and no species can ever multiply beyond it. But in civilized society, it is only among the inferior ranks of people that the scantiness of subsistence can set limits to the further multiplication of the human species; and it can do so in no other way than by destroying a great part of the children which their fruitful marriages produce.'

High wages, on Malthusian lines, will increase the number of workers. If there is an increased demand for labour, wages must rise to stimulate the production of workers. Wages, in fact, reflect the demand for labour:

'It is in this manner that the demand for men, like that for any other commodity, necessarily regulates the production of men, quickens it when it goes on too slowly, and stops it when it advances too fast.'

This sentence summarizes Malthus with a terseness and incisiveness which Malthus himself might have envied.

In the main, then, Adam Smith's discussion of wages is interesting because he gropingly anticipates so much of later thought. The doctrine on which he lays most stress is that which makes wages the resultant of the bargaining strength of the two parties to the contract, and the bearing on this of what he calls the progressive, the declining and the stationary state.

In turning, in the ninth chapter, to profits, Smith emphasizes that these also, like wages, depend upon the increasing or declining state of wealth of a country, but the relationship is in the opposite direction. Increase of stock, by leading to competition, will mean a diminution of the rate of profit. An indication of the rate of profit is to be found in the current rate of interest, inasmuch as a high rate of interest betokens that a profitable use can be made of capital. The general theory thus presupposes that wages and profits will move in opposite directions, not because of the exploitation of labour by capital, but because the increasing abundance of capital, on which high wages depend, leads likewise to capital commanding a lower reward. To this general tendency there are two exceptions: in new colonies, wages and profits may be high simultaneously, and in a stationary state, in a country with its full complement of riches, both may be low.

So much for wages and profits in general. What, however, will determine their variations as between different employments? This, so far as wages are concerned, leads to one of the most hackneyed passages in Smith (chap. 10). Broadly, wages will vary in employments, according to their agreeableness, the ease in learning them, the constancy of employment they offer, the trust imposed, and the probability of success. His treatment of this question is apparently one of those things which age cannot wither, however much custom may stale its finite variety. His observations throughout are just and pertinent; but as a general criticism, it may be suggested that Smith's explanations only account for wage-differences in employments between which labour is easily transferable. He overlooks the fact that the reservoir of labour is not one, but rather that labour consists of many groups which are isolated from each other. Smith's five causes rather inadequately explain the difference in re-muneration between a fashionable doctor and an unskilled navvy, between a Hollywood star and a professor of Political Economy. Of these five causes of variation, it should be added that Smith regards two only as applicable to profits, viz., the agreeableness or disagreeableness of the business and the risk involved. Moreover, agreeableness affects the employers far less than the worker. Therefore, on general grounds Smith infers that rates of profit will vary less than rates of wages. On the general treatment of profits, it is noteworthy that for Smith, profit is equivalent to the total return to capital, and that therefore interest is merely a constituent element in profits. Otherwise expressed, there is no systematic analysis of gross profits or net profits.

Lastly, there is Rent (chap. 11), with regard to which Smith remains ambiguous. His main statement tends to look upon rent as mere extortion. It is 'naturally the highest which the tenant can afford to pay in the actual circum-stances of the land.' What is left over 'is evidently the smallest share with which the tenant can content himself, without being a loser, and the landlord seldom means to leave him more.' So far from rent representing a reasonable profit on money sunk in improvements, the landlord, he goes on, demands a rent even for unimproved land. Ricardo, later, boggling at the 'even,' would say that this alone was rent. The rent of land is therefore 'naturally a monopoly price.' Conjointly with this, there is, curiously, the purely Physio-cratic doctrine that rent springs from the bounty and generosity of Nature:

'Land, in almost any situation, produces a greater quan-tity of food than what is sufficient to maintain all the labour necessary for bringing it to market, in the most liberal way in which that labour is ever maintained. . . . Something, therefore, always remains for a rent to the landlord.'

With all its confused thought, this is precisely the Physiocratic view. Here there is no Ricardian finesse, no subtle juggling with land at the margin.

For a conspectus of the economic views of Adam Smith, the second book dealing with ' the nature, accumulation, and employment of Stock' (i.e., capital) is of less importance than the first, but here also there are points which reveal the essential Smith. His analysis of the meaning of capital and his account of fixed and circulating capital need not detain us, but his discussion of the accumulation of capital and the distinction between productive and unproductive labour have been the occasion of so much criticism on the part of those writers who are unsympathetic to Smithianismus that these points ought not to be passed over in silence.

The distinction between productive and unproductive labour, as has been seen, was an evil legacy of the Physiocrats; but with Smith the words have a new meaning. Productive labour is now that labour which adds value to the material worked upon; unproductive labour is labour which, however useful, results in no increase of value. In Smith's vigorous language, ' the labour of the manufacturer fixes and realizes itself in some particular subject or vendible commodity, which lasts for some time at least after that labour is past.'[9] It has therefore been productive. On the other hand, the services of a menial servant, taking him as an example of unproductive labour, ' generally perish in the very instant of their performance' – and forthwith into this galley, along with the menial servant, goes the sovereign, accompanied by all the army, the navy and the civil service, followed by churchmen, lawyers, buffoons and opera

  [9] *The Wealth of Nations*, Book II, chap. 3.

dancers. All these – and it is hard saying – render services which perish in the very instant of their performance.

But do they? the ordinary man asks. Adam Smith's test of productive labour is that the labour should realize itself in a 'vendible commodity' – or result in a higher vendibility. On this, as much as anything, is based the charge of materialism which the German idealist school brings against Smith. His view of wealth, it is said in criticism, is that it consists of things that can be and are brought to the market and sold; and consequently that an increase of wealth occurs whenever there is an increase of exchange values. The whole controversy with regard to productive and unproductive labour strikes us nowadays as rather futile – a fertile field for suggesting insoluble conundrums which are sometimes not unamusing. Two things only need be said; firstly, there may be all manner of occupations which are unproductive in the Smithian sense, but yet indirectly are of the ·highest productivity. The doctor who saves the life of a worker should be allowed some share in the worker's later productivity,[10] and a nation whose existence has been saved by an army of mercenaries, ought not, in writing their epitaph, to record that their services perished in the instant of their performance. Secondly, precisely the same services may or may not result in an increase of exchangeable values. The pastry-cook who produces a pie and sets it in the shop window, may pride himself on the productive labour which he has fixed in a vendible commodity; but what of the cook-general, a menial servant, whose pie perishes in the instant of its production?

The other point in the same chapter which is pre-eminently characteristic of Smith is his emphasis on parsimony as the basis of accumulation, not merely of private wealth, but also of the wealth of the State. To parsimony, indeed,

[10] As Mill, later, realized; but it only led him deeper into the bog.

rather than to industry, the increase of capital must be attributed. Though unacceptable later to Lauderdale, this pæan, admirably adapted to further the Savings Movement, is on reasonably orthodox lines. Every prodigal is a public enemy, and every frugal man is a benefactor; and reasons for this faith are vigorously annexed. What is important in Smith's exposition is, however, the manner in which he links this up with his fundamental principle of self-interest, which is, by its impulse to economy, a power capable of saving the State, the errors of government notwithstanding:

'This frugality and good conduct, however, is, upon most occasions, it appears from experience, sufficient to compensate, not only the private prodigality and misconduct of individuals, but the public extravagance of government. The uniform, constant, and uninterrupted effort of every man to better his condition, the principle from which public and national, as well as private opulence is originally derived, is frequently powerful enough to maintain the natural progress of things towards improvement, in spite both of the extravagance of government, and of the greatest errors of administration. Like the unknown principle of animal life, it frequently restores health and vigour to the constitution, in spite not only of the disease, but of the absurd prescriptions of the doctor.'

Here self-interest becomes the very life force of society, saving the State in spite of itself.[11]

[11] Another passage in the same chapter lays even greater stress on the permanent pervasive influence of self-interest, though without linking it up with the public benefits flowing therefrom: 'But the principle which prompts to save, is the desire of bettering our condition; a desire which, though generally calm and dispassionate, comes with us from the womb, and never leaves us till we go into the grave. In the whole interval which separates these two moments, there is scarce perhaps a single instance, in which any man is so perfectly and completely satisfied with his situation, as to be without any wish of alteration or improvement of any kind. An augmentation of fortune is the means by which the greater part of men propose and wish to better their condition,' etc. etc.

The last chapter in the second book (chap. 5) deals with the various ways in which capital may be employed, and their relative advantages from the point of view of giving encouragement and support to productive labour. Smith's argument is remarkable, firstly, for the notable infusion of Physiocratic doctrine, of which Smith was never able wholly to rid himself, and secondly, for its enunciation of *laissez-faire* doctrine, more fully elaborated at a later stage. The problem is to determine in what order the various possible employments of capital should be ranked, having regard to their comparative advantageousness to society. At the head Smith places agriculture: 'No equal capital puts into motion a greater quantity of productive labour than that of the farmer.' But the reasons he assigns are almost exclusively Physiocratic in character, based on the assumption that in agriculture, Nature is herself an active co-operating agency:

'Not only his labouring servants, but his labouring cattle, are productive labourers. In agriculture, too, Nature labours along with man; and though her labour costs no expense, its produce has its value, as well as that of the most expensive workmen.'

Nature herself, in short, produces something which has a value; it is Turgot's 'pure gift' over again. After agriculture, Smith places manufacturers, and in the third place the 'trade of exportation.' Smith here is at one with the Physiocratic reversal of the mercantilist scale of values. So far as concerns trade, the home trade, from the point of view of employment, is preferable to the foreign trade of consumption, and that again is preferable to the carrying trade. But natural forces 'without any constraint or violence' should determine the distribution of capital between the different employments:

'The great object of the political economy of every

country is to increase the riches and power of that country. It ought, therefore, to give no preference nor superior encouragement to the foreign trade of consumption above the home trade, nor to the carrying trade above either of the other two. It ought neither to force nor to allure into either of those two channels a greater share of the capital of the country than what would naturally flow into them of its own accord.'

Thus does Adam Smith, the great apostle of *laissez-faire,* deploy his forces for the grand argument in the fourth book.

The fourth book, designated 'Of Systems of Political Economy,' is devoted largely to a criticism of the mercantilists, and to a smaller extent of the Physiocrats; and it is here, as against the mercantilists, that the full argument for Free Trade and against Protection is developed. Adam Smith's statement of the mercantilist position, crudely that 'wealth consists in money, or in gold and silver,' is not wholly above reproach, but we are here concerned with the development of his own views rather than with his representation of the views of others. With becoming brevity, his view may be taken to be that gold and silver are commodities on the same footing as any others, and that the natural course of trade will bring to any country the gold and silver it requires:

'A country that has wherewithal to buy wine will always get the wine it has occasion for; and a country that has wherewithal to buy gold and silver will never be in want of these metals. They are to be bought for a certain price, like all other commodities; and as they are the price of all other commodities, so all other commodities are the price of these metals.'[12]

The freedom of trade that brings us the wines we require

[12] *Ibid.,* Book IV, chap. I.

can be relied on to bring us the gold and silver we require.
Moreover, on account of their small bulk and great value,
no commodities regulate themselves more easily or perfectly
to the effective demand for them than do the precious
metals.

Not only so, but on lines familiar to modern monetary
theory, Smith argues that is a futile proceeding to endeavour
to restrain gold and silver from leaving the country, if the
natural course of trade would lead to their withdrawal. 'All
the sanguinary laws of Spain and Portugal' cannot prevent
the exportation of gold and silver from these countries if,
owing to excess of the metals there, they should fall in
value below what they command elsewhere. This is merely
the familiar point, already encountered in Hume, that excess
of gold will result in high prices which, by making the
country a good country to sell to and a bad country to buy
in, will result in a drain of gold until equilibrium and
stability are again established. Gold and silver are, indeed,
less essential than other commodities. 'If provisions are
wanted, the people must starve'; but there are expedients,
as in a paper currency, for getting along without gold and
silver. It is only a small part of a nation's produce that is
required for purchasing gold and silver from neighbouring
countries; the greater part is circulated and consumed at
home; even of that which is sent abroad, the greater part
is destined for the purchase of foreign goods. All this could
go on without the mercantilist itch for gold. The whole of
Smith's argument thus tends to look upon gold not merely
as a commodity stripped of mystic qualities, but as a
commodity which is really subservient to other commodities,
and therefore less important:

'Goods can serve many other purposes besides purchasing
money, but money can serve no other purpose besides purchasing goods. Money therefore necessarily runs after goods,

but goods do not always or necessarily run after money.'[13]

'Look after trade, and the gold will look after itself,' is, in effect, the sum of Smith's teaching on this point. Claims that gold is a more durable form of wealth rest on a misconception. Hardware is more durable than wine, but we do not therefore heap up hardware 'to the incredible multiplication of the pots and pans of the country.' The number of pots and pans which it is expedient a country should possess is limited by the use there is for these utensils, and in the same manner the use there is for the precious metals sets a limit to the quantity of these which any country may wisely or profitably possess. Increase the use of gold and silver, 'and you will infallibly increase the quantity'; if you artificially increase the quantity beyond the use there is for them, nothing will prevent the metals from going elsewhere.

If foreign trade does not exist for the purpose of acquiring gold and silver, wherein lies its advantage? Adam Smith replies that it brings two distinct benefits. It carries out surplus produce, and it brings back something for which there is a demand. More significantly for Smith's general standpoint, as a result of foreign trade 'the narrowness of the home market does not hinder the division of labour in any particular branch of art or manufacture from being carried to the highest perfection.' Foreign trade is, in fact, for Adam Smith, merely an extension of domestic trade. It extends division of labour; it increases specialization; it multiplies exchanges.

So much for Smith's general criticism of mercantile assumptions. It is difficult to resist the impression that he somewhat overstates his case in arguing that gold is a commodity exactly like any other. Originally it doubtless was; but when one commodity, for whatever cause and

[13] *Ibid.*, Book IV, chap. I.

whatever it may be, becomes the universally accepted medium of exchange, it attaches to itself qualities which it did not possess before its elevation to the rank of money; and henceforth it is bound to be a commodity somewhat different from all others. The fact that gold is universally acceptable, that it is consequently wealth which can be potentially applied in any direction, sufficiently distinguishes this utensil from Adam Smith's pots and pans.

Smith next proceeds to consider the various expedients whereby the mercantilists had sought to secure a favourable balance of trade. His most instructive and illuminating chapters are those which relate to restraints upon imports. Of such restraints he distinguishes two kinds, the first being restraints upon the importation of such commodities as might be made at home, irrespective of the country they come from; while the second class is represented by the more mercantilist idea of restraints on all goods which happen to come from countries with which the balance of trade is unfavourable. The first is the typically straightforward protective duty, aiming at giving a monopoly to the home producer. Such a protective duty, Adam Smith admits, may give encouragement to any particular industry to which it is applied, and may direct labour and capital in that direction; but as industry is limited by capital, such a regulation cannot increase the quantity of industry in any country beyond what the capital will maintain. A protective tariff will therefore merely divert industry from one trade to another.[14]

Moreover, Adam Smith argues, it will divert it from a more advantageous to a less advantageous channel. And this for two reasons. Firstly, from motives largely of security, the merchant will prefer to put his money in the home trade rather than in the foreign trade of consumption, and in the

[14] *Ibid.*, Book IV, chap. 2.

foreign trade of consumption rather than in the carrying trade. But that is the order in which the possible uses of capital are to be arranged, viewing them from the point of view of their advantageousness to the country. The second reason is more fundamental, and leads to the core of Smith's doctrine. Every individual is aiming at a profit, and therefore uses his capital where the produce is likely to be of the greatest value. But the annual revenue of society is the sum total of all that is produced. Therefore each individual, pursuing his own ends, is unconsciously helping to increase the wealth of the whole:

'He generally, indeed, neither intends to promote the public interest nor knows how much he is promoting it. By preferring the support of domestic to that of foreign industry, he intends only his own security; and by directing that industry in such a manner as its produce may be of the greatest value, he intends only his own gain; and he is in this, as in many other cases, led by an invisible hand to promote an end which was no part of his intention.'

Such is the invisible hand whose intervention miraculously harmonizes the pursuit of gain with the promotion of the public good – the quasi-religious sanction of *laissez-faire*. Moreover, in the pursuit of his own interests, each one is a reasonably competent judge; certainly, knowing the local circumstances, he is a better judge than any Government. It is a 'most unnecessary attention' on the part of a statesman to direct private people how they shall apply their capital, and this is what is done when, by restraints placed on imports, trade and industry are diverted into channels which they would not have taken of their own accord. Protective tariffs are, in short, either useless or hurtful – useless, if without them the home product is as cheap as the foreign; hurtful, if it prevents people buying in the cheapest market:

'It is the maxim of every prudent master of a family never to attempt to make at home what it will cost him more to make than to buy. . . . What is prudence in the conduct of every private family, can scarce be folly in that of a great kingdom.'[15]

Such, in somewhat condensed from, is the substance of Adam Smith's argument for Free Trade. Fortunately it is not necessary here to try the great issue; but, without in any way impugning or even considering the case for Free Trade, it is worth noting how essentially Adam Smith's argument is based on the ideas and the circumstances of his time. The basic arguments are two: firstly, that there is a natural order in which men direct their capital and their enterprise, and that this natural order follows a descending grade of advantageousness from the country's point of view. This corresponds to the conditions of the time when capital was relatively immobile, and when men were timorous of letting it out of their sight. 'Home is, in this manner, the centre,' says Adam Smith, 'round which the capitals of the inhabitants of every country are continually circulating.' With the development of foreign investment and the inter-nationalization of finance and enterprise, no one would say this to-day. The second main argument is that of the invisible hand, the divinity which shapes our selfish ends to public purposes. Frankly, we do not believe it; rather have we learned that the interests and the prosperity of the individual may be in conflict with the well-being of the community, that no such simple process of mathematical integration as Smith suggests is permissible. If so, there must be a restraining power, and the restraining power can be vested nowhere but in the State itself. We have thus lost faith in the fundamental assumptions of *laissez-faire*, and

[15] *Ibid.*, Book IV, chap. 2.

Adam Smith's observations on the 'folly and presumption' of Government intervention, the outcome of many irritating restrictions on trade, do not awake the ready response that once they did. Yet Adam Smith was far from being the doctrinaire free-trader of the type which a later generation produced. He notes two cases where some burden should be placed upon foreign, for the encouragement of domestic, industry; and two others where the matter is, as he says, one for deliberation. Two of these at least are such that Adam Smith's authority may be, and has been, invoked in support of fairly wide departures from Free Trade policy. The first definite exception is 'when some particular sort of industry is necessary for the defence of the country.' Defence is of more importance than opulence, in Smith's famous dictum; and Smith, an ardent patriot in spite of cosmopolitan tendencies, approves of the Navigation Act on this ground. In these days, when in the event of war the whole nation and all its resources are pitted against the enemy, it is obvious that this exception, if admitted, will claim a wider application than in Smith's time.

The second definite exception is of little importance in these days: it relates to the imposition of an import duty where a tax of the nature of an excise duty is already imposed on the domestic production of a commodity. This merely equalizes the conditions as between the home and the foreign goods, and it is therefore merely a step towards equality of treatment. The first of the two matters of deliberation relates to the vexed question of retaliation, where high duties are imposed by a foreign country, and where the object of introducing duties is to persuade the foreigner to remove his. Of such duties, Smith gives a vague approval, if they are likely to succeed; but whether or not they are in any case likely to succeed he refers to that 'insidious and crafty animal vulgarly called a statesman or politician.' The

fourth of the exceptions (the second of the cases for deliberation) relates to how far and in what manner it is proper to
restore Free Trade when it has been lost. The argument is
not without interest in modern times. Smith realizes that
the sudden introduction of Free Trade may result in wide
unemployment in industries suddenly exposed to foreign
competition, and he adds that 'humanity may in this case
require that the freedom of trade should be restored only
by slow gradations, and with a good deal of reserve and
circumspection.' Smith's willingness, in the interests of
humanity, to postpone the restoration of Free Trade in
order to prevent the emergence of unemployment, is of
some interest in an age deafened with pleas for protection to
cure existing unemployment.

From Adam Smith's criticism of the second class of
restraints on imports (restraints on all goods from countries
with which the balance of trade is unfavourable[16]) two
points of general interest emerge. Firstly, as against the
mercantilist tendency to consider that the interest of each
nation consisted in beggaring its neighbours, he emphatically
asserts the common interests of all nations in these matters.
It is a point familiar alike to the Physiocrats and to David
Hume. A trade carried on 'without force or restraint' is
advantageous to both parties; and, whatever may be the case
during war, it is in peace to the advantage of every nation to
be surrounded by wealthy and prosperous nations. 'As a
rich man is likely to be a better customer to the industrious
people in his neighbourhood than a poor, so is likewise a
rich nation.' The second point is his adumbration, as against
the balance of trade, of another and more important
balance, the balance of the annual produce and consumption. This is the real test of prosperity, and it may exist in a
country without foreign trade, cut off from all other nations,

[16] *Ibid.*, Book IV, chap. 3.

just as it may exist in the world viewed as a whole. A country may enjoy a balance of produce over consumption when its balance of trade, estimated on mercantilist lines, is unfavourable. But Adam Smith does little more than hint at this idea without developing it.

The criticism of the Physiocratic system (entitled 'Of the Agricultural Systems') which follows the campaign against the mercantilists is a shorter encounter. Its chief interest perhaps lies in the revelation of the extent to which Smith remained, unconsciously and despite his protestations, in the Physiocratic line of thought. In criticizing the Physiocratic use of the words 'productive' and 'unproductive' he says, and with evident truth:

'We should not call a marriage barren or unproductive, though it produced only a son and a daughter, to replace the father and the mother, and though it did not increase the number of the human species, but only continued it as it was before.'[17]

True, but the Physiocrats, and not merely the Physiocrats, would say that such a marriage was not ultimately productive of an increased population, which is the essential Physiocratic point. And even more emphatically of the Physiocratic train of thought is a subsequent sentence:

'As a marriage which affords three children is certainly more productive than one which affords only two, so the labour of farmers and country labourers is certainly more productive than that of merchants, artificers, and manufacturers. The superior produce of the one class, however, does not render the other barren or unproductive.'

In admitting the greater productivity of agriculture, Adam Smith accepts the essence of Physiocracy. As Mr. Gonnard

[17] *Ibid.*, Book IV, chap. 9.

has well put it, Smith, in protesting against the word, accepts the idea.[18]

Other points, and these by no means the least interesting for a comprehension of the complete Adam Smith, must here be passed over. In particular there is his scheme of Imperial Federation, a by-product of his criticism of the mercantilist colonial policy; there is his discussion of the principles of taxation which has lived on in so many text-books; there is his chapter on the expenses of the Sovereign, from which inferentially may be deduced his views on the functions of Government, and the exceptions (again consider-able) which he would allow to the general principle of non-intervention. But enough, it is hoped, has been said to indicate the main features of Adam Smith's system of thought viewed as a whole, and his commanding place in the development of economic doctrine. For undoubtedly he is not merely the central and greatest figure in the develop-ment of Political Economy as a separate branch of study, his influence, both in thought and practice, has been greater than that of any other economist. His great merit lay in presenting an interpretation of life which, up to a point, corresponded, and still corresponds, with the facts of the case. He saw society on its economic side working automatic-ally through competition and self-interest, the whole being knit together by division of labour and the multiplex process of exchange resulting therefrom. The efficiency of this self-adjusting machinery was such that all he demanded was liberty for its fuller and better functioning. Much of this, it is true, is *a priori* in its character, but the Adam Smith who took refuge in the shadow of an invisible hand is constantly corrected by another Adam Smith, a hard-headed, shrewd, far-seeing, somewhat cynically wise and slightly sceptical

[18] Gonnard, *Histoire des Doctrines Économiques*, Vol. II, p.211.

Scot, such as every village on the eastern sea-board of Scot-land produces in large numbers, though few may attain to the eminence of the most eminent son of Kirkcaldy.

The Adam Smith of the large unproved assumptions is indeed admirably balanced by that other Adam Smith who knew so much about his fellow-men that he is never sur-prised into anything more than a biting phase which is almost kindly even when it cuts. Smith, perhaps for the same reason, is full of contradictions; putting it more gener-ously, he is many-sided. A cosmopolitan, if ever there was one, no one was ever more patriotic; the supreme exponent of *laissez-faire* and of the ultimate beneficence of the indivi-dualistic and self-centred instincts, he is under no illusions regarding the consequences of unrestrained selfishness. The oracle of Free Trade from his own to the present day, he has furnished the Protectionist Party with the motto which, if it were wise, it would inscribe on its banner. That Smith contains something for all men and for all causes, is the supreme proof that he was a giant compared to all who stand around him.

Yet Smith has not escaped criticism, and to one school of thought he has apparently continually acted as an irritant. Smith's feet were so firmly planted on the ground that those whose heads are lost in the clouds have never realized how secure his footing was. The idealist school and those whose patriotism is barbed with enmity for others, have been uniformly unkind to Adam Smith. Hildebrand, List, Müller, and in our own day Spann, represent a well-defined line of criticism. It may be as well to note wherein hostile criticism suggests that the weakness of Adam Smith lies.

Firstly, it is suggested that his view of wealth is too narrow. His starting point, it has been seen, leads to the idea of exchangeable value, and he therefore identifies wealth with exchangeable value. His theory, therefore, merely relates to the 'formal laws of value and of price,'[19] and consequently the wiler aspects of national welfare elude him. Here, as in most of these points, Smith is his own best corrective, and a perusal of *The Wealth of Nations* in its totality will rectify any erroneous impressions based on particular passages.

Secondly, there is the charge of excessive individualism, that he is, in the German phrase 'atomistisch,' viewing society as a vast crowd of individuals, unrelated except by the interaction on each other of their self-interested motives; consequently, that he misses the significance of the State in which, on one view of politics, the individual alone attains true significance. That Smith is not one of those who regard the State as a Holy Leviathan may be frankly admitted; that he did not recognize the need for the protective functions of the State can hardly be a charge against one who, in fact, wrote before the Industrial Revolution, since the modern idea of the State as a protective agency is largely the result of conditions which became apparent after Adam Smith's day.

Thirdly, the critics have found in Smith a certain materialism, an absence of idealism. Partly this is an extension of the first point mentioned above, the limitation of wealth to things that can be bought and sold. But partly also the criticism goes beyond this, and suggests that Smith does not approach questions relating to the right consumption of wealth or the higher ends and uses of wealth. Superficially again, there may be some substance in the criticism, especially if based on isolated passages; in fact Smith's treatment has a comprehensiveness which will be sought for in vain in most of his successors. So far as there is any foundation in the criticism, two answers may be suggested. Firstly,

[19] See Spann in the translation now available under the title *Types of Economic Theory*.

deliberately and of intention, *The Wealth of Nations* is only a half of Smith; designedly it embodies his thought on the economic and material side of life alone. And secondly, like all (or most) Scots, Adam Smith did not easily wear his soul on his sleeve, and was rather tongue-tied in the presence of the lofty theme. The true Scot shrinks from speaking of the ideal, fearing lest he may thereby look silly.

And so we take leave of Adam Smith.

CHAPTER VI

Malthus and Ricardo

Malthus

THOMAS ROBERT MALTHUS[1] (1766-1834) the second of the trinity who laid the foundations of classical English Political Economy, is, for a fairly prolific writer, surprisingly the author of one book, the protagonist of one idea. That book is his *Essay*, to which it is scarcely prudent to give a more precise title, since it varied with the years; the idea is the so-called 'Principle of Population.' It is safe to say that no reputable citizen has ever been so vilified and abused as Malthus; no writer of the first magnitude has been so often 'refuted' – even though, as must be added, by writers who give so copious evidence of neither having read nor understood the object of their hatred.

Yet, in a sense, Malthus neither wrote anything very new nor anything very startling. If by Malthusianism is meant the doctrine of Malthus – which is perhaps a large assumption – then Malthusianism was not without its clear exponents before the days of the *Essay on Population*. In that chapter on wages, in which so many wage theories are hinted at, Adam Smith, as has been seen in the passages already quoted, had observed that 'the demand for men, like that for any other commodity, regulates the production of men.' Here, if one so chooses to regard it, is the quintessence of Malthusianism, and many other writers in the

[1] Born near Dorking, 1766; ninth wrangler; Fellow of Jesus College; entered the Church; Professor of Political Economy at Haileybury College (East India Company). In addition to the *Essay on Population*, wrote a considerable number of pamphlets (as on Rent and Importation of Corn), and also *Principles of Political Economy*.

second half of the eighteenth century, including the elder Mirabeau – to name but one – might be drawn upon to furnish quotations in the Malthusian line of thought. Such originality as may be claimed on behalf of Malthus, lies in the fact that he realized the importance of a principle which others had casually stated; what others had disposed of in an *obiter dictum* became for him a central and dominating principle illuminating all things.

Malthus is comprehensible only in the light of the impulse to which the *Essay on Population* owes its origin and the curious stages by which Malthus's doctrine developed. The essay sprang from a domestic debate betwen Malthus and his father, Daniel Malthus, a man of left-wingish views and a friend of Rousseau. The air was then full of beatific visions of terrestrial paradises, represented by the glowing enthusiasm of Condorcet, and crystallized in this country in the *Political Justice* (1796) and *The Enquirer* (1797) of Godwin. Godwin, if anything, is a political theorist, and only by his repercussions concerns economic doctrine; it is therefore sufficient to say that the state which he prophetically foresaw was an anarchic society, in which happy men, freed from the fetters of property, of the passions and of marriage, would live blissfully at the cost of half an hour's labour a day. On such day-dreams, based on the perfectibility of man, and indeed his ultimate immortality here on earth, father and son disputed; and the dispute being ended or suspended, young Malthus, moved by the *esprit d'escalier*, proceeded to commit to paper the arguments which would most effectively have cornered his father, had he thought of them in time.

Thus arose the first edition of the *Essay on Population* issued in 1798, and its character corresponds to its origin. It is indeed a work full of the vigour and fire of youth, a dashing polemic against Godwin and Condorcet, designed to disprove the 'perfectiblity of man' in the Godwinian sense, by proving the instability of the state of society foreseen by Godwin.

In the first edition Malthus, for the routing of Godwin, makes two postulates, firstly that food is necessary to the existence of man, and secondly that 'the passion between the sexes is necessary, and will remain nearly in its present state.'[2] Population, in short, has a greater power of increase than the means of subsistence – the celebrated geometrical and arithmetical progressions appear in a hardened and somewhat dogmatic form in the first edition. Thus armed, Malthus has much enjoyment in disposing of Godwin; for assuming the Godwinian society safely launched, it would be impossible to imagine a state of society more favourable to population. Apply the geometrical and arithmetical progressions, and where would it be in the brief period of fifty years? Back come the hateful passions; the mighty law of self-preservation reasserts itself, and 'the whole black train of vices that belong to falsehood are immediately generated.' The thesis of the first edition is simple; if it be granted that population has a greater power of increase than the means of subsistence, there must be forces keeping the population within its due bounds. Now since these checks on population are reducible to vice and misery, the Godwinian Heaven upon earth is but a beautiful fabric of the imagination which vanishes at the severe touch of truth.

Having fired his squib, Malthus proceeded systematically to get up his subject, and he travelled and read extensively with the object of turning his earlier impulsive production into a mature discussion of the whole question. The result was the second edition of 1803, in some respects a very different book from its forerunner. In one particular the criticisms and discussion of the intervening years led

[2] First edition reprinted by the Economic Society, p.11.

Malthus to make an alteration which fundamentally altered his argument. In his first sketch he had allowed only two checks on population, namely vice and misery; but, as has been hinted, there are many old bachelors who are obviously not unhappy and who are not obviously vicious. To meet this difficulty, Malthus now introduced a third possible check on population, represented by moral restraint; but in thus varying his original doctrine to meet an obvious criticism, Malthus in effect knocked the bottom out of his original argument. For with moral restraint as a third possible check on population, the argument against the perfectibility of man (within reason) was clearly deflated, since the Godwinian earthly paradise might never be exposed to the insidious attack of the black train of vices, if it were a possible (even if unlikely) contingency, that the inhabitants might practice the necessary amount of moral restraint. Consequently, Condorcet and Godwin, whose names had figured on the title page, tend to fade out of the picture.

In the more careful statement of the second (and subsequent) editions, Malthus obligingly summarizes what he has to say in the opening chapter where his doctrine is conveniently compressed into his three celebrated propositions:

1. Population is necessarily limited by the means of subsistence.
2. Population invariably increases where the means of subsistence increase, unless prevented by some powerful and obvious check.
3. These checks, and the checks which repress the superior power of population, and keep its effects on a level with the means of subsistence, are all resolvable into moral restraint, vice and misery.[3]

[3] *Essay on Population*, Book 1, chap. 2, pp.18-19 in Vol. 1 of Everyman edition, to which, for convenience, subsequent references relate.

Of these three propositions the first requires no proof; there cannot be more people than the means of subsistence will support. The second is obviously regarded by Malthus as an excessively cautious statement, and he hankers in a footnote after a more precise formula to the effect that ' population always increases where the means of subsistence increase,' and throughout he argues on the more precise conception that where the food is increased, there will the population also be increased, so that food is in effect a demand for population. On this point hinges the discussion of the two ratios, the geometrical and arithmetical progression, which plays so large a part in Malthusian controversy. Malthus assumes that the impulse to increase of numbers in the human race is constant at all times and in all circumstances. As he phrases it in one place, ' the passion between the sexes has appeared in every age to be so nearly the same, that it may always be considered, in algebraic language, as a given quantity.'[4] This is, of course, a mere assumption, incapable of proof, and the denial of this assumption furnishes later one of the lines of attack on Malthus. But granting for the moment that this assumption is justified, then if population is capable of doubling itself in twenty-five years (as seemed to be evidenced by contemporary American experience), in successive periods of twenty-five years population would have the power of increasing according to the progression, $1:2:4:8:16:32$, etc.

The reasoning establishing the arithmetical ratio as governing the increase of the means of subsistence is less happy. It is indeed no proof at all, and is by no means creditable to a ninth wrangler. All that Malthus says is that if we allow that the produce could be doubled in the next twenty-five years, it will be ' probably a greater increase

[4] *Ibid.*, Book ii, chap. 13, Vol. i, p.312.

than could with reason be expected';[5] and with regard to subsequent periods of twenty-five years, he merely makes a supposition that in each period there would be a uniform increase of production equal to the amount at present produced. But there is no proof of the arithmetical progression; it is merely what Malthus regards as an outside estimate, a 'supposition, which, without pretending to accuracy, is clearly more favourable to the power of production in the earth than any experience we have had of its qualities will warrant.'

Accepting these ratios, there must be forces restraining the increase of population within the limits of subsistence. In the revised version these are comprehensively described as moral restraint, vice and misery, but a no less important cross division classifies them under the preventive and the positive checks. The preventive check denotes all those influences which lead to a diminution of the birth-rate. Moral restraint, if the restraint is carried far enough, clearly falls under this head; so also for Malthus do all vicious practices which result in a reduction in the number born. Positive checks, on the other hand, are all those influences which increase the death-rate, 'the whole train of epidemics, wars, plagues and famines.' If these are brought upon us by the laws of Nature, they are exclusively misery; if they are caused by our own actions, they may be described as vice, and their consequences are misery. How far this latter distinction is logical might furnish matter for argument; it may be that by foresight and knowledge, pestilence and famine and the devastation of many waters are no less avoidable than wars. It is a sign of man's coming of age that he is prepared to shift the responsibility for such happenings from the Almighty to himself.

[5] *Ibid.*, Vol. I, p.9.

Moral restraint, it has been observed, is an innovation in the second edition; yet the innovation is more apparent than real.[6] In the first edition Malthus in substance repeatedly emphasizes the principle of moral restraint; but for the purpose of his argument against Godwin, it had to be assumed, rather violently, that the single state was a state of misery, or, alternatively, was productive of vice. Something very like this conclusion was in fact reached by the Malthus of 1798.[7] It is perhaps not an unjust comment on Malthus to say that in the first edition he recognized in substance the principle of moral restraint, but that his argument compelled him to regard it as equivalent to misery.

In one respect Malthus provides a curious complement to the work of Adam Smith, who, in his attacks on the mercantilists, had shown the superfluousness, indeed the injuriousness, of Government intervention with a view to the increase of wealth. These things were subject to law, and it was merely mischievous for authority to seek by artificial restraint to increase the amount of bullion in a country.[8] This idea of law Malthus now applied to the increase of man himself. Here also there was law, not arbitrarily to be set aside. Here also it was vain for governments to seek arti-

[6] Malthus uses the expression in a very restricted sense. ' By moral restraint I would be understood to mean a restraint from marriage from prudential motives, with a conduct strictly moral during the period of this restraint.' Book I, chap. 2, footnote, Vol. I, p.14.

[7] ' This restraint almost necessarily, though not absolutely so, produces vice ' (First edition, p.29). ' Every obstacle in the way of marriage must undoubtedly be considered as a species of unhappiness ' (p.89). ' Even the slightest check to marriage, from a prospect of the difficulty of maintaining a family, may be fairly classed under the same head ' (i.e., a species of misery) (p.108). The cynic may be tempted to observe that Malthus married between the dates of the first and of the second edition.

[8] Malthus himself draws attention to this analogy. Book III, chap. 14.

ficially to stimulate population, which would not increase unless the means of subsistence increased, and which would assuredly increase, apart from Government encouragement, if these means were multiplied. Encouragement of population, as practised by most governments, was perfectly futile, and could only lead to increased mortality;[9] indeed, death was the most powerful of all the encouragements to marriage by its action in opening the way to the marriages of the younger generation. To act consistently, those who desire to encourage early unions should, if they shrink from famine, at least 'sedulously encourage the other forms of destruction which we compel Nature to use.'[10] So, following the same train of thought, a country cannot be depopulated merely by emigration; those who depart will merely make room for others; but 'take away its industry, and the sources of its subsistence, and it is done at once.'[11] Prosperity does not depend on population, but population depends on prosperity. It is not true that God never sends a mouth without sending food; but it is true, such is the pestering of the unborn, that wherever there is food, there also a mouth will appear. Food takes the lead, and the only precept for increased population is to increase the food supply, and leave the matter to individual enterprise, which assuredly will not fail.

But if Malthus in one respect completed the doctrine of Adam Smith, in another he was diametrically opposed to him. For Adam Smith postulated an essential harmony in things, typified by that invisible hand which, out of the conflict of individual interests, would bring the greatest good for the community. He was thus entirely and sturdily optimistic, even if the invisible hand is but an act of faith.

[9] *Ibid.*, Book II, chap. 4, Vol. I, pp.195, 196.
[10] *Ibid.*, Book IV, chap. 5, Vol. II, p.179.
[11] *Ibid.*, Book II, chap. 10, Vol. I, p.272.

Malthus, on the other hand, is profoundly pessimistic. Here, too, there is law, but how different is its character! Apart from moral restraint, in which he has clearly no great practical confidence, the sanctions lurking behind his laws are vice and misery. The laws of Nature to which he frequently refers are essentially punitive, and these laws of Nature, as he reminds us, are the laws of God. Natural evil is the instrument by which God warns us from any mode of conduct which is not suited to our being. 'If we are intemperate in eating and drinking, our health is disordered . . . if we multiply too fast, we die miserably of poverty and contagious diseases.' Such are the laws of Nature and of God, warning us that we have followed our impulses too far; and if we are heedless, 'we justly incur the penalty of our disobedience, and our sufferings operate as a warning to others.'[12] The note of gloom and pessimism which distinguishes so much of the economic doctrine of the nineteenth century is in no small measure the legacy of Malthus.

When it comes to practical proposals, Malthus is somewhat ineffective. Contrary to the usual view as to what is involved in Malthusianism, he restricts himself to telling us not to be in too great a hurry to get married, with a special appeal to his women readers, who, 'if they could look forward with just confidence to marriage at twenty-seven or twenty-eight,' should (and would) prefer to wait until then, 'however impatiently the privation might be borne by the men.'[13] This is the voice of a dear and kindly old uncle, rather than of the monster for whom Malthus has so frequently been mistaken; and it is as ineffective as the advice of an uncle in such matters usually is. For even with marriage at twenty-eight there is time for a discon-

[12] *Ibid.*, Book IV, chap. 1, Vol. II, p.152.
[13] *Ibid.*, Book IV, chap. 2, Vol. II, p.163.

certing and devastating torrent of children. Unlike Mill, Malthus in no wise suggests the exercise of moral restraint after marriage. His view is rather that while man may exercise his discretion in postponing marriage, the responsibility for what may happen after marriage must rest elsewhere. 'When a man marries, he cannot tell what number of children he shall have'; and he even gives a mild blessing to a modified form of family endowment in the case of very large families, and almost speaks the language of the movement when he discusses the question of relieving such a one 'from a species of distress which it would be unreasonable in us to expect that he should calculate upon.'[14]

His other practical proposal, which hardly concerns economic theory, relates to the gradual abolition of the Poor Law. His suggestion, explicable by reference to the conditions of the time, is that the State should formally disclaim the *right* of the poor to support, that there should be incorporated in the marriage service a short address emphasizing the obligation on every man to support his children, and making clear that those who erred in the face of these express warnings should be left to the punishment of Nature, the punishment of want – or to the pity of some kind benefactor. Moreover, we can rely on God (or Nature) to apply the appropriate punishment, so that no conscience need be seared. 'When Nature will govern and punish for us, it is a very miserable ambition to wish to snatch the rod from her hand and draw upon ourselves the odium of executioner.'[15] It is the laws of Nature, which are the laws of God, that have doomed him, and society at large may look the other way while punishment is being inflicted. It is one of the least pleasing aspects of Malthus

[14] *Ibid.*, Book IV, chap. 13, Vol. II, p.255.
[15] *Ibid.*, Book IV, chap. 8, Vol. II, p.202.

that in his scheme of things the poor are entirely responsible for their poverty. Neither the rate of wages, nor the parish, nor the institutions of society, nor Providence, nor the State are to be blamed: 'they are themselves the cause of their own poverty.'[16] In particular, 'the inference . . . drawn against governments from the unhappiness of the people is palpably unfair,' inasmuch as the principal cause of want and unhappiness is only indirectly connected with government.[17] It is scarcely necessary to emphasize the close connection of this doctrine with the *laissez-faire* view of government.

It should be redundant at this date to defend Malthus against the old assumption that he was a monster who gloated over pestilence, famine and war, and who prayed nightly for the periodic recurrence of such scourges as the divinely appointed method of ridding the world of superfluous babies. Malthus himself thought it at least expedient formally to disclaim any approbation of his various checks,[18] yet it is difficult to read his work consecutively without feeling that he was asking for trouble. Probably in the first edition Malthus was trailing his coat, a posture which is always picturesque in the young; as against all visionaries, he takes obvious delight in administering the cold douche of reality, and he manifests a singular sang-froid and imperturbability in constituting himself the chronicler of death and pestilence. He uses his very great literary skill to invest his views with a pungency which, if not designed to wound, was almost certainly intended to shock. And at times he sails rather near the wind, as in his studiously callous reference to the 'unhappy persons who in the great lottery of life have drawn a blank,'[19] or again when he

[16] *Ibid.*, Book iv, chap. 3, Vol. ii, p.170.
[17] *Ibid.*, Book iv, chap. 6, Vol. ii, p.193.
[18] *Ibid.*, footnote to Book i, chap. 5, Vol. i, p.53.
[19] *Ibid.*, Book iii, chap. 2, Vol. ii, p.20.

speaks of the preventive checks superseding ' the necessity of great and ravaging epidemics to destroy what is redundant,' apologetically interjecting that he is using an expression ' which certainly at first appears strange.'[20] When he contemplates the response made by Nature confronted with a redundant population, there is an air of complacency in his voice as he states that ' though we cannot always predict the mode, we may with certainty predict the fact.'[21] Nor is it possible for the ordinary person to read, without a slight shudder, his lucid objective account of the process whereby, when we close up any of the channels through which the great stream of mortality is constantly flowing, others will become proportionally more fatal.[22] Malthus has been much misrepresented and much misunderstood, but it is difficult to exonerate him from all responsibility for the caricature which did service throughout a large part of the nineteenth century.

Malthus is in many ways a peculiar and striking figure. By a premature and incautious statement of his thesis, he gained a degree of attention which would probably not have been bestowed upon him had he been guided by the academic rather than the journalistic instinct. Though original in his method rather than in his substance, he was fortunate in the moment of his exposition, since on the one hand the growth of population in Great Britain was attract-

[20] *Ibid.*, Book II, chap. 13, Vol. I, p.312.
[21] *Ibid.*, Vol. I, p.312.
[22] ' The small-pox is certainly one of the channels, and a very broad one, which Nature has opened for the last thousand years to keep down the population to the level of the means of subsistence; but had this been closed, others would have become wider, or new ones would have been formed ' (Book IV, chap. 5, Vol. II, p.183). But the whole chapter reveals Malthus in his happiest vein. Characteristic also of the ' brutality ' of Malthus is his curt dismissal of the illegitimate child : ' The infant is, comparatively speaking, of little value, as others will immediately supply its place ' (Book IV, chap. 8, Vol. II, p.203).

ing attention, and on the other hand the positive checks, as represented by bad harvests and in the consequences of war and in the prevailing squalor, were visible to all men. Moreover, though his detached air offended many, yet in an age of dominant *laissez-faire*, his subtle suggestion that the poor were responsible for their poverty, and that the Government had no responsibility for the prevailing misery, commended his doctrine to those who were thus exonerated. Yet, taking the revised text as the statement by which Malthus should be judged, there is little in his doctrine that one need hesitate to accept. Nevertheless, though the European War led to a marked revival of interest in Malthus, the problem has in large measure lost its terrors for the present generation. Nor is the reason far to seek. The fundamental assumption of Malthusianism in the strict sense is the uniform power of increase of population; subject to the operation of the preventive checks, this means in effect a potential uniform birth-rate. But one of the most marked features of population statistics is the steady decline in the birthrate during the last fifty years – so marked, indeed, that in some countries the fear is of depopulation, and children are consequently at a premium. This, fortunately, is not the place to consider the cause of the decline in the birth-rate; but, without expressing views on a matter with regard to which no one will enter the witness-box, it is clear that the cause must lie either in a diminishing reproductive power, such as Godwin, and later Carey, postulated – in which case the fundamental assumption of Malthus would be proved false – or, alternatively, in a deliberate and intentional restriction of births after marriage. This last, as has been seen, was in no wise contemplated by Malthus. As applied to present-day conditions, therefore, it must be conceded either that his fundamental assumption of a uniformity of prolific power was stated too

dogmatically, or alternatively, that the preventive checks
require restatement to include points of view with which
Malthus was wholly unfamiliar.

Even a brief account of Malthus calls for some reference
to his doctrine on the subject of rent, as expounded in *An
Inquiry into the Nature and Progress of Rent* (1815), in
which to a very considerable extent he anticipated the
essential points of the teaching of Ricardo. Malthus, in his
tract, is concerned at the outset with the causes of the high
price of agricultural produce, and dissents from the view
expressed by those of his predecessors who, like Say and
Sismondi, had regarded the high price as solely the result of
a monopoly. The high price of raw produce he attributes to
three causes, the first being that quality of the earth which
enables it to yield more than is necessary for the maintenance of those employed on the land (a Physiocratic remnant), and the third being the comparative scarcity of the
most fertile land. The second cause, which fits in with his
general doctrine of population, is the ingenious point that
agricultural produce, in contradistinction to any other commodity, produces its own demand. In other commodities,
demand is exterior to, and independent of, the production
itself, so that abundance leads to cheapness; whereas, contrariwise, since food is a demand for population, the
demand for the necessaries of life is dependent upon the
produce itself. Hence it follows, paradoxically, that here
the cause of the high price is to be found in abundance
rather than in scarcity.

The explanation of rent follows from these considerations.
' While fertile land is in abundance . . . nobody, of course,
will pay a rent to a landlord.' Later, ' land still poorer, or still
less favourably situated, may be taken into cultivation.' But
the produce is in each case sold at the ' natural or necessary
price,' since ' the price of produce, in every progressive

country, must be just about equal to the cost of production on land of the poorest quality actually in use.' How closely Malthus came to the Ricardian and the ordinarily accepted statement of the doctrine of rent, will be apparent from the following passage which is based on the comparison of the earth to a ' vast machine ' – a simile later so dear to the heart of Carey:

'The most fertile lands of a country, those which, like the best machinery in manufactures, yield the greatest products with the least labour and capital, are never found sufficient to supply the effective demand of an increasing population. The price of raw produce, therefore, naturally rises till it becomes sufficiently high to pay the cost of raising it with inferior machines, and by a more expensive process; and as there cannot be two prices for corn of the same quality, all the other machines, the working of which requires less capital compared with the produce, must yield rents in proportion to their goodness ' (p. 38).[23]

Ricardo
According to the point of view, David Ricardo[24] (1772-1823) is the evil genius who switched Political Economy on to the wrong lines, diverting it to a harsh, barren and inhuman orthodoxy, or, alternatively, by virtue of his incisive logic and ruthless pursuit of an argument, he is about the

[23] It should be noted that Malthus is more subtle than Ricardo on a point on which Ricardo has been frequently criticized, inasmuch as he makes it clear that price rises and rents emerge *before* resort to an inferior soil, and that these are indeed conditions of such a resort: ' No fresh land can be taken into cultivation till rents have risen or would allow of a rise upon what is already cultivated.' Again, ' it can never answer to take fresh land of a poorer quality into cultivation, till rents have risen or would allow of a rise, on what is already cultivated.' (Pages 27 and 28.)

[24] Born in London in 1772 of Jewish extraction, his father (a banker) having been born in Holland; on the Stock Exchange from a very early age; made a fortune; became a landowner and entered Parliament. In addition to his *Principles*, his various pamphlets, e.g. on the high price of bullion, are of the highest importance.

greatest economist of all times – though perhaps one should hasten to add that little of the Ricardian edifice has endured. Nevertheless no one has been more influential than Ricardo, even if it may have been in ways which would have surprised Ricardo himself. His has indeed been a curious fate. It is round him more than anyone that controversy has raged. In his hands classical English Political Economy reaches its final and complete form, so that, for the next generation, the leaders of economic thought can do little more than repeat the perfected blend of Adam Smith, Malthus and Ricardo; yet – curious example of the irony of human effort – it is in Ricardo that there are to be found all the conclusions which, gratefully accepted by the scientific socialists, became an armoury of arguments with which to attack 'bourgeois economy' and the established order of things. If Marx and Lenin deserve busts, somewhere in the background there should be room for an effigy of Ricardo.

As to the form rather than the substance of Ricardo's writings, it is perhaps sufficient to say that he was no writer. He himself dimly realized that he was a bad writer, but it is doubtful whether he can have known the whole truth. It is undiscerning flattery to regard his chief work, *The Principles of Political Economy and Taxation*, as a book at all. Rather does it suggest the sweepings of a busy man's study – chapters of very varying length, which he clearly found it difficult to arrange in the right order, brusque notes and memoranda on points which interested the author. In defence, it may be admitted that Ricardo had the plea, on which few authors can rely, that he did not mean to write a book. These were indeed memoranda written for himself and his friends, published on his friends' incitement. But this is poor consolation to the lonely traveller befogged in the Ricardian jungle.

It is customary to say that Ricardo is the supreme example of abstract reasoning in economics. This is true, yet it is not the whole truth. Ricardo does indeed proceed from certain principles accepted as true, and he follows these to their bitter – sometimes very bitter – conclusions. If to-day we are frequently aware of the gulf between his conclusions and the world we know, it is as well to remember that probably the gulf did not yawn so widely in Ricardo's time. It is true also that his book is a horrible concatenation of 'supposes,' so that one seems to gasp for breath in a world of abstract suppositions. Yet if Ricardo appeared to write in a world of abstract assumptions, he did not live in such a world. On the contrary, no economist ever knew the world better, or made so handsome a fortune out of it. Moreover, in all his occasional writings, which are no less important than his *Principles*, Ricardo always had before him a very practical and urgent question of the day.

Perhaps the dominant factor in making Ricardo what he was from a literary point of view is to be found in a certain inherited Jewish subtlety. Mr. Gonnard has elaborated, on the basis of their common racial origin, an impressive comparison between Ricardo and Marx, who certainly have many spiritual points of kinship. To this must be added his experience on the Stock Exchange, where the Ricardian assumption of free competition is most fully realized. His literary work is, in fact, the production of an unliterary Jewish stockbroker who had neither time nor skill to give grace or clarity to his writings, and who made the mistaken assumption that his readers would be as ingenious as he himself was.

One general point as to Ricardo's views on the scope of Political Economy meets the reader on the threshold. In his preface he lays it down that the produce of the earth is divided into rent, profit and wages, and that 'to determine the laws which regulate this distribution is the principal problem in Political Economy';[25] and more emphatically in a letter to Malthus (20th October 1820) he says:

'Political Economy, you think, is an inquiry into the nature and causes of wealth: I think it should rather be called an inquiry into the laws which determine the division of the produce of industry amongst the classes who concur in its formation. No law can be laid down respecting quantity, but a tolerably correct one can be laid down respecting proportions. Every day I am more satisfied that the former inquiry is vain and delusive, and in the latter only the true object of the science.'[26]

Attention is thus concentrated on the problem of distribution, above all with a view to determining the proportions of the various claims made on the national dividend – a programme which Ricardo hardly fulfilled. If many of the Ricardian theories are admirably fashioned to the hands of Marx, the new emphasis on distribution is no less significant. For if in the field of production the ultimate test is efficiency, in distribution the underlying question which sooner or later thrusts itself forward is that of justice.

For an understanding of Ricardo's place in the history of economic thought, it is almost sufficient to study his *Principles*. Here his starting point – whether it was in fact the starting point of his thought may be doubted – is the venerable question of value, to which he consecrates his first and longest chapter. Here his doctrine, at the first blush simple and comprehensible, trails off into modifications which leave the reader who pushes so far, not quite sure how much of the original simplicity is left, and which indeed later left Ricardo himself somewhat doubtful of the whole doctrine.

[25] *Principles of Political Economy and Taxation*, Everyman edition p.1.
[26] *Letters of Ricardo to Malthus*, p.175.

He starts off in the footsteps of Adam Smith, distinguishing between value-in-use and value-in-exchange, and points
out that to have exchangeable value, a commodity must
have utility, though utility cannot be the measure of
exchangeable value. Assuming the presence of utility, the
exchangeable value of commodities comes from two sources:
(1) their scarcity, and (2) the quantity of labour required to
obtain them. But how are we to apportion the influence of
these operative causes? Here Ricardo, with magnificent
daring, effects a simple dichotomy of all commodities. There
are some of which no labour can increase the quantity, and
therefore their value cannot be lowered by an increased
supply. In these cases value is determined by scarcity alone.
Of such are 'rare statues and pictures, scarce books and
coins,' and all the other objects of the type of the Great
Auk's egg, which figure in the economist's museum. On the
other hand, there are those commodities which can be
multiplied 'almost without any assignable limit' by the
exertion of human industry. Here, the foundation of exchangeable value is 'the comparative quantity of labour
expended on each,' though even in his general statement at
the beginning of the chapter, Ricardo limits this by restrict-
ing the proposition to the 'early stages of society,' and
further slips in a modifying 'almost exclusively.'[27] Apparently, however, in all stages of society, it remains the
foundation.[28]

It may be suggested that such a bold division of the problem involves its own condemnation. The problem of value
is one, and a theory of value should explain value wherever
it occurs. It is in the highest degree unlikely that value
should flow from one group of causes in the case of one type
of commodity, and should be determined by wholly dif-

[27] Originally he had said 'solely' Ricardo's doubts soon set in.
[28] *Principles*, chap. 1, On Value, section 1.

ferent causes in another. Ricardo's fundamental error here lies in the assumption that there is a sharp line of division between things which may only be increased in quantity by the operation of a miracle (the possibility of which may be ignored in an economic text-book), and those which can be increased 'almost without any assignable limit,' if people so choose. It might be argued that neither of these classes really exist; it is certain that, if they do exist, they fade into each other by a series of infinitely small gradations. The truth is that all commodities at a given moment are limited in quantity; it is indeed because they are so limited that the question of increasing their quantity arises. At the other extreme, though it may savour more of sophistry, there are few goods which are for practical purposes so limited that they cannot under any circumstances be increased. Old Masters and Great Auk's eggs are probably the traditional examples. It is true that the works of any particular Old Master are obviously limited, so long as the ingenuity of the trade is restrained. But the production of Old Masters goes on, though the products may take five hundred years to mature. In the year 2400 the market for Old Masters may conceivably be flooded with Augustus Johns. So with our friend the Great Auk, the eggs she has left are indeed numbered, but it is certainly possible, though it might be troublesome, to increase the eggs of extinct birds, if only by sending sparrows and starlings the way of the Great Auk. He would be a bold man who should say that the complete success of the Farmers' Anti-Sparrow League would have no influence on the value of Great Auks' eggs. It would, because thereby the supply of eggs of extinct birds would be increased; and though admittedly the new supply would in a sense be a substitute for the Great Auk's egg, nevertheless some consumers of these eggs would doubtless be prepared to accept a substitute.

It may be observed that Ricardo, less daring than Marx, in fact gives no proof that the increasable commodities exchange in accordance with the quantity of labour expended on each. The nearest approach to a purported proof is in the passage where he states that, to convince ourselves of the truth of the proposition, we have but to 'suppose any improvement to be made in the means of abridging labour.' And the result? Clearly, a fall in the value of the final product – a proof of the proposition which rests on the truth of the proposition.[29]

But the principle thus advanced as the 'foundation' is immediately made subject to a number of reservations, the effect of which is to damage the foundation more than Ricardo was prepared to admit – at least in *The Principles*. The first difficulty arises from the different qualities of labour. Ricardo here tells us that 'the estimation in which different qualities of labour are held comes soon to be adjusted in the market with sufficient precision for all practical purposes.' A scale is thus arrived at which, 'when once formed, is liable to little variation.'[30] It ought to be clear, however, that a theory of value designed to explain what happens in the market cannot base itself on what does in fact happen in the market. It is the old problem which so pervades all economic discussion, of determining which of two phenomena is cause and which effect. Is the scale of values attached to different kinds of labour something which we arrive at, Heaven knows how, and which is subsequently reflected in the market in the values of the commodities produced; or is the value of commodities determined independently in the harsh, unsympathetic market and thereafter reflected back in the relative values attached to different kinds of labour? A theory which makes value in

[29] *Ibid.*, chap. 1, section 3, p.15.
[30] *Ibid.*, chap. 1, section 2, pp.11-12.

the market the expression of the amount of labour involved is clearly debarred from going to the market to find in what ratios different kinds of labour ought to be weighted.[31]

Other modifying conditions noted by Ricardo relate to the time and labour necessary to produce the capital involved; its distribution as between fixed and circulating capital; the greater or less degree of durability of the capital, and the time that must elapse in bringing the commodities to market. Though Ricardo professes to regard all these as relatively unimportant, his own statement leaves doubts which, it is known, disturbed Ricardo's own peace of mind. Nevertheless in *The Principles* a brave show is made in identifying, as far as might be, value and the amount of labour necessary for production. His many qualifications and hesitations were easily overlooked, and Ricardo was assumed to have presented to the world a labour theory of value.

How far, it may be asked, is the doctrine that value is the expression of the labour involved, affected by the appropriation of land and the consequent payment of rent? The answer brings us to what is, if not the central, at any rate the most celebrated of Ricardian doctrines, namely the Ricardian theory of rent. That the Ricardian theory of rent had previously been stated in its essentials by others is true; nevertheless, Ricardo enunciated it with a fullness and clarity which has made it peculiarly his, for what it is worth, to all time. The Physiocrats, it will be remembered, had looked on rent as proof of the bounty of Nature; Adam

---

[31] It is curious to note how similar are the words of Marx on the same point: 'The different proportions in which different sorts of labour are reduced to unskilled labour as their standard, are established by a social process that goes on behind the backs of the producers, and, consequently, appear to be fixed by custom.' (Marx, *Capital*, chap. 1, section 2, p.52.) This mysterious process behind the backs of the producers is once again, of course, merely the judgment of the market.

Smith, with confused Physiocratic remnants in his composition, was perhaps inclined to the same view. Malthus, not to
refer to less celebrated names, had shown the way to a
theory of rent based, not on the bounty, but on the mean-
ness of Nature.

The Ricardian theory of rent has for us, in these latter
days, something of the obvious and platitudinous, once
Ricardo's restricted definition of rent is swallowed. It is, in
a too familiar phrase, ' that portion of the produce of the
earth which is paid to the landlord for the use of the original
and indestructible powers of the soil.'[32] Ricardian rent is
therefore a very different thing from rent as understood by
landlords, farmers, and the other vulgar, in whose minds
rent always has been, and always will be, a payment in
which are contained elements in respect of farm-buildings,
capital sunk in improvements, and all the rest of it. A
colonist might say that the soil had no original powers except those put there by the devil; an incompetent farmer
might protest that it had no powers which were indestructible. The ordinary person would say that, even assuming
that there are such powers, they are so inextricably intermingled with others which have a later and more human
origin, that it is futile even to attempt to visualize a separation of rent, as vulgarly understood, between the Ricardian
or economic rent proper, and the other ingredients which
are rather of the nature of interest.

The text-books have made the Ricardian theory of rent
so familiar that the merest bones may suffice. Assuming ' an
abundance of rich and fertile land ' in the case of a new
settlement, there will be no rent, as no one will pay for that
of which there is an abundant quantity not yet appropriated.
But this best land not being unlimited in quantity, it is
necessary, with the progress of population, to resort to land

[32] *Ibid.*, chap. II, p.33.

of inferior quality. Rent will then arise on the land of higher quality; and so progressively, with each increase in population which 'obliges' recourse to land of inferior quality, the land last cultivated will yield no rent; rent will emerge on that which had previously been on the margin, and the existing rent on all the higher grades will be correspondingly increased.

It is possible, however, to render the theory more precise. 'Suppose' (if we may borrow Ricardo's favourite word) that three grades of land, with an equal employment of capital and labour, yield a net produce of 100, 90 and 80 quarters of corn. So long as the first only is cultivated, there will be no rent; with resort to the second quality land, a rent equivalent to 10 quarters will appear on the first grade, since there can only be one price in the market, and that price must be such as to enable farming to make ends meet with a yield of 90 quarters. So with the descent to the third quality land, the no-rent land will now be that which yields 80 quarters; the previous marginal land (yielding 90 quarters) will yield a rent of 10 quarters, and the rent of 10 quarters hitherto payable on the highest quality land will rise to 20 quarters. And so on indefinitely.

It will be seen in what way the Ricardian theory of rent is connected with the labour theory of value. Value is determined by cost of production, but in the case of agricultural produce, there is clearly no uniform cost of production. With which of the possibly infinite number of costs-of-production is value to be equated? Clearly, with the highest, since if the needs of society require resort to production under unfavourable conditions, the costs there incurred must be covered by the price received. Price is therefore determined by the costs of those who continue to produce under the most unfavourable circumstances, and inasmuch as there is uniformity of price, there will be a surplus in the case of those who produce under better conditions. The Ricardian theory of rent thus reduces itself to the comparatively obvious statement that if there is (as there must be) uniformity of price in the market, then whenever two identical commodities are produced at different costs, a surplus will accrue on that which is produced under more favourable conditions. Rent, as Ricardo specifically states, is 'always the difference between the produce obtained by the employment of two equal quantities of labour and capital,' and as so defined, rent is clearly not confined to the sphere of agriculture, but may, as later theory realized, appear in any department of economic life.

The critical may suggest that the whole of Ricardo's account of rent is vitiated by that fruitful source of confusion, the mistaking of cause and effect. His statement is that the progress of population 'obliges' a country to have recourse to land of inferior quality, and that in consequence prices rise to support the increased cost of production. It is, of course, an imaginary world in which Ricardo moves, but even in such a hypothetical state, it is clear that the rise in price would precede, and not follow, recourse to inferior land. The true sequence would obviously be that when scarcity was felt, the price would rise, and the rise in price would then enable recourse to be made to land of inferior quality. It is unnecessary to underline the bearing of this point on the general Ricardian theory of value. It suggests a reversal of the statement that 'that corn which is produced by the greatest quantity of labour is the regulator of the price of corn ';[33] on the contrary it may be the price of corn which determines how far it is profitable to carry cultivation.

Certain footnotes to, and inferences from, the Ricardian

[33] *Ibid.*, pp.40-41.

theory of rent may be noted. While the theory implies that there is somewhere a grade of land that pays or would pay no rent, Ricardo realizes that subsequent 'doses' of labour and capital (if a later phrase be admissible) may be applied to land of higher quality in preference to resort being made to lower grade lands. Such less efficient applications to land already cultivated will, however, give rise to rent in exactly the same way, since rent 'invariably proceeds from the employment of an additional quantity of labour with a proportionally less return.'[34] (Here the Law of Diminishing Returns is clamouring for fuller expression.) To put it once more in modern terms, this means that the Law of Rent may operate intensively as well as extensively.

The most important inference from the theory is that rent (in the Ricardian sense) does not enter into the cost of production, and that consequently the remission of rent would have no effect on price. This follows from the fact that price is determined by production under the most unfavourable conditions, on land which by hypothesis pays no rent – rent being merely an emergent surplus, representing the differential advantage of the superior land. A further conclusion implicit in the Ricardian theory is that rent, the surplus which falls into the lap of the landlords, will tend to increase as society advances. It is the effect of the increasing wealth of the country, and, with increasing wealth, there will (according to the true Malthusian doctrine) be increasing population, compelling for its maintenance the cultivation of inferior land. Such a tendency to increasing rents might, of course, be checked by improvements in agriculture which would enable the additional quantities required to be obtained from land already under cultivation. Anything that diminishes the inequalities of lands necessarily

[34] *Ibid.*, p.37.

cultivated will diminish rent, and as Ricardo observes in one luminous sentence, rent increases most rapidly as the remaining disposable land decreases in its productive powers – that is to say, the most favourable position for the landlord is when, after the best lands have been exhausted, the population is forced down with a bump to the cultivation of the Bass Rock.

It will be seen how far-reaching are the implications of the Ricardian theory. Before any other claims are considered, a slice of the produce of the earth is assigned to the landlords in return for no service rendered, a slice, moreover, which grows progressively with the increase of population, so that there is scarcely (from the point of view of Ricardian theory) any limit to the proportion of the annual produce which may be absorbed in this way. So, too, there is a complete reversal of the Physiocratic point of view which not merely assigned to the landlords a place of conspicuous honour and usefulness, but viewed the exis-tence of rent as proof of the motherly benevolence of a bountiful Nature. Nature has now become stepmotherly: 'The labour of Nature is paid, not because she does much, but because she does little. In proportion as she becomes niggardly in her gifts she exacts a greater price for her works.'[35] Gloom is settling down on the economic horizon.

Of the other influential doctrines of Ricardo, the most important is that which is concerned with wages. Wages, that is the price of labour, is of course merely an example of value. Value, as has been seen, is determined by the amount of labour necessary for production; but while this is the 'natural price,' there may be accidental and temporary deviations occasioned by the fact that no commodity is supplied for any length of time in precisely the required

[35] *Ibid.*, chap. 2, footnote, p.39.

degree of abundance. It is under the influence of such deviations that capital is properly apportioned between the various lines of production, and the Ricardian scheme envisages constant oscillation in the market price, tending always to return to the natural price represented by the labour cost of production.[36] Applying these principles to wages, the price of labour, there will here also be a market price and a natural price. The market price will be the price actually paid, depending on the proportion of supply and demand, excess of labour depressing and scarcity of labour raising the market price. But whatever these deviations, there will be a tendency, here as elsewhere, to return to the natural price.

What, then, is the natural price of labour? The answer is to be found in what later, following Lassalle, came to be known as the Iron or Brazen Law of Wages. If there be obloquy attaching to the authorship of this law, it must rest, not on Ricardo, but on many others who expressed what was tending to become a commonplace view in the late eighteenth century. The very precise statement of Turgot has already been noted.[37] According to Ricardo, 'the natural price of labour is that price which is necessary to enable the labourers, one with another, to subsist and to perpetuate their race, without either increase or diminution.'[38] According as the price of food and necessaries rises and falls, so will the natural price of labour rise and fall. The market price of labour will tend towards the natural price, because it obviously cannot remain below it without leading to a reduction in the volume of labour, while, if it rises above it, the population will increase, and with redundancy of labour the market price will again tend to fall. For

[36] *Ibid.*, chap. 4, On Natural and Market Price.
[37] See above, p.116.
[38] *Ibid.*, chap. 5, On Wages, p.52.

Ricardo, a complete Malthusian, 'no point is better established than that the supply of labourers will always ultimately be in proportion to the means of supporting them.'[39]
The natural price of labour, in short, is the minimum cost
of producing men.

Such is Ricardo's first brutal statement which suggests
that the natural rate to which wages will always tend to
fall is the bare minimum necessary to allow a labourer and
his wife to bring up a family of approximately two; but as
so often with Ricardo, the theory is imperceptibly modified,
if not seriously undermined in subsequent discussion. He
admits in the first place that in what he calls an 'improving society,' in which one increase of capital follows another,
the market rate may be above the natural rate for 'an
indefinite period.' Apart from the fact that the operation of
the law may be indefinitely suspended, there is the further
damaging concession that even when estimated in food and
necessaries, the natural price of labour is not absolutely
fixed and constant. It not only differs in different countries,
but it varies in the same country at different times. In
short, 'it essentially depends on the habits and customs of
the people.' The standard represented by the Ricardian
wage is thus not a standard of subsistence, but a customary
standard. If the natural rate is merely the customary rate,
it is somewhat tautological to say that wages tend to
return to their natural rate. What that may be depends
entirely on 'the habits and customs of the people.' Ricardo
emphasized the importance of a 'taste for comforts and
enjoyments' as a security against a superabundant population; we should regard it to-day as buttressing the conventional standard of life. Clearly, if in one of these periods
when the market rate is, for an indefinite period, above

[39] *Ibid.*, chap. 21, p.194.

the natural rate, such a taste for comforts is developed, then at the end of this indefinite period, the 'habits and customs of the people' will have changed, and Ricardo's natural price of labour will have to take account of the fact.

So far from being rigorously adamant, Ricardo's statement of the 'iron' law of wages suggests something peculiarly adjustable. Even taking it in its cruder and more popularly accepted form, it must be remembered that in two respects the doctrine that wages tend to be depressed to a minimum – a doctrine that probably did not seriously misrepresent the position in the period between Turgot and Ricardo – has been undermined since Ricardo wrote. In the first place, he viewed the worker entirely in isolation, and as at a grave disadvantage when confronted with the employer; he could not foresee the reaction on wages of Combinations and Trade Unions. Secondly, it is clear that the Malthusian generalizations, which lurk behind the Iron Law, require restatement. The preventive check is not what it used to be; it is certainly no longer so true as it was, that children rush into the world on the slightest suggestion of food. On the contrary, a rise in the standard of life may, and generally does, lead to a decline in the birth-rate. To these two considerations, above all, is due the fact that the so-called Iron Law of Wages is to-day of little importance except for the examinee.

Ricardo's professions would lead the reader to expect a discussion of the proportion in which the 'produce' is allotted among the various claimants. While his discussion nowhere approaches such a quantitative computation as might be anticipated, he does indicate how, in accordance with his theory, the proportion will tend to vary in future. Rent, as we have seen, will rise; wages will tend to rise nominally, owing to the increased cost of food occasioned by resort to inferior land, but real wages (being governed

by subsistence considerations) will not rise. Indeed, though
it may appear to be in contradiction with the stricter interpretation of the Ricardian law, the normal rise in wages
will not be sufficient to compensate the worker for the rise
in prices of commodities in general.[40] With regard to profits,
along with which interest is lumped, Ricardo is not entirely
clear, but to one general proposition he adheres with the
utmost tenacity. It is that whatever increases wages necessarily reduces profits, and indeed nothing can affect profits
but a rise in wages.[41] No place here for the 'economy of
high wages,' or for a consideration of those causes which
may lead to variations of the output of labour. Wages and
profits are diametrically opposed, and a fall in the one means
a rise in the other. In the long run, as has been seen, money
wages will rise, so that the rate of profit will tend to fall.

Such is the Ricardian scheme of distribution; in place of
the old harmony of interest, he has placed dissension and
antagonism at the heart of things. 'The interest of the
landlord is always opposed to that of the consumer and
manufacturer.'[42] So also the interests of the worker and the
employer are eternally and irreconcilably opposed; when
one gains, the other loses. Further, the outlook for all, except the landlord, is a process of continual pejoration. Gone
is the large-hearted optimism of Adam Smith, transmuted
into a pessimism that will not be comforted. Yet Ricardo
remains immovably non-interventionist. 'These, then,' he
says, 'are the laws by which wages are regulated'; and he
adds inconsequently, 'like all other contracts, wages should
be left to the fair and free competition of the market, and
should never be controlled by the interference of the
legislature.'[43] In a world of Ricardian gloom one might

[40] *Ibid.*, chap. 5, On Wages, p.57.
[41] *Ibid.*, chap. 6, On Profits, pp.70-71.
[42] *Ibid.*, chap. 24, p.225. It is true that there is a slight exception.
[43] *Ibid.*, chap. 5, On Wages, p.61.

ask, and did in effect ask, why there should not be interference. An optimist carolling that God's in His Heaven, and that all's right with enlightened self-interest has a right to nail the *laissez-faire* flag to the mast, but a pessimist who merely looks forward to bad days and worse times ought not in principle to be opposed to intervention, unless his pessimism is so thorough-going as to lead to the conviction that, bad as all diseases are, all remedies for all diseases are even worse.[44]

Much might be said, but cannot be said here, with regard to Ricardo's writings relating to the theory of foreign trade and in the field of currency problems. It must suffice here to say that, as Ricardo's starting point was in the urgent problems of the day, so in these more technical discussions his importance is as great as in the more general parts of economic theory. He explained the laws which govern the distribution of the precious metals among different countries as a result of international trade; in currency matters he expounded the quantity theory of money, and with much subtlety analysed the meaning of depreciation; he advocated economy in the use of gold and silver, and indeed he argued that 'a currency is in its most perfect state when it consists wholly of paper money, but of paper money of an equal value with the gold which it professes to represent.[45] He anticipated in his writings the peculiar features of the Gold Standard, as reintroduced in 1925. But the temptation to discuss the currency expert in Ricardo must be resisted.

Even if little of the main Ricardian structure be left to-

[44] Mr. Gonnard has very properly drawn attention to the illogical combination of pessimistic belief and the cult of individual liberty, characteristic of the school of Ricardo, which he ascribes to the Calvinistic and puritanical element in the British character. But in Ricardo's case it must go further back than Calvin. See Gonnard, *op. cit.*, Vol. II, p.250.
[45] *Ibid.*, chap. 27, p.244.

day, it nevertheless remains true that Ricardo was one of the dominant influences of the nineteenth century, and that, moreover, in directions which would have made Ricardo shiver to contemplate. His primary purpose was to elaborate the theory of distribution, and in particular to consider the incidence of various types of taxation. He did so on certain assumptions regarded as sacrosanct, and ruthlessly pushed on to certain logical conclusions. There is no place in Ricardo for the waywardness of human action or for the multiplicity of causes of friction which place mere logic at a disadvantage in explaining the mechanism of society. Above all, competition – omnipresent, unrestrained and instantaneously operative – is assumed as the driving force of all action. It is not so now, nor indeed was it ever so. 'Why should the manufacturer continue in the trade if his profits are below the general level?'[46] He himself knows the answer, as he shows two chapters later, namely that people while losing money may continue in a trade for the very excellent reason that they cannot get out of it, that a shipbuilder overnight cannot turn his capital to agriculture. But such distracting knowledge of the real world has little influence on the march of Ricardo's argument. Again, despite occasional sympathetic observations, his whole attitude to the working class is that they are merely a means to production. 'Suppose the circumstances of the country to be such that the lowest labourers are not only called upon to continue their race, but to increase it; their wages would be regulated accordingly.'[47] Marx's Industrial Reserve Army does not more definitely set the workers aside as a separate race maintained for the high ends of enterprise. Again in another celebrated passage which very properly stuck in the throat of Sismondi, he argues against Smith for magnifying

[46] *Ibid.*, chap. 17, footnote, p.160.
[47] *Ibid.*, chap. 16, p.143.

the advantages of a large gross income rather than a large net income. It is, says Ricardo, the net income that matters, and if the net income can be obtained with a smaller population, what purpose is served by the superfluity?[48] His logic would lead to the desirability of the population being reduced to one, and that last remnant producing a vast net surplus with the aid of sorcery and mechanical contrivances. The repellant doctrine that man exists for the production of wealth, rather than that wealth exists for the use of man, here finds its classical utterance.

All Ricardo's doctrines were left in a form to invite mis-quotation and abuse. They are so easily remembered in their abridged form; it is so easy to forget (it was perhaps difficult ever to understand) the subsequent reservations in which Ricardo did so much to complicate and modify his simple doctrines. It is therefore not surprising that the crude and unrefined Ricardo should have been taken and applied to other purposes. Above all, he provided, all unwittingly, the foundation stones of so-called scientific socialism. The labour theory of value, with which he appears to have been increasingly dissatisfied, is the basis of Marx and the source of the claim to the ' whole produce of labour.' The doctrine of rent, especially if one forgets that Ricardian rent is an abstraction, appears as an instigation to agrarian socialism. The Ricardian doctrine of wages, shorn of those reservations which go far to deprive it of all meaning, became the battle-cry of socialism. His opposition of wages and profits seems to symbolize the class war. For the ironically minded, noth-ing is more curious to observe than this supreme exponent of classical English Political Economy providing arguments to Marx and his followers. That the Ricardian refinements were left behind in the transplantation is true but im-

[48] *Ibid.*, chap. 26, On Gross and Net Revenue, p.235.

material. Perhaps the final lesson to be learned from Ricardo is that the literary graces are not merely ornamental but useful, and that he who is deficient in the art of expression has only himself to blame if he is misrepresented.

CHAPTER VII

Lauderdale, Rae and Sismondi

WITH Adam Smith, Malthus and Ricardo, the structure of 'classical' Political Economy is, in a sense, complete. From this point onwards, it is, for a time, by no means easy to decide in what sequence our chosen representatives of economic thought should be marshalled, or how best they should be grouped for purposes of exposition. The classical school had made certain assumptions with regard to the relationship existing between the individual and the State; they had in their later developments arrived at a generally pessimistic outlook, as exemplified in the 'principle' of population and the Ricardian Law of Rent; their defence of *laissez-faire* and Free Trade had given them cosmopolitan sympathies; they had been hardened individualists. Against each of these aspects of the classical body of thought, reaction was inevitable; it was likewise inevitable that some should continue to croon, with modifications, the accepted and orthodox doctrine.

There are thus, in the next generation, critics of the excessive individualism of the classical school denying the assumptions on which *laissez-faire* is built. There are advocates of Protection. There are those who struggle towards a more optimistic view of the universe. There are those who plead the case of the nation against what they regard as a wishy-washy cosmopolitanism. On a larger canvas, these various lines of reaction against the classical school might be traced consecutively. Unfortunately, the authors concerned do not consistently group themselves along different lines of development; and therefore in the next four chapters a rough and ready grouping is all that is possible. In this chapter a brief account will be given of three early critics of Adam Smith, viz., Lauderdale, Rae and Sismondi. Lauderdale and Rae are largely concerned with what they regard as Smith's erroneous views on the nature of wealth. Rae and Sismondi have this in common, that both are led to reject *laissez-faire* and to insist that extensive duties rest on the State. It is true that while this reaction leads Rae to a somewhat paternal state, it rather urges Sismondi in the direction of socialism. In the next chapter three German writers, Müller, List and von Thünen, will be considered. Müller and List have much in common, and represent the reaction to nationalism and Protection, though indeed Müller's criticism of Smith is extensive and comprehensive. Von Thünen is rather a star that dwells apart, but he would probably be happier beside his German compatriots than anywhere else. In the ninth chapter, the reaction to optimism will be discussed (very briefly) as it is represented in Carey and Bastiat, though here again Carey might better be grouped with List as jointly representing, on the commonly accepted view, the leading exponents of Protection. Lastly, in the tenth chapter, the continuation of the orthodox school will be exemplified by Say, Senior, Mill and Cairnes.

Lauderdale

Of the group assigned to this chapter, two, it is to be noted, are Adam Smith's own countrymen. Though they have not succeeded in retaining a large place in the general memory, they are noticeable for their fundamental criticisms of certain of the assumptions of Adam Smith. While Smith was the embodiment of common sense and shrewdness, these critics are, however, rather to be regarded as interesting and curious, if not indeed eccentric. Doubtless this eccentricity was more marked in James Maitland, eighth Earl of Lauderdale, than in John Rae.

Lauderdale[1] (1759-1830) was in his time a striking figure, much given to entering protests in the journal of the House of Lords. His contribution to economic literature is to be found in a work of which the complete title is *An Inquiry into the Nature and Origin of Public Wealth, and into the Means and Causes of its Increase*, a book of commendable brevity and of few ideas, pushed home with much pertinacity and ingenuity, and indeed carried to the point of habitual paradox. In his 'advertisement,' he claims that his views 'are not only new, but even repugnant to received opinions.' The central point of Lauderdale's theorizings is foreshadowed in the title of his treatise. 'Public Oeconomy,' he tells us, 'is of necessity in all stages of society, a subject of discussion, even amongst the most vulgar and illiterate, whose rude and erroneous conceptions must naturally lead to expressions founded on inaccuracy and pregnant with error.'[2] Lauderdale throughout shows a truculent and carping spirit wherever Adam Smith is concerned,[3] and the implication of the whole discussion is that Smith likewise is a victim of these rude and erroneous conceptions. The particular example of the Idol of the Market-Place with which Lauderdale is concerned is that which confuses the wealth of a nation with the riches of an individual, and which assumes that whatever increases the riches of an individual will *pro tanto* increase public wealth,

---

[1] Born 1759; entered Parliament 1780; succeeded to Scottish peerage in 1789, and in 1790 was elected a representative Scots peer. Politically he moved, during his lifetime, from the extreme left to the extreme right. In the language of his countrymen, 'a crotchety body.'

[2] *Public Wealth*, pp.3-4.

[3] E.g., 'There is no opinion that has been anywhere maintained on the subject of the sources of national wealth, which does not appear to have been adopted in different parts of the inquiry into the *Wealth of Nations*' (*Public Wealth*, p.116).

Lauderdale, it may be observed, consistently uses the word
'wealth' when the appropriate adjective is 'public,' whereas in speaking of the individual, he uses the word 'riches.'
The passage in Smith which Lauderdale regards as particularly peccant is that in the third chapter of the second
book of *The Wealth of Nations*, wherein the 'eminent
philosopher' discusses the accumulation of capital. 'As the
capital of an individual,' says Smith in this passage, 'can be
increased only by what he saves from his annual revenue or
his annual gains, so the capital of a society, which is the
same with that of all the individuals who compose it, can be
increased only in the same manner.' It is the concluding
part of this dictum which particularly displeases Lauderdale. So far from it being possible to identify the capital
(or wealth) of society with the sum total of the capital (or
riches) of all the individuals, they are indeed fundamentally
opposed. To find the basis for the distinction, indeed
antagonism, between public wealth and private riches, we
must follow Lauderdale into that unending morass where
economists and others assiduously and eternally discuss the
meaning of value, and find no end in wandering mazes lost.
That value may be conferred on any commodity, two conditions are, he says, requisite: firstly, the commodity, as being useful or delightful to man, should be an object of his
desire; and secondly, the commodity should exist 'in a
degree of scarcity.'[4] If the circumstances with regard to
demand remain the same, value will accordingly increase
with scarcity, and be diminished with abundance. But if
the individual's 'riches' are increased by scarcity (existing
elsewhere), there must, argues Lauderdale, be an antagonism between public wealth and private riches, and the
increase of the two must depend on different causes. The
popular idea regards public wealth as the integration of all

[4] *Public Wealth*, p.12.

private wealth, and, as exemplified by Adam Smith, holds
that parsimony, ' the most usual means of increasing private
fortune,' is likewise the 'parent of public wealth.'[5] In fact,
as has been seen, private riches postulate scarcity, and 'the
common sense of mankind would revolt at a proposal for
augmenting the wealth of a nation by creating a scarcity
of any commodity generally useful and necessary to man.'
He continues in a passage which has been frequently
quoted:

'For example, let us suppose a country possessing abundance of the necessaries and conveniences of life, and universally accommodated with the purest streams of water:—
what opinion would be entertained of the understanding of
a man, who, as the means of increasing the wealth of such
a country, should propose to create a scarcity of water, the
abundance of which was deservedly considered as one of
the greatest blessings incident to the community? It is
certain, however, that such a projector would, by this means,
succeed in increasing the mass of individual riches; for to
the water, which would still retain the quality of being useful and desirable, he would add the circumstance of existing in scarcity, which of course must confer upon it value.[6]

The converse case is also forcibly argued:

'Let us for a moment suppose it possible to create as
great an abundance of any species of food as there exists of
water: what would be thought of the advice of a man who
should cautiously recommend, even at the moment of the
pressure of scarcity, to beware of creating this boasted
abundance? for, however flattering it might appear as a
remedy for the immediate evil, it would inevitably diminish
the wealth of the nation. Yet ridiculous as this opinion
might appear, as everything which partakes of the abundance of water or air must at once cease to possess value, it
follows that, by occasioning such an abundance, the sum-

[5] *Ibid.*, p.40.   [6] *Ibid.*, pp.43-44.

LAUDERDALE, RAE AND SISMONDI 181

total of individual riches would most certainly be diminished, to an extent equal to the total value of that species
of food whose value would by this means be destroyed.'[7]

There is thus complete antagonism between public wealth
and private riches; the community is interested in abundance, the individual (who possesses) is interested in scarcity.
Indeed Lauderdale goes so far as to affirm generally that
'an increase of riches when arising from alterations in the
quantity of commodities, is always a proof of an immediate
diminution of wealth; and a diminution of riches is evidence
of an immediate increase of wealth.'[8] Thus Lauderdale
arrives at his definition of wealth as consisting 'of all that
man desires, as useful or delightful to him,' while individual
riches consist of 'all that man desires as useful or delightful
to him; which exists in a degree of scarcity.'[9] As scarcity
increases, the former diminishes, while the latter must
increase.

In an elaborate discussion of the four causes which lead
to variations in value (diminution and increase of quantity;
diminution and increase of demand), Lauderdale is led to an
analysis of what would now be known as the principle of
elasticity of demand. Thus, taking the first of these causes,
that of diminution of quantity (or scarcity), the effect of
competition in raising value may be far beyond what might
be expected. It will depend upon the extent to which people
are willing to deprive themselves of a portion of other enjoyments, the governing consideration being the 'desire of
mankind to continue their usual enjoyments'; and their
obstinacy in attempting to acquire the same quantity of any
commodity as formerly is 'proportioned to the degree of
inclination which either necessity, habit or taste has created
for it.' This explains the difference between the effects of

---

[7] *Ibid.*, pp.45-46.   [8] *Ibid.*, pp.55-56.   [9] *Ibid.*, pp.56-57.

scarcity on the value of different articles; in the case of necessities there may be a rise in value in the ratio of one to fifty, whereas articles of taste or luxury hardly ever rise to double or treble their usual value.[10] As Lauderdale says in another part of the same discussion:'No rise in value can induce men to renounce the acquisition of the necessaries of life, provided any sacrifices they can make will procure them.'[11]

Lauderdale is also notable for his closer analysis of the function of capital in the production of wealth. Land, labour and capital are, he says, all three, original sources of wealth, though at different stages of development they contribute to this end in very different proportions. So far as the function of capital is concerned, the view which Lauderdale criticizes is that implicit in certain statements of Adam Smith (Book I, chap. 6) to the effect that the profit of stock is paid out of and derived from the value added by the workman to the raw material, a doctrine which, as interpreted by Lauderdale, seems to savour of Marxian doctrine. On this view, says Lauderdale, capital would not be an original source of revenue, since profit would be 'only a transfer from the pocket of the labourer into that of the proprietor of stock.'[12] As against this view, Lauderdale argues that the profit which capital receives is not a simple transfer of this nature; the profit it receives arises from its own independent services, that is to say 'from its supplanting a portion of labour which would otherwise be performed by the hand

[10] *Ibid.*, pp.65-66.
[11] *Ibid.*, p.76.
[12] *Ibid.*, p.158. He also quotes from Book II, chap. 3, of *The Wealth of Nations*, a sentence which seems to be peculiarly susceptible of a Marxian interpretation: 'The labour of a manufacturer adds generally to the value of the materials which he works upon, that of his own maintenance and of his master's profit.' 'Manufacturer' has, of course, in this passage, its eighteenth century and true significance of one who does things with his hands.

of man; or from its performing a portion of labour which is beyond the reach of the personal exertion of man to accomplish.'[13] A man with a spade can do the work of fifty people using their nails (surely an underestimate); this portion of capital, therefore, supplants the necessity of forty-nine people, who are thereby rendered superfluous. So with each and all of the five methods in which, according to Lauderdale, capital may aid production, the profit which accrues to capital arises essentially from the displacement of labour.[14] So far from its being the case, then, that capital is profitable in putting labour into motion, or in 'adding to the productive powers of labour,' its real function is to supplant labour. And the consequeces of this view are far-reaching. On what, for convenience and following Lauderdale, may be taken as Smith's view, labour is limited by and proportioned to the quantity of existing capital, and therefore an increase of capital is the 'sovereign and unbounded means of augmenting wealth.' On Lauderdale's view, a country cannot be benefited by the possession of a greater portion of capital than can be advantageously employed in supplanting labour.[15]

This leads, on the practical side, to the central point in Lauderdale, carried to the excess of paradox. It might reasonably have been inferred that wealth could only be increased by those means by which it is originally produced, but popular prejudice, confusing the means whereby an individual may properly increase his private riches with the policy proper for the increase of public wealth, has pointed

[13] *Ibid.*, p.161.
[14] In a characteristic footnote, Lauderdale observes: 'It is a strange confusion of ideas that has led Dr. Smith to describe the operation of capital as increasing the productive powers of labour. The same process of reasoning would lead a man to describe the effect of shortening a circuitous road between any two given places, from ten, to five miles, as doubling the velocity of the walker ' (p.185).
[15] *Ibid.*, pp.203-205.

to parsimony as the path of enrichment.[16] But Lauderdale will have nothing to do with parsimony, 'the baneful passion for accumulation'; nor does he support the orthodox and Smithian doctrine that every prodigal is a public enemy, and that every frugal man is a benefactor. In the more primitive agricultural state, when a man is in possession of as much capital as he can use, it is neither advantageous to himself nor to others that he should abridge consumption merely to obtain more than he can use, and at all times there is a point beyond which capital cannot be profitably increased.[17] Hence the folly of sinking funds; hence also the importance of stimulating demand, on which industry depends. Lastly, Lauderdale strikes a note suggestive of much to come later when he argues that great inequality of fortune . . . has everywhere been the principal impediment to the increase of public wealth,' and that a proper distribution of wealth insures the increase of opulence by sustaining a regular progressive demand in the home market.[18]

Rae

John Rae[19] (1786-1873) has many points in common with Lauderdale, and though a flabbier and less pungent writer, he is not so markedly a disgruntled voice *et præterea nihil*. In large measure he also is critical of the foundations on which Adam Smith builds, and in particular of two assumptions, firstly, that the national wealth can be increased by

[16] *Ibid.*, p.208.
[17] *Ibid.*, p.228.
[18] *Ibid.*, pp.345 and 349.
[19] Born at Footdee (or Fittie), Aberdeen, in 1796; educated at Marischal College; later studied medicine at Edinburgh. He seems to have emigrated under the double spur of financial and matrimonial misfortune. Led a very miscellaneous life in Canada and elsewhere, teaching, doctoring, etc. He ended up, a rather pathetic exile, as a kind of administrator in the Sandwich Islands.

the accumulations of private wealth, and secondly, that there is a natural harmony between private and national interests. These are the views expounded in his chief work, *New Principles on the subject of Political Economy*[20] (1834). Individual accumulation, as a means of advancing the national capital, has, he argues, limits beyond which it cannot pass.[21] There is, as in Lauderdale's example, a limit to the number of flails a country can profitably use; Adam Smith, indeed, had in one place spoken to the same effect regarding pots and pans. Beyond this point, mere accumulation in itself will do no good; that the national capital may increase further, the nation must be hitched up to a higher level of development. Flails must be replaced by threshing machines; that is to say, there must be invention and progress.[22]

This, for Rae, is the fundamental point of distinction. In a passage too long for quotation, he argues that individuals in general increase their capitals by acquiring a larger portion of the common funds. One grows rich, while another grows poor; but while one man may add house to house and farm to farm the national capital itself may remain but little changed. Neighbouring nations, on the other hand, advance and decline in wealth together. Thus, in a characteristic summary:

'As individuals seem generally to grow rich by grasping a larger and larger portion of the wealth already in

[20] The full title is really much more cumbrously lengthy. Rae's book was re-edited by Dr. Mixter in 1905, under the title *The Sociological Theory of Capital*. Unfortunately, in this edition, the contents have suffered a complete reshuffling in order to attain what the editor regards as a more logical arrangement. This is what Adam Smith would have called a 'most unnecessary attention'. Reference is, however, made to this edition as being the most accessible.

[21] *Sociological Theory of Capital*, p.157.

[22] *Ibid.*, pp.152-153.

existence, nations do so by the production of wealth that did not previously exist. The two processes differ in this, that the one is an acquisition, the other a creation.'[23]

It is a consequence of this view that Rae assigns to invention a place of primary importance in his scheme of things; indeed his work is largely a study of the place of invention in social development. Invention can alone be said to create, and as such it is an essential element in the process of the increase of national wealth; but, having regard to the distinction indicated between national and individual wealth, it cannot be assigned a similar place in the increase of individual wealth.[24] Allied to this is his dissent from Adam Smith on the question of division of labour. Smith had noted the encouragement of invention as one of the consequences of division of labour; but this, argues Rae – not without cogency – is to invert the true order of events. Knowledge and discoveries mean the multiplication of instruments; and variety of tools means diversity of trades. It would be wasteful for all men to possess all tools, as in that case the great bulk of implements would in general be lying idle.[25] Thus division of labour proceeds from, and is dependent on, the antecedent progress of invention; indeed, monotonous occupation, which is in part synonymous with division of labour, will rather tend to dull and cramp men's faculties and so discourage further inventions in the victims of a monotonous regime. Here he is doubtless right in his readjustment of emphasis, as also perhaps in his inclination to minimize the place of ' dexterity' in Smith's theory of division of labour. For dexterity is of importance only in the beginning of art, and with progress ' the hand does less, the instrument more.'[26] Division of Labour, in short, is for Rae not a cause but a result of progress; it is but the mani-

[23] *Ibid.*, p.383.　　[25] *Ibid.*, pp.102-103.
[24] *Ibid.*, p.386.　　[26] *Ibid.*, pp.237-242.

fest consequence of that inventive faculty which raises society to a higher level.

The fact that on Rae's view private accumulation rests largely on mere acquisition implies further that there is no natural identity between national and individual interests. ' Do the labours of the cool, calculating gambler, or of the sharper, add to public wealth? Does the spirit of keen bargaining add to public wealth? In these and countless other ways self-interest may not be guided by an invisible hand to the promotion of larger ends.[27] Rae is thus led to a reasoned refutation of the doctrine of *laissez-faire*, to a plea for enlightened government interference. When men are united in large societies it is impossible for each to take an active part in what concerns the public good; this is the function of the legislator. On the theory of *laissez-faire* each individual, seeking his own good, unintentionally and indirectly increases the national wealth. Admittedly, then, it is only the legislator who can *of design* act with a view to increase the national opulence; but as his interference would disturb the course which events would otherwise take, this interference, being opposed to the course of Nature, is presumed, on *laissez-faire* principles, to be injurious.[28]

This presumption Rae holds to be unfounded; it is by no means demonstrable that the art of the legislator is powerless to promote the prosperity of nations, and indeed the assumption should rather be the other way.[29] The example which bulks most largely in his mind is that of the passage

[27] *Ibid.*, p.345.
[28] *Ibid.*, pp.357, 362.
[29] Rae's analogy is interesting, if not wholly to the point: ' If a number of people have occasion to pass frequently between two points, they will without design produce a natural footpath. Will this, which was no part of their intention, be a better footpath than one artificially and intentionally created by the community, acting as an organized unit? ' (p.362). An argument for the continued existence of the Parish Council.

of the useful arts from one country to another. These transplantations were originally due to violent causes; they were the consequences of war, revolution and exile. But if such evil influences no longer operate, must we also sacrifice the indirect good which such causes may have produced, or is it not rather the duty of 'the intellectual part of our nature' to achieve the good and prevent the evil?[30] The original violent methods of dissemination of the knowledge of the arts should therefore be replaced by the direct efforts of the legislator to draw them there. Thus the legislator is called upon to act, but to act cautiously; and the weapons which Rae places in his hands for this purpose are represented by premiums, bounties and duties.[31] This argument Rae further buttresses by the contention that cases in which private effort succeeds in transferring an industry to a new country are very rare, and that it is scarcely ever likely to be profitable. 'It would be more just and judicious,' he says, 'that the necessary first cost of the scheme should be borne by the whole community' rather than that we should wait 'till the miscalculations of some unfortunate projector confer on us a public benefit.'[32] Thus does the infant industry argument gently crow from its cot.

Rae's central doctrine is open to the criticism which must so often be passed on those who are determined to be critical. While he suggests useful correctives, his main contentions, when generalized, are as untenable as those which he attacks. It is curious to observe that he regards the theory which identifies increase of national wealth with accumulation of private capital as inconsistent with itself, merely because Adam Smith admits the importance of the introduction of the new arts.[33] It would be equally logical to regard Rae's theory as ship-wrecked by his admission

[30] *Ibid.*, p.365.   [32] *Ibid.*, p.419.
[31] *Ibid.*, pp.369-370.   [33] *Ibid.*, p.407.

'that individuals, as well as nations, acquire wealth from other sources than mere saving from revenue; that skill is as necessary, and consequently as valuable, a co-operator with the industry of both, as either capital or parsimony; and that therefore the expenditure which either may be called on to make to attain the requisite skill is very well bestowed.'[34]

This is an impeccable statement which even Adam Smith in his more obtuse moments might have accepted, but it somehow torpedoes the crisp distinction between the sources of national and individual wealth which elsewhere Rae attempts to draw.

Rae is an interesting study for those who are fascinated by the reaction of mind on mind. Perhaps in part owing to a common American environment, there is a good deal in him that foreshadows Carey, notably in his treatment of land as an instrument, indistinguishable from other instruments, and in a doctrine that approaches Carey's theory of value as determined by cost of reproduction.[35]

So also there are hints of List, whose views likewise were moulded by his experiences and his study in America. When Rae emphasizes the importance of introducing a new industry to serve later as a source of wealth, and indicates that the legislator may 'by means of a small expenditure, effect an increase of the productive powers of the com-

[34] *Ibid.*, p.428.
[35] Thus, in discussing 'instruments,' he explains that 'a field fitted for use is an instrument. . . . The power which has made it an instrument is the agriculturalist's labour' (p.16). And again, 'a portion of cultivated land, considered as an instrument actually subject to the operations of the husbandman, does not differ from any other instrument' (p.40). On the question of value where articles are produced with less labour than formerly, they 'procure for their owners less of other articles in exchange than they did before. They exchange, not for what labour has been actually wrought up in them, but for what is now required to make others similar to them' (p.107).

munity,' he is anticipating not merely the thought but the phraseology of the German economist. Lastly, if it be not too fanciful, his comments on luxury and vanity, and his conjuction of the words 'conspicuous' and 'consumption' are a curious anticipatory echo of Thorstein Veblen.[36]

Sismondi

Sismondi[37] (1773-1842), as a writer of economics, is extremely difficult to 'place.' This is due to the fact that his was a mind in transition; he never quite lost contact with his starting point, yet he never quite arrived at his natural destination. While having kinship with many schools, he is consequently at home with none. In his first important work, *De la Richesse Commerciale*[38] (1803), his position is simple; he is, as becomes a young man, content to be a not very critical follower of Adam Smith. Moreover, there is a refreshing honesty about his discipleship. Of certain chapters he tells us that they contain no ideas really new to anyone who has studied Adam Smith,[39] and further that his object is to appropriate to France the counsels which Adam Smith had intended primarily for England.[40] There is an engaging candour in his later confession that if in this book he did not make any discoveries, he was at least well aware of the fact.[41]

---

[36] *Ibid.*, p.245 et seq.
[37] Born in 1773 in Geneva, where he also died. Spent a considerable time in Italy, where he engaged in agriculture and wrote his sixteen-volumed work on the history of the Italian Republics in the Middle Ages. Later also he embarked on a history of the French, of which twenty-nine volumes were written, and other works less markedly voluminous. He visited England in his youth and also later.
[38] The full title is significant: *De la Richesse Commerciale ou Principes d'Économie Politique appliqués à la Législation du Commerce.*
[39] *De la Richesse Commerciale*, Vol. I, p.xx.
[40] *Ibid.*, Vol. I, p.12.
[41] *Nouveaux Principes*, p.vii.

In the main, then, the central point of this first work is to be found in Sismondi's restatement of the harmony of interests, the necessity of *laissez-faire* and the folly of Government interference. When commerce is left free, he explains in one place, capital naturally takes the direction which is most advantageous to the nation which possesses it,[42] and there is more than an echo of the invisible hand in his assertion that 'all men, in seeking their own interest, incessantly tend to serve the national interest.'[43] Thus we arrive at the glowing optimistic conclusion that 'the capitalist, who consults his own interest, always works for that of the nation';[44] and the *sans cesse* and the *toujours* stand forth brazenly without modification. He thus quotes as a *noble réponse*, the alleged reply of the British business world to a Government anxious to help them that the only favour they desired was 'la grâce de nous oublier.'[45] All this savours of the clotted cream of *laissez-faire*; but there are pointers in the direction of the later Sismondi, as when he exclaims that 'no man of sensibility can without grief see the most interesting class in the nation, that which supports the whole by the fruit of its labours, deprived of its enjoyments in order to share it with people who are a charge upon it.'[46]

When Sismondi, after an interval of sixteen years spent in historical research, returned to economics in his *Nouveaux Principes d'Économie Politique*[47] (1819) he may be a respectful admirer of Adam Smith, but he is certainly no longer a meek disciple. In the interval he had seen the

---

[42] *De la Richesse Commerciale*, Vol. I, p.267.
[43] *Ibid.*, Vol. I, p.329.
[44] *Ibid.*, Vol. II, p.152.
[45] *Ibid.*, Vol. II, p.143.
[46] *Ibid.*, Vol. I, p.109.
[47] The full title is again of interest: *Nouveaux Principes d'Économie Politique, ou de la Richesse dans ses Rapports avec la Population.*

world in a period of rapid transition and industrialization, a world urged from every quarter to produce more, and to produce more cheaply. He had looked upon it, and had found little to admire. Behind all this feverish accumulation there lurked the teaching of orthodox political economy; but for the maturing Sismondi, political economy ought to be something else. It was 'la théorie de la bienfaisance';[48] its object was to increase the physical well-being of man. But in the Europe of 1819, above all in the England of that day, what had happened to the enjoyment of life? In sombre phraseology, in contrast to which Malthus appears a radiant optimist, Sismondi describes a world, hungry, suffering, degraded, and he is tempted to curse division of labour and the invention of manufactures as the rock on which the human race has made shipwreck.[49] To Sismondi, it appears appropriate to ask the disturbing question: 'Where are we going?' Where are the happy people in this world in which everywhere one observes the progress of things, everywhere the suffering of men?[50]

Sismondi's central theme is simple, and it is so omnipresent that he tends to be a man of one idea. That idea is to be found in his emphasis on the evils which flow from unrestrained competition, above all as evidenced in the excessive production of goods for which there is not, and cannot be, any demand. This over-production which so haunts Sismondi is, it will be observed, a general over-production of all commodities, and not merely over-production of certain commodities relative to others. It is, in his view, a direct result of division of labour and large-scale production. In isolation, a man produces for himself and knows when to stop and 'repose'; in society he is producing

[48] *Nouveaux Principes*, Vol. ii, p.248; Vol. i, pp.8-9.
[49] *Ibid.*, Vol. ii, p.313.
[50] *Ibid.*, Vol. ii, p.329.

for others, and cannot know when enough has been produced.[51] To the man in isolation there is therefore a clear
limit to the extent to which he should amass. The purpose
of accumulation is subsequent enjoyment and rest, and it
would be folly to accumulate in excess of the power to
consume. With a complex society, the efforts of men are
separated from their natural rewards, so that one man
labours and another man rests. Yet, though thus obscured,
it is as true of society as it is of the individual that there is
a limit to the power of consumption. But as this limit is no
longer obvious, men are urged on by the 'zeal to produce
which every writer stimulates and which every Government
encourages.'[52] Demand should precede production; but
what, in fact, the producer considers is whether he is capable
of producing more, not whether there will be a demand for
the commodity when it is produced.[53] Production, that is to
say, is based on the extent of capital at the disposal of the
producer. These evil consequences are accentuated by the
fact (which has much later been no immaterial factor in the
tendency to industrial combination) that it is always easier
to expand than to contract, that it is indeed almost
impossible, for a variety of reasons, to restrict the size of an
undertaking or to close down.[54] To Sismondi, looking
around, the world everywhere presented the spectacle of
overstocked markets, of production for which there were no
consumers – the consequence of apportioning production
not to demand but to available capital.[55]

Sismondi's theory of distribution, on which the doctrine of

[51] *Ibid.*, Vol. I, p.68.
[52] *Ibid.*, Vol. I, pp.77-80.
[53] *Ibid.*, Vol. I, p.317.
[54] 'Les producteurs ne se retireront point du travail, et leur nombre
ne diminuera que lorsqu'une partie des chefs d'atelier aura fait
faillite, et qu'une partie des ouvriers sera morte de misère' (*ibid.*, Vol.
I, p.310).
[55] *Ibid.*, Vol. I, p. 338.

over-production rests, is one of those things which are better left in their natural obscurity. His distinction between the annual production and the annual revenue, and his view that the annual production of any year is bought by the revenue of the preceding year, reveal a mind which was a stranger to strict reasoning. On this side Sismondi's doctrines merely possess the value of antiquarian curiosities, and as such should not be withdrawn from the museum, even for purposes of examination.[56] His strength lay in the force of his general contentions, not in the abstract reasoning on which these were based. Out of incomprehensible reasoning there emerges for Sismondi a sure conviction which is at least comprehensible, that there ought to be an equilibrium between production and consumption, and that nations may be ruined either by spending too much or too little.[57] His is, in fact, a doctrine of under-consumption.

Probably the economic foundation is so tangled and uncertain because the main inspiration may have come from elsewhere. His view of man is that of the moralist; there is indeed an almost religious fervour in his denunciations. For Sismondi, man is a creature with whom rest, *le repos*, is a natural taste, and in the scheme of things this natural taste should also find its gratification.[58] 'L'homme travaille pour que l'homme se repose,' as he says with an air of benediction; but in the urge to produce, we forget the end of all labour and the purpose of life.

Inasmuch, then, as it is not merely accumulation of wealth that matters, but control of wealth and the direction of wealth to secure the increase of happiness, the blessedness

[56] The reader who desires fully to understand Sismondi may be referred to Book II, chapters 5 and 6 of the *Nouveaux Principes*, on 'The division of the national revenue between the various classes of citizens,' and on 'The reciprocal determination of production by consumption and of expenditure by revenue.'

[57] *Ibid.*, Vol. I, pp.120, 122.

[58] *Ibid.*, Vol. I, p. 78.

of unlimited competition vanishes. *Laissez-faire* tends to incredible suffering, and it is therefore essential that there be a large measure of Government intervention.[59] For the function of the State is to be the protector of the weak against the strong, the defender of the defenceless, the representative of the permanent interest of all against the temporary interest of each. And in the light of experience (since the days of Adam Smith, as he hints) it had become abundantly evident that there was need of such an authority ' to prevent men being sacrificed to the progress of a wealth from which they will derive no profit.'[60]

The doctrine of the harmony of interests and of the potency of the invisible hand accordingly receives short shrift from the later Sismondi, and though he does not use the phrase, he realizes how *laissez-faire* may break down on inequality of bargaining power. There may be self-interest displayed in highway robbery, and self-interest may likewise dictate to the victim the expediency of offering no resistance, if acquiescence is calculated to increase his prospects of escaping unmurdered.[61] The institutions of society have, argues Sismondi, given rise to a similar kind of restraint, though it may not be accompanied by such obvious violence. 'It has as often as not placed the poor man under the necessity of submitting to increasingly onerous conditions, under the penalty of dying of hunger; in placing him in this perilous condition, it falls to society to undertake his defence.'[62] Left to its natural course, the conflict of interests, since it may be to the interest of the weak not to resist, may lead to the triumph of injustice.[63]

Thus we arrive in the most general terms at the functions

[59] ' Nous invoquons presque constamment, pour surveiller le progres de la richesse, cette intervention qu' Adam Smith repoussait ' (*ibid.*, Vol. I, p. 54).
[60] *Ibid.*, Vol. I, p.55.
[61] *Ibid.*, Vol. I, p.197.
[62] *Ibid.*, Vol. I, p.197.
[63] *Ibid.*, Vol. I, p.379.

of government. Each individual, pursuing his interests, tends to increase the speed of the machine; the task of the Government should be to slow down and regularize its movement; to exercise, in the pursuit of wealth, 'une action régulatrice et modératrice.'[64] The difference between other economists and Sismondi, as he himself expressed it, was that while they had applauded the new industrial ardour, and had urged to greater rivalry and speed, he had felt merely alarm, and had summoned the friends of humanity to assist 'in retarding the social chariot which, in its accelerated course, seems to be on the point of plunging us in the abyss.'[65]

Easy enough to speak of slowing down; but how? Take, for instance, the vexed question of inventions and machinery on which Sismondi has unusual views. In the main he detests inventions; they usually, though not necessarily, lead to evil consequences. Man loses in intelligence, in bodily vigour, in health and gaiety, all that he gains in increased power to produce wealth.[66] Even children, it is true, may make stockings from their most tender years, before they have tasted any of the enjoyments of life. But at what an odious price are these things bought! The normal effect of inventions is to diminish the labour demanded, and thereby make the country poorer, even though this broad effect may be concealed by the operation of foreign trade which, while creating prosperity in the producing country, may concentrate elsewhere the real ruin created. Thus in the case of English manufacturers, 'all the suffering has fallen on continental producers, all the enjoyment has remained with the English.'[67] It is not, however, all inventions that are to be condemned; the criterion which Sismondi applies is to be found in the pre-existence of an unsatisfied demand. 'When-

[64] Ibid., Vol. I, pp.381-385.
[65] See Études sur l'Économie Politique, Vol. II, p.211.
[66] Nouveaux Principes, Vol. I, p.366.
[67] Ibid., Vol. I, p. 322.

ever demand for consumption surpasses the means of production, any new discovery is a benefit for society, because
it provides the means of satisfying existing needs. On the
contrary, wherever production is fully sufficient for consumption, any similar discovery is a calamity because it does
not add to the enjoyment of the consumers anything else
than that of satisfying their needs at a lower price, while it
suppresses the very life of the producers.'[68] The market
must first be extended; if this is done, there is room for
invention. Modifying the argument, Sismondi contends that
when an invention extends the market by putting the commodity at the disposal of a poorer class, it is beneficial. But
if the market cannot be extended, either because all needs
are already supplied or because, no matter what reduction
in price is made, the poor will never be consumers, then the
discovery is a calamity for the human race, for in this case
it will only advantage certain manufacturers at the cost of
others – or, it may be, certain nations at the cost of others.[69]
So also, when Sismondi assumes the part of a *laudator
temporis acti*, it is one of the marks of happier times that
then men only thought of inventions when a new need had
made itself felt.[70]

It remains to be considered what can be done to protect
society and the worker against the rage of inventors. Here
Sismondi does not get beyond a very tentative and curious
suggestion. He realizes that it would be idle to forbid the
use of a pernicious invention, if other countries were still
free to make use of it. The sole measure of protection which
he suggests is the suppression of the privileges accorded to
the inventor; if all inventions are at once made known and
available to all, then, as he says, revealing the individualist

[68] *Ibid.*, Vol. II, p.317.
[69] *Ibid.*, Vol. II, p.321.
[70] *Études*, I, p.34.

at his heart, 'the zeal for such discoveries will grow cold.'[71]

With regard to population, that apple of discord which Malthus had lightly tossed to the economists, Sismondi's views are likewise peculiarly his own. Population, he holds, is limited by revenue. In contradistinction to what Malthus had said, population never reaches and probably never will reach the limit of possible subsistence. It is checked because it becomes impossible to buy the means of subsistence, or because people are not allowed to work in order to produce it. The check thus comes, not from the means of subsistence, but from the 'will' of man, above all of the landowner who will not allow others to work unless he receives a revenue for his assent.[72] This, of course, is scarcely in opposition to Malthus; but in his further elaboration of the element of human *volonté*, his views as to the natural action of man differ profoundly from those of Malthus. The vital thing on which population depends is the demand for labour.[73] Given employment and an assured revenue, people will marry and have children; the vice of the new society is that there is no security as to the worker's revenue, and the worker being deceived as to his position, children are born for whom there is no provision. It is a firm article of faith with Sismondi that the worker will not marry until he can afford to marry, and that he will proportion his family to his revenue – that is, assuming there is stability and a fixed revenue. But if there is no stability, if the workers are displaced by machinery, how grave is their situation! The workers' revenue is no longer within their calculation; it may be altered by others without their knowledge; the

[71] *Nouveaux Principes*, Vol. II, pp.331-333.

[72] *Ibid.*, Vol. II, pp.267-270.

[73] The similarity to Malthus and the different emphasis are alike interesting: 'La population se mesure toujours, en dernière analyse, sur la demande du travail. Toutes les fois que le travail sera demandé et qu'un salaire suffisant lui sera offert, l'ouvrier naîtra pour le gagner' (*ibid.*, Vol. II, p.284).

entrepreneur himself may miscalculate.[74] So living from day to day, the 'proletarians become content that their children should do the same'; moreover, do not the children become a title to charity, and may they not spasmodically earn wages from the age of seven? Thus the restraint on marriage disappears and children are born for whom society has made no provision.[75] It is not then so much demand for work that is important, as regular and perpetual demand; for if the demand is intermittent, it merely creates workers in order to condemn them to death.[76]

We are back, it will be observed, at the old point. Excessive population is the offspring of instability, which itself is the offspring of over-production and of all the devilish inventions of the era of the Industrial Revolution. His views, by way of suggested remedy, even if impracticable are of interest. He accepts as almost obvious the view that the obligations of celibacy rest on the married as soon as they have the family to which they are entitled – which would appear to be one boy and one girl. To have more would be unjust and cruel, since such a course is tantamount to depriving others, either of the joys of marriage in youth or of the comforts of children in old age.[77] Beyond this, the remedies which Sismondi hints at, rather than suggests, are drastic[78]; he would be prepared to prohibit the marriage of the poor, or at least to require certain guarantees. The aim of the Government, so far as the agricultural population is concerned, should be to unite labour and property, and Sismondi's suggestions would ultimately rest marriage on a property qualification. In the towns, though the task is not so easy, the end should be the same, namely, to abolish the

[74] *Ibid.*, Vol. II, p.259.
[75] *Ibid.*, Vol. II, p.263.
[76] *Ibid.*, Vol. II, p.285.
[77] *Ibid.*, Vol. II, p.295.
[78] He was more definite in earlier editions.

precarious position in which the workers live, to make it possible for them to attain to a certain status, and to forbid marriage until that has been reached. This means among other things a guarantee from the employer; it means vesting in the employer the right to veto the marriage of his employees; it means, on the other side, that the worker is to be a permanent charge on his industry.[79]

In summary, Sismondi is a protesting voice, and it is from this point alone that he is significant. In so far as he presented a body of 'doctrine' to the world, he is negligible. His chief obsession, that of a general overproduction of goods as an explanation of glutted markets and commercial crises, is obviously untenable, and the orthodox spokesmen have never had any difficulty in showing that while there may be over-production in respect of particular commodities, a uniform over-production of all commodities simultaneously is unimaginable.[80] Over-production, indeed, means disproportionate production; it means, within limits, that too much is produced, having regard to the volume of other products; that is to say, it involves under-production elsewhere. So also, in his doctrines with regard to machinery and improvements, and in his insistence on the existence of a previous demand before expansion is justified, Sismondi turns a blind eye to half the facts of economic life, and neglects the possible reactions which variations in the conditions of supply may exercise on demand. It is scarcely too much to say that none of the peculiar tenets of Sismondi has stood the test of time. Yet he is not thereby negligible. In an age when the protest was necessary, he affirmed that wealth was made for man and not man for wealth, as the 'chrematistic' doctrine seemed to imply;[81] in the darkest

[79] *Ibid.*, Vol. ii, pp.339, 363, etc.
[80] See Mill, *Principles of Political Economy*, Book iii, chap. 14.
[81] See *Études*, Vol. i, p.62.

days of the Industrial Revolution he asked, very pertinently, where the world was going, and insisted on the importance for the worker of stability and status. But in truth he gets nowhere in particular. He never reached Socialism, though it would be easy to collect a nosegay of Socialist sentiments from his works, and it would be folly to ignore his influence on later Socialist writers. But his final attitude is rather one of helplessness and bewilderment before a problem of which he cannot find the solution.[82] He is perhaps a moralist rather than an economist, reminding us, as certain of our own poets have done in these latter days, of the folly of those whose vision is machines for making more machines, of the poverty of a life which leaves no time to stand and stare. Righteous indignation, such as inspired Sismondi, is a noble passion, and the indignant prophet fulfils a useful purpose, even if indignation not infrequently leads to bad logic.

[82] The pathetic words with which (in some editions) the *Nouveaux Principes* closes have often been quoted: ' Je l'avoue, après avoir indiqué où est à nos yeux le principe, où est la justice, je ne me sens pas la force de tracer les moyens d'exécution; la distribution des profits du travail entre ceux qui concourent à les produire me paraît vicieuse; mais il me semble presque au-dessus des forces humaines de concevoir un état de propriété absolument différent de celui que nous fait connaître l'expérience.'

CHAPTER VIII

Müller, List and von Thünen

Müller

OF the group of three German writers discussed in this chapter, Adam Müller[1] (1779-1829) is the least known in this country. His has been a curious fate. If not entirely forgotten, he at least suffered a considerable measure of neglect until, quite recently, the neo-romantic school in Germany, elaborating a point of view similar to his, have recalled him from his oblivion and have engineered for him a reasonably successful revival. Dr. Spann would persuade us (according to the edition consulted) that Müller was the greatest economist of all, or of his own, times. As his contemporaries included a Ricardo and a Malthus, even the more cautious eulogy savours of extravagance. To others, again, it may appear that Müller was not an economist at all, but rather that he was merely one who wallowed in windy words. Yet even if doubts be entertained on this point, he is rightly admitted here as representing a distinct line of criticism and because of his spiritual kinship with List.

Müller would probably have regarded himself as primarily a political writer, and only secondarily as an exponent of economic doctrine. His views on politics, it is true, are such that in his presentation politics and economics become inextricably intertwined; yet at the same time it is abundantly

[1] Born in Berlin, 1779; studied in Berlin and Göttingen; received into the Roman Catholic Church in 1805; ultimately entered the Austrian State Service, and finally became Councillor in the State Chancellory in Vienna. His chief works were the *Elemente der Staatskunst* (1809) and the *Versuche einer neuen Theorie des Geldes* (1816), but there is in addition a good deal of miscellaneous writing.

clear that his mind is preoccupied with considerations usually regarded as non-economic. To him more than to anyone else is due the reaction against certain aspects of Adam Smith's teaching. Smith, without doubt, had raised his theory on the instincts and actions of the individual, though he had been by no means so one-sided as later criticism suggested. Without violent injustice, Adam Smith's state could therefore be represented as being a conglomeration of individuals, the national wealth as the summation of individual substances; and for him the economic impulse was to be sought in the individual heart, moved by highly enlightened self-interest. In the phrase which later became so much beloved, Adam Smith was 'atomistic'; the public interest, so far as it was considered, was a by-product, due to the silent functioning of an unseen hand. With Adam Müller, on the other hand, the State comes first, and the individual has only significance in relation to the State. It is therefore necessary to approach Müller's contribution to economics by way of his more general political doctrine.

Two dominant influences are obvious in the writings of Müller. In the first place, he was part and parcel of the so-called Romantic movement, and the leading representative of that movement on the political and economic side. As to the precise significance of the Romantic movement, as it existed in Germany, the phrase is one of those which are better left vaguely sensed than precisely defined. As a school the Romantics strove for the unseen and the eternal, for the intangible and the infinite; they concerned themselves with the ultimate riddles of life, and so tended to a mysticism incomprehensible to those entangled in the seen and the temporal. The other primary influence is that of Burke, to whom Müller consistently refers in words of the highest eulogy.

The central point in Müller's theory is the Aristotelian

doctrine that man is inconceivable outside the State. Every individual is in the centre of civil life, interwoven with the State on all sides, just as every individual is at the central point in the life-period of the State, with a past lying behind, which must be respected, and a future which must be cared for. The State, then, is not an artificial creation, begotten for the attainment of particular ends and objects in civil life; it is the sum-total of civil life itself. In a phrase to which Müller constantly recurs, it is not merely a fundamental human need; it is the supreme human need.[2]

Moreover – a point in which the influence of Burke becomes apparent – the State represents a continuity through time. In the great warfare which man wages with the earth, he has need of allies, and the alliance extends not merely to all those who are contemporaries in the struggle, but it also embraces all past generations, since no generation can successfully conduct this warfare, relying on its own strength alone. The State, then, is this double alliance, not merely of all who are at any time living together, but also of all those who follow each other in time.[3] It is thus immortal and to be viewed not as something static, but as in continual motion. The mutual interdependence of all, in the stream of time, is thus made fundamental. The analogy of the household continually recurs in Müller; each individual can produce and possess only in so far as he is a member of a group which together makes up a household,[4] and it is because Müller believed that in the Middle Ages society was in fact constituted on such a family basis that his writings are so full of eulogies of the feudal system and of the place and function of a nobility in the

[2] *Elemente der Staatskunst*, Vol. I, pp.29-31. The State is 'das Bedürfniss aller Bedürfnisse des Herzens, des Geistes und des Leibes.' References are to the recent editions in the Herdflamme Series.
[3] *Ibid.*, I, pp.59-60.
[4] *Theorie des Geldes*, p.10.

State. That the State should be a leviathan, consuming the individual, is of the essence of Müller's political doctrine, and it is a not uncommon point of view in German speculation; what is more peculiar to him is that he somehow persuaded himself that his ideal was embodied in the feudal system.

With such a hasty sketch of the political background, it is possible to approach the more specifically economic doctrines of Müller. And first of all, his antagonism to individualism leads him to reiterated condemnation of absolute private property, that evil legacy of the Roman law, so gloriously absent under the feudal system. The result of cutting the individual off from the whole is that each and all will live in poverty, possessed by a lust for exclusive possession which no wealth, however great, may satisfy.[5] As the members of a family, on an equal share-out, are all poorer than they were before, although arithmetically there has been no change in the sum-total of wealth, so in society there is a force present which heightens all values.[6] Müller, indeed, finds that there are three kinds of property: (a) pure private property; (b) corporative property; and (c) State property. Moreover, all these elements are, or should be, present in all property, and the individual only possesses in so far as he is at all times prepared to share with others what is peculiarly his, and, should occasion arise, to surrender it to the State. Real property exists only in common possession, and all private property is but a right of usufruct.[7] Müller's devotion to the feudal system is due to the fact that in his view it embodied this principle; and indeed in one place he oddly defines feudalism as embracing all the legal hindrances in the way of private property.[8]

[5] *Ibid.*, p.7.　　　　[7] *Ibid.*, pp.19-20.
[6] *Ibid.*, p.11.　　　　[8] *Staatskunst*, I, pp.268-269.

Turning more to the nature of wealth and the meaning of production, Müller repeatedly emphasizes his divergences from Adam Smith. In opposition to the doctrine of *laissez-faire*, what should be the task of the statesman? It should be to consider the totality of the needs of his State, viewed in the light of eternity. Non-intervention is but the consecration of the right of absolute property, the renunciation of the claims of the State to all property.[9] The doctrine which appeals to a law of Nature is 'revolutionary' in so far as it implies that human institutions and laws are bankrupt.[10] For Müller, the State is always in the centre of all things, and consequently all wealth, all production, all consumption must alike be viewed in the light of their reaction on this eternal thing which we call the State. Value itself, as distinguished from price (which relates to the moment), is indeed but the significance which a thing has in the State, and for the perpetual rejuvenation of the State,[11] and it is Müller's central criticism of orthodox Political Economy that it is a theory of wealth which takes no account of the value of things in this high sense.[12] It concerns itself with things, never with persons. Adam Smith, in Müller's indictment, is concerned only with tangible things that can be bought and sold; and admittedly, Smith's discussion of productive and unproductive labour, if viewed apart from the development of that rather foolish controversy, does seem rather harsh on the philosopher whose philosophizings are not embodied in a vendible book. But the question 'What is wealth?' cannot, according to Müller, be considered apart from the other question: 'How does wealth come about?'[13] A system of Political Economy which aims at the multiplication of 'products,' and which removes all hindrances to the further increase of products, may result in a wealth which

---

[9] *Theorie des Geldes*, pp.102-103.   [10] *Ibid.*, p.132.
[11] *Ibid.*, pp.58-59.   [12] *Ibid.*, pp.96-97.   [13] *Staatskunst*, i, pp.35-36.

has no guarantee of its continued existence.[14] Adam Smith, in limiting wealth to products which possess exchangeable value, had, like his predecessors, neglected other equally important questions. Amongst other things, for instance, he had forgotten to consider what is the force or activity in the State which maintains wealth.[15]

Thus we arrive at a view of Political Economy which is largely emancipated from external things which, if important, are important only because they increase the productive powers of the persons concerned.[16] We have to discard the habit of counting wealth by sums and by figures. As Müller, with characteristic Romantic affectation, observes: 'Nothing is worthy of admiration that can be expressed in numbers.'[17] He is indeed at one with Lauderdale, to whom he refers with approval, in rejecting current views on production and parsimony. The economic activity of society is at once an unending consumption and an unending production, and an excess of production over consumption is only apparent. National wealth is not to be arrived at by subtracting the nation's needs from the nation's products; that merely leaves a 'dead deposit of possessions'; on the contrary, true consumption is itself a source of national wealth, which exists in use as well as in possession.[18] Out of the everlasting conflict between production and consumption there arises a higher product, which may be called the national credit, the national power, faith in the State, the State itself.[19] The State is thus not merely the cradle in

---

[14] *Ibid.*, I, pp.356-357.
[15] 'Welche Kraft oder Thàtigkeit im Staate ist erhaltend?' (I, p.375).
[16] *Theorie des Geldes*, p.14.
[17] *Ibid.*, p.46.
[18] See *Theorie des Geldes*, p.66; Staatskunst, I, pp.348, 474.
[19] *Theorie des Geldes*, pp.70-72. It is characteristic of the rather meaningless jargon which Müller loves that credit should be called 'dieses Produkt aller Produkte.'

which all wealth is produced and the guarantor of all wealth; it is at the same time the end of all production and consumption.

Akin to this is Müller's position with regard to what he termed spiritual capital. It is in keeping with his reverence for tradition and continuity that he should replace the familiar trinity of 'land, labour and capital' by 'Nature, man and the past.'[20] Capital is the contribution made by past generations to the present race of men for use in their struggle with Nature, and as such it belongs to the whole race of men and to all generations of men, subject to a right of usufruct.[21] But so viewed, the legacy of the past is not merely material; it is also spiritual in character; hence alongside capital, as interpreted by Smith, it is necessary to find a place for spiritual capital. To this idea Müller constantly recurs in one form or another. In this sense the wealth of the State comprises, among other more obvious things, the arts of administration, the constitution, the laws, and all great national memories.[22] At times particular emphasis is laid on the element of legislation, as when he declares that the legislation of a Christian state is the only real wealth of that state, a proposition in an especial degree true of England, for England's power rests not on the soil or on labour, but on capital – the divine capital of laws, customs, national reputation and credit.[23]

[20] *Staatskunst*, II, p.6.
[21] *Ibid.*, I, p.161.
[22] *Theorie des Geldes*, p.12.
[23] *Theorie des Geldes*, pp.107-108; *Staatskunst*, II, p.16. In a curious elaboration of the distinction between 'physisches' and 'geistiges' capital, Müller typifies them by the two great common possessions, money and language, thus giving four elements in national wealth: land, labour, physical capital (money) and spiritual capital (speech, learning and writing). Corresponding to these, since even a philosopher cannot resist the allurement of jingle, are the four classes of society: Lehrstand, Wehrstand, Nährstand, and Verkehrstand. (*Staatskunst*, II, pp.29-33.)

Another point on which the polemic of Müller is directed against Adam Smith relates to division of labour. The citizen, he says truly, must not cease to be a complete man merely because he looks after his own business; and in an imaginative passage he pictures man in the beginning of society revealed in the comprehensive fullness of his capacities. The whole State is then but a single man; but likewise the individual man is no less than the State. All those who come after this original man together make up the complete man in whom the various occupations of life are in as natural equilibrium as they were in him. Thus division of labour (or of the various functions of society) is only possible by a personal relationship among those concerned, so that together, by their union, they shall represent a great and complete person.[24] But while by progressive division of labour there is on this side an ever greater departure from the original man, in whom all activities were combined, the needs of each individual remain the same. Each one can therefore labour only on condition that all others labour for him. He needs the totality of all others; in short, society, the union of all economic functions, the State, remains the 'need of all needs,' and this uniting force must become stronger as division of labour is carried further.[25]

Adam Smith's curious explanation of division of labour, as due to a 'propensity to truck,' is mildly described by Müller as incomplete. Division of labour springs from, and is dependent on, capital, or in Müller's use of the word, 'the past,' which furnishes a guarantee to the worker while he is devoting himself to his particular task. Yet division of labour (and it is to Müller's credit that he realized it) may in itself reduce men to the level of slaves and machines,

[24] *Theorie des Geldes*, pp.123-124.
[25] *Ibid.*, p.138.

unless there is a true national capital, the inheritance of the past, active in the minds of the workers to counteract these dangers.[26]

In the course of his criticisms of Adam Smith, Müller constantly recurs to one point in partial extenuation of Smith's one-sidedness. It is that Smith's doctrines are the peculiar product of Great Britain, and comprehensible when one has regard to the conditions prevailing in this country; and further, that the elements which Smith's doctrine neglected were those of most importance to continental nations where the conditions were different. Müller constantly speaks with an embarrassing appreciation of England. Smith, he says, could afford to neglect the element of spiritual capital, because everyone in England took that side for granted. Production might there be emphasized to the apparent exclusion of the conservation or maintenance of wealth, because the principle of maintenance (*Erhaltung*) and of national unity had for centuries been instinctively implanted by the constitution and by the customs of the country. So also in Great Britain the application of the principle of division of labour would not have the evil effects it might have elsewhere, because of the existence there of a reintegrating national spiritual capital, whereby every citizen in this blessed island is again inspired and ennobled by the all-pervading spirit of former times and of common achievements in the past. It almost reads like a far-off echo of a verse in 'Rule, Britannia.' Whether or not Müller's doctrine be accepted, it is at least illuminating.

As one of Müller's chief works is ostensibly devoted to a theory of money, a slight reference to his views on this aspect of economic doctrine may be expedient. Yet here, even more than elsewhere, Müller trails off into the mystical, the nebulous, the symbolic and, indeed, it is to be

[26] *Staatskunst*, ii, pp.17-23.

feared for most, the entirely incomprehensible. It has been shown that the fundamental need of man is for reunion with his fellows; the desire for money is a reflexion of this desire for union or, otherwise expressed, for the State. Men and things require to be linked together, and the great uniting force is the State. Money is the economic expression of this need for union, just as the law is its juridical expression. It is in fact a substitute for the State, and like the State, and, indeed, all property, it should be a common possession. Only in the moment of circulation, in passing from hand to hand, is money money; if it becomes an object of private possession and 'rests,' it ceases to be money. In so far, then, as the essence of money is that it is the mortar that links society together, money for Müller is something that goes beyond the ordinary conception of the market-place. In so far as any object is desired by two persons, it becomes money. Money is thus a property inherent in all individuals (and things) in civil society by virtue of which they enter into relationship with other individuals. The citizen himself, in so far as he becomes more necessary to others, becomes money; the more excellent he is, the more he is money. So, elsewhere, the State is money; the law, likewise, is the purest form of money. Money, thus representing the need of society, is something eternal, a primitive need, existing at all times in its two forms, later represented by metallic money and the ' Word.'[27] It is, of course, open to anyone to define money (or anything else) as he or she chooses; but a theory of money as so defined is scarcely calculated to furnish much illumination, either at the Treasury or the Bank of England. Into the abstruseness and the curious symbolisms with which Müller's theory of money

[27] For examples of the peculiar interpretation of money see *Staat-skunst,* I, pp.351-354; II, pp.78, 97-101; *Theorie des Geldes,* pp.180, 212.

is adorned and obscured, it is, happily, unnecessary to enter here, but it is interesting to observe that Müller notes as one of the fortunate consequences of a paper circulation the fact that it links those who hold it more closely to their particular state. World-money or metallic money, on the contrary, fosters the illusion that the holder's interests are dependent on the stream of world trade, and thus conceals the fact that he is much more directly dependent on the internal trade of his own country and on his own sovereign. Gold and silver encourage the belief that wherever the language of metallic gold is heard, there is a man's father-land; paper money attaches him to his own soil.[28]

List

Apart from the recent revival of interest in the origins of Romanticism, Müller's claim to consideration rests on the fact that his point of view is so largely reflected in Fried-rich List[29] (1789-1846). List was no visionary dreamer. He played a very practical part in the affairs of his day; and though the world broke him, he was yet a man of the world. But, to a large extent, the substance of his views is in line with Müller's thought. What Müller saw darkly through a haze of mysticism and symbolism, and expressed in a cloud of words, List wrote and expounded in the spirit of a political pamphleteer.

For all practical purposes, List's contribution to economic doctrine is to be found in *The National System of Political*

---

[28] *Staatskunst*, I, p.453.
[29] Born at Reutlingen in 1789; became Professor of Economics at Tübingen in 1817. Obliged to resign in 1819, he entered the Würtenberg Chamber. His agitation for reform led to his expulsion. Being released he emigrated to America, where he remained for seven years as journalist, etc. Returning to Germany, he took up the causes of railway development, and of the Zollverein. Suffering ill-health and financial embarrassment, he died tragically in 1846.

Economy.[30] It suffers to a considerable extent from being very largely a tract for the times, issued for the encouragement of the Germany of List's day; and as such it is highly polemical in tone, the opponent to be disembowelled being a somewhat distorted Adam Smith, or an amalgam of Adam Smith and his less careful followers, known throughout List's volume as 'the school.' The attack on Adam Smith is lively and spirited, even if the book suffers from frequent and indeed intolerable repetition. Without aiming at a comprehensive review, certain ideas may be selected as representing the essential core of List's criticism of 'the school.'

Fundamental in his criticism is his contention that Adam Smith gives merely a theory of value, that his doctrine is nothing more than a shopkeeper's theory built up on the conception of 'value in exchange.'[31] Wealth and the causes of wealth represent two entirely different ideas, and it is more important to consider the latter than the former.[32] A person may possess wealth, but if he does not possess the power of producing objects of more value than he consumes, he will become poorer. 'The power of producing wealth is therefore infinitely more important than wealth itself; it insures not only the possession and the increase of what has been gained, but also the replacement of what has been lost.'[33] On these lines List stresses throughout the contrast between what he calls the theory of values and the theory of productive powers, and illustrates the distinction by the example of two fathers, each with five sons and a surplus of one thousand thalers a year. The one invests his savings at interest, and keeps his sons at common hard work;

[30] References to English translation by S. S. Lloyd.
[31] *National System of Political Economy*, p.279.
[32] Müller's phraseology in making the same point is interesting; he contrasts 'Nationalreichthum' and 'Nationalbereicherung' (*Theorie des Geldes*, p.44).
[33] *National System of Political Economy*, p.108, and indeed all chap. 12.

the other uses his savings to educate two of his sons as 'skilful and intelligent landowners,' and in enabling the other three to learn a useful trade. The former, acting on the theory of values, is the richer at his death; on the theory of productive powers, it is the latter who is to be commended.[34]

Throughout, therefore, it is the 'development of productive powers' that has to be kept in view, and the causes that may influence this are infinite:

'The Christian religion, monogamy, abolition of slavery and of vassalage, hereditability of the throne, invention of printing, of the press, of the postal system, of money, weights and measures, of the calendar, of watches, of police, the introduction of the principle of freehold property, of means of transport, are rich sources of productive power. . . . We can scarcely conceive of any law or any legal decision which would not exercise a greater or smaller influence on the increase or decrease of the productive power of the nation.'[35]

This, it will be observed, is nothing less than the sum total of the human legacy as incorporated in our national life, and indeed List so expresses it:

'The present state of the nations is the result of the accumulation of all discoveries, inventions, improvements, perfections, and exertions of all the generations which have lived before us; they form the *mental capital of the present human race,* and every separate nation is productive only in the proportion in which it has known how to appropriate these attainments of former generations and to increase them by its own acquirements. . . .'[36]

This leads to the second and even more deliberate line of attack made by List on 'the school,' viz., their neglect of the national element. Quesnay had extended his investigations to the whole human race, and Adam Smith, following him, had likewise neglected true Political Economy. Taking

[34] *Ibid.,* p.112.   [35] *Ibid.,* p.113.   [36] *Ibid.,* p.113.

the literal meaning of the words, Political Economy ought to have reference to the life of a nation; the school had substituted for it 'cosmopolitical or world-wide economy.'[37] Assuming a universal union or confederation of all nations, the Free Trade position is justified, but 'the popular school has assumed as being actually in existence a state of things which has yet to come into existence.'[38] The position, however, as we know it, is that between each individual and the whole of humanity stands the nation, the embodiment of a tradition which List praises in words reminiscent of Burke and Müller.[39] Individuals are not merely producers and consumers, they are also citizens of states and members of nations,[40] and moreover, the producing power of all individuals is to a great extent determined by the social and political circumstances of the nation.[41] The function of political economy, then, is to accomplish the economic development of the nation.

It follows, therefore, that any attempt to keep economics free from politics is mistaken, and that the doctrine of *laissez-faire* is a delusion. As List says in one place – and he has been justified by the event – 'the necessity for the intervention of legislative power and administration is everywhere more apparent the further the economy of the nation is developed.[42] *Laissez-faire* is a maxim which sounds no less agreeable to robbers, cheats and thieves than to the merchant.[43] It is not the function of the statesman to do nothing: 'A statesman will know, and must know . . . how the productive powers of a whole *nation* can be awakened, increased, and protected, and how, on the other hand, they are weakened, laid to sleep, or utterly destroyed.'[44]

[37] *Ibid.*, p.98.   [38] *Ibid.*, p.102.   [39] *Ibid.*, p.141.
[40] *Ibid.*, p.140.   [41] *Ibid.*, p.65.   [42] *Ibid.*, p.139.
[43] *Ibid.*, p.208.   [44] *Ibid.*, p.284.

How, then, is this task of the statesman to be accomplished? The answer brings us to what is perhaps the central point in List's doctrine. Adam Smith had emphasized the advantages of division of labour as applied to any individual trade, as, for example, pin-making; he had 'no perception of the division of labour as affecting a whole nation,'[45] and as applied to a whole nation the principle of division of labour means the symmetrical development of all the powers of which the nation is capable:

'The popular school, inasmuch as it does not duly consider the nature of the powers of production, and does not take into account the conditions of nations in their aggregate, disregards especially the importance of developing in an equal ratio agriculture, manufactures and commerce, political power and internal wealth, and disregards especially the value of a manufacturing power belonging especially to the nation and fully developed in all its branches.'[46]

This is the text on which List preached to the Germany of his times the imperative need for the encouragement of manufactures. His doctrine has obvious reference to the circumstances of his age as List saw them. England was the workshop of the world, intent on nipping continental manufactures in the bud; was it safe for other countries to be content with a position of subordination, accepting this 'insular supremacy'? List's argument is that the agricultural state is definitely inferior to the state which combines both agriculture and manufactures, and he is led, in emphasizing this point, to not a little disparagement of agriculture and to enthusiastic praise of the effects of manufactures in a community. Thus, while it would hardly be proper to say that he reverts to mercantilist views, it is certainly true that he is led to a position entirely antagonistic to the

[45] *Ibid.*, p.280.   [46] *Ibid.*, p.114.

Physiocrats. He constantly recurs to the argument that navigation, inland and foreign trade, and agriculture itself, flourish only where manufactures have reached a high state of prosperity.[47] A nation which possesses merely agriculture lacks the most essential division of operations among its inhabitants; it will attain not a half, scarcely a tenth, of the material wealth of the perfect nation.[48] As against a 'crippled state of agriculture,' it is urged that in the state which introduces manufactures at the right time, the agricultural and industrial productive powers will react on each other, reciprocally promoting an increase – 'indeed *ad infinitum*' says the optimistic List.[49] A nation which carries on agriculture alone is like an individual who lacks one arm,[50] and how unhappy (with all respect to Varro and the Physiocrats) is the condition of such a country; for there (to quote only one outburst) 'dullness of mind, awkwardness of body, obstinate adherence to old notions, customs, methods and processes, want of culture, of prosperity, and of liberty prevail.'[51] Manufactures, on the other hand, are 'the offspring, and at the same time the supporters and the nurses, of science and the arts.'[52] It is indeed only under the influence of manufactures that agriculture itself is raised to a skilled industry, an art, a science. Into the glories of the manufacturing state, where inventions are encouraged, where genius is valued and rewarded, where the gift of time is appreciated[53] it is unnecessary to enter; it is enough

[47] *Ibid.*, p.89.   [48] *Ibid.*, p.124.   [49] *Ibid.*, p.126.
[50] *Ibid.*, p.130.   [51] *Ibid.*, p.159.   [52] *Ibid.*, p.161.
[53] 'How can the shepherd learn to estimate the value of time, to whom time is simply a burden which his pastoral pipe or sleep alone makes tolerable to him?' (p.163). This beautifully idyllic conception of the shepherd's life still seems to survive from eighteenth-century pastoral poetry. See Mr. Hearnshaw on the labour of the shepherd: 'He sits and contemplates the stars, Nature does the rest, and he is rich' (*Survey of Socialism*, p.351). As Mr. Robert Burns said of something else, supposed to be easy: 'Let them try.'

that 'all the mental powers of a nation, its State revenue, its material and mental means of defence, and its security for national independence, are increased in equal proportion by establishing in it a manufacturing power.'[54] Moreover, as has already been implied, this development of manufactures is required for the full development of agriculture itself. The farmer requires manufactures at his door, not in another country; manufactures increase the value of land tenfold, to the manifest advantage of the agricultural interests, as is evidenced by the fact that in a suitable nation the internal manufacturing production will occasion from ten to twenty times more demand for ordinary agricultural products than the most flourishing exportation of such products could do.[55]

These considerations indicate the functions of the State, for with List economics remains political and national. It is essential, in general terms, to promote the productive powers of the nation; in particular, it is imperative at the right time to secure the development from a lower to a higher stage – in the case which List had particularly in mind, from the purely agricultural state to the state combining agriculture and manufactures. In his complete statement, there are five stages of development through which a nation has to pass, and these he describes under the names of original barbarism, pastoral condition, agricultural condition, agricultural manufacturing condition, and agricultural manufacturing commercial condition. It is in fact, however, only with the latter three that he is concerned.[56] The primary weapon whereby a nation may progress from a lower to a higher stage is Protection in one form or another; but the common view that List is a stout, uncompromising

---

[54] *National System of Political Economy*, p.168.
[55] *Ibid.*, pp.194, 200.
[56] *Ibid.*, p.143.

advocate of Protection is as erroneous as the not uncommon impression that Adam Smith was a free-trader *sans phrase*. It is true that in List the emphasis is all on Protection, because he is primarily concerned with the stage at which, on his view, Protection is appropriate. But in a complete statement of his theoretical position, List is properly to be described as being neither a Protectionist nor a free-trader. Neither policy is for him an end in itself; each is merely a means, and the appropriate policy will depend on the needs of each case. 'History teaches us,' as he says, 'how nations . . . may and must – without on that account forfeiting the end in view – modify their systems according to the measure of their own progress.'[57] In the earlier stages they will adopt Free Trade with more advanced nations as a means of raising themselves from a state of barbarism, and of making advances in agriculture; in the next they will promote the growth of manufactures, fisheries, navigation and foreign trade by means of commercial restrictions; and in the last, when they have reached the highest degree of wealth and power, they will revert to the principle of Free Trade – in order to preserve their agriculturalists, manufacturers and merchants from indolence. He cites Spain, Portugal and Naples as examples of the earliest of these stages where Free Trade is appropriate; Germany and the United States of America as examples of the next where Protection is the expedient policy, with France near the boundary of the highest stage; and Great Britain as the only example where the ultimate adoption of Free Trade is appropriate.

It is desirable to examine more closely the place, the purpose and the extent of Protection in the system of List. The ultimate goal is Free Trade, but there can be Free Trade only among equals; hence 'in order to allow freedom of

[57] *Ibid.*, p.93.

trade to operate naturally, the less advanced nations must first be raised by artificial measures to that stage of cultivation to which the English nation has been artificially elevated.'[58] The artificial measures are, of course, represented by Protection, which is the only means of placing backward nations on terms of equality with a predominant nation.[59] In speaking of the adoption of Protection, List has in mind, however, only nations of a considerable magnitude, and he speaks throughout rather contemptuously of small states. 'A small state,' he says, 'can never bring to complete perfection within its territory the various branches of production. In it all Protection becomes mere private monopoly.' It is only by alliances with more powerful nations and by excessive sacrifices that such a small state can with difficulty maintain its independence.[60] But even where Protection is appropriate, List is under no illusion on the point that it represents an immediate sacrifice. It is a sacrifice of present advantages in order to insure future ones;[61] but these sacrifices, he contends, are made good a hundredfold, and they are therefore properly to be regarded as reproductive outlay by the whole nation.[62] He would doubtless have approved of the contrast recently drawn between the principle underlying a national debt and that implicit in Protection. In the case of a national debt it is thought proper that a part of the burden incurred for the benefit of the present generation should be borne by the future; under a protective system, expenditure for the benefit of the future is borne by the present; in either case, the apportionment is effected by the State, which alone has a sufficiently roving eye over time. When we turn to the extent of the Protection to be afforded, there are considerable limitations. In the first

[58] Ibid., p.107.   [59] Ibid., p.103.
[60] Ibid., p.142. See also p.247.
[61] Ibid., p.117.   [62] Ibid., p.183.

place, it is argued, on wholly orthodox lines, and in accordance with the principles of the school, that, so far as concerns the interchange of raw products, the 'most extensive liberty of commerce' is always advantageous both to the individual and to the entire State. Manufactured goods are in a different case, because here restrictions on importations 'call into life and activity a mass of natural powers.'[63] The case for Protection is then limited to those states which, so far as manufactures are concerned, are capable of reaching the highest degree of civilization, 'but which are retarded in their progress by the competition of a foreign manufacturing power,' and even so, such a measure is specifically designed for the purpose of industrial development only, and 'is justifiable only until that manufacturing power is strong enough no longer to have any reason to fear foreign competition.'[64] Moreover, it should not 'exclude foreign competition at once and altogether, and thus isolate from other nations that nation which is thus protected.' Nor should all branches of industry be protected in the same degree; it is only the most important that require Protection.[65] The importation of machinery should also be free until such time as the country is in a position to produce it for itself. As to the height of the protective barrier, List says in one passage that when an industry cannot be established by means of an original protection of from forty to sixty per cent., and cannot continue to maintain itself under a continued protection of from twenty to thirty per cent., 'the fundamental conditions of manufacturing power are lacking.'[66] It is also essential that the duties should be known in advance and maintained inviolably; and on this point he attacks Adam Smith, not without reason, on the ground of his (rather half-hearted) approval of retaliation

[63] *Ibid.*, p.175. [65] *Ibid.*, pp.144-145.
[64] *Ibid.*, p.144. [66] *Ibid.*, p.251.

– a principle which would lead, in List's eyes, to 'the most absurd and most ruinous measures,' consequent on the disturbing influence of duties imposed and again immediately removed.[67]

It will be observed that, for List, Protection is strictly a transitional phase, yet there is a strange contradiction between the List who is concerned with a world of warring nations, and the List who appears almost as a prophet of the League of Nations. In the one case, he proclaims the doctrine that 'Germany must care for Germany, and Russia for Russia'; and urges that 'instead of hoping and waiting and expecting the Messiah of a future Free Trade, it would be better that the cosmopolitan spirit should be thrown into the fire.'[68] In this mood also, inspired by a love of the big battalions, List is a pan-Germanist, making it clear that Holland and Denmark must come within the German Bund;[69] elsewhere that Germany, with Holland, Belgium and Switzerland, should become a 'commercial and political whole,'[70] and finding war itself beneficial, if it leads to Protection and the advancement of a state from the purely agricultural stage to the stage of manufactures.[71] Yet elsewhere, and doubtless with sincerity, he contemplates in the by-no-means remote future, the union of all nations, and indicates the forces making in that direction; Protection is indeed but the most efficient means of furthering such a union, and hence also of promoting true freedom of trade.[72] It is of the highest interest in illuminating List's position that in his criticism of the mercantilist system, one of the reproaches he urges against it (again doubtless with sincerity) is that 'chiefly owing to its utterly ignoring the principle of cosmopolitanism, it does not recognize the future union of all nations, the establishment of perpetual

[67] Ibid., pp. 254-255.   [68] Ibid., p.75.   [69] Ibid., p.143.
[70] Ibid., p.332.   [71] Ibid., p.148.   [72] Ibid., pp.101, 103.

peace, and of universal freedom of trade, as the goal towards which all nations have to strive, and more and more to approach.'[73]

Von Thünen

Despite laudable efforts, such as those of Dr. Spann, it is hardly possible to regard Johann Heinrich von Thünen[74] (1783-1850), the third of the present group, as having any great spiritual kinship with Müller or List. He is indeed an economist by accident, because of his interest in one problem which was every day before his eyes as a practical agriculturalist. Also he was a man of a kindly heart who thought of his fellows, and was therefore led to jot down his reflections on the social conditions of his humbler neighbours. But it is fairly safe to say that Müller would have bored him, and he showed small interest in the problems which excited List. On the vexed question of the claims of nationality, he merely says that nations should cease to regard themselves as the 'middle-point of the earth,' and recommends that they should take as their aim the well-being of humanity, adding a word in praise of England for having recently shown a disposition to follow this self-sacrificing path.[75] One gets the impression that the political side of economics (fundamental with Müller and List) had little attraction for von Thünen. He was a landowner, interested in his estates and his workmen on the estates, with a passionate hobby for keeping accounts in the evening.

Von Thünen's position in the development of economic theory is due to the work to which he gave the title of *The*

[73] *Ibid.*, p.272.
[74] Born 1783, the son of a landed proprietor in Oldenberg; for a time a student at Göttingen. In 1810 he bought the estate of Tellow and remained there. Died 1850.
[75] *Der Isolierte Staat*, p.514. (References to the edition in the *Sammlung Sozialwissenschaftlicher Meister*.)

Isolated State (*Der Isolierte Staat*), a work for which the whole of his life was in a sense the background. He acknowledges himself as the disciple of Adam Smith, but Smith, as he rightly says, had been confused on a number of points. He had confounded profits and interest; he had not properly explained rent; on numerous other points he was 'incomplete.'[76] His reverence for the master urged him to complete Smith's doctrine. The result is *The Isolated State*, a book which grew in the course of its author's life.

The Isolated State is among the most remarkable (and one is tempted to add, most curious) books in economic literature, alike in form, method and substance. In its final form it is almost formless, an obvious bringing together of notes, comments, and arithmetical examples, with little unity of subject between the abstractions of the isolated state and the consideration of the social problem, which is jointly attacked by humanitarian aspirations and algebraic formulæ.

It is in regard to its method that *The Isolated State* is most obviously original. Von Thünen had a fresh mind, not overburdened with the learning of others: a premature engagement had snatched him betimes from the snares of excessive study and of the University of Göttingen. The whole conception of the isolated state, with which his mind had amused itself from an early age, is highly abstract, and in a sense the kernel of von Thünen's work is concerned with unrealities. The spirit of the mathematician hangs heavily on von Thünen. On his first page he carefully sets out his 'postulates' (*Voraussetzungen*), followed immediately by a statement of the *Aufgabe*, the problem to be solved. Euclid, as known to our younger days, would have smiled approval. The postulates are, in short, a definition of

[76] *Ibid.*, p.402.

the unrealities implicit in the isolated state. Imagine a large town in the midst of a fruitful plain, traversed neither by navigable river nor canal; the plain consists of uniform soil capable of cultivation, ending in the remote distance in an uncultivated wilderness, so that the town supplies all the manufactures for the plain, and in return draws all its sustenance from the surrounding country. Such being assumed, there arises the question how the land will be tilled, and what effect greater or less distance from the town will exercise on agriculture.

An abstract unreal problem, it will be observed; yet, curiously, von Thünen contrives to make his discussion bristle with reality. Indeed, it may be said that von Thünen and Ricardo, the two masters of the abstract method, knew, better than any other economist, what they were talking about. Von Thünen had had practical experience of farm management on his estate at Tellow; heaven knows how he had kept accounts. His problem, being one solely of distance from the market, reduced itself ultimately into that of cost of transport, and no one had ever known, so accurately as von Thünen did, what everything on his estate had cost. The isolated state, in fact, is built up on the experience gained at Tellow, and the carefully studied accounts of years provide the concrete material from which conclusions are drawn.

It requires little proof that in the unreal conditions postulated (which also inferentially exclude the existence of any main roads), cultivation will automatically be arranged in a series of concentric circles round the town, according to the cost of transport of the commodity and the ratio in which its value stands to its bulk and weight. But von Thünen's reputation does not depend on his success in unveiling the obvious. The order in which he arranges his six circles is in part in accordance with what might be

226   THE DEVELOPMENT OF ECONOMIC DOCTRINE

expected, and in part somewhat surprising;[77] but in any case the actual conclusion on this point is unimportant. What is significant throughout is the use of a technique suggestive, and indeed in places an anticipation, of much later methods of approach. Thus he points out that in the inner circle devoted to garden produce, milk must also be included, both by reason of cost of transport and perishability; and he goes on to explain that, accordingly, the price of milk must rise so high that the land devoted to the production of milk cannot be used more advantageously for any other product.[78] After a careful analysis of the cost of transport (with due allowance for the maintenance of the horses on the journey) he presents a diminishing scale of values for grain at different distances from the town until, at a distance of 49.95 miles, the grain becomes valueless, and beyond this distance cultivation becomes impossible, even if the grain could be produced without cost.[79] It is but a simple elaboration of this idea to arrive at von Thünen's conception of rent, one of the points on which he was consciously acting as a corrective of Adam Smith. A farm or estate (*ein Gut*) is always provided with buildings and other equipment which can be separated from the soil; the income which the farm yields does not therefore spring wholly from the soil, but is also in part interest on capital sunk in these valuable objects. That part which remains after deduction from the total income of what is represented by interest on all capital sunk in objects which can

[77] Market-gardening, forestry, *Fruchtwechselwirthschaft, Koppelwirthschaft, Dreifelderwirthschaft,* cattle. (It is perhaps prudent not to translate words which can only be mistranslated.) Spann comments on the high place assigned to forestry, that its relegation in practice to remote regions is largely due to the fact that forestry is assigned to places not suitable for other culture.
[78] *Ibid.,* p.13.
[79] *Ibid.,* p.18.

be disassociated from the soil (and which thus belongs to the soil itself) is termed the rent of land,[80] and on this definition a negative amount of rent is theoretically conceivable. A consideration of the causes that determine the price of grain naturally leads to an explanation of the origin of rent. In order to obtain the corn it needs, the town must be prepared to pay a price which is sufficient to pay the cost of production and the cost of transport in the case of the most remote producer whose grain is required. On this, von Thünen frames a general law (for the isolated state and reality) that 'the price of corn must be so high, that the rent of that farm whose cost of production and delivery is highest, whose cultivation is at the same time necessary for the satisfaction of the demand for grain, shall not fall below zero.'[81] But, for the purchaser, grain produced in the vicinity of the market is of equal value with that produced at a distance, and he is indifferent which of the two has cost most to bring to market. 'What the producer in the neighbourhood of the town receives over and above what it costs him, is for him pure gain'; it is a gain, moreover, which is perpetual and yearly recurrent, so that the soil of his farm yields a yearly rent. Hence we get the explanation of rent: 'The rent of a farm arises from the advantages which it possesses over the worst farm, whether in situation or soil, the production of which is necessary for the satisfaction of demand.'[82]

It is obvious at what point von Thünen has arrived; he has evolved the Ricardian theory of rent, although primarily in terms of situation and distance from the market, and not,

[80] *Ibid.*, p.23. The test of 'separability from the soil' (*die vom Boden getrennt werden können*) obviously covers an ambiguity; does the interest on the cost of improvements not so separable fall within or without von Thünen's conception of rent?

[81] *Ibid.*, p.226.

[82] *Ibid.*, pp.229-230.

as in the case of Ricardo, in terms of quality.[83] When he comes to discuss taxes on rent, it is obvious that he has very clear ideas as to what the conception involves. If a portion of 'land-rent' has to be surrendered to the State, this will, he says, in no way alter the form or the extension of agriculture. The farms whose rent is near zero, will contribute very little to such a tax, and the most remote and the worst will not be affected. Such a tax, therefore, could not detrimentally affect the extent of cultivation, the population, the application of capital, or the quantity of produce; indeed, if the whole of the rent were taken away by the tax, the cultivation of the soil would remain as before.[84]

In elaborating his theory of rent, von Thünen has in effect made use of the idea of the margin, and it is surprising how, throughout his speculation, he anticipated the technique of the later marginalist school. Thus, with regard to wages, he lays down the principle that on an estate, beyond a certain point, each additional worker will yield a smaller addition to the product, the twenty-second less than the twenty-first, the twenty-third less than the twenty-second and so on, and that the increase in the number of workers must therefore be continued until the additional value yielded by the last worker is equal to the wage which he receives.[85] Further, the wage which the last worker receives must act as the norm for all workers, since unequal remuneration cannot be made in respect of the same work.[86] Here, undisguised, is the theory of the marginal productivity of labour. So again, in discussing the relation of interest and wages, he emphasizes 'the diminishing effectiveness of capital' in a wholly modern manner. By

---

[83] The whole argument of *The Isolated State* postulates uniformity of soil, so that situation would be the only variable, yet von Thünen shows a disposition to speak of superiority in 'Lage und Boden.'

[84] *Ibid.*, p.346.   [85] *Ibid.*, pp.415-416.   [86] *Ibid.*, p.577.

means of a lengthy table, such as von Thünen delights in, he shows that capital, as it increases in amount, can only find less profitable outlets, and that at each stage of its increase, competition will force down the rate of interest to that which the least profitable opening can afford to pay. Consequently, interest (the rent which capital yields) is determined by the yield of the last portion of capital applied; and it is notable that in determining the rate of interest von Thünen regards the successive increments of capital as being infinitely small.[87]

Even a brief notice of von Thünen would be incomplete without reference to an aspect of his writings which is somewhat remote from the abstract isolated state. He was troubled by the condition of the worker and the lowness of his wages, and he sought for something more satisfying than he could find in the pages of Ricardo. In a section ' on the lot of the workers,' incorporated in the second part of *The Isolated State*, he gives expression to what he calls ' a dream of grave substance.'[88] It is a great evil, he says, that the most numerous class, that of the common hand-worker, is unrepresented in the State. The reward of the hand-worker is disproportionately low compared with that of those who conduct industry, and there is no remedy by transference from one class to the other, because of the absence of ' school-knowledge,' which the worker cannot afford for his children owing to his low wage. These low wages, again, are due to the fact that, by reason of early marriages, the supply of workers is always greater than the demand. To remedy this, nothing short of a change in the character of the people is required, and von Thünen pleads

---

[87] *Ibid.*, pp.496, 498, 558. ' Es folgt hieraus dass wir das zuletzt entstandene und angelegte Kapitalteilchen, durch dessen Nutzung der Zinsfuss bestimmt werden soll, sehr klein – genau genommen, unendlich klein – annehmen müssen.'
[88] *Ibid.*, p.440.

for greater prevision, postponement of marriage and better education, from all of which such astonishing results are anticipated, that even the word *Paradies* does not appear out of place.

Viewed apart from this dream, there are two aspects of the wage-problem with which von Thünen grapples: firstly, why cannot wages rise so as to absorb the rent which the owner draws without labour? Secondly, is the low rate of wages founded in the nature of things, and thus in accordance with the will of Providence, or is the present position the result of force and oppression? On the first point von Thünen traces, in the most approved manner, the effects of a rise of wages 'at the margin of cultivation, where the soil gives no rent,'[89] leading ultimately to a drawing-in of the margin of cultivation towards the town, with displacement of labour and subsequent depression of wages. On the problem of the true rate of wages, von Thünen rather tends to provide one of the curiosities of economic literature. He points out that wages must comprise two constituent parts: (1) what the worker must expend for his maintenance in order to remain efficient; and (2) what he receives as a reward for his exertion,[90] so that Roscher hails him as one of the earliest to view wages as something more than the price of a commodity, 'labour.' But beyond this, his contribution to the theory of wages is somewhat bizarre. In the pursuit of a natural and a just rate of wages, von Thünen proves, with a vast display of mathematical formulæ, and indeed along various lines, that the true formula for wages is represented by $\sqrt{ap}$, where a represents subsistence, and p the productivity of the worker. The proof, such as it is,

[89] It is perhaps worthy of notice that von Thünen uses the word 'Grenze,' now irremediably consecrated: 'An der Grenze der kultivierten Ebene des isolierten Staats, wo der Boden keine Rente gibt' (*ibid.*, p.463).
[90] *Ibid.*, p.490.

rests on assumptions which are unreal, and the very celebrated formula cannot therefore be regarded as more than
a symbol of the view that the worker should share in the
prosperity which he produces. In practice, von Thünen
would appear to have introduced a kind of profit-sharing
scheme on his estate, which doubtless represented a distant
obeisance to $\sqrt{ap}$. Von Thünen himself, however, regarded
the formula as his crowning achievement, and desired that
it should be inscribed on his tombstone – a medium of
publication in which strictness of proof is seldom exacted.

CHAPTER IX

The Optimists: Carey and Bastiat

I T has been said that classical Political Economy, as represented by Malthus and Ricardo, tended to certain pessimistic conclusions, above all in the inferences to be drawn
from the Law of Rent, based on a Law of Diminishing
Returns, and from the so-called Principle of Population,
especially if this latter be carelessly apprehended. Moreover, apart from the disconcerting vision of a future in
which an increasing proportion of the world's produce would
be diverted to an idle class, in which for an ever-increasing
number there would be 'no place at Nature's feast,' it is
to be noted that the classical school tended to a system of
disharmonies and conflict. Even if outward peace might be
preserved, there was at the heart of things incompatibility
of interest.

Carey

The reaction to a more optimistic view of things is
primarily and most conveniently represented by Henry
Charles Carey[1] (1793-1879), who indeed was at one time
regarded as the representative of a peculiarly American

---

[1] Born in Philadelphia in 1793, the son of an Irish emigrant who
had become a successful publisher. Carey succeeded to the business,
but retired while still young (1835), and devoted the rest of his life
to producing economic literature. Few authors surely can have written
quite so much. His larger works cover some thirteen volumes, and
his pamphlets are at least fifty-seven in number, not all of which are
mercifully small. His chief works are: *Essay on the Rate of Wages*,
Principles of Political Economy (three volumes), *The Past, the
Present and the Future*, *Harmony of Interests*, and *The Principles of
Social Science* (three very large volumes).

Political Economy. In his time he exercised great influence, though less so in this country than in America and on the Continent; for us, at least, he has now faded into comparative insignificance, cursed by his own voluminousness and repetitiveness, and, it must be added, by a rather naïve foolishness. But to the persevering and buoyant reader he is not without interest. He had ideas which are not wholly unjust; he is, above all, the supreme example of the truth that the economist reflects his environment. Moreover, there is always profit in reconsidering an author who, like Carey, has continued to rank higher elsewhere than with us. While others may have been more than generous, we may have been less than just.

The central point in Carey's theorizing is probably most conveniently found in his theory of value.[2] Labour is, for him, the sole cause of value, but Carey's labour theory of value has variations which lead to his peculiar conclusions. In the earliest Robinson Crusoe stage of economy (to which Carey is much addicted) articles will be measured or exchanged in proportion to the labour required; but with the appearance of capital on the scene, a change is effected in all existing values, and things will now exchange in accordance with their cost of reproduction. But with the progress of humanity, this cost of reproduction steadily falls, and there is thus a steady decline in the value of all existing capital. Value, in Carey's rather peculiar phrase, is an 'estimate of the resistance to be overcome before we can enter upon the possession of the thing desired.' It follows from this that, as labour aided by capital is superior in quality, the exchange value of labour expressed in commodities will constantly increase; while at the same time existing capital will experience a corresponding decline in

[2] *Principles of Political Economy*, Vol. I, chap. 2, especially pp. 19-20.

values, expressed in labour, since at each stage its value is limited by its cost of reproduction, which by hypothesis is constantly falling. Moreover, not only is the labour value of all previously existing machinery constantly declining, but Carey also shows, by reasoning which is by no means impeccable, that there is likewise a diminution in the proportion of the product of labour that can be demanded for granting the use of it. The position of the labourer, that is to say, is constantly improving; the capitalist's reward tends to increase absolutely, but it is a diminishing proportion of an increasing product.[3]

Carey extends the sphere of his harmony by entirely identifying land with other forms of capital, and thus eliminating rent as a separate category. He held that 'capital in land differs in no respect from that invested in other machinery, that rent is only interest for capital invested, and that the value of all landed property is due, like that of all gifts of Nature existing in unlimited quantity, solely to the labour employed in its appropriation and improvement.'[4] The analogy with other forms of capital also holds inasmuch as with the progress of society, later farms are brought under cultivation at less cost, so that here also the cost of reproduction is constantly falling. This is proved by the fact that land invariably sells at less than its cost of subjugation, which sufficiently refutes the Ricardian assumption that a payment is made for the 'original and indestructible powers' of the soil. These last, in fact, have no existence.

It will be observed that Carey's views are the expression of a belief in the progress, and indeed the indefinite progress, of society. Everywhere he reflects the spacious days of the early settler, when every new man added to the

---

[3] Social Science, Vol. I, p.158; Vol. III, p.133.
[4] Political Economy, Vol. I, pp.129-130.

primitive community represented a fresh ally in the struggle against Nature. It is characteristic of Carey that, like Müller, though with a different emphasis, he makes association the fundamental need of man: 'The first and great desire of man is that of association with his fellow men; and it is so because he feels that improvement of his condition, physical, moral, mental and political, is its uniform accompaniment.'[5] The development and growing strength of the early community in which 'the carpenter comes to exchange his labour for food,' or the farmer rejoices in the arrival of the black-smith, furnish, in his writings, a constantly recurring idyllic picture.

Thus, viewing life from the point of view of a settler in a new country, Carey is led to deny, and indeed with vituperation and abuse, the Law of Diminishing Returns (and with it the Ricardian Law of Rent), as also the Malthusian Principle of Population. Ricardo, he says – and it is a significant sentence – 'had never witnessed as at the moment we do from the window at which we write, the progress of a new settlement.' In his restatement of Ricardo's theory, the whole doctrine is represented as resting on the proposition that in the commencement of cultivation, the best soils alone are cultivated. 'That fact exists, or it does not. If it has no existence, the [Ricardian] system falls to the ground.' Accordingly a very large part of Carey is taken up with a wide inductive survey tending to prove, and with success, that the order of cultivation is the reverse of that which he regards as the essential basis of Ricardo's theory. It is the inferior soil that is first cultivated, and it is first cultivated because it is less cumbered with vegetation and therefore more manageable in the earlier stages. It is only with increased power and with association that a descent is made from the hill-sides to the richer valleys. 'We know of no

[5] *Harmony of Interests*, p.52.

exception to this rule, and we feel assured that none exists or can exist.'[6] In accordance with his identification of land with other forms of capital, 'the earth,' for Carey, 'is a great machine given to man to be fashioned to his purpose,' but it is of the essence of all progress that man everywhere begins with the worst and proceeds to the best. First of all there are axes of stone, then of iron and lastly of steel. It is only in regard to the machinery for obtaining food, if we accept Ricardo's theory, that man begins with the best and proceeds to the worst.[7]

It may be conceded that as a matter of historical investigation, Carey amply establishes his point regarding the order of settlement. There are, however, two obvious comments. In the first place, despite Carey's dogmatism, Ricardo's theory in no wise postulates a historical progress from the best soils in the beginnings of cultivation to inferior soils later. Ricardo was concerned with comparative fertility at any given time. That, for a time, there may be increasing returns in agrictulture, that the more fertile soils at one time may be less fertile later, would have left Ricardo cold. In his voluminous criticisms of Ricardo, Carey proves primarily that he had failed to understand what Ricardo meant, just as elsewhere he manifests a similar lack of comprehension with regard to Malthus. But Carey's work is not in vain. Apart from the historical interest of his researches, he has doubtless compelled a more careful statement of the Law of Diminishing returns by necessitating emphasis on these blessed words: 'beyond a certain point.' The other aspect provoking comment is the obvious fallacy involved in the constantly recurring analogy of the stone, the iron and the steel axe, as typifying progress from inferior to superior instruments. In the first place, when men advance

[6] *The Past, the Present and the Future*, pp.21-39.
[7] *Political Economy*, Vol. I, p.25.

THE OPTIMISTS: CAREY AND BASTIAT 237

beyond the stone axe, the stone axe is scrapped. Not so with
the inferior land first cultivated; even if temporarily abandoned, it is kept in reserve. And secondly, when, if ever,
the human race, made strong by association, has gone down
into the valleys everywhere, there will obviously be no
more valleys to descend, no lands of still higher fertility to
cultivate, and the only course will be to return to what may
have been temporarily abandoned. In short, with regard
to machinery the human race tends to restrict itself to the
best known at any time, so that the instruments in use tend
to be of uniform efficiency. It is quite otherwise in land,
where 'instruments' of different efficiency are necessarily
used simultaneously; and herein lies the whole of the
Ricardian theory of rent.

But these things do not trouble Carey, for to him the
world is limitless, nor is there any obstacle to the constant
progression of increasing returns in agriculture. And indeed, greatly daring, he has the courage to say so expressly.
'There is now, and always has been, an abundance of unoccupied land'; there is an 'almost infinite extent of soil
capable of yielding food' which yet remains unoccupied and
unproductive. The earth is the great labour savings bank,
the only bank 'whose dividends are perpetually increasing
while its capital is perpetually doubling,' and it will continue
to do so for ever, provided it receives back the refuse of its
produce – a point of importance in connection with Carey's
protectionist views. In short, agriculture is the only field
'in which an almost unlimited amount of labour and capital
might be employed at a constantly increasing rate of
return.'[8]

These considerations, in themselves, indicate in part the
nature of Carey's reply to Malthus. It is fundamental to his

---

[8] e.g., *The Past, the Present and the Future*, pp.77, 99.

doctrine that under natural conditions, and unless prevented by disturbing causes, capital will tend to increase more rapidly than population.[9] This merely reflects the virtue of association and the increasing power of numbers over the forces of Nature, when 'each successive addition to the population brings a consumer and a producer,'[10] when the first early settlement, poor by reason of the paucity of its numbers, advances in efficiency and the power to produce wealth with each accession. All this is true. Men cannot live alone, and when population is sparse, the first condition of an increase of welfare is an increase of population. But beyond this caveat, perfectly justifiable in view of the conditions of America in the early nineteenth century, Carey advances to a jumble of curious arguments against Malthus. The one which weighed most with him is theological in origin, for whereas God had said: 'Be fruitful and multiply,' the modern school of Political Economy says: 'Be not fruitful; do not multiply.' 'It prescribes disobedience to the earliest of God's commands; it ascribes poverty and wretchedness to the erroneous arrangements of the Deity.'[11] In a curiously confused criticism of Malthus, he points out that the Malthusian theory inverts the true order of things.[12] It is when population increases that food is abundant. Again, on the Malthusian theory when the Malthusian checks are operative, food ought to be most redundant; but during war there is distress: 'Peace comes – the remedy is withdrawn – and capital begins again to increase.'[13] Put tersely: 'Is war required to correct an error of the Creator, or has the Creator Himself provided the corrective required for removing the effects of human

[9] *Wages*, p.81.
[10] *Harmony of Interests*, p.86.
[11] *Harmony of Interests*, p.201; *Wages*, p.232.
[12] *Wages*, p.244.
[13] *Political Economy*, Vol. III, p.54.

error?'[14] All this is to betray a naïve misunderstanding of Malthus, but Carey in crusading against Malthus is largely inspired by a desire to justify the ways of God to man, and his arguments directed to that end have a child-like simplicity distantly reminiscent of Fourier.

One other argument, in itself inexpressibly foolish, which nevertheless has done good service in its time, finds its highest expression in Carey, and might also have been to the liking of Fourier. Even if man has a tendency to in-crease in a geometrical progression, is he not for his sus-tenance dependent on lower animals and vegetables, and do they not manifest a similar tendency to increase in a geo-metrical ratio? But Carey would have us believe that the situation is even more comforting for man than this general reflection would indicate. Men, the devourers, and rabbits, the devoured, may alike tend to increase geometrically, but it is notorious that rabbits are the more potent multipliers. The increase in numbers is everywhere, he holds, in the inverse ratio of development; as the riddle used to put it, 'the higher, the fewer.' But on the Malthusian doctrine, when we come to man, 'we learn the existence of a new and greater law, in virtue of which man increases in a geo-metrical ratio, while the increase of herrings, rabbits, oysters, potatoes, turnips and all other commodities required for his use is limited to the arithmetical one! '[15] Elsewhere he tells us that 'rapid as has been the growth of American popula-tion, that of the supply of oysters has been far more so.'[16] On Carey's philosophy, the obvious remedy for unemploy-ment is for the unemployed to take to the breeding of rabbits, or still better the cultivation of oysters.

Equally deserving of note, if only as a curiosity, is the

[14] *Social Science*, Vol. III, p. 270.
[15] *Social Science*, Vol. I, p.92.
[16] *Social Science*, Vol. III, p.351.

argument which centres in carbonic acid. With progress and advancing civilization, the larger lower animals die out, with a consequent disturbance of the supply of carbonic acid necessary for the maintenance of plant life. Hence, if only as producers of carbonic acid, there is need for more men to compensate for the extirpation of their larger but lower fellow-creatures. Men must breathe more, if lions breathe less. This is but another example of the 'beauty of all natural arrangements.'[17]

In themselves such arguments are not sufficient to lay the Malthusian devil, and Carey realizes it. In his early writings he admitted that the time might come when 'there will not be even standing room,' but he is content to 'leave that distant future to the benevolent care of the Deity.'[18] There is no immediate necessity for becoming idle, intemperate and profligate with a view to increasing the supply of food. He admits, at this stage, that possibly, and even probably, the world will some day be over-peopled, 'but we must leave it to our successors to adopt the remedies whenever they shall see cause to believe that they will thereby improve their condition.'[19]

Nevertheless, to an apostle of harmony, such a postponement of trouble to a future, however remote, could not be satisfactory, and in his final statement he admits that if, as he puts it, 'the procreative tendency is a positive quantity,' slavery will be the ultimate condition of the great mass of the race, and man will ultimately be subdued by Nature.[20] To meet this difficulty, there is one obvious method of argument. If it can be proved that the procreative power is not constant, but is in fact a variable quantity, it will be possible to re-establish the harmony so dear to

[17] *Social Science*, Vol. III, pp.319-320.
[18] *The Past, the Present and the Future*, pp.77.
[19] *Political Economy*, Vol. III, p.91.
[20] *Social Science*, Vol. III, p.265.

Carey's heart. Such, in fact, is Carey's line of argument. He cites (although there is much unconscious Malthusianism mixed up with the argument) many instances of variable procreative power, and advances the general argument that there is a relationship between the nervous and the reproductive powers.[21] As energy is diverted from the muscular to the nervous system, so will the ratio of procreation diminish. Sterility goes with mental eminence, and as the race progresses there will be a natural diminution in the rate of increase. Thus harmony is again established; the Malthusian checks become superfluous, because there is a divine, self-adjusting mechanism which will temper the flow of population.

Carey is usually regarded as being the twin-exponent of Protection, alongside List. But indeed his Protection is of a most unscientific kind, springing from instinct rather than from reason. It is not for him to pursue the intricacies of the incidence of import duties. His protectionism, when it comes, is again the natural ejaculation of a backwoodsman, girding at his primitive environment. At the outset Carey was an orthodox free-trader, regarding Protection as a device 'to frustrate the beneficent designs of the Deity,'[22] but with his growing appreciation of the advantages of association, he became rapidly and somewhat foolishly protectionist. Here Carey's fundamental idea, from which all others radiate, is the importance of bringing the producer and the consumer into close proximity; thus Protection represents an instinctive effort to obtain that combination which elsewhere he so fervently lauds. With Carey there are no half-lights. 'Protection is right or wrong. Free Trade is right or wrong. . . . Half-way measures are always wrong.'[23]

[21] *Social Science*, Vol. III, p.299.
[22] *Wages*, p.14.   [23] *Harmony of Interests*, p.67.

Another idea constantly recurs in Carey, so that it almost acquires the importance of an *idée mère*. It is his own peculiar distinction between commerce and trade. Commerce is the natural interchange between members of a community and is blessed; trade is the carrying of things to far countries and is accursed. Epigrammatically put, the followers of commerce desire to effect exchanges *with* their fellow-men; those engaged in trade desire to effect exchanges *for* them.[24]

Carey's protectionism, then, is largely summed up in his proposition that 'the first and heaviest tax to be paid by land and labour is that of transportation,' and in a phrase of which he never wearies, he desires to eliminate this tax by bringing 'the loom and the anvil to take their natural places by the side of the plough and the harrow.' Most of his arguments, indeed, are but variants of this fundamental contention that ' the object of Protection is that of diminishing the distance and the waste between the producer and the consumer,' that it is no more than an instinctive effort to attain combination.[25] Some of the variations of the theme, however, are interesting, and others not unamusing. Protection promotes concentration; Free Trade dispersion. Protection is competition for the purchase of labour; Free Trade for the sale of labour. As war is encouraged if men are cheap, Free Trade encourages war. Free Trade, again, stands for distant markets; Protection for the home market; but those who seek distant markets are separated from their wives and children, spend much time on the road and in taverns, and are thus liable to be led into dissipation. Free Trade thus stands for the dissipation of the tavern; Protection for the blessedness of the home. But these, and

---

[24] *Social Science*, Vol. III, p.44.
[25] *Harmony of Interests*, pp.52, 101, etc.

other striking points, are perhaps but the embroidery of the argument.[26]

But there is one subsidiary argument of a different character. The unprotected country which is restricted to agriculture is in effect selling its own soil. The principle of returning waste products to the soil as a condition of the land playing its part in yielding ever-increasing returns exercised a curious fascination over Carey's mind, and it involves as a consequence that the place of consumption must be sufficiently near to enable the earth to get back its own.[27] Thus we arrive at a further conclusion, suggestive of List, that 'manufactures always precede, and never follow, the creation of a real agriculture. In the absence of the former, all attempts at cultivation are limited to the work of tearing out and exporting the soil in the form of rude products.'[28] The reader who desires economic comment on this argument will find it in its appropriate place (Book V, chap. 10) in John Stuart Mill, who apparently thought it worthy of his heaviest artillery.

Despite a certain tendency to foolishness,[29] Carey is an important figure in the development of economic doctrine. He represents primarily a reaction against the pessimism of the classical school. His theory of value, resting on the idea of constant depreciation of existing wealth consequent on progress, was designed to prove the ultimate harmony of all things. There is 'a perfect harmony of real and true interests among the various classes of mankind'[30] – an idea to reappear in Bastiat. This is his central doctrine, but it is

[26] *Harmony of interests*, pp.193, 202, 209, etc.
[27] *Social Science*, Vol. I, p.273.
[28] *Social Science*, Vol. III, p.333.
[29] 'Truth being simple, simple ideas are generally true' is one of Carey's favourite aphoristic observations. It is hardly a promising foundation-stone for any system of thought.
[30] *Social Science*, Vol. III, p.113.

naturally buttressed by vigorous attacks on the two chief sources of classical pessimism, the Law of Diminishing Returns and the Principle of Population. Much of his criticism has at least the minor merit of compelling in others a greater fastidiousness of statement, if only in order to avoid being misunderstood and misrepresented by the Careys of this world. His glaring and most obvious defect is that for which he reproached others, that he is, namely, so restricted and limited by his environment. He is pathetically the economist of the earliest stage of colonization, imbued with a touching faith that there will always be wild waste places, that there will always be room, and that men will never have cause to fear the stinginess of the earth or the embarrassing fecundity of women.

Bastiat

Time has perhaps hardly been kind to Frederic Bastiat[31] (1801-1850), yet he deserves a place among the landmarks. His curse was that he was pre-eminently an *esprit vulgarisateur* in the convenient French phrase. Not the least remarkable feature in Bastiat's career is the fact that he began to write so late in life, and, since he died young, his very considerable literary output was the result of about five years' feverish activity. Primarily, Bastiat was a journalist, not using the word with any highbrow condescension, but merely implying its literal sense, that he was a man who served the needs of the day. And as a journalist Bastiat has had few equals. No one has ever been quite so skilful in

[31] Born at Mugron, near Bayonne, in 1801, and lived obscurely on his farm until 1844, though influential in the intellectual and public life of his area. Thereafter accident and the Free Trade cause revealed his supreme journalistic powers, and he entered a larger life. He was a member of the Assemblée Constituante in 1848, and of the Assemblée Legislative in 1849. His last six years were years of exhaustive labour, and he seems to have died of overwork (at Rome) in 1850.

making the case of his antagonist look extremely foolish. Even now his most ephemeral work remains a joy to read, by reason of its wit, its merciless satire and the neatness wherewith he pinks his opponents.

Bastiat, being a journalist, was, however, never able to remove himself from the controversies of the day; and his very skill in scoring off others has created a posthumous suspicion that, if not exactly a quack in the austere eyes of science, his was at least a shallow, if an agile, mind. Bastiat was moved to write by two of the most seductive (because inexhaustible) and most enduring of journalist topics – the Free Trade and Protectionist controversy, and the eternal dispute concerning Socialism. His objection to Protection is fundamentally the same as that which he urges against Socialism; they are both devices of exploitation. The manufacturer who cannot make a profit invokes Protection, whereby the State will guarantee him a profit at other people's expense; so likewise Socialism involves a denial of individual responsibility. Thus, in one of his most amusing skits,[32] he arrives at his definition of the State as 'the great fiction, by means of which everybody contrives to live at the expense of everybody else.' It is true that it is a rather crude Protection against which he tilts, just as there is not much subtlety in the Socialism against which he inveighs; but how effective his satire can be, is seen in the immortal petition of the candle-makers against the competition of the sun, or in the less well-known proposal to renounce the use of the right hand with a view to the attainment of greater wealth, based on the following train of reasoning: 'The more one works, the richer one is; the greater the obstacles to be overcome, the more one has to work; therefore the greater the obstacles to be overcome, the richer one is.' Perhaps it is all slightly puerile, and his reputation as a

[32] *L'Etat.*

serious writer has doubtless suffered from the faint aroma of the very junior class-room which hangs about his fables and his allegories. Nevertheless, the cause is fortunate which enlists the services of a Bastiat.

The assault on Protection and on Socialism represents the negative, destructive side of Bastiat, and it is seen at its best in *The Economic Sophisms*. Before his death, he embarked on a more ambitious statement of the positive side of his doctrine, of which, however, only one volume appeared. The title of this work, *Economic Harmonies*, sums up the essence of Bastiat. He had attacked Protection and Socialism because they represented an unnatural organization of society – each of them devices whereby certain people could sponge on others. Himself an orthodox *laissez-faire* economist, he was troubled by the inferences drawn from the teaching of Smith, Ricardo and Malthus, pointing to an ultimate antagonism of interests. As becomes an obdurate believer in liberty, he harks back to something like a natural order of society, and speaks reverentially of 'les grandes lois providentielles.' But where are we, if these great providential laws precipitate society towards evil, as the doctrines of Ricardo and Malthus would seem to indicate?[33] Bastiat, however, cannot accept the view that the various economic laws (as of rent, of population and of value) are silently thrusting society towards injustice and inequality. Herein lies the significance of Bastiat, regarded as something more than a crusader in current controversy. A non-interventionist to the finger-tips, he sets out to prove that under the reign of liberty, so far from there being antagonism at the centre of things, there is complete harmony of all legitimate interests.

The essence of his doctrine is found in a rather peculiar

[33] See the address *A la Jeunesse Française* prefixed to the *Harmonies Économiques*.

view of value, and in a rigid distinction between value and utility.[34] Utilities are of two kinds; there are, firstly, those that are accorded gratuitously by Providence, and there are those which are bought by our own efforts. Now the whole essence of progress consists in making proportionately more use of the former than of the latter class, so that a continual process is going on whereby onerous utilities are displaced by gratuitous utilities. Turning to the idea of utility, Bastiat seeks to evade difficulties by linking up the conception with that of a service. 'To accomplish an effort in order to satisfy the needs of another is to render him a service.' Services are exchanged against services, and when exchange is free, the services which are exchanged are equivalent in value. There, then, we have 'value'; it consists in the comparative appreciation of reciprocal services, or, more briefly, it is 'the relation of two services exchanged' – a phrase which covers as miry a bog as any other definition. To introduce the optimistic tinge, it must be remembered that, on this interpretation, the free gifts of Nature have no value. The essence of value lying in human service, it follows that where no service is rendered or received, there can be no value. Thus utility springs from the collaboration of two agencies, which we may call Nature and man's efforts. The former is gratuitous; the latter alone carries value. But, as has been seen, the meaning of progress and invention is that Nature is constrained to render a more efficacious assistance. Thus utility tends to become more and more gratuitous (since the gifts of Nature are gratuitous) while value, which corresponds to man's share in the proceedings, tends to fall relatively to the utility. While value rests in the service, and not in the 'materiality,' it may nevertheless be trans-

[34] For a first approach, the most important chapters in the *Harmonies Économiques* are: Chapter 2, 'Besoins, Efforts, Satisfactions'; chapter 3, 'Des Besoins de l'Homme'; chapter 5, 'De la Valeur.'

ferred from the service to the product, and in a sense be incorporated therein; but even when so incorporated in the product, it remains subject to all the hazards which might befall the service itself. If the service goes down in value, so will the value which has temporarily been incorporated in the product associated with that service.

But this, assuming progress, is what must normally happen. By continually making greater use of the gratuitous gifts of Nature, everything should cost less effort to make in future than it does to-day. Utility may remain unimpaired, but capital tends to depreciate. In the exchange of present labour against past labour, the advantage will always lie on the side of present labour. The workers, therefore, freed from the nightmare of the Iron Law of Wages, may look forward to a rosy future.

So also, Bastiat undertakes the defence of the landed interests. Land is not immune from the general law of slow depreciation. With Carey, he holds that the payment for land is not in respect of a gratuitous gift of Nature; it represents payment for past services in draining, fencing and all the rest of it; and as all these operations become easier, so the value of land must fall. Thus rent is likewise a legitimate payment for services rendered in the past. Nor is capital overlooked in Bastiat's bounty. It is not merely that he defended with the utmost vigour the legitimacy of interest, but he further proved, to his own satisfaction, that the progress of labour to a better position would be in no wise bought at the expense of the capitalist's reward. The capitalist's share might decline proportionately, but it would increase absolutely. In all this there is much of that other optimist, Carey, whom indeed Bastiat has been accused of plagiarizing. Even in his more serious work he can hardly escape the charge of special pleading, and of being unduly influenced by the case he desires to make. He would have the reader believe that he is not blind to the imperfections of this world, but a perusal of the *Economic Harmonies* leaves the impression that, if only there be enough liberty, everything in the economic garden will be increasingly more and more beautiful.

CHAPTER X

The Classical Tradition: Say, Senior, J. S. Mill and Cairnes

THE later development of the orthodox school of Political Economy (meaning thereby those writers who accepted in the main the body of doctrine which had been formulated by Adam Smith, Malthus and Ricardo) hardly calls for any detailed discussion in such a broad outline as this. Theirs was, in the main, a work of elaboration and systematization; yet not a few of them succeeded in emphasizing a point or, after much labour, gave birth to a phrase or an idea which long survived. It may be permissible to lump together in this chapter a few of these writers, some of whom are of considerable importance in themselves, yet for our purposes are necessarily less important than those who founded a tradition or opened up a new line of thought.

Say

Among these, pride of place, or at least priority of time, may be assigned to Jean Baptiste Say[1] (1767-1832), who later has tended to suffer the neglect which is so often the Nemesis of overestimation by one's contemporaries. It is perhaps true that primarily his great achievement was to interpret to the French people and to the world the work

---

[1] Born in 1767 at Lyons; at first in business. After various ups and downs, and more experience of business, he occupied a Chair of Political Economy at the Conservatoire des Arts et Métiers, and later for a short time at the Collège de France. In addition to the *Traité d'Économie Politique* (1803), he also wrote a *Cours Complet d'Économie Politique Pratique* (1828-1829).

of Adam Smith. In the most interesting preliminary discourse prefixed to his treatise of Political Economy, he alternates between high appreciation of the work of Smith and somewhat scathing remarks upon his method or lack of method in the presentation of his arguments. 'The work of Smith,' he says in an often quoted passage, 'is only a confused assemblage of the soundest principles of Political Economy, supported by luminous examples and by the most curious notions of statistics, mingled with instructive reflections; but it is a complete treatise neither of the one nor of the other; his book is a vast chaos of just ideas, jumbled with positive knowledge.'[2] There is some truth in the criticism, and Ricardo likewise, as has been seen, had been a most disorderly writer. It was Say's mission to put an end to this vast chaos, to bring order and method into the statement of economic principles; also to 'render the doctrine popular,' that is to say, to write a book which would be comprehended not merely by the expert.

In both respects he achieved an astounding success. He had a very clear idea of what Political Economy should be. Like other exact sciences (for such he claimed it to be), it consisted of a small number of fundamental principles, and of a large number of corollaries and consequences of these principles.[3] These principles are derived from the nature of things quite as surely as are the laws of the physical world. The stage is thus set for the treatment of economics as a science, and in the title-page we have consecrated the triple division into production, distribution and consumption of wealth – exchange at this stage being quite soundly regarded as a mere step under the first head of the trilogy. So also land, labour and capital (with the entrepreneur looming large), and the corresponding revenues due to these

[2] *Traité d'Économie Politique*, Vol. i, p. 16-17.
[3] *Ibid.*, p.27.

productive agents, provide the framework of Say's exposition. The shadow of Say does indeed lie heavily across the text-books of the nineteenth (and perhaps the twentieth) century.

He was equally successful in his other main object, that of rendering the subject 'popular,' in the sense explained by him. Say had an orderly mind, and a peculiarly lucid and limpid style. Even to-day he can be read with pleasure, whereas the re-reading of Ricardo calls for fortitude and a stout heart. As a result, Say was translated into many tongues, and was something of a best-seller, and in consequence it was perhaps he, more than anyone else, who taught the early nineteenth century its economics.

Apart from this great and meritorious work of vulgarization, certain ideas were peculiarly Say's own. Of these, the one which had in its time most renown, and which was indeed for long regarded as Say's passport into the company of the immortals, was the once celebrated 'theory of markets' (la théorie des débouchés).[4] This theory, which perhaps does not come to much, is to the effect that goods and services are only superficially bought with money; they are, in fact, bought with other goods and services. The money is merely the 'carriage' which, having effected the exchange of two commodities, will forthwith proceed to exchange others. But in reality, products are always exchanged against other products. Consequently, he tells us one ought not to say: 'Sale does not take place because money is scarce, but because other products are so.' It is likewise an integral part of the theory that a product, when created, offers from that very moment a market for other products. General over-production is thus an impossibility. If certain products are in excess, it is because there is a

[4] *Traité d'Économie Politique*, Vol. I, chap. 15, Des Débouchés, pp.148-165.

deficiency elsewhere, and the cure for 'over-production' in one direction is therefore more production elsewhere to serve as a *débouché* for this excess.

From his theory of markets Say draws three conclusions. Firstly, the more numerous and extensive the markets are, the more will they prove to be lucrative, for there will thereby be an increased demand, tending to raise the price. Secondly, from his theory he draws the time-honoured conclusion that everyone is interested in the prosperity of everyone else. It is a foolish distinction to divide the nation into producers and consumers; everyone is both. The prosperity of A makes him a good customer for B, C and D, who should therefore jointly pray for his success, just as the devout Hume prayed for the prosperity of France. In the field of the nation's life, Say draws the conclusion (more suggestive of List and Carey) that agriculture, manufactures and commerce should flourish together, and in the international sphere (as in Adam Smith) that a nation is directly interested in being surrounded by wealthy neighbours: 'car on ne gagne rien avec un peuple qui n'a pas de quoi payer.' The third conclusion, drawn from the theory of markets (and it is of the essence of Free Trade doctrine), is that imports can in no wise be detrimental to home production or industry, since what is bought from abroad is purchased with home products, for which a market has thus been opened.

There is perhaps in all this *Théorie des Débouchés* nothing very original. The essence of the doctrine can be found, for instance, in Quesnay's *Dialogue du Commerce*, where he says categorically: 'que tout achat est vente, et que toute vente est achat,' and where he contends, as has been noticed in an earlier chapter, that the mercantilist doctrine of selling more than is bought merely aims at a 'commerce commencé.' Nor are the conclusions drawn by Say from the *Loi des Débouchés* different from those to be found in Smith or Quesnay. His conclusion with regard to foreign trade, for instance, is but an echo, not merely of certain famous observations of Smith and Hume, but also of Quesnay's dictum: 'si ceux avec qui nous commerçons n'etaient pas riches, nous ferions un pauvre commerce.'

There is more active dissent from Smith in Say's doctrine of immaterial products, which may be noticed briefly.[5] Smith, misled by his idea that wealth must be 'susceptible of conservation,' has classified all manner of services as examples of unproductive labour. But take the case of the doctor who cures a sick man. Who (least of all the sick man) would say that this labour was unproductive? Further, was the 'product' of the doctor incapable of being made the subject of an exchange? 'In no wise, since the advice of the doctor has been exchanged against his fees; but the need of this advice ceased the moment it was given. Its production consisted in saying it; its consumption in hearing it; it has been consumed simultaneously with its production.'[6] Such, then, are Say's immaterial products, where consumption—the consumption of a song, for instance— necessarily coincides with production. While these may linger in the memory they have no exchangeable value once the moment of production is past, and clearly, as they are incapable of accumulation, they cannot increase the national capital. And for this reason there are dangers (which almost bring him back to Smith's point of view) in an excessive amount of immaterial products, since in increasing this kind of productive labour, the consumption is inevitably at the same time correspondingly increased, and nothing is left over. If the consumption is a pleasure, good and well, but who is benefited if the complexity of the law merely

[5] *Ibid.*, Vol. I, chap. 13.
[6] *Ibid.*, Vol. I, chap. 13, p.121.

gives employment to lawyers, and puts up their fees?[7] Adam Smith smiles approval in the background.

On one other point, at least, Say went some distance towards breaking new ground, though he did not tarry long enough to harvest the fruit. Ricardo, in his twentieth chapter, pillories Say for his confused statements on value, setting out fourteen quotations and wringing his hands despairingly over the inconsistencies involved. It would indeed be difficult to summarize succinctly Say's views on value, nor perhaps do they greatly matter. Inconsistency may spring from muddleheadedness, or from a laudable groping away from an untenable theory, even if the journey be never completed. Say, in brief, was prepared to attach much more importance to the idea of 'utility' than were his English contemporaries. Indeed by a careful choice of extracts, it is possible to find in Say an exponent of a theory of value which is wholly psychological, and in which the idea of cost of production is more or less eliminated. Doubtless these could be rebutted by other extracts, in the compilation of which Ricardo will be found serviceable. It is not, he says in one place, 'the value of the productive services which determines the value of the products.' On the contrary, 'it is the utility of the product which makes it sought out, and which confers upon it a value; and it is the faculty of being able to create this utility which makes the productive services be sought out, and which confers upon them a value.'[8] So also he speaks of the utility of a commodity raising its price to the cost of production; if it fails to do so, nothing is of course produced.[9] Even more

---

[7] *Ibid.*, Vol. I, pp.124-125. It is curious to note the *laissez-faire* doctrine come out at this point: 'Administrer ce qui devrait être abandonné à soi-même, c'est faire du mal aux administrés, et leur faire payer le mal qu'on leur fait comme si c'était un bien.'
[8] *Ibid.*, Vol. II, chap. I, p.9.
[9] *Ibid.*, Vol. II, p.17.

emphatically, he states that 'the value of the means of production comes from the value of the product which may result, which is founded on the use which can be made of this product or the satisfaction which can be drawn from it.'[10] These, in the history of the theory of value, would be interesting utterances, even if they led nowhere. Ricardo was dissatisfied internally with his theory of value; Say was more vocal in expressing his doubts.

Lastly, Say sings the praises of the entrepreneur, is strictly non-interventionist, and represents the aspirations of an industrial age.

Senior

In such an introductory narrative as this, in which stars of the second magnitude must suffer extinction, some who are almost of the first rank must be accorded a brevity of notice which hardly corresponds with their real deserts. Of the considerable tribe of spiritual sons of Ricardo, Nassau William Senior[11] (1790-1864) is the one who in the next generation most calls for notice, firstly because he was himself an interesting personality, and secondly he also has to his credit a phrase which has been tossed down the years on the waves of economic controversy. Two points in Senior are perhaps worthy of mention here, the first relating primarily to his views regarding the 'scope and method' of Political Economy, the second relating to his analysis of the function of capital in production.

On the first point, Senior represents a definite narrowing

[10] 'Un champ ou une usine ne procurent directement aucune satisfaction appreciable a leur possesseur; leur valeur vient donc de la valeur du produit qui peut en sortir, laquelle est fondée sur l'usage qu'on peut faire de ce produit, sur la satisfaction qu'on en peut tirer' (Vol. ii, p.24).
[11] Born 1790; called to the Bar; Professor at Oxford; member of the Royal Commission on the Poor Laws, 1832.

of the sphere of economics, and an accentuation of the tendency towards a certain aloofness and rigidity. He is indeed in theory (he is less so in practice) the supreme exponent of that view which regards economics as an abstract and deductive science which can be most appropriately pursued in a comfortable arm-chair by the fireside, in an inspiring cloud of tobacco smoke. For him Political Economy is, in its strictest sense, the science which deals with the nature, the production and the distribution of wealth, and the economist who knows his job must stop short of anything which might be called an art. Practical questions, no matter of what kind, 'no more form part of the science of Political Economy . . . than navigation forms part of the science of astronomy.' Moreover, the conclusions of the economist, 'whatever be their generality and their truth, do not authorize him in adding a single syllable of advice.' His business is neither to recommend nor to dissuade, but solely to state general principles.[12]

This represents an admirable spirit of aloofness, though it is perhaps asking too much of the economist to expect him, by a pure process of ratiocination, to arrive at conclusions, and to be thereafter content to leave them to someone else to chew. Yet Senior is herein probably merely overstressing a truth which assumes a more palatable form when he suggests that in the tangled problems of this world it may be 'neither advisable, nor perhaps practicable' to regard the economic consideration as providing the sole, or perhaps even the principal, guide. In the abstract science which Senior contemplates, it will be observed, reasoning is more important than observation.[13] Not only so, in his hands it professedly becomes very largely a matter of the precise meaning of terms. Thus he warns his readers that

[12] *Political Economy*, pp.2-3.
[13] *Ibid.*, p.5.

his treatise will consist, in a great degree, 'of discussions as to the most convenient use of a few familiar words.'[14] Had Senior lived up to his professions, Political Economy, as practised by him, would have become a useful exercise in the Socratic art of definition.

But on what is reasoning to operate, if economics is primarily a matter of reasoning rather than of observation? The answer almost takes away our breath by its calm daring. All Political Economy is comprised in what flows from a few general propositions, 'the result of observation and consciousness.' These propositions, to be precise, are four in number. As they are so typical of a certain phase of economic doctrine, it may be as well to reproduce them in abridged form. The first is 'that every man desires to obtain additional wealth with as little sacrifice as possible.' Here is the economic man stalking abroad as a postulate on which economic science is built. The second proposition is a statement of the Malthusian law, to the effect that the population of the world is 'limited only by physical or moral evil.' The third proposition is a statement which, according to the point of view, may either indicate the functions of capital or the principle of increasing returns in industry. It lays down that 'the powers of labour, and of the other instruments which produce wealth, may be indefinitely increased by using their products as the means of further production.' The last of the four fundamental propositions is a statement of the Law of Diminishing Returns as applied to agriculture. The first of these propositions, Senior obligingly tells us, is a matter of consciousness; the three others are matters of observation. Now nothing could be easier than to make hay of Senior's four fundamental propositions or postulates. The first is presumed to be a truism; like most truisms, it is probably funda-

[14] *Ibid.*, p.5.

mentally untrue. The Malthusian generalization is certainly not true of all times and places (as Malthus assumed it was), and to many it has not been a matter of observation. The Laws of Increasing and Diminishing Returns again require a nicety of statement of which Senior was singularly insensible. It is certainly a crude generalization to say, with Senior, that 'additional labour when employed in manufactures is *more*, when employed in agriculture is *less*, efficient in proportion.'[15] This may be the result of observation, but not much is gained if the observation is inaccurate. His first principle, embodying a raw hedonism, may therefore by some be rejected. The other three propositions are anything but observations to be swallowed at sight; they are the end of a long process of economic reasoning and observation, rather than tolerably axiomatic postulates from which reasoning may begin. This, however, for our present purpose is relatively of minor importance. What is of interest is the abstract view of Political Economy as a branch of knowledge which is wholly enfolded in four postulates which, at the bidding of a sufficiently imperious mind, can be summoned to yield up their hidden economic profundities.

Such a programme, if rigorously adhered to, might have been expected to lead to a wholly academic science resting on barren logomachies. Fortunately, however, Senior did not turn economics into a logical exercise in the inferences to be drawn from four propositions. He had an acute, a penetrating and a logical mind; and his passion for accuracy in the use of his terms and in his definitions enabled him in many respects to be usefully critical of his predecessors. In particular on one point he introduced a phrase which embodies a range of suggestive ideas, even though the phrase has likewise occasioned merriment in certain quarters. In

[15] *Ibid.*, p.81.

his analysis of the agents of production, he carefully avoided the word 'capital' on the ground that it 'has been so variously defined that it may be doubtful whether it have any generally received meaning.'[16] (Senior, careful in his nomenclature, is also careful in his use of the subjunctive.) Accordingly his instruments of production are labour, natural agents – which is certainly preferable to the fatuous use of the word 'land' – and *abstinence*. He rejects the word 'capital,' because in the ordinary acceptation of the term it has come to mean 'an article of wealth, the result of human exertion, employed in the production or distribution of wealth.'[17] But capital, as thus defined, is not a simple productive instrument; it is itself the result of the co-operation of labour, of the natural agents, and of the other thing which Senior calls 'abstinence.' By 'abstinence' Senior means 'that agent, distinct from labour and the agency of Nature, the concurrence of which is necessary to the existence of capital, and which stands in the same relation to profit as labour does to wages.'[18] It will be seen what Senior has done. He has replaced capital, which is normally conceived as a dead and objective thing, by a human sacrifice, obviously entitled to a reward. For that there is here a human sacrifice, Senior has no doubt: 'To abstain from the enjoyment which is in our power, or to seek distant rather than immediate results, are among the most painful exertions of the human will.' Consequently, when we come to an analysis of cost of production, the elements into which it is resolved are wholly subjective. By cost of production is meant 'the sum of the labour and abstinence necessary to production.[19] The reward of the capitalist is thus seen to be the reward due to abstinence, the price which it is necessary to pay in order to induce

[16] *Ibid.*, p.59.   [17] *Ibid.*, p.59.   [18] *Ibid.*, p.59.
[19] *Ibid.*, p.101.

people to abstain from claiming, in the present, rights which have accrued. The word 'abstinence' is perhaps unfortunate, because of its regrettable psychological association with 'total'; but it is only because 'abstinence' in a restricted sense has come to connote a monastic asceticism that it is possible to find amusement in the idea of a Rothschild being rewarded for his abstinence.

J. S. Mill

To withhold from John Stuart Mill[20] (1806-1873) the compliment of a separate chapter, and to bundle him into a second-class compartment along with Say, Senior and Cairnes may appear little short of high treason. For all but the greatest of the dead, however, life is a continuous decline until the indignity of a recording footnote is reached. Yet there are more substantial reasons for holding that in such an introduction as this, Mill need not be subjected to a lengthy examination. With regard to Mill's position in the development of Political Economy, there is singular unanimity among the commentators. For one, Mill briefly represents the 'restatement'; in the eyes of another, he provides 'a skilful statement of the chief results of the previous generation'; a third regards him as presenting the classical doctrines in their final crystalline form; a fourth looks on his *Principles* as an *œuvre d'assemblage*. Where so many agree, Mill himself not dissenting, it may be assumed that truth lies somewhere in the direction of these concurring pointers. Ricardo and Malthus had introduced the main themes of the economic symphony – not perhaps remarkably harmonious themes; in the interval, these themes had been somewhat distorted by critics like Rae

[20] Born 1806, the son of James Mill, and the victim of an extraordinary educational experiment which might have been expected to produce worse results than it did. For thirty-five years at the India Office. For a short time in Parliament.

and Lauderdale, and discordant motifs of an entirely different character had been introduced by the wind instruments of the early socialists like the St. Simonians and the Fourierists. The confused listeners were beginning to be doubtful as to what it was all about. It was time for the main theme to be restated, with the confidence and the assurance that comes from a liberal use of brass, and to work into the restatement just sufficient of the intervening dissident and dissentient themes as might be necessary for the æsthetic satisfaction of the hearers. This was the task Mill took in hand; his work is a restatement of the main doctrines of Ricardo and Malthus by one not insensible of the criticisms of the intervening thirty or forty years.

Mill's pre-eminence rests on the extraordinary skill with which he accomplished his mission. The high moral tone which pervades the *Principles* made it acceptable to an age which, in essentials, was austere; and its literary competence was a feature which had not been too common a characteristic of Mill's predecessors. In the result, it is probably true that Mill, for a period of two generations, taught this country its economics, either through his own *Principles*, or through other works for which these *Principles* cannot shake off responsibility. While this may be an excellent reason for erecting a bust of Mill in a Political Economy lecture-room, it is also a reason for assigning him disproportionately small space in an introductory history of economic doctrine. For the people who are most interesting for our present purpose are those who, however gropingly, first state a fruitful idea, not those who at the end of a generation's discussion sum up and present the world with a restatement. Apart from certain elaborations of the theory of foreign trade, it is doubtful whether Mill added much, or anything, to the body of economic doctrine. A recent somewhat severe critic has indeed stated that, objectively, Mill

teaches us nothing new, adding that it is easier to point
out the doctrinal errors committed by Mill than to indicate
his contribution to the development of theory.[21]

It does not of course follow that Mill's presentation is
colourless, or that there are not degress of emphasis, and
indeed modifications, of the traditional classical doctrines.
Mill, like everyone else, had his hobby horses, though they
were conspicuously absent from his nursery. Without
attempting to present consecutively his main ideas, which
were largely the ideas of Malthus, of Ricardo and of his
father, it may be permissible to indicate some of the points
which, owing to the emphasis laid upon them by Mill,
stand out as pre-eminently revealing the mind of the
writer.

The first point of interest strikes one in the preface and
on the title-page. Mill professedly set out to write an up-to-
date Adam Smith. That, in fact, he rather wrote a 'read-
able Ricardo' is immaterial. What is of interest is the
reason that impelled Mill to take Smith as his model; it is
that Smith 'invariably associates the principles with their
applications,' and 'perpetually appeals to other and often
far larger considerations than pure Political Economy
affords.' This point of view also affects the title-page, where
after the orthodox 'Principles of Political Economy,' there
appears the words: 'with some of their applications to
social philosophy.' Political Economy, in short, was for
Mill part of something larger, and in his own mind he was
not content to be merely a theorist. Like his master,
Bentham, he was as much as anything a social reformer.
Senior might declare that the economist, *qua* economist,
was never authorized in adding a single syllable of advice.
For Mill, to give advice was the very essence of life. His
theory may, to a large extent, be a modified restatement;

[21] Bousquet, *Essai sur l'Éolution de la Pensée Économique*, p.91.

264   THE DEVELOPMENT OF ECONOMIC DOCTRINE

the essential Mill is rather to be found in his proposals for reform, whether these are to be sought in his advocacy of peasant proprietors, of co-operation, of the taxation of rent, or of restriction of inheritance.

With this general view of economics as a study which almost becomes subservient to its practical applications, it is necessary to take one tenet which is peculiarly Mill's, and which indeed he himself regarded as the chief merit of his treatment of the subject. This is his famous distinction between the nature of the laws of production and those of distribution. The laws of the production of wealth, Mill held, 'partake of the character of physical truths. There is nothing optional or arbitrary in them.' Whatever be our likes or dislikes in the matter, such principles as the Law of Diminishing Returns are there. Our opinions and our wishes have no control over the things themselves. It is, however – so Mill held – entirely different when we turn to the distribution of wealth; there we are in the realm of 'human institution solely.' 'The things once there,' men can do with them as they like, and it follows therefore that 'the distribution of wealth depends on the laws and customs of society.'[22] Such is Mill's rigid distinction between the field of production where inexorable law, uncontrolled by man, prevails, and the other field of distribution, which is also doubtless subject to a law, but to a law of man's making and revising. It is almost unnecessary to observe that Mill's strict line of differentiation is indefensible. Doubtless 'the things once there,' an omniscient, omnipotent, omnicompetent Parliament may decree any distribution which, in its lack of wisdom, may seem good to it; but if in these matters it errs against popular sentiment, it will not be long until the things are not there. An unquestioned

[22] *Principles, Book* II, chap. I.

power to control distribution brings little comfort, if the exercise of that power dries up the stream of production, and so leaves nothing to distribute. The difference here from the older classical economists is obvious. For them the laws of distribution were as inexorable as any other. Mill, in sweeping all this into a sphere controlled by human volition, made it possible for him to be the speculative reformer, calmly contemplating the coming of the communistic state.

For increasingly, as Mill grew older, his reforming zeal led him to a Platonic and sentimental flirtation with socialism, though he was never brought to the point of seriously declaring his intentions. If the choice were between communism and individual property – not as it might be, but as it now is – then, he says, 'all the difficulties, great or small, of communism, would be but as dust in the balance.'[23] The socialism of Mill is a curious study, but only this need be said here. Mill was unable to resist suggestions or ideas from whatever source they came; he was likewise constitutionally incapable of assimilating these ideas with the creed in which he was brought up and which was more peculiarly his own. In consequence there is at times a considerable incongruity, not to say inconsistency, in ideas which he advances concurrently. His socialism is a deposit of a period later than his main ideas; and when a socialist outcrop is detected, it is obvious that it lies very uncomformably on the older strata. In fact, in his heart Mill remained an unregenerate individualist to the end, and even his socialism is rooted in individualistic ideas. When he speaks of legislation favouring equality of fortunes, the incorrigible individualist adds: 'so far as is consistent with the just claim of the individual to the fruits, whether great or small, of his or her own industry.'[24]

[23] *Ibid.*, Book II, chap. I, sec. 3.
[24] *Ibid.*, Book IV, chap. 6, sec. 2.

He boggles at such an embryonic socialistic proposal as progressive taxation, on the ground that 'to tax the larger incomes at a higher percentage than the smaller, is to lay a tax on industry and economy; to impose a penalty on people for having worked harder and saved more than their neighbours.'[25] He ties himself into knots in the chapter on Bequest and Inheritance, because even in his zeal for reform he is obsessed with the individualistic idea that bequest, as one of the sacred rights of property, must not be tampered with, and hinting at the desirability of a system which would 'restrict, not what anyone might bequeath, but what anyone should be permitted to acquire, by bequest or inheritance.'[26] The reforms dearest to his heart, the extension of peasant proprietorship and the fusion of labour and capital in a system of co-partnership, are of the essence of individualism, and his utterances in defence and praise of competition[27] fit in badly with socialism, which, if it means anything, means the elimination of competition. Mill's socialism was perhaps scarcely a 'gesture,' as the current jargon has it; but it was a sentimental infusion which never harmonized with the rest of Mill's system of thought, even though Mill himself was happily unaware of the fact.

Apart from the question of Mill's general standpoint, a hint may be added regarding some of the points emphasized, or supposed to be emphasized, in his restatement. It is impossible to glance through Mill without being struck by the influence exercised on him by the Malthusian generalization; and as an increase of population is terrifying only because of the base question of food, the Law of Diminishing Returns is placed by Mill in a place of high

[25] *Ibid.*, Book v, chap. 2, sec. 3.
[26] *Ibid.*, Book ii, chap. 2, sec. 3.
[27] *Ibid.*, Book iv, chap. 7, sec. 7.

honour or dishonour. It is the 'most important proposition in political economy.'[28] In writing on the population question, his voice quivers with a righteous indignation which leads him to a violence of language nowhere to be found in Malthus. Excessive procreation is for Mill on the same level as drunkenness or any other physical excess, and those who are guilty should be discountenanced and despised accordingly.[29] To appreciate his crusading fury in this cause, it is necessary to turn to his views regarding wages. The celebrated wages fund doctrine has, not with entire justice, become peculiarly associated with Mill—probably because when the fallacy was exposed, Mill publicly recanted, and the recantation has tended to hang round Mill's neck the faith in respect of which he expressed his recantation. But indeed the wages fund doctrine was more or less common property. It can be deduced from Malthus; amongst other places it is to be found concisely stated by Senior in the form that wages depend 'on the extent of the fund for the maintenance of labourers, compared with the number of labourers to be maintained.'[30] Mill has some difficulty in getting a convenient phrase for 'the aggregate of what may be called the wages fund of a country'; but his theory is essentially that of a pre-determined fund set aside for wages, a definite number of workers among whom that fund must be shared, and a distribution effected under the influence of competition. From this Mill draws the inference that 'wages cannot rise, but by an increase of the aggregate funds employed in hiring labourers, or a diminution in the number of competitors for hire.' The wages fund, in the sense of a portion of the capital of the country irrevocably set aside for the payment of wages, is, of course, a

[28] *Ibid.*, Book I, *chap.* 12, sec. 2.
[29] *Ibid.*, Book II, chap. 13, sec. 1.
[30] Senior, *Political Economy*, p.154.

pure myth, but it led Mill to consider that only one method of raising wages could escape the charge of futility. That method lay in a due restriction of population.

Mill's discussion of value is perhaps memorable, not so much by reason of its substance or conclusions, as on account of his unfortunate assurance that here at last all ghosts were laid. 'Happily,' he observes, 'there is nothing in the laws of value which remains for the present or any future writer to clear up; the theory of the subject is complete.'[31] By a strange Nemesis this threatens to become the most frequently quoted of all Mill's utterances, furnishing, as it does, to the young, a useful warning that it is never safe to be sure of anything.

One last curiosity in Mill is represented by his conception of the stationary state,[32] a curious blend of economics, philosophy and poetry. Like Sismondi, Mill felt impelled to ask 'to what goal' society is tending by its industrial progress, and 'when the progress ceases, in what condition are we to expect that it will leave mankind?' Mill, it will be observed, assumes that progress must cease, just as the same Mill was flung into an agony of gloom, reflecting that as there is but a limited number of musical tones and semitones, and also a limited number of ways in which these may be combined, the world would one day – and that before long – have whistled its last tune.[33] The annual publications of Messrs. Francis, Day and Hunter give no indication that the day is yet imminent. But to Mill it is axiomatic that, as the increase of wealth is not boundless, so beyond the progressive state, there must lie the stationary state, when the stream of human industry shall 'finally

[31] *Principles*, Book III, chap. I, sec. I.
[32] *Ibid.*, Book IV, chap. 6.
[33] 'I was seriously tormented by the thought of the exhaustibility of musical combinations. . . . Most of these, it seemed to me, must have been already discovered.' (*Autobiography*, chap. 5.)

spread itself out into an apparently stagnant sea.' To some
this prospect of the stationary state may appear depressing,
ending in shallows and in miseries; but not so to Mill, who
draws a pleasantly coloured picture of a state with population and industry alike held in equilibrium, with no extremes of wealth or poverty, with no undue hustle, and over
it all a faint suggestion of the indolent charm of the island
of the lotus-eaters. But though stationary, so far as capital
and industry are concerned, it need not be a stationary
state of human improvement. It will still be open to the
grandsons of Angus to write books with philosophic uplift.
It is a curious epilogue to classical Political Economy,
which at its beginnings – or so its critics suggested – had
exalted the thruster and the climber.

Cairnes

A survey of the orthodox school, the spiritual descendants
of Ricardo, may fittingly conclude with a brief reference to
John Elliott Cairnes[34] (1823-1875), in some ways the last of
the line. When Mill recanted on the wages fund doctrine,
Cairnes continued to show cause why the Master should
not have succumbed to the attacks of Longe and Thornton.
Among the faithless, faithful only he – or almost so, for one
must not forget Professor Fawcett. A perusal of Cairnes's
works reveals an acute, a vigorous and a subtle mind, engaged in refining the achievement of Mill; a mind, nevertheless, which was rather impervious to new ideas. Only
two points need detain us here; firstly, his views as to
the scope and function of Political Economy, and secondly,
his doctrine with regard to 'non-competing groups,'

[34] Born in Ireland in 1823; educated at Trinity College, Dublin;
studied law; Professor at Dublin and Galway, and later at London.
His chief works are *The Character and Logical Method of Political
Economy*, and *Some Leading Principles of Political Economy*.

which represents the most vital and enduring idea of
Cairnes.

To the general question of the purpose and nature of
Political Economy as a study, Cairnes devoted one of his
chief works, *The Character and Logical Method of Political
Economy*. The main argument is somewhat reminiscent of
Senior. Political Economy, in Cairnes's view, has suffered
from the intrusion of alien elements, represented by 'considerations of equity and expediency.'[35] But so long as
Political Economy is given the task of accomplishing
definite practical ends, it can have none of the characteristics of a science. Economics, then, for Cairnes, is to be
rigidly scientific, and in order that it may be so, it is to be
cut off from all practical considerations, and issue an unlimited declaration of neutrality, standing 'apart from all
particular systems of social and industrial existence.'[36]
Political Economy, he says in a passage frequently quoted,
is to be regarded as

'standing neutral between competing social schemes;
neutral, as the science of Mechanics stands neutral between
competing plans of railway construction, in which expense,
for instance, as well as mechanical efficiency, is to be considered; neutral, as Chemistry stands neutral between competing plans of sanitary improvement; as Physiology stands
neutral between opposing systems of medicine. It supplies
the means, or more correctly, a portion of the means for
estimating all; it refuses to identify itself with any.'[37]

'Economic Science,' in short, 'has no more connection with
our present industrial system than the science of mechanics
has with our present system of railways.'

[35] *Character and Logical Method*, pp.14-16.
[36] *Ibid.*, p.20
[37] *Ibid.*, p.21.

This, even if truth, is an over-accentuation of truth. If this austere doctrine were honoured in practice, it would mean the separation of economics from its living inspiration; and the effect of taking at their face-value the views expressed by Cairnes elsewhere, is to accentuate the abstract, detached, academic nature of economic study. His whole argument tends to make economic science exclusively a deductive study.[38] For induction, experiment is necessary, and in the nature of things this is excluded from the armoury of the economist. The facts, moreover, are too overwhelming:

'He [the economist] must take economic phenomena as they are presented to him in the world without, in all their complexity and ever-changing variety; but from facts as thus presented, if he declines to avail himself of any other path than that of strict induction, he may reason till the crack of doom without arriving at any conclusion of the slightest value.'[39]

But as against this handicap, the economist, compared with the physicist, has one mighty advantage. 'Mankind has no direct knowledge of ultimate physical principles'; and it is only as a result of long groping, 'after a long period of laborious inductive research,' that the scientist can arrive at the generalizations from which he reasons.[40] But 'the economist starts with a knowledge of ultimate causes'[41] —happy man! 'He is already, at the outset of his enterprise, in the position which the physicist only attains after ages of laborious research.' These ultimate causes, needless to say, centre round the behaviour of the economic man; they consist of 'certain mental feelings and certain animal propensities in human beings.' These ultimate

[38] Ibid., p.64.
[39] Ibid., pp.65-66.
[40] Ibid., pp.70-71.
[41] Ibid., p.75.

causes, of which we have direct knowledge, are obviously closely akin to Senior's four fundamental propositions.

The cold philosophic truth is again, perhaps, over-emphasized in Cairnes's views regarding the nature of an economic law. He rightly indicates in what sense Political Economy must be regarded as a hypothetical science.[42] Its conclusions are true when no disturbing causes intervene—a condition, as Cairnes adds, which is scarcely ever realized. An economic law, in short, expresses not a positive but a hypothetical truth, and it follows also that a law relating to economic phenomena 'can neither be established nor refuted by an appeal to the records of such phenomena.' The proof must rest on an appeal to certain principles of human nature, operating under certain physical conditions. So also to refute an economic law, it is necessary to show that the 'principles' (i.e. of human action, etc.) do not exist, or that the economist, on the way to his conclusion, has fallen a victim to a logical gin. Putting it briefly, the nature of an economic law is such that it can neither be established nor refuted by an appeal to facts.[43]

Viewed merely as a question in epistemology, it may be that Cairnes's views are defensible. It is not merely desirable, but essential, that periodically we should test the basis and limits of our knowledge—indeed, ask ourselves whether we can properly know anything at all. For this purpose a wise society maintains a staff of philosophers and metaphysicians. But the plain man has difficulty in resisting the impression that an undue addiction to questions of scope, method and what-not, betokens an unhealthily introspective frame of mind. Much of what Cairnes says, as he himself realizes, is applicable to other branches of knowledge; but so far as he

---

[42] *Ibid.*, p.51.   [43] *Ibid.*, pp.99, 107.

was understood (or misunderstood), his influence was in the direction of making economics an abstract, formal study. It does not require much perversion of Cairnes to see in him an exponent of the view that economics is solely a deductive study, reasoning from certain general principles, proud of its impartiality in the world's affairs, and arriving at conclusions which, in the nature of things, cannot be refuted by an appeal to the hard facts of reality. Should the facts appear to be in contradiction with economic law, so much the worse for the facts. Even if this be perversion, the fact that classical Political Economy came to appear in this guise was, in large measure, its undoing.

Apart from questions of methodology, Cairnes is chiefly to be remembered for his conception of 'non-competing groups' and the inferences drawn therefrom. His opening chapter on value (in *Some Leading Principles*) is primarily interesting because of his manifest failure to understand Jevons. His own view of value is in the orthodox line, but with critical reservations. He criticizes Mill's analysis of 'cost of production' with a subtlety which never abandoned him. No two ideas, he says, are more opposed to each other than 'cost' and 'reward of cost.'[44] Cost and remuneration are 'economic antitheses of each other.' Wages and profits of capital, into which, in the main, Mill analyses cost of production, are not costs at all. Costs are sacrifices,[45] and these factors in Mill's analysis are the rewards of sacrifices, not the sacrifices themselves. Thus, in the orthodox form of the doctrine which Cairnes combats, cost of production is resolved solely into capitalist's costs, and it follows likewise that the principle that cost of production determines value becomes the assertion of an identical proposition.[46] Thus in place of the capitalist's objective costs, Cairnes outlines a

---

[44] *Leading Principles*, p.50.
[45] *Ibid.*, p.60.   [46] *Ibid.*, p.53.

theory, reminiscent of Senior, in which cost of production is based on subjective considerations, and is represented by the various sacrifices made – the labour, the abstinence, the risk, not the money rewards of these various elements.[47]

The possibilities of determining such a subjective 'cost of production,' however, need not detain us; we are concerned merely with the disentanglement of the idea of non-competing groups. It is to competition that we must look as the agent which brings remuneration into proportion with the sacrifices undergone; so also competition is the 'security for the correspondence of the values of commodities with the costs of their production.'[48] Cost of production will only regulate values if there is 'effective competition.' Cairnes was thus led to consider how far such effectiveness of competition did exist, since, if there be any obstacle, 'whether law, ignorance or poverty,' competition will be defeated, and consequently it will not follow that commodities will exchange according to their cost, i.e., the amount of sacrifice involved.[49] Cairnes, somewhat too easily satisfied, finds that capital has a reasonable fullness of choice, since capital, while in a disposable form, may be applied in any direction.[50] It it not so with labour. Labour, whose occupation is not yet finally determined, does not have a choice over the entire range of industry:

'What we find, in effect, is, not a whole population competing indiscriminately for all occupations, but a series of industrial layers, superposed on one another, within each of which the various candidates for employment possess a real and effective power of selection, while those occupying the several strata are, for all purposes of effective competition, practically isolated from each other.'[51]

---

[47] *Ibid.*, p.81. [48] *Ibid.*, p.63. [49] *Ibid.*, p.64.
[50] *Ibid.*, p.70. [51] *Ibid.*, p.72.

Thus we are 'compelled to recognize the existence of non-competing industrial groups as a feature of our social economy.' The point, sufficiently obvious in itself, becomes important, because Cairnes uses it to make considerable modifications in the theory of value. For it is only within any group that commodities will exchange according to their cost of production; as between two non-competing groups, exchange will take place on another principle, which indeed is none other than that of reciprocal demand, familiar in the theory of foreign trade. The failure of the principle of cost in the case of non-competing groups is exemplified in the relative remuneration of the producers of different articles. Remuneration is in proportion to sacrifice within a group, but not when the comparison is instituted between two groups. The advantageousness of one group compared with another – as in the case of foreign trade – will depend on the reciprocal demands of one group for the produce of the other.[52]

Cairnes's theory of non-competing groups is chiefly of interest because he uses it to undermine the traditional cost-of-production theory of value; and moreover, in shifting the emphasis to the subjective idea of the sacrifice involved, he went farther than he realized in the direction of Jevons and the Austrians. Had he gone a little farther, he would probably have gone a great deal farther. Thus in discussing why skilled labour receives higher wages than unskilled, he rightly explains that this is not in fact necessarily the case, that skill itself is not an element of cost, and that 'the result in question [i.e., a higher remuneration] only occurs where skilled labour represents a monopoly.' The decisive consideration is to be sought in 'the circumstances which limit the possession of this skill to a small number of persons as

[52] *Ibid.*, pp.75-79.

compared with the demand for their services.'[53] A later generation would have said that when the workers are limited in numbers, the marginal productivity of labour is high; it is what Cairnes, innocent of the margin, is trying to say.

[53] *Ibid.*, p. 85.

CHAPTER XI

Karl Marx

IN a volume of ampler proportions than this, the early history of socialism might claim, and might deservedly receive, the tribute of an independent chapter, though doubtless it might be urged that these early socialists were dreamers and not economists. Here they must be content with such notice as is indispensable for a comprehension of the works of Marx. Socialism, according to taste, begins with Plato, in virtue of his advocacy of communism; or with More's Utopia, where the evils of private property are denounced and the doctrine of exploitation expounded. But viewed from the Marxian angle, the socialism which preceded Marx, and which earned his undisguised contempt, was that of the so-called Utopian socialists, whose writings date from the earlier part of the nineteenth century.

It is among these that we must look for the 'father of socialism,' though the number of claimants to paternity is embarrassingly large. Firstly, there is St. Simon (1760-1825) – *not* the writer of the memoirs – an eccentric nobleman who foresaw the coming of a new age which would be industrial in character, and who sought assiduously, in many pamphlets and what-nots, to discuss where spiritual leadership in this new and uncharted age was to be found. The mark of this new world, intent on the exploitation of the globe, was to be the abolition of privileges. St. Simon's socialism is of the weakest, if indeed it exists at all, but his followers, the propagators of a strange religion, extended his doctrine to include the abolition of the greatest of all privileges, that of inheritance, and thus, making the State the residuary legatee, they found a short cut to State socialism. Then there is Fourier (1772-1837), a man of a disordered mind, full of the disconcerting flashes which so frequently enlighten the deranged. His vision was of a re-organized world on the basis of the 'phalanx,' a co-operative group, and with such phalanges the world would ultimately be covered to the number of 2,985,984. His is the socialism of co-operation, designed to replace the horrible waste and inefficiency, the divided and clashing interests of civiliza-tion, where all men profit by each other's misfortunes. There is our own Robert Owen (1771-1858), a man greater in his earlier practical years, when he figured as the ideal employer, than in the adventures and the speculations of his later life. For him also the path of salvation lay in co-operation, and in the establishment of settlements more or less communistic in character, as evidenced in New Harmony. Fourthly (and lastly here), there was Louis Blanc (1813-1882), a transitional mind, pointing rather to later socialism and therefore scarcely Utopian. His idea likewise was to eliminate competi-tion by association; but in his case, the State, the banker of the poor, was to be the agent to initiate the great scheme of reform, launching the co-operative bodies, which later were to drive the capitalist from the field.

Such were the Utopians, most of whom were also 'associa-tionists.' They were Utopians because they believed that the realization of socialism was essentially an affair of getting someone to 'launch' something, and thereafter the business would be done. They were 'associationists,' because in the main they visualized the coming of socialism through the formation and extension of groups living together on socialistic principles. Fourier, waiting at home for one hour a day for the unknown capitalist who should enable him to establish his first phalanx, is the pathetic symbol alike of the lovableness and ineffectiveness of the earlier socialists.

With Karl Marx[1] (1818-1883) all this changes. Socialism now definitely enters the main current of economic doctrine because, with Marx, socialism becomes a body of doctrine relying on the support of economic argument – also, in Marx's case at least, a body of prophecy resting on the interpretation of recent and current economic phenomena. Herein lies the significance of the transition of socialism from the former type, somewhat contemptuously dubbed 'Utopian,' to that newer variety, rather vaingloriously branded as 'scientific.' To the new age the Utopian socialists appeared as dreamers, men who had touching faith in the power of an Act of Parliament to serve as the basis of an ideal commonwealth, who were even so childish as to believe that an appeal to justice, mercy and right had power to move the hearts of men. The Utopian socialists might appeal to sentiment to prove the desirability and the æsthetic beauty of socialism; such a procedure would cut no ice. It was better policy to prove, by economic reasoning, the inevitablity of socialism; to mingle together economic argument and an interpretation of history, and thereby to show that, things being as they are, their consequences will be what they will be; and that the only outcome, ineluctable and inescapable, is the establishment of the socialist state.

The literature of Marxism is such a Sahara of books, and the controversies as to what Marxism means, even among the faithful and the expert, are so perennial that it is even more necessary here than elsewhere to discard all but the

[1] Born at Trier, 1818. Studied at Bonn and Berlin. Engaged in journalism on the *Rheinische Zeitung* (1842). Obliged to move about continually between Germany, France, Belgium and England until 1848. Thereafter, with few interruptions, he remained in London until his death in 1883. He played a leading part in the formation of the First International in 1864, and its subsequent proceedings; but in the main his life in London was devoted to reading and writing. The first volume of *Capital* appeared in 1867; the second and third appeared, after his death, in 1885 and 1894 respectively.

essential, even if that may lead to the driest of bare bones. And at the outset, in pursuance of this policy, the other commonly accepted founders of scientific socialism may be left aside. Rodbertus (1805-1875) was primarily a philosopher, evolving socialist doctrine in dignified retreat; something of a Fabian; in the immediate insistent present, rather a conservative and an aristocrat. The bitter controversy centring round Marx's alleged appropriation of the ideas of Rodbertus merely provides some slight refreshment in an otherwise arid waste. The third of the trinity, Lassalle (1825-1864), was essentially the agitator, the silver-tongued orator who, after a stormy life ending in a stormy death, became a legend, and who, for English readers, has had the good fortune to be embalmed in one of George Meredith's novels.

But Marx remains; and except for the antiquarian explorer into origins, Marx is to be identified with scientific socialism. Jealous, if misplaced patriotism may point out that he probably received a large measure of inspiration (and perhaps something more) from that remarkable early group of English socialists which comprised men like Hodgskin, Thompson and Bray; the disciples of Rodbertus may feel that their master has been shorn of his appropriate glory. These are trivial questions. Heaven may, or may not, deal justly in these matters. The indubitable fact is that all subsequent socialism has been dominated by Marx; and that even when subsequent schools have disowned him, they have owed their existence to a reaction from Marx. It is therefore permissible to confine this chapter to Marx, and to Marx alone.

More than most writers, Marx requires to be read with some knowledge of his life and character. From the conclusion of his student days until the age of thirty he lived the life of a rebel and an intriguer, at war with all governments, editing papers which were promptly suppressed, and uneasily flitting from one country to another, according to the exigencies of the situation. But from the age of thirty, that is to say following the Revolution of 1848, there began in 1849 the second part of Marx's life, the long period of his exile in London, which continued until his death in 1883. Though interrupted by occasional visits to the Continent, and though in part occupied with various revolutionary activities, Marx's life during this long period was primarily that of a recluse, whose waking hours were spent in the British Museum in devouring blue-books. Add to such a morbid life all the cares, privations, hardships, jealousies and suspicions inseparable from the existence of a political exile and, on the materialistic conception of history, some progress may be made towards a comprehension of Marx and his writings.

With regard to these writings, it is doubtful whether any man living has read, may read, or should read them all. For in the nature of things, Marx was a voluminous journalist and (horrid word) a publicist. In addition to his greater *pièces de résistance* (and the resisting power is great) he is therefore responsible for a copious pamphlet literature. And there is his correspondence. But for the ordinary man and the intelligent woman, three publications are sufficient, even if of these the whole may not be necessary. There is, first of all, *The Critique of Political Economy*, dating from 1859, which is rather by way of being a preliminary draft for *Capital*. Vastly more important, dating from 1848, is the *Communist Manifesto*, written in conjunction with the faithful Engels, which is of interest as showing how completely, apart from the psuedo-economic and scientific frills, the main elements of the Marxian system had been outlined by that date. Thirdly, there is *Capital*, the complete and overwhelming statement of the Marxian system, of which the first volume appeared in 1864. The second and third volumes did not appear in Marx's lifetime, but were edited by Engels, whose function it was to glue together the fragments and chips of the Marxian workshop. Everyone has a duty to endeavour to read the first volume of *Capital*; no one need be ashamed to admit defeat at the hands of Volumes II and III.

As an aid to a comprehension of the essential doctrines of Marx, it may be convenient (even at the risk of repetition) to endeavour to reduce his theories to a number of propositions. The greater the complexity of a country, the more is a preliminary study of a map a wise precaution. Leaving aside *obiter dicta* regarding the organization of society after the coming revolution (a topic on which Marx shows restraint) as being concerned with politics rather than with economics, and therefore outside our sphere, Marx's doctrines may essentially be described as a theory of value and of profit-making (exploitation), rooted in a certain view of the march of history, and pointing forward to the subversion of the existing capitalistic system. Putting aside, therefore, doctrines regarding the dictatorship of the proletariat as lying outside the immediate purpose of this chapter, Marx may, accordingly, be summarized without injustice in six propositions, or – since the propositional form is hardly necessary – in six catchwords, two relating to the interpretation of history, two being economic in character, relating to value and inferences therefrom, and two being rather of the nature of prophecy.

Firstly, there is the so-called materialistic conception of history, by which is meant that the dominating and determining factor in all history is economic in character.

Secondly, this materialistic conception of history finds its expression in an unintermittent class struggle. History is merely a record of class struggles; as soon as one is resolved, another is engendered. The materialistic conception of history and the class struggle furnish the sociological basis of the Marxian structure.

Thirdly, and coming now to economics, there is the Marxian theory of value; that is to say, the value of any commodity is merely the amount of labour, that is, of socially necessary labour, congealed in it.

Fourthly, applying this, we get the notion of surplus value. The workman sells his labour power, which produces more than it is necessary to give the worker in the form of wages. The difference is surplus value, which is pocketed by the capitalist and constitutes the exploitation of labour. Herein lies the impulse to the class struggle between the capitalist and the proletariat. These two last propositions together form the economic kernel of Marxism.

Fifthly, and approaching prophecy, the uncontrollable thirst of capital to increase the surplus value in every possible way leads, and will lead, to increasing misery and degradation of the working classes, and to the formation of an increasingly large Industrial Reserve Army of unemployed and under-employed.

Sixthly, and lastly, there is the Law of Capitalistic Accumulation. The large capitalist devours the smaller, so that the means of production become concentrated in ever fewer hands. Society becomes increasingly rent by commercial crises until the auspicious moment when the expropriators will be expropriated and the proletariat will enter into their heritage.

While an elementary discussion of Marx may be confined to an elucidation of what is involved in these six propositions, it is perhaps wise to preface a more detailed consideration by noting three points of more general interest. Firstly, as to the nature of Marx's masterpiece; *Capital*, viewed merely as a book, is surely one of the most bewildering of human productions. It is safe to say – indeed it is obvious from the *Communist Manifesto* – that the conclusions to be arrived at were firmly implanted in Marx's mind before he began to evolve his reasons. This in itself would be quite proper, if nevertheless an open mind were kept throughout. But in reading Marx, one feels that he was so convinced of the truth of his conclusions that he became careless as to the arguments used, and in some of the argumentative passages it is difficult to resist the impression that he is intent on befogging rather enlightening the reader. The pedantic parade of learning, the display of rather puerile mathematical formulæ, the dexterous skating on thin ice, the subtlety approaching at times perilously near to sophistry, produce on the unsophisticated reader the impression that he is confronted with a juggler or a necromancer who could without difficulty elicit from the most unpromising hat a teeming progeny of rabbits. In a book which, after all, attains the reasonable spaciousness of approximately 2,500 pages, an author ought to have room to turn round and make his meaning clear; yet despite this, there are chapters, and these among the most crucial, where condensation is carried to the extreme limit of unintelligibility. As an economic argument, the whole array of these three volumes depends on the proof of the labour theory of value which is contained in the first fifteen pages or so of the first volume. Yet nowhere is there in print such a miracle of confusion, such a supreme example of how not to reason. If at the end of these fifteen pages, Marx has gained the assent of his readers, it is assuredly the assent of despair and weariness, and not the assent of enlightenment.

The second point relates to the influence of Hegel, the hero of the young men of Marx's youth. Marx doubtless outgrew his Hegelian period, and could even claim that his dialectic method was the direct opposite of the Hegelian, turning right side up what he had found 'standing on its head.'[2] These are forbidden pastures; it is sufficient to note that he never outgrew the Hegelian phraseology and its implications. Fundamental to Hegel is the idea of development. Every positive calls forth its negative, which again creates the negation of the negation, which, however, is not the original positive but something which unites the original positive and its negative. Otherwise expressed, there is firstly the thesis which calls forth its antithesis, which again leads to the synthesis, in which both thesis and antithesis are combined. Traces of philosophic phraseology do no one any harm, but a reperusal of the essential parts of *Capital* is apt to countenance the suggestion that, with Marx, the philosophic formula came first, and that the world was interpreted in accordance therewith. The class struggle is but the thesis begetting and wrestling with the antithesis; when the dominant class is engulfed, then we have the synthesis, a new starting point in development. Despite Marx's affected omniscience, *Capital* reveals very little real knowledge of the world, as indeed Marx, throughout life, was singularly obtuse with regard to the feelings of his fellow-men. He was too much in the British Museum, and too little on the Epsom Downs on Derby Day; and the more one reads *Capital*, the more one feels that these things which he calls the capitalist and the proletariat are anæmic abstractions who, with as little vitality as Tweedledum and Tweedledee, fight out their battle to its appointed end in order that a philosophical formula may be fulfilled.

The third general point is Marx's relation to the classical economists, in particualr to Adam Smith and Ricardo. The finest flower of Marx's contempt is reserved for what he calls 'vulgar economy'; yet there is truth in the jest which describes Marx as the last of the classical economists. Smith and Ricardo had groped, with hesitation and limitations,

[2] *Capital*, Preface, Vol. I, p. 25 (Kerr).

towards a labour theory of value. Marx accepted the doctrine without hesitation and, greatly daring, added a proof of his own. In other respects also, as in regard to the theory of wages, it has already been noted how generous Ricardo had been in furnishing bricks for the construction of the edifice of scientific socialism. Not the least entertaining aspect of the great Marxian riddle is to observe Marx railing at the vulgar economists while he is meanwhile complacently arraying himself in their discarded rags and outgrown garments.

The *Manifesto of the Communist Party* has been so pre-eminently the most influential of the writings of Marx that a slight consideration of this brief pamphlet is desirable, if only to indicate how far the leading Marxian positions had been reached by 1848. It differs from *Capital* above all in its terseness, its twenty-two fiery pages comparing most favourably with the interminable dreariness of its bigger brother. Of its four sections,[3] it is the first, dealing with 'Bourgeois and Proletarians,' that is most relevant to the question of Marxian doctrine. It begins by striking a characteristic note : 'The history of all hitherto existing society is the history of class struggles.' And in amplification :

'Freeman and slave, patrician and plebeian, baron and serf, guildmaster and journeyman, in one word, oppressor and oppressed, standing constantly in opposition to each other, carried on an uninterrupted warfare, now open, now concealed; a warfare which always ended either in a revolutionary transformation of the whole of society or in the common ruin of the contending classes.'

[3] Section 1, 'Bourgeois and Proletarians,' contains most of the essence of Marxism; section 2, 'Proletarians and Communists,' leads up to the programme of the communists; section 3, 'Socialist and Communist Literature,' is an entirely unfair attack on previous socialist literature; section 4 is little more than peroration : 'The proletarians have nothing to lose but their chains. They have a world to win.'

This is followed by an analysis of the existing situation and the process which has led to it, and above all a discussion of what has been done by the bourgeoisie. Despite its brutality, the bourgeoisie has not been useless, having indeed played its appointed part in history in destroying feudalism. It has given a cosmopolitan character to the production and consumption of all countries. 'To the despair of reactionaries,' as the manifesto says, it has cut from under the feet of industry its national basis, so that national narrowness and exclusiveness have become daily more and more impossible. Further (a characteristic note), it has rescued a great part of the population from the idiocy of country life. But just as feudal relations became so many fetters on production and had to be burst asunder, so also the day of the bourgeoisie is past:

'The weapons with which the bourgeoisie conquered feudalism are now turned against the bourgeoisie itself. But the bourgeoisie has not only forged the weapons that bring death to itself; it has also produced the men who will wield these weapons—the modern workers, the PROLETARIANS.'

In the next passage the manifesto approaches the question of exploitation, without, however, relying on later refinements as to labour-power, value and surplus value. 'These workers, forced to sell themselves piecemeal, are a commodity like every other article of commerce. . . . The cost of production of the worker is in consequence reduced almost entirely to the means of subsistence that he requires for his maintenance and for the propagation of his race.' The price of a commodity, and therefore of labour, is at this stage equated to its cost of production. Exploitation consists in the worker receiving 'his bare money wage,' and the burden of labour is increased (as is later, in *Capital*, the degree of exploitation) by prolongation of the working hours, increased speed of machinery, and the employment of women and children.

The increasing separation of society into two opposing camps is also a cardinal point in the manifesto:

'The little middle class, the small shopkeepers, trades-people, peasant proprietors, handicraftsmen and peasants, all these classes sink into the proletariat, partly because their small capital is not sufficient for modern industry and is crushed out in the competition with the large capitalists, and partly because their specialized skill is depreciated by the new methods of production. Thus is the proletariat recruited from all classes of the population.'

The increasing misery of the working classes is likewise more comprehensible here than in *Capital*:

'The modern worker, on the contrary, instead of rising with the progress of industry, sinks ever deeper beneath the social conditions of his own class. The labourer becomes the pauper, and pauperism increases even more rapidly than population and wealth.'

This means that the bourgeoisie can no longer assure exist-ence in slavery to its own slaves, and that therefore society can exist no longer under its rule. In the celebrated phrase: 'it produces its own grave-diggers.'

Enough, and perhaps too much of the *Communist Manifesto*. Its significance lies in the fact that in a few brief pages it enables the reader to grasp the leading ideas of Marx, free from the mathematical and economic obfuscations which too frequently mar *Capital*. Here, in 1848, supreme emphasis is already laid on the continuity of the class struggle; there is the sharp differentiation into two classes, into the lower of which all but a few are inevitably thrust; there is the idea of the exploitation of the worker, though the conception may lack precision of definition; and lastly there is implied the inevitable march of history, so that the capitalistic system engenders within itself the seeds of its own destruction. All these are pure Marxism, and except for some psuedo-scientific elaboration (particularly with regard to value and surplus-value), Marxism is little else.

Having seen how far the essential Marxian positions are already enunciated in the *Communist Manifesto*, it may be convenient to consider in slightly more detail the series of propositions on page 282, where in an attempt was made to reduce Marx to tabloid form. The first two – the materialistic conception of history and the class struggle – may be taken together; and inasmuch as they are scarcely, if at all, matters of economic doctrine, they may be disposed of summarily. Although it is customary to regard the materialistic conception of history as of the essence of Marx's doctrine, the beginner may nevertheless search diligently in Marx's better-known works and find no clear explanation of what the great principle involves. It is, apart from a few occasional passages, rather a pervading assumption, and for a relatively clear statement one must turn to Engels rather than to Marx. Perhaps the most definite statement in Marx's own writings is contained in the preface to the *Critique of Political Economy*, in which the most crucial sentences are these:

'The mode of production in material life determines the general character of the social, political and spiritual processes of life. It is not the consciousness of men that determines their existence, but, on the contrary, their social existence determines their consciousness.'[4]

[4] p.11. Still better known as a *locus classicus* is the passage in the preface to the *Communist Manifesto*, written by Engels after Marx's death: 'The pervading and basic thought of the manifesto is: that in every historical epoch, the prevailing mode of economic produc-

In its original form, if one may appropriate a phrase from Engels, this meant that 'the final causes of all social changes and political revolutions are to be sought, not in men's brains, not in men's better insight into eternal truth and justice, but in changes in the modes of production and exchange.'[5] It is not the philosophy, but the economics, of each particular epoch that provides the essential cause of change. In consequence, art, religion, law and all the rest of it do not mould economic conditions; on the contrary, they are the outcome of these conditions. The far-fetched illustrations of the materialistic conception of history, which were at one time put forward, need not detain us. It is sufficient that in its original form the doctrine was untenable, and was not indeed maintained by Engels without devastating modification. That history, to be comprehensible, must take account of the kitchen larder, is a truth which few would deny; but equally, there is a great deal more in history than the economic factor. Man does not wholly or exclusively crawl on his belly; there are all manner of enthusiasms, loyalties, inspirations spurring men to action, which are nevertheless entirely uneconomic but which may yet react on economic conditions. Above all, the action of mind on mind which, with its remoter consequences, is one of the greatest of all influences in the world, eludes economic explanation. Assuming that it may be possible to explain how Dante, Mahomet, Calvin, Marx, Mr. Lloyd George and Mr. George Robey could only have occurred when they did in fact occur, there remains the much more difficult question

---

tion and exchange, and the social organization necessarily following from it, form the basis upon which is built up, and from which alone can be explained, the political and intellectual history of that epoch; that consequently the whole history of mankind . . . has been a history of class struggles.'

[5] *Socialism, Utopian and Scientific*, p.45.

of explaining how or why they occurred at all. It is even more difficult to explain how the great man finds his 'sounding-board,' which may carry his influence erratically to different parts of the world; for Calvin might not have found his Knox; Marx might have had no Lenin. In interpreting history it is well to be humble and perhaps even agnostic, realizing that the history of man is moulded by many factors, of which the economic is merely one, and that perhaps not necessarily the most important.

The class struggle is likewise merely an unjustifiable generalization of a very partial truth. In the true Marxian statement, the existence of the class struggle is linked to the materialistic conception of history by a 'consequently' (as in Engels). But it is surely the most inconsequent consequence. The economic factor (and it is not to be underrated) may manifest itself otherwise than in the class struggle. Moreover, one could only postulate the ubiquitous existence of the class struggle if men were everywhere, predominantly if not exclusively, moved by economic motives, and were moreover conscious where their economic interests lay. In more orthodox and hackneyed phrase, they should be moved by enlightened self-interest. But, on the contrary, men are moved by all sorts of ideas – patriotism, religion, fanaticism and love of liberty – which may conflict with their interest, or the interest of their 'class,' whatever a class may be. But indeed, waiving the wider point, the whole idea of a class struggle is perhaps a *petitio principii.* The dividing lines in society are many, but men do not feel themselves to be a group or a class until they have acted as a group or a class. The consciousness of solidarity is not the cause of common action, but is rather the consequence of such common action. Whenever men act together with any measure of continuity, then there will emerge a feeling of solidarity, which will continue so long as in fact they act together. Nor need the bond connecting them be economic in character. But the idea of an inevitable, universal, all-embracing solidarity of the working classes is the merest delusion. There may be conflict of interests between different grades in the same industry; between different industries in the same country; between the workers in different countries.

The fundamental error in the Marxian statement of the class struggle has two aspects. Firstly, Marx visualized the proletariat as an idealized worker, and he was therefore able to invest the proletariat with a unity which it does not in fact possess. Secondly, he regarded this unified 'proletariat' as being endowed with the peculiar properties of the 'economic man.' It is curious once again to observe how, when that anæmic ghost the 'economic man' was falling into disrepute, Marx seized on the remnants of the classical school, and produced not one, but a whole race of economic men. The final trumpet-call of the *Communist Manifesto* provides a curious commentary on all this interpretation of history. For there should be no need to summon, with the aid of the largest capitals, the workers of all lands to unite, unless in fact they had been previously disunited. But if previously disunited, one is tempted to inquire whether their disunion had by any chance been caused by conflicting interests, or ideal causes such as patriotism and religion.

Turning to the economic kernel, we are confronted with the Marxian theory of value, which makes value merely the expression of the amount of labour embodied in a commodity. Up to a certain point this is merely a transplantation from Ricardo; but whereas Ricardo allowed for modifications, and was obviously increasingly beset with doubts, Marx pushed to its rigid and universal extreme the doctrine that all value springs from, and is, labour – impelled thereto, doubtless, by the necessity of proving the central doctrine of exploitation. Further, whereas Ricardo did not really attempt to prove the proposition, Marx, more courageous, essayed to give a rigorous and exact demonstration; and indeed on this demonstration rests the whole vast superincumbent weight of the three volumes of *Capital*.

The demonstration, such as it is, meets the reader in the first section of the first chapter of *Capital*, and it may have proved a contributory cause in deterring many readers from faring further. Briefly – very briefly – the argument is that wealth is an immense accumulation of commodities, a commodity being a thing that satisfies human wants. Every useful thing is an assemblage of many properties, and may therefore be of use in various ways. If a thing has utility, it is a use-value; but commodities are also the depositories of exchange-value. Approach now the question of exchange-value, which at first appears as a quantitative relation. If a number of things – x blacking, y silk, z gold – exchange for each other, then each as an exchange-value must be replaceable by any of the others. If we take, then, an equation representing equality of exchange (e.g., 1 quarter corn=x cwt. iron), then we may infer that in 1 quarter of corn and in x cwt. iron there exists in equal quantities something which is common to both; and to this third thing, which is neither of them, both must be reducible.

What, then, is this mysterious property which lies concealed in equal quantities in a shilling's worth of fresh butter and a shilling's worth of tin-tacks? Firstly and obviously, it is not the geometrical or chemical or physical properties. These only engage our attention so far as they affect the utilities of the commodities. Nor has the undetected common property anything to do with the utilities of the things. As Marx somewhat pedantically expresses it, 'the exchange of commodities is evidently an act characterized by a total abstraction from use-value.' It is indeed just because things have different use-values that they are exchanged, and it is certainly true that a wise man will not confuse the uses of butter and tin-tacks. Then, says Marx, taking a mighty leap, the commodities represented in our equation 'have only one common property left, that of being products of labour.' If things are of equal exchange-value, this merely means that each contains, congealed in it, the same amount of human labour.[6]

Such, leaving aside a good deal of unnecessary mystification, is the essence of Marx's proof of the labour theory of value. Certain points at once strike even the most befogged reader. In the first place, Marx assumes that everything that has value is the product of human labour; at the crucial point of the argument, it is found that this is the only quality common to two things of equal exchange-value. 'Virgin soil, natural meadows,' Marx allows to have use-value, but not value.[7] This, however, is too obviously to shut one's eyes to half the problem. Whether we like it or not, things which are not the product of human labour may, and do in fact have, exchange-value; but all such things are inferentially excluded before Marx begins his winnowing process in search of the meaning and cause of value. In Böhm-Bawerk's famous phrase, he acts like one who, urgently desiring to bring a white ball out of the urn, takes care to secure this result by putting in white balls only.

The second noticeable peculiarity of the Marxian demonstration is that it rests on the perfectly legitimate, but highly dangerous, method of exclusion. There is no direct proof that value expresses the amount of labour congealed in a commodity; this conclusion, at best, merely emerges from the purported exclusion of every other possible solution. But

---

[6] *Capital*, Vol. I, chap. I, sec. I, pp.41-44. (Edition published by Kerr, Chicago, but the pagination is not uniform in all editions.)
[7] *Ibid.*, Vol. I, p.47.

a generation familiar with detective literature should know
that this is the kind of proof on which a well-advised jury
will convict, only with the utmost hesitation. You dare not
hang the heroine merely because everyone else supposed to
have been on the premises on the fatal night can show a
clean pair of hands. You never can tell. A closer inspection
might have revealed the butler behind the curtain or the
pantry-boy under the sofa. In the present case, Marx turned
a blind eye to a whole regiment of pantry-boys who, so far
from being concealed, were sitting ostenatiously in the most
conspicuous chairs. In particular, there is the important
element of scarcity in relation to human desire, the fact that
things may have value in proportion to the desires of men
to possess them. Otherwise expressed, Marx, here as elsewhere neglects the whole side of human demand. He
approaches value solely from the side of supply. His demonstration is fallacious because, resting on exhaustion, it
obviously does not exhaust.

Thirdly, Marx's attempt at the outset to side-track the
element of utility is again little more than mystification. It
may be true that the use-value of blacking is different from
that of silk, and that exchange only takes place because
these articles serve different purposes. But the fact that each
of these commodities has utility is assuredly not ignored in
the process of exchange. Nor indeed does Marx for any
length of time maintain the contrary. The idea of utility is
an inconvenient thing to have about the premises while he
is establishing his main proposition; so he incontinently
bundles it out at the front door. But when his labour theory
of value has been proved, he gently opens the back door for
its readmission. 'Lastly,' he says at the end of the section,
'nothing can have value without being an object of utility.'[8]

[8] *Ibid.*, Vol. I, p.48.

Here, then, after the fair is over, is one overlooked factor common to things which have value.

The objection that identical commodities may represent different amounts of labour Marx meets, quite legitimately, by the contention that it is not the labour of this or that worker (which may vary according to his resources and his industry) which determines value. What is decisive is the labour time socially necessary to produce an article, and this implies the normal conditions of production at the time, as also the average degree of skill and intensity of labour.[9] If articles continue to be produced by antiquated methods, the amount of labour so involved will not determine value, since in this case an amount of labour greater than is socially necessary will have been expended. More open to objection are the further refinements necessary to make the theory fit the facts. It has been shown that utility was grudgingly admitted to be essential to value; if the thing turns out to be useless, so also was the labour involved.[10] As Marx imperturbably puts it, 'the labour does not count as labour' – though there might be difficulty in persuading the worker to accept on pay-day the consequences of this point of view. So also a glut proves the expenditure of more time than was socially necessary; generally speaking, labour spent on anything 'counts effectively only in so far as it is spent in a form that is useful for others.'[11] Somewhat similar is Marx's treatment of the difference between skilled and unskilled labour, and between labour of different qualities. For Marx all labour is reducible to what he calls 'human labour in the abstract,' or 'simple average labour' – a curious fiction which implies that there is labour which is neither the labour of the tailor, nor the weaver, nor of any other specific

[9] *Ibid.*, Vol. I, p.46.
[10] *Ibid.*, Vol. I, p.48.
[11] *Ibid.*, Vol. I, pp.97-98.

worker. But if, as is admittedly the case, there are different qualities of labour, how are they to be expressed in terms of that underlying jelly to which labour is ultimately reducible? Marx's explanation is illuminating:

'Skilled labour counts only as simple labour intensified, or rather, as multiplied simple labour, a given quantity of skilled being considered equal to a greater quantity of simple labour. Experience shows that this reduction is constantly being made. . . . The different proportions in which different sorts of labour are reduced to unskilled labour as their standard, are established by a social process that goes on behind the backs of the producers, and, consequently, appear to be fixed by custom.'[12]

This, clearly, is to argue in the most vicious of circles; for this mysterious social process that goes on behind the backs of the producers is nothing else than the rude determination of the market-place. The world's coarse thumb and finger determine that the products of A and B shall exchange in the ratio of $5:4$, and Marx thereupon says that B's labour 'counts' as $1\frac{1}{4}$ times as much as that of A. When the ratio as so determined in the market changes to $10:9$, there will be a consequent change in the ratio in which the labour of the workers is 'counted.' But a theory designed to explain what takes place in the market cannot appeal to the market to provide a varying formula which, when applied to the theory, will make the theory tally with the facts. But this is what Marx does throughout. Labour determines value; but to the extent to which it is misapplied or applied in excess, it 'does not count as labour,' or requires to be graded down. Different kinds of labour are to be regarded as simple labour multiplied: if you would know to what extent any kind of labour must be multiplied in order to yield the right

12 *Ibid.*, Vol. I, pp. 51-52.

answer, all that is necessary is to look at the right answer as supplied by the market, and deduce therefrom the necessary multiplicator. Thus by ignoring labour where necessary, by grading it up or down as the situation requires, it ought to be possible to secure that the facts and the theory are happily mated.

The analysis of surplus value is enveloped in a considerable mass of metaphysical subtlety; but the essence of the idea is not obscure. The problem, putting it popularly, is to ascertain wherein lies the secret source of the increase of capital. Marx makes much play with the two formulæ representing the circulation of commodities, C-M-C (where a commodity is exchanged for money, and subsequently reconverted into a commodity), and the alternative circuit, M-C-M (in which money purchases a commodity which is again transmuted into money), or since the capitalist is marked by a boundless greed after riches, the formula should more properly be M-C-M^1 (where M^1=M+δM). The wise reader will waive aside the three points in which the formulæ are similar and the nine in which they are dissimilar. In the first formula (C-M-C) there can be no increase, because equivalents are exchanged for equivalents; in a sentence which sums up the perverseness of the Marxian theory of value, at least as expounded in Volume I, 'the value of a commodity is expressed in its price before it goes into circulation, and is therefore a precedent condition of circulation, not its result.'[13] Nor can a surplus emerge from circulation of commodities merely by selling them above their value; for in that case what one gains another loses. After further refinements, Marx concludes that the source of increase of wealth must be sought in the first portion of M-C-M, though not in the value of the commodity bought, which is indeed

[13] *Ibid.*, Vol. I, pp.175-176.

paid for at its full value.[14] The source must lie in its use-value. There must be somewhere in the market a mysterious commodity ' whose use-value possesses the peculiar property of being a source of value, whose actual consumption, therefore, is itself an embodiment of labour and, consequently, a creation of value.'[15] This mysterious commodity is labour-power, which, as he elsewhere expresses it, is a ' source not only of value, but of more value than it has itself.'[16]

Divested of its wrappings, the doctrine of surplus value becomes clear. Labour-power, like everything else, has its value; it is (we are back at the unrefined Ricardo) ' the value of the means of subsistence necessary for the maintenance of the labourer.'[17] But when put to use, labour-power will produce more than this. If five hours' labour are sufficient to produce what is required for the maintenance of the labourer, and if the worker, having sold his labour-power for the day, is required to work ten hours, these five additional hours, representing surplus labour, will yield surplus value. The Marxian doctrine on this point may be summed up in two contentions, firstly, that all value springs from labour; but, secondly, that labour in return receives merely the means of subsistence. The difference is the exploitation effected by capital.

That all value comes from labour is further accentuated by a point on which Marx lays much emphasis, and which ultimately leads to the undermining of the Marxian edifice. This is the important distinction betwen constant capital and variable capital.[18] By constant capital is meant the means of production, the instruments of labour, etc. –

[14] *Ibid.*, Vol. i, p.185.
[15] *Ibid.*, Vol. i, p.186.
[16] *Ibid.*, Vol. i, p.216.
[17] *Ibid.*, Vol. i, p.190.
[18] *Ibid.*, Vol. i, chap. 8, especially pp.232-233.

loosely, we may say machinery. By variable capital is meant that part of capital represented by labour-power – in effect, wages. Capital may therefore be of different organic composition (high or low) according as the ratio of constant to variable capital changes. Now it is of the essence of the Marxian theory that the whole of the surplus value comes from the variable capital. Whatever be the longevity of a machine, its total value will be gradually transferred to the product during the years of its working period.[19] 'In the value of the product, there is a reappearance of the value of the means of production,'[20] but no more. Even more tersely, 'machinery, like every other component of constant capital, creates no new value, but yields up its own value to the product that it serves to beget.'[21] The consequences of this doctrine, that all surplus value (i.e., all profits) springs from variable capital, and from variable capital alone, will call for consideration later.

Such, then, is surplus value, but inasmuch as 'capital has one single life impulse, the tendency to create value and surplus value,'[22] the capitalist machine, once it has begun to grind, will strive to make the surplus value a maximum. The obvious method is to extend the hours of labour.

$$
\begin{array}{ccccc}
A & B^1 & B & C & C^1 \\
| & | & | & | & |
\end{array}
$$

If AB is the 'necessary labour time,' then a prolongation of the working hours from AC to AC^1 will increase the surplus value; so likewise will a curtailment of the necessary labour time from AB to AB^1. To this latter is to be ascribed the

[19] *Ibid.*, Vol. I, pp.226-227.
[20] *Ibid.*, Vol. I, p.231.
[21] *Ibid.*, Vol. I, p.423.
[22] *Ibid.*, Vol. I, p.257.

immanent tendency in capital 'to heighten the productiveness of labour, in order to cheapen commodities, and by such cheapening to cheapen the labourer himself.'[23] Surplus value will also be increased by 'nibbling at meal-times,' by day and night work, by the relay system, by roping in the labour of women and children. All these represent the 'vampire thirst for the living blood of labour.'[24]

The defects of the foregoing analysis are sufficiently patent. It is common to observe that Marx, in the first place, entirely omits the element of time, and that his doctrines therefore imply the illegitimacy of interest. His discussion of interest, when it comes (Volume III), is wholly inadequate; in the place where a discussion would be in point, he tells us that 'interest is a mere fragment of surplus value.'[25] For Marx, money is still barren, and his objection to the

[23] *Ibid.*, Vol. I, p.351.

[24] *Ibid.*, Vol. I, p.282. It is perhaps worth while to quote one of the purple passages with which Marx studs his volume: 'But in its blind unrestrainable passion, its were-wolf hunger for surplus labour, capital oversteps not only the moral, but even the merely physical maximum bounds of the working day. It usurps the time for growth, development, and healthy maintenance of the body. It steals the time required for the consumption of fresh air and sunlight. It higgles over a meal-time, incorporating it where possible with the process of production itself, so that food is given to the labourer as to a mere means of production, as coal is supplied to the boiler, grease and oil to the machinery. It reduces the sound sleep needed for the restoration, reparation, refreshment of the bodily powers to just so many hours of torpor as the revival of an organism, absolutely exhausted, renders essential. It is not the normal maintenance of the labour-power which is to determine the limits of the working day; it is the greatest possible daily expenditure of labour-power, no matter how diseased, compulsory, and painful it may be, which is to determine the limits of the labourers' period of repose. Capital cares nothing for the length of life of labour-power. All that concerns it is simply and solely the maximum of labour-power that can be rendered fluent in a working day. It attains this end by shortening the extent of the labourer's life, as a greedy farmer snatches increased produce from the soil by robbing it of its fertility' (Vol. I, pp. 291-292).

[25] *Ibid.*, Vol. I, p. 644.

public debt is that 'it endows barren money with the power of breeding, and thus turns it into capital.'[26] So also the importance of directive and managerial functions is almost unmentioned.[27] Yet it is a well-known fact that of two businesses, with apparently similar advantages, one may prosper and the other may head determinedly for the bankruptcy court, even though the labour-power exerted in the two cases may be identical. But apart from these difficulties, the Marxian explanation suffers from two inner inherent contradictions (or two aspects of the same contradiction) from which it never escaped, and on which it finally made shipwreck in the third volume. In the first place, if all profit springs from variable capital and none from machinery, then it is the height of folly ever to introduce machinery, and it is a poor explanation to suggest that the capitalist does not know what he is doing. Marx realizes the difficulties of this 'contradiction which is immanent'[28] in the application of machinery, but his observations leave it barking for solution in the minds of all readers. On the Marxian theory, with every progress of capital to a higher proportion of constant capital, there will be a diminution of profits, since profits come solely from labour, which admittedly represents a continually smaller proportion of total capital. With every step forward which the capitalist makes, he thus more deeply cuts his own throat. Surplus value calls for, and can only arise from, the existence of vast masses of workers; the Marxian analysis shows an increasing army of

[26] *Ibid.*, Vol. I, p.827.

[27] Possibly the only reference is in the chapter on Co-operation, where it is argued that wage-labourers cannot co-operate unless they are employed simultaneously by the same capitalist, and therefore, 'that a capitalist should command on the field of production, is now as indispensable as that a general should command on the field of battle' (Vol. I, pp.362-363). This says nothing, and what is said rather sounds as if Marx's tongue were in his cheek.

[28] *Ibid.*, Vol. I, p.445.

unemployed, displaced by machinery which can yield no profit.

The other flaw is a variant of this, and is in a sense even more fatal. If profit springs only from the labour employed, and in no wise from the constant capital, then the rate of profit in different industries will vary according as the proportion of variable capital is high or low. When there is much variable capital (i.e., in more primitive and undeveloped industries) the rate of profit will be high; in industries which have had extensive resort to machinery, the rate of profit will be low. Marx admitted with praiseworthy frankness that the observed facts were in glaring contradiction with the law so ascertained:

'This law clearly contradicts all experience based on appearance. Everyone knows that a cotton spinner, who, reckoning the percentage on the whole of his applied capital, employs much constant and little variable capital, does not, on account of this, pocket less profit or surplus value than a baker, who relatively sets in motion much variable and little constant capital. For the solution of this apparent contradiction, many intermediate terms are as yet wanted, as from the standpoint of elementary algebra many intermediate terms are wanted to understand that o/o may represent an actual magnitude.'[29]

The subsequent history of this conundrum furnishes one of the few comedies of economic literature. The promised solution did not appear in Volume II, but references to it figure largely in the preface written by Engels, above all in the form of a challenge addressed to the followers of Rodbertus. For if, as was claimed, Marx had plagiarized Rodbertus, now (and that right early, before the publication of Volume III) was the time for those who had championed

[29] *Ibid.*, Vol. I, p.335.

Rodbertus to vindicate his claims by producing the correct solution of the riddle. The odd thing is that many socialists and economists did in fact respond, and took part in the competition to the extent of speculating as to what the Marxian solution was to be. But indeed it ought to have been clear *a priori* that there could be no solution, since irreconcilables cannot be reconciled, nor can harmony be established betwen two contradictory propositions – unless by the simple expedient of dropping one of them overboard. Contemplating the 'Russian campaign of disaster' organized by Engels, Loria, an enthusiastic admirer of Marx, even suggests that the procrastinations of Marx in getting on, with Volumes II and III were due to a realization of the impending ruination of his life's work: 'Is there any reason for surprise at Marx's hesitation to punish this so-called defence; need we wonder that his hand trembled, that his spirit quailed, before the inexorable act of destruction?'[30]

The solution offered to the undiscerning in the third volume in explanation of the existence of a uniform rate of profit is embedded in a good deal of arithmetical illustration. Briefly, it amounts to this. Employers are not to be viewed in isolation. A group of enterprises, with different proportions of variable and constant capital, should be replaced by an imaginary enterprise, comprising the total of all the capitals of the members of the group. As this process of averaging cannot be limited, it means that all employers are to be regarded as one group, in which the surplus value gained by all is distributed among all. The possibility of a uniform rate of profit thus emerges; but it is on condition that some things sell above and some below their value.[31] This uniform rate of profit is arrived at by

[30] Loria, *Marx*, p.78.
[31] *Capital*, Vol. III, p.186.

competition, and capital everywhere looks for the average profit. Thus, there emerges a difference between value and price; and henceforth it will only be on rare occasions, indeed only by accident, that the surplus value really produced in any given branch of industry will correspond to the profit contained in the selling price of the commodity – the accidental case arising where the composition of the capital (as between constant and variable) is exactly the average of the sum total of all capitals.[32] Elsewhere the products of industries, with a proportion of constant capital above the average, will sell at a price above their value, while in the contrary case they will sell below their value. Thus the desired uniform rate of profit is established, but at the cost of sacrificing the whole of the first volume of *Capital*; for the inspired doctrine of the first volume, that things exchange in accordance with the congealed labour they contain, is ignominiously tossed overboard. This is the 'solemn mystification' of which Loria speaks. In fact, Marx has replaced Volume I by a mere cost-of-production theory such as a vulgar economist like Adam Smith might have evolved in his most vulgar and least enlightened moments. Things exchange according to their cost of production (which includes a normal rate of profit).[33] It is true that they still have a 'value' which differs in general from the price; but in a 'value' which is an abstract metaphysical conception, and which is uniformly ignored in the market-place, few of us have any lively interest.

The remaining parts of Marx – relating to the Industrial Reserve Army and the Law of the Concentration of Capital – are perhaps in the field of vaticination rather than of

[32] *Ibid.*, Vol. III, p.198.
[33] 'That price of any commodity, which is equal to its cost price plus that share of average profit on the total capital invested . . . in its production . . . is called its price of production' (Vol. III, p. 186).

economic analysis, and may therefore be dealt with more summarily. The existence of the Industrial Reserve Army is, above all, due to the progressive use of machinery; and all that Marx says on this subject is in a sense vitiated by the flaw which he openly admits, that as no profit can arise from machinery, the progressive introduction of machinery must lead to a curtailment of surplus value. Accepting, however, the were-wolf greed of capital for surplus value, it is clear that surplus value may be increased either by increasing the amount of labour exacted, or by diminishing the number of hours during which the worker must labour to provide his necessary maintenance[34] (the distinction between absolute and relative surplus value). Herein, as has been noted, lies the interest of capital in increasing the productivity of labour; it makes the worker cheaper. Hence also the significance of division of labour, which calls for production on a considerable scale, and therefore requires that the minimum amount of capital should be constantly increasing.[35] But once introduced, machinery clamours to be increasingly used. It is to the interest of the employer that the machinery be used as long each day as possible;[36] apart from prolongation of hours, there is a similar impulse to intensification by increasing the speed of the machinery and by requiring the worker to tend more machines. But all this means the displacement of the worker: 'the workman becomes unsaleable, like paper money thrown out of currency by legal enactment.'[37]

Putting the point in technical Marxian phraseology, the advance of accumulation connotes an increasing proportion of constant to variable capital; in other words, the demand for labour must fall progressively.[38] There is thus a relative

[34] Ibid., Vol. I, p.351.
[35] Ibid., Vol. I, p.395.
[36] Ibid., Vol. I, p.441.
[37] Ibid., Vol. I, p.470.
[38] Ibid., Vol. I, p.690.

surplus population produced, which forms a 'disposable Industrial Reserve Army,' which still belongs to capital, and which is retained to provide 'the possibility of throwing great masses of men suddenly on the decisive points without injury to the scale of production in other spheres.'[39] The Industrial Reserve Army plays a quite peculiar part in Marxian theory. Its expansion and contraction is implicit in the explanation of 'crises'; the general movements of wages are explained by what happens to the Industrial Reserve Army. In periods of stagnation it weighs down the active labour army, while in times of activity it keeps its pretensions in check.[40]

To complete the picture, it is necessary to bear in mind what is happening at the other end, in the Law of Capitalist Accumulation. 'One capitalist always kills many.'[41] Marx here has implicit faith in the big battalions. The battle of competition is fought by cheapness, but cheapness depends on productiveness, and productiveness on the scale of production. 'Therefore the larger capitals beat the smaller. . . . Competition . . . always ends in the ruin of many small capitalists, whose capitals partly pass into the hands of their conquerors, partly vanish.'[42] Such, then, is the diagnosis of the natural trend of events. At one end, the larger capitalists devour each other like monstrous pike in a pond, growing ever larger in size, ever fewer in number: at the other end there is a vast Industrial Reserve Army of unemployed and intermittently employed sunk in increasing misery – at one pole accumulation of wealth; at the other, accumulation of misery, agony of toil, slavery, ignorance, brutality, mental degradation. So, increasingly, until the

[39] *Ibid.*, Vol. I, p.694.
[40] *Ibid.*, Vol. I, pp.699-701.
[41] *Ibid.*, Vol. I, p.836.
[42] *Ibid.*, Vol. I, pp.686-687.

final catastrophe, which can be fittingly presented only in the words of Marx himself:

'Along with the constantly diminishing number of the magnates of capital, who usurp and monopolize all advantages of this process of transformation, grows the mass of misery, oppression, slavery, degradation, exploitation; but with this too grows the revolt of the working-class, a class always increasing in numbers, and disciplined, united, organized by the very mechanism of the process of capitalist production itself. The monopoly of capital becomes a fetter upon the mode of production, which has sprung up and flourished along with, and under it. Centralization of the means of production and socialization of labour at last reach a point where they become incompatible with their capitalist integument. The integument is burst asunder. The knell of capitalist private property sounds. The expropriators are expropriated.'[43]

It is unnecessary to consider how far Marx in these matters has proved a prophet of repute, or by what glosses it may be possible to make him appear as such. To the doctrine of the Industrial Reserve Army – in the sense in which Marx used the term – subsequent history has given no support; with regard to the increasing degradation of the working classes, he is equally at sea. In extenuation, it should be borne in mind that all Marx's ideas were formed before 1848, and that his subsequent reading was very largely devoted to a study of the more repellent aspects of the Industrial Revolution in the halcyon days of unrestrained *laissez-faire*. The functions of trade unions, the possibly beneficent activity of the State were outside the scope of Marx's vision. A better case can be made in justification of the law of capitalistic concentration. Concentration there certainly has been; but it has been concentration

[43] *Ibid.*, Vol. I, p.837.

of control, not of ownership, and the whole Marxian thesis demands concentration of ownership as of the essence of the doctrine. So likewise, between the two extremes, the Marxian prophecy has found no fulfilment. The population has not been thrust ruthlessly into two opposing camps; there is still an intermediate grade which somehow contrives to pay its taxes and survive.

But quite apart from the minor question of the justice of the Marxian prophecy, the state of society visualized by Marx is in itself sufficiently curious to provoke wonder. A society consisting largely of an army of unemployed (and that in pre-Insurance Act days), leavened by a few remaining capitalists relying increasingly on the use of machinery (which on the Marxian theory yields no profits), is in itself a bundle of glaring contradictions. For whom, under these conditions, are the dark satanic mills supposed to grind out goods? Obviously not the Industrial Reserve Army, whose home is the workhouse, and who have no purchasing power. As before, Marx entirely overlooks the side of demand. Production cannot go on unless there is a market for the goods, and in reading Marx and in contemplating the population drifting into the Industrial Reserve Army and sunk in increasing misery, one inevitably wonders where the market is to be found.

Marx remains, and probably always will remain, one of the riddles of the nineteenth century. He set out to be 'scientific,' to produce what the reviewers would call a cogent piece of reasoning; and, undoubtedly, the whole system is extraordinarily closely knit together; the various points are admirably dove-tailed. Yet no system of thought has suffered such complete bankruptcy as the Marxian. His philosophy of history was to all intents disowned by Engels; the fallacies of his economic doctrine have been so ruthlessly and frequently exposed, that they scarcely any longer furnish even satisfactory examination questions; his prophecies have perversely refused to be fulfilled. All this, moreover, is acknowledged even by those who honour him most. Take, for instance, Mr. Beer, who says that Marx's theory of value and surplus value have rather the signifi-cance of a political and social slogan than of an economic truth;[44] or take Mr. Laski, who dismisses the theory of value as one that has not stood the test of criticism, as out of harmony with the facts, and as far from self-consistent.[45] Yet, despite this bankruptcy, Marx continues to live and to be a vital force. Indeed, Marx is one of those writers in whose case refutation is a singularly futile exercise. He is a legend; he is, in the Sorelian sense, a promulgator of 'myths' where truth is a secondary consideration, so long as the myth embodies what one wishes to believe, and so long as the belief has power to inspire action. This point of view is admirably, if somewhat unblushingly, put by Mr. Beer, who, having dismissed the Marxian economics as a 'political slogan,' adds that 'such militant philosophies need not in themselves be true, only they must accord with the sentiments of the struggling mass'; and (a page later) the doctrines of Marx 'will for long have the force of truth for the masses, and will continue to move them.'[46] This is somewhat too blatantly to reduce Marx to a sacred lie, whose falsity is known to the elect, but which serves its pur-pose so long as it misleads others.

An entirely different line of defence is, however, possible. It consists in arguing that Marx has been completely mis-understood, that he was not, in fact, discussing the market-places of the world and the employers and the employed

[44] Beer, *The Life and Teaching of Karl Marx*, p.129.
[45] Mr. Hearnshaw's *Survey of Socialism* contains an interesting nosegay of socialist utterances on Marx in a similar sense.
[46] Beer, *op. cit.*, pp.130-131.

who elbow each other there, but an abstract world of his own thought and his own creation. Here, for instance, is Croce:

'The capitalist society studied by Marx, is not this or that society, historically existing, in France or in England, nor the modern society of the most civilized nations, that of Western Europe and America. It is an ideal and formal society, deduced from certain hypotheses which could indeed never have occurred as actual facts in the course of history.'[47]

It is interesting to observe that Croce prefaces his remarks by saying that it does not appear that Marx himself always realized fully the peculiar character of his investigation. Whatever contortions may have resulted from the conflict between the first and third volumes, it is indeed abundantly evident that Marx would have been genuinely surprised had he been told that he was discussing a state of society which could never have existed in the course of history;[48] and it is also obvious that those with whom Marx has had most influence, have in fact shared his failure to realize the peculiar character of his investigations.

Whatever may be thought of the riddle of Marx, it remains beyond question that he has been the dominant force in the whole of the subsequent development of socialism. Whether that influence has been a beneficial one may perhaps be doubted, and there are at last some indications of a tardy realization of the fact that Marx, shifting the car of socialism on to the wrong lines, has had a degrading effect on the whole socialist movement.

[47] Croce, *Historical Materialism*, p.50.
[48] So also a perusal of the little book by the Master of Balliol would probably have caused Marx to raise his eyebrows. Marx, of all men, would have objected to being explained away.

Délivrons-nous du Marxisme is the significant title of a recent French volume, and Mr. de Man's thoughtful work[49] is a reasoned statement, from the socialist point of view, against the assumptions of Marxism. What Marx did for socialism may be seen by contrasting his spirit and that of his despised predecessors, and a socialist indictment of Marx would probably concentrate on three points. In the first place, in putting forward a 'scientific' type of socialism, he deliberately and ostentatiously eliminated the moral basis of socialism and the appeal to justice. Marx cared for none of these things; the coming of socialism was to be scientifically demonstrated. But after the moral appeal had been thrown aside as mawkish sentimentality, the scientific proof, which was to take its place, has collapsed. Socialism can only regain its moral basis by being delivered from Marxism. The second main criticism was urged long ago by Mazzini in a frequently quoted phrase: 'Hatred,' he said of Marx, 'outweighs love in his heart.' The early socialists had been inspired by a large-hearted love; the gospel of Marx is a gospel of hatred and envy and malevolence, setting the class struggle in the centre of things, and appealing to all the ignobler passions. Consistently he looks downwards and not upwards. The third point of criticism is akin to this. It is that with Marx, socialism definitely becomes sectional. There is a grand catholicity about the early socialist visions; theirs was a paradise into which all might enter. But the Marxian heaven rests on a strict separation of the elect from those fore-ordained to damnation. Such has been the legacy of Marx to the socialist movement; he has shorn it of its idealism, and to the utmost of his influence made it sordid; he has infused into it a leaven of hatred and intolerance; he has deprived it of its universality. Sufficient reason indeed for the devout socialist

[49] Translated as *The Psychology of Socialism*.

to pray to be delivered from Marxism! How far these baser elements were the reflection of Marx's warped and cankered personal character would furnish material for an interesting, but perhaps an irrelevant, study. Those who desire enlightenment may find instruction in the biography recently written by that enthusiastic Marxian, Mr. W. Rühle.

CHAPTER XII

The Austrian School. The Theory of the Margin

THE present chapter is designed to give some account of the leading members of the Austrian school, which in popular acceptation has become identified with the development of the 'margin' as an economic tool with far-reaching ramifications. The Austrians, however, are scarcely to be apprehended without some reference to their predecessors, and it may therefore be expedient in this case to make a slight departure from the procedure followed in previous chapters, in which, so far as might be, all but the leaders have been jettisoned for the purposes of elucidation. The Austrians represent the culminating point of a well-defined line of thought, and although the word 'Austrian' has become consecrated, it is further significant that, quite independently of the work of the leading Austrians, the main tenets of the Austrian point of view were expressed almost simultaneously by Jevons in England, and by the younger Walras in Lausanne. The net must therefore be spread wider in this chapter, though the mesh must still be sufficiently large to allow some quite considerable fish to escape.

Putting it crudely, and subject to later refinements, the essentials of the Austrian school may be reduced to three cardinal points. Firstly, as against all cost-of-production theories of value, they held that value essentially springs from utility, that it reflects the mind of a person who finds something useful; secondly, that this value is determined at the 'margin,' that is to say, that, successive portions of a good having diminishing utility, the crucial use which determines value is the least important use to which the good, having regard to the amount available, can be put; and thirdly, that value is reflected back from things consumed to the agents which produce these commodities, that is to say, that value sanctions costs and is not caused by costs.

Earlier Anticipations

Before the appearance of the Austrian school, these essential points had frequently gained expression, though at times rather incidentally and without a full realization of their import. Reference has been made in Chapter X to some interesting passages from Say in this sense. When Archbishop Whately opined that pearls were not valuable because men dived for them, but rather that men dived for them because they were valuable, he was expressing, without its refinements, one aspect of the essence of Austrian doctrine. Of the very considerable number of early writers who might be, and have been, cited as foreshadowing, in one way or another, the Austrian school, the most interesting is perhaps Condillac (1714-1780), who in Le Commerce et le Gouvernement, published in 1776, maintained that the value of things was 'founded on their utility, or what comes to the same thing, the need we have of them, or what again comes to the same thing, the use we can make of them.' Not only so, but the value of things, he held, increases in rarity and diminishes with abundance, so that, with sufficient abundance, it may fall to the point of being nil. Thus, with Auguste Walras later, he makes value depend on 'rareté,' if only this 'rareté' could be assessed: 'The greater or less degree of value, utility being the same, would be based solely on the degree of 'rareté,' if this degree could be known with precision.' But since it cannot, there enters an element of human estimation which, in times of dearth, for instance, magnifies the shortage. Thus the 'true value' remains unknown and, assuming constant utility, value is founded not so much on the 'rareté' or abundance of a commodity, as on the opinion we form regarding its 'rareté' or abundance. On these lines Condillac adumbrates a wholly subjective theory of value; it is only necessary to add further his essentially Austrian dictum that 'une chose n'a pas une valeur parce qu'elle coûte, comme on le suppose; mais elle coûte, parce qu'elle a une valeur.'

Turning to this country, an interesting place among the forerunners of the marginal theory is occupied by W. F. Lloyd (1794-1853), who, as Professor in the University of Oxford (1832-1837), was under obligation to publish one lecture a year. The lecture for 1833 on 'The Notion of Value'[1] is a remarkable anticipation of the general line of thought of the Austrians, and indeed the usual type of illustration relating to the housekeeping worries of Robinson Crusoe is here in abundance. From the case of the hungry man having one, two or three ounces of food at his command, Lloyd deduces the general principle that

'while he is scantily supplied with food, he holds a given portion of it in great esteem—in other words, he sets a great value on it; when his supply is increased, his esteem for a given quantity is lessened, or, in other words, he sets a less value on it.'

Even more interesting is his 'good rule for distinguishing between utility and value.' 'To obtain the idea of the utility of an object,' he says, 'imagine what would happen,

[1] Reprinted in the 'Economic History Supplement,' No. 2. of the *Economic Journal*, May 1927.

what inconvenience would arise, from the loss, not of that object alone, but of the whole species to which that object belongs.' In the case of water, for instance, in what predicament should we find ourselves if we lost, not a particular pailful, but the whole element of water? But value represents a different kind of idea; it attaches to an object in possession, which cannot therefore be unlimited. In the case of the overturned pail of water, the value is at once determined for us, either by the inconvenience of leaving unsatisfied the particular want for which the consignment of water was designed, or by the trouble of going back to the well for more water. Here is clearly prefigured the idea of total utility, and the marginal utility (the determinant of value) arrived at by considering the inconvenience resulting from the destruction of the last unit of a store.

Auguste Walras

About the same time France supplies an important anticipator of certain of the essential ideas of the marginalists in Auguste Walras[2] (1801-1866), who in 1831 published a work entitled *De la Nature de la Richesse et de l'Origine de la Valeur*. It is a book which is marked in the crucial parts of the argument by a convincing clarity which is peculiarly French, and throughout by a tendency to repetitiveness which is peculiarly his own. His incursion into economics was, in the first place, a by-product of other studies. He was primarily interested in natural law and the theory of property, and turning to writers on economics for enlightenment on the meaning of wealth, he found himself, in the confusion of tongues, turned empty away.

---

[2] Born at Montpellier, 1801; Professor of Rhetoric at Evreux, 1831; Professor of Political Economy at the Athénée, Paris, 1835; later Professor of Philosophy at Caen. His son, Leon Walras, perhaps a greater man, carried on his tradition.

Wealth and property, he argued, have a common origin in the limitation of certain goods, 'la rareté de certains objets utiles.' It is this limitation, or 'rareté,' that gives things value; it makes them capable of being appropriated, and thus value is an idea prior to that of property. Value is thus a complex idea, implying a comparison with other things, and ultimately their exchange; exchange implies property, and property implies limitation; for if all desirable things were unlimited, there would be no property, just as there would be no exchange.[3]

Walras proceeds to analyse with great incisiveness current views on the source and origin of value. In the main he holds that these fall into two schools, those who base it on utility, represented by French writers, and those who, like the English economists, tended towards a labour or cost-of-production theory.[4] Taking the first of these explanations, if utility be the explanation, then, wherever there is utility, there also should value exist. But sunshine and rain are standing proofs to the contrary. They exist in such abundance that everyone can take 'à son aise et à foison' without anyone being thereby deprived. It is different with other things; there are some who possess them, and some who do not.[5] It is, in short, a characteristic of all wealth, of all things possessing value, that they should be limited, and this limitation establishes a natural disproportion between the sum total of these goods and the sum total of needs which claim the possession of these goods.[6] It is this that constitutes 'rareté' – a word not used in the popular sense which clings to 'rarity,' but merely denoting an insufficient supply to meet all claimants. It is to this 'rareté' alone that value is due. Whatever has value owes its value entirely to this principle of limitation. Utility is not the cause, though

[3] *De la Nature de la Richesse*, pp.18-19.
[4] *Ibid.*, p.21.   [5] *Ibid.*, pp.37-38.   [6] *Ibid.*, p.41.

it may be a necessary condition.[7] Having regard to the principle of 'rareté' which underlies all value, Walras in an acute phrase suggests that one might be tempted to call Political Economy not so much the science of wealth as the science of poverty.[8]

Turning to the other explanation, the cost-of-production theories, Walras holds that the underlying assumption here is that all values are products, and that the value of any object represents the time and the labour lost in obtaining it, assuming – as is sometimes done – that all the other productive services can be resolved into labour. But this does not carry the analysis far enough. 'The value of the products (on this view) represents the value of the productive services, and it is only because the productive services have a value that their product can have one. But we are concerned to know why the productive services have a value, and if the productive services are merely labour, why labour has a value'[9] – and this latter question is one which, according to Walras, Adam Smith never asked.

That the value of labour comes from its 'rareté' is a proposition hard to advance in an age that knows the problem of unemployment, which indeed was known likewise in the time of Walras. But with the utmost ingenuity he avoids the obvious pitfall, shifting the weight of the argument to the element of time:

'There is no work that can be accomplished but with time and on certain conditions. But time is not for any of us an unlimited good. . . . Our life is short and our days are numbered. Time is for each of us a precious thing because it is rare. And since labour can only be accomplished with time and on conditions more or less onerous, it follows that labour has a value.'[10]

[7] Ibid., p.44.
[8] Ibid., p.81.
[9] Ibid., p.166.
[10] Ibid., p.167.

So with the other agents of production. Land and capital are alike limited, and therefore both have a value. Their services command a price, and the price is obviously merely the natural consequences of their limitation or 'rareté.'[11] There is here an obvious kinship with Cassel's principle of scarcity. So, Walras claims, the principle of demand and supply consecrates under another name the principle he has developed; for supply is merely the sum or quantity of the product, while demand is the sum of needs which demand satisfaction; 'rareté' is merely the relation which exists between the two. But even more fundamentally, that a thing may be demanded, it must be limited; that a thing may be supplied, it must be limited likewise. Only on the assumption of 'rareté' do the operations of the market-place acquire a meaning.

Walras has great merit in underlining one aspect of the problem of value, which later became an essential point in the Austrian structure. His weakness is equally obvious. He leaves the idea of 'rareté' somewhat vague, and makes no approach to correlating value with increasing degrees of 'rareté.' The furthest he gets is to define 'rareté' as existing in a certain disproportion between goods and the need of these goods. How various degrees of 'rareté' would react on value, he leaves undiscussed.

Gossen

It is now generally accepted that, apart from such incidental anticipations as are indicated above, the first reasonably complete statement of marginalist doctrine was given by Hermann Heinrich Gossen[12] (1810-1858) in an extra-

---

[11] *Ibid.*, p.177.
[12] Born 1810 at Düren; in the Government service without conspicuous success; retired in 1847, and devoted himself to writing his book.

ordinary work published in 1854.[13] The history of this book is one of the curiosities of economic literature. Entirely neglected on its publication, the unsold copies (which must have been virtually the whole stock) were called in by its disappointed author shortly before his death in 1858. Its life hung by a footnote in Kautz, which was sufficient, a generation later, to stimulate the interest of the economic bloodhounds and set them on its track. It has since then, of course, been reprinted, but it may be doubted whether the number of those who conscientiously read its two hundred and seventy-seven pages has thereby suffered any material increase.

Gossen's book is indeed one of those that are made not to be read. It is repellently mathematical, with whole pages given over to symbols or to lists of numbers; even worse, it is chaotic; worse still, one can hardly escape the impression that the authors had a bee, or several bees, in his bonnet. The reviewers of 1854 are hardly to be blamed if they left Gossen to languish in the list of 'Books received.'

Yet to us to-day, dipping into *The Laws of Human Intercourse* in the light of all that has since then become commonly accepted doctrine, Gossen's is a sufficiently remarkable book. His attitude is brazenly utilitarian; he outbenthams Bentham in his assertion that the object of every man is to raise his enjoyment of life to a maximum. But, Gossen hints, we cannot run bald-headed at our enjoyments. There are after-effects, and there are disappointments; a pleasure may generate later a feeling of the opposite kind. The fundamental principle, then, is that man should so direct his actions that the sum of his enjoyments in life

---

[13] *Entwicklung der Gesetze des menschlichen Verkehrs und der daraus fliessenden Regeln für menschliches Handeln.* References are to the recent edition published by Prager, Berlin.

should be a maximum; and this, moreover, is in accordance with the will of the Creator.[14]

We are therefore acting in accordance with the divine command when we seek to find out the laws which regulate our pleasures. Enjoyments, in fact, are marked by two characteristics: firstly, the magnitude of an enjoyment diminishes progressively until satiety supervenes; and secondly, there is a similar diminution in repetitions of the same enjoyment. Not only is the initial satisfaction lower, but its duration is also shorter; and, moreover, both kinds of diminution are more marked, the more frequently the repetition occurs. Gossen cites the usual illustrations: the first bite tastes the best, the second less good, still less the third. The second principle is illustrated by the poor man who finds much more pleasure in his Sunday roast than does the plutocrat who is so unfortunate as to have one every day in the week.[15]

From his analysis of enjoyments, Gossen elicits three fundamental principles which illustrate his pleasure-and-pain philosophy. Somewhat abridged, the essence of these is as follows:

1. In the case of each enjoyment there is a manner of enjoyment, chiefly dependent on the frequency of repetition, which will make the sum of enjoyments a maximum. If this maximum is attained, a more frequent or less frequent repetition will diminish the total enjoyment.
2. When there is a choice between several enjoyments, but insufficient time to enjoy all completely, maximum enjoyment requires that all should be partly enjoyed, even before the greatest of these enjoyments has been exhausted. At the moment of breaking off, the enjoyment which is being derived from each of the possible lines should be the same.

[14] *Entwicklung der Gesetze des menschlichen Verkehrs*, p.3.
[15] *Ibid.*, pp.4-6.

3. Thirdly, and rather oddly, the possibility of increasing the sum total of enjoyments is presented whenever a new enjoyment (however small in itself) is discovered, or an existing enjoyment extended. Blessed indeed is he who invents a new pleasure.[16]

Gossen's theory of value is intimately interwoven with this principle of diminishing satisfaction. The prevalent confusion in economic doctrine, he holds, springs exclusively from different conceptions of value. Nothing has led to such unfortunate results as the 'fiction of an absolute value,' whereas in fact there is nothing in the external world which possesses such an absolute value.[17] External things have value for us, he declares, according as they help us to attain the purposes of life; in more utilitarian language the magnitude of value is measured by the extent of the enjoyment or satisfaction which anything yields.[18] On this he enunciates the essentially marginalist principle that the individual 'atoms' (this is Gossen's word) of any consumption-good have highly different values. Moreover, for any man only a determinate number of these atoms has value, and beyond this point an increase is valueless; the point of valuelessness, however, is only reached after value, as represented by successive atoms, has gradually passed through the most diverse grades of magnitude. The first atom has the highest value; each additional increment has a smaller value until worthlessness supervenes.[19]

Moreover, in his analysis of value, Gossen is led to a classification of goods which is strongly suggestive of that advanced by Menger at a later date, and in his use of this classification in connection with the problem of the determination of value, he is the angel of Wieser. He divides

---

[16] *Ibid.*, pp.11, 12, 21. [18] *Ibid.*, p.24.
[17] *Ibid.*, p.46. [19] *Ibid.*, pp.31, 33.

goods into three classes: firstly, consumption-goods (*Genuss-mittel*), and above this goods of the second and of the third class. Goods of the second class are complementary goods – the pipe and the tobacco, the oven and the coal, the cart and the horse. The third class comprises productive-goods, whose purpose is to create consumption-goods.[20] The significant thing with regard to Gossen is that, in discussing the value of the goods of the second and third classes, he plots out, if he does not lose himself in, the field in which later Wieser was to disport himself. In the case of complementary goods, value is to be ascribed (*Werth zuzuschreiben ist*) because they are of assistance in preparing the way for a satisfaction, but what value should be so ascribed is not easy to determine. The combined value of the goods will be given by the satisfaction which in combination they yield; but beyond this one cannot go with precision, since they have value only when combined, and individually they 'will have value only so far as there is an intention to supply the missing units.' So, in the case of goods of the third class, the estimate is 'mediate' (*eine mittelbare*); value can only be ascribed to these in so far as they are of assistance in producing a consumption-good, and they are worth exactly as much as is represented by the assistance they lend in producing these. Here – except that Gossen uses the word 'zuschreiben' whereas Wieser uses 'zurechnen' – is the core of Wieser's productive contribution.

In two other respects Gossen's anticipations of the future deserve at least to be recorded. His lengthy and rather peculiar definition of 'work' need not concern us unduly, except to the extent that it is based on the idea of 'work' as a 'disutility' which is to be balanced against the utility resulting from it. It follows, therefore, that work should be continued until a negative balance emerges from the pro-

[20] *Ibid.*, pp.24, 25, 26.

cess. Work, he tells us, is something undertaken to produce a satisfaction, that is, to create something of value, and it follows that we are in a position to increase the sum total of the enjoyments of life by work, so long as the satisfaction created by the work is to be estimated as higher than the inconvenience caused by the work.[21]

So also, in his study of the question of exchange and the limits to which exchange should profitably be carried, he uses the machinery of marginalism and the conception of equi-marginal value. For any given person, exchange will continue to be advantageous until the last atoms of the objects under consideration have for him equal value.[22] In the light of these illustrations, it is not too much to say that in Gossen's long-neglected work there may be found all the essential ideas and much of the technique of the Austrian school.

Jevons

The importance of William Stanley Jevons[23] (1835-1882) lies in the fact that simultaneously with, and independently of, the Austrian school, he elaborated ideas fundamentally identical with theirs, and can thus claim to be one of the originators of the marginal school.[24] Jevons's *Theory of Political Economy* (published in 1871, the same year as Menger's *Grundsätze*) is inspired throughout by a 'fear of the too great influence of authoritative writers on Political

[21] *Ibid.*, p.38.
[22] *Ibid.*, p.84.
[23] Born at Liverpool in 1835. For a time in the Mint of Australia; 1866-1875 Professor of logic and mental and moral philosophy at Owens College, Manchester, and lecturer in political economy; 1875-1880 Professor in London.
[24] The other non-Austrian founder of the Austrian school, Leon Walras (son of Auguste Walras), must be crowded out here. His *Elements d'Économie Politique Pure* dates from 1874, and he is thus slightly later than Menger and Jevons.

Economy,' and there is in him not a little of conscious revolt against great names. So far as concerns method, he is an uncompromising advocate of the mathematical character of economics. 'Economy, if it be a science at all, must be a mathematical science.'[25] It is bound to be a mathematical science because it deals with quantities, with things which are capable of being more or less in magnitude; indeed there cannot be a true theory of Political Economy which dispenses with the aid of the differential calculus. Accepting sound utilitarian principles, Political Economy thus becomes a calculus of pleasures and pains; and if Jevons has doubts as to how far it is possible to conceive a unit of pleasure or pain, he takes refuge in the thought that the mind of the individual is the balance which makes its own comparisons. If we may not estimate, we may at least compare, since 'pleasures, in short, are for the time being as the mind estimates them.'[26] And for the immediate purpose, to compare is even more important than to measure.

Jevons's central doctrine, which he challengingly places in the forefront of his book, is what he calls 'the somewhat novel opinion that value depends entirely upon utility,'[27] and he claims that it is possible to arrive at a satisfactory theory of exchange (including as a consequence the ordinary laws of supply and demand) merely by tracing out the natural laws of the variations of utility 'as depending upon the quantity of commodity in our possession.' This, of course, is merely the core of Gossen, as it is of the marginal school. Utility is not an inherent quality; rather is it 'a circumstance of things arising out of their relation to man's requirements,'[28] and in which the amount already possessed is therefore a material factor. Taking the too familiar case of water, 'all that we can say, then, is that

[25] *Theory of Political Economy*, p.3.
[26] *Ibid.*, p.10.   [27] *Ibid.*, p.2.   [28] *Ibid.*, p.52.

water up to a certain quantity is indispensable; that further quantities will have various degrees of utility; but that beyond a certain point, the utility appears to cease.'[29] And in general the same principle holds: 'the very same articles vary in utility according as we already possess more or less of the same article.'

Jevons is thus led, with the aid of curves now known to every beginner, to distinguish between the total utility, which may be great – indeed infinite, when a question of maintaining life is involved – and the utility belonging to any particular portion which, if it is possible to increase the supply, may become as low as we choose. For the utility of the last portion, Jevons uses the phrase 'final degree of utility,' and much confusion in the past has, he contends, been caused by failure to distinguish between the total utility of a commodity which may be very great and the final degree of utility, which, by abundance verging on superfluity, may be reduced to zero.[30] Such old conundrums as the comparative value of gold and iron, of water and benedictine, and all the other usual examples, rest fundamentally on a confusion with regard to the meaning of the word 'value.' Water, if we talk sloppily with our eyes on value-in-use, may be said to be of infinite value; but weighed drop for drop in the balance of exchange, it makes a poor show against benedictine. Jevons would say that, so far as there is a mystery, it is because we confuse total utility with the final degree of utility.

Here, then, is what for Jevons is the 'all-important point in all economical problems,' viz., the variation of the function expressing the final degree of utility, a function which 'varies with the quantity of commodity, and ultimately decreases as that quantity increases.'[31] The same principle explains, for Jevons, the distribution of a commodity be-

[29] *Ibid.*, p.53.   [30] *Ibid.*, pp.58-61.   [31] *Ibid.*, p.62.

tween various possible uses, a classical point in the later statement of the Austrian school. Barley may be used to make beer, spirits, bread, or to feed cattle and so on. The theory of utility shows that the distribution between the various uses should be so assigned that the final degree of utility in the various directions should be equal.[32]

With this doctrine of diminishing utility, Jevons works out a theory of exchange. The word 'value,' owing to its horrid confusions, he would discard, and substitute for it the expression 'ratio of exchange,'[33] a suggestion which has not prevailed against the power of custom. The value of a commodity, if the 'dangerous term' may be permitted, is measured not by total utility, but by the intensity of the need we have for it; in even more precise language, 'value in exchange is defined by the terminal utility.'[34] The theory of exchange corresponds; the result of exchange is that all commodities sink to the same level of utility in respect of the last portions consumed.

The opposing doctrine that value is caused by labour, or that it is proportional to labour, Jevons dismisses very curtly as one 'which cannot stand for a moment.'[35] As he truly says, labour once spent has no influence on the future value of any article; in this sphere of life bygones are for ever bygones.[36] Yet though he holds that the value of labour is determined by the value of the produce, and not the value of the produce by that of labour,[37] his complete statement contains concessions which would considerably placate an upholder of the labour theory. For labour, though never the cause of value, may be the determining circumstance, and indeed he proves as a rider to his own theory that in the case of articles which can be produced in greater or less quantity, exchange will take place in the ratio of the quanti-

[32] *Ibid.*, pp.68-70. [33] *Ibid.*, p.83. [34] *Ibid.*, pp.83, 130.
[35] *Ibid.*, p.157. [36] *Ibid.*, p.159. [37] *Ibid.*, p.161.

ties produced by the same quantity of labour.[38] In this
case, then, Jevons's view would appear to be that what is
wrong with the labour theory of value is not that it is untrue, but that it gives the wrong reason for the truth which
it declares.

As distinguished from the earlier forerunners, Jevons
and Leon Walras (whom we can but distantly salute) are
almost entitled to be regarded as extra-mural founders of
the Austrian school, which we are now in a position to consider. The outstanding leaders of this group were Menger,
von Wieser and Böhm-Bawerk, with perhaps Sax as the
leading representative of those who might be called
followers.

Menger

Of these, Karl Menger[39] (1840-1921), though the least
known in this country, has distinct priority in time, and,
notwithstanding a smaller literary output, was probably the
most influential of the group. His *Grundsätze der Volks-
wirthschaftslehre*, published in 1871, really established the
school. Menger starts with a bold assertion of the universality of cause and effect. The transition from a state of
want to a state in which want is satisfied is, like everything
else, the result of causation. Here, then, is the subject of his
analysis. Those things which have the capacity of being
placed in a causal relationship with the satisfaction of
human needs are called utilities. In so far as we have power
to place them in this connection they are called ' goods.'[40]

[38] *Ibid.*, p.182.
[39] Born 1840 at Neu Sandez in Galicia; student at Prague, Vienna
and Cracow; Professor of Economics at Vienna, 1873; private tutor to
Prince Rudolf of Austria. Returned to academic work, and finally
retired from the university in 1903. In 1900 was made a life member
of the Austrian Upper House.
[40] *Grundsätze*, pp.1-2.

That a thing may be a 'good,' four conditions are necessary. There must be a human need; the thing must have such qualities as enable it to be placed in relationship with the satisfaction of the want; this causal relationship must be recognized; and, lastly, there must be a power to dispose of the thing in such a way that it can satisfy the want. All these things are essential; if any of the four is lacking, the thing loses its quality as a 'good.'[41] This looks horribly abstract; but it is subtly devised with a view to further argument.

The satisfaction of needs, then, is the primary consideration; but at once we come to a distinction, and it is the first fundamental point in Menger. There are goods which can be immediately applied to the satisfaction of our needs, as, for instance, bread. Such he defines as 'goods of the first order.' But apart from these, there are many things which indubitably possess the marks of 'goods,' but which nevertheless stand in no immediate causal connection with the satisfaction of our needs. Their function is to produce goods which do; these are goods of the second order, and exist to produce goods of the first order with which, directly and without any mediation, we satisfy our needs. Beyond these are goods of the third order, which produce goods of the second, and so on, as far as human ingenuity cares to go. Beyond the bread is the flour; beyond the flour, the grain; beyond the grain, the field and the plough; beyond the plough, the iron. While, then, it is essential that a good should stand in causal relationship to the satisfaction of our needs, this relationship need not be direct.[42]

Menger at once proceeds to use his theory of the order of goods in such a way as to foreshadow one of the cornerstones of the marginalist theory. To produce goods of a lower order, the co-operation of several goods of a higher

[41] *Ibid.*, p.3.   [42] *Ibid.*, pp.8-9.

order is required; to produce bread calls not merely for meal or flour, but also for water, all the baker's contrivances, fuel, and the baker alone knows what else. These are complementary goods. With regard to these Menger lays down two propositions which are significant, even if reasonably obvious. The first is that goods of a higher order only retain their quality as goods, if we can dispose of the corresponding complementary goods – though it is true that they may retain this quality in respect of other goods which they may also assist in producing. Thus pipes cease to be goods when the tobacco crop entirely fails, except in so far as they may remain goods for the purpose of producing soap-bubbles. The second proposition is that goods of a higher order only remain goods so long as the goods of a lower order, whose production they serve, retain the quality of goods. When golf goes wholly out of fashion, not merely do the golf-clubs become useless, but all the machinery used specifically and exclusively for the production of golf-clubs will also, in that fell day, cease to be goods.[43]

It will be seen to what distant end Menger is tending. The decisive position is occupied by the goods nearest the consumer, the goods of the first order; all others derive their importance from these, and have their justificaton in these; and they only live as goods to the extent to which they are countenanced by goods of a lower order.

The next important point in Menger arises from his distinction between economic and non-economic 'goods,' and the inferences drawn therefrom. It requires time to produce goods of a lower order from those of a higher, and the man who regulates his life on economic principles (*der wirthschaftende Mensch*) looks ahead and balances the want (*Bedarf*) against the quantity of goods available. Three cases may arise. The want or need may be greater than, less

[43] *Ibid.*, pp.11-17.

than, or exactly covered by the supply.[44] The first is the important case, and when this situation arises, it must further be recognized that no part of the supply can be withdrawn without leaving unsatisfied some concrete need for which previously provision had been made. In practice there are various consequences: the owner has to make a choice between the more important needs which he will continue to satisfy, and the less urgent which he must reconcile himself to leaving unsatisfied. Otherwise expressed, he must plan out the most expedient manner in which the available supply of goods can be used. This is the meaning of economics (*wirthschaft*), and these are economic goods.[45] Economic goods, in short, are goods which we are compelled to economize because the supply is inadequate; we have to decide that they may be applied to certain purposes and should not be applied to others. In the case of non-economic goods, on the other hand, where the supply exceeds the need, there is no occasion to arrange possible uses in a descending order of importance, or to plan out the wisest employment of the available supply.[46]

It follows from this that the economic or non-economic character of a good is no inherent immutable property. It arises from the proportion between the want or the need and the quantity available; in short, it expresses the 'rareté' of Auguste Walras. Accordingly, and further, it follows that goods may pass from one class to another by virtue of changes in this proportion. Increase of population, development of wants, the progress of men in the knowledge of what may be serviceable to their well-being, any or all of these may lead to a change in the character of the good.[47]

So armed, we are prepared to meet the idea of value. Value springs from the same causes as confer on certain

[44] *Ibid.*, p.51. [46] *Ibid.*, p.57.
[45] *Ibid.*, pp. 52-53. [47] *Ibid.*, p.62.

goods the quality of being 'economic goods'; it arises from the relation of wants and supply, and from the fact that in economic goods a diminution of supply leads to a want unsatisfied, or a want less adequately satisfied than before. Speaking generally, it expresses the importance or the significance which goods acquire in our eyes owing to our consciousness of the fact that we are dependent on our disposal of them for the satisfaction of our needs. Value, then, is a judgment of the mind; not a property of the thing or an independent entity.[48]

Different needs are of different importance. Some preserve life; some minister to our comforts; some are mere luxuries. But even so, taking the most fundamental, the importance attached to various concrete acts of satisfying the desire for food varies greatly. Up to a certain point it maintains life; later it may result in mere enjoyment. If continued (gloomy prophet!) it may turn to pain, and finally imperil life and health itself. This too familiar illustration is, however, primarily introduced in order to illustrate his scale of the importance of needs. Admittedly the demand for bread serves a more important purpose than the demand for tobacco; at least it starts off with a higher importance. But it may, and does happen, that later satisfactions from bread are less than the earlier satisfactions from tobacco. Economically, after eating for a certain time, it is wise to smoke.[49]

Turning to the more objective problem of the determination of value in any case, the question is complicated by reason of the fact that where a quantity of the good is in existence, different portions, applied in different directions, may yield entirely different satisfactions. Menger's example is of the farmer who has a reasonably adequate supply of grain, which after harvest he divides into different portions

[48] *Ibid.*, pp.78, 86.   [49] *Ibid.*, p.91.

and mentally allots to various purposes. The first is to preserve the lives of his family, and so we descend through next year's seed, the brewing of beer and brandy, until we end (since the farmer has enough) with a supply of what Menger pleasingly calls 'luxus-thieren' – presumably chinchillas and guinea-pigs.[50] The more familiar example rings the changes on Robinson Crusoe, his man Friday, his dog and his parrot. Under these circumstances, what is the value of the quantity of corn which we take as the unit? The answer, as so often, is found by asking another question: What want would remain unsatisfied in the event of the destruction or loss of the last portion in question?[51] In the cases supposed, the farmer would get rid of his chinchillas; Robinson Crusoe would wring his parrot's neck; and all other needs would remain satisfied as before. Further, as all like portions of the commodity are interchangeable, they must all have the same value; any of the sacks of grain may be the last. In the case supposed by Menger the value of the unit of corn is represented by the pleasure of keeping 'luxus-thieren.' Thus in general we get the determination of value. The value of any portion of goods, when a supply exists, is represented by the least important use to which such a portion is applied.[52]

In the case of those goods which are in direct touch with the consumer, goods of the first order, the determination of value is thus a problem which admits of a solution which

[50] *Ibid.*, p.96.
[51] *Ibid.*, p.98.
[52] *Ibid.*, p.99. The exact words may be given: '. . . der Wert einer Teilquantität der verfügbaren Gütermenge ist für jede Person demnach gleich der Bedeutung, welche die am wenigsten wichtigen der durch die Gesamtquantität noch gesicherten und mit einer gleichen Teilquantität herbeizuführenden Bedürfnisbefriedigungen für sie haben.' This is merely a fragment of a longer statement; Menger's sentences and paragraphs, which are sometimes indistinguishable, frequently seem to call for dynamite.

is easily comprehensible. To put the point of the previous paragraph in a slightly different form, value will be determined by the use which would first be sacrificed in the event of a curtailment of supply. And it is further clear that with a curtailment of supply, the value will rise. Crusoe, with his six sacks of grain, evaluates each by the pleasure he derives from his parrot's conversation. When the rats eat one sack and the stuffed parrot adorns the mantelpiece, each sack assumes the value of a dog – and so on through rising stages until, when there is only one, it has for Crusoe the supreme value he attaches to Robinson.

When we come to goods of a higher order, we are, however, confronted with complexities which the Austrian school, despite the utmost ingenuity, never satisfactorily resolved. It is fundamental to the Austrian view that value is reflected back, as against the erroneous cost-of-production theory which attributes value to a product, because goods possessing value have been spent and consumed in its production, and which thus derives the value of goods of a lower order from the value postulated to be already existing in goods of a higher order. As Menger says: 'The value of goods of a higher order is always, and without exception, conditioned by the value of goods of a lower order towards the production of which they are subservient.'[53] There is, indeed, the further complication that the element of time enters, so that the value of goods of a higher order to-day reflects the prospective values, some time hence, of the goods they are instrumental in producing.[54]

But to determine how much value each of the goods of a higher order derives from the value of the final product is clearly no easy matter. Menger's solution is obviously inadmissible. The difficulties are patent. Each product is the result of the co-operation of a group (which may be large) of

[53] *Ibid.*, p.124.   [54] *Ibid.*, p.138.

goods of a higher order, not all of which may, however, be essential. Menger notes that grain results from the co-operation of land, manure, agricultural machinery and labour, and there may be much more.[55] But, though the use of manure increases the supply obtained, nevertheless, even without any manure, the crop will not entirely fail; so also the absence of manure might be counteracted by increased labour in other directions. Moreover, there is the further complexity that complementary goods, which enter into a given combination with a view to the production of one commodity, may also, in another combination, stand in a similar relationship to an entirely different good of a lower order. There is more than one kind of agricultural produce, and very different values attach to each of them. In this criss-cross of uncertainty, how much value may we allow the manure to derive from the value of the grain? Menger rightly says that the value of a higher good cannot be equivalent to the satisfaction yielded by the whole product which it helps to create. What he suggests is that the value of a higher good is represented by the difference which its presence makes, or the loss which would be sustained by its withdrawal from the group.[56] This, however, is clearly inadmissible. It is unnecessary to go into refined arithmetical examples to realize that the withdrawal or destruction of land would have a devastating effect on agriculture, and therefore, on Menger's principles, the whole value of the product should pass to land; yet the contribution of agricultural implements and of manure cannot be denied. To the ordinary man, therefore, it would seem that, on Menger's solution, goods of a higher order might jointly derive from a good of a lower order a greater value than that good itself possesses. Menger, it should be noted, applies, although in a very brief discussion, the

[55] *Ibid.*, p.139.   [56] *Ibid.*, p.142.

same principle to the question of the determination of wages. The value of labour in any given case is represented by the loss we should suffer in the event of that labour being withdrawn.[57]

Lastly (or at least lastly for our purposes), Menger applies the general principles underlying his doctrine to the problem of the motives prompting to exchange, and the extent to which exchange should be carried. Daring to make game of Adam Smith's odd phrase regarding the 'propensity to truck,'[58] he shows that exchange is rooted in the ordinary individualistic impulse striving for the completest satisfaction of needs. Wherever A has possession of certain quantities of a good which have for him a less value than certain quantities of another good which are in the possession of B (and the reverse position holds the other way round), it will be advantageous for both that exchange should take place; and it is only necessary to confront the six horses and the one cow which A possesses against the six cows and the one horse which B has, specifying the diminishing value which each successive unit of cow and horse has in the eyes of A and B, to see up to what point exchange should take place. It is necessary to mention this point, but unnecessary to expand it, since this is one of the points more fully developed by Böhm-Bawerk[59]

Before leaving Menger, it is perhaps worthy of mention that he does not use the word 'margin,' which was lying ready to hand in the writings of von Thünen. It is to Wieser that this familiar friend is due; Menger himself periphrastically speaks of the 'least important' use.

Wieser
As we are here concerned only with the general ideas of the Austrian school, the other leading members must be more

[57] *Ibid.*, pp.149-150.   [58] *Ibid.*, pp.153-154.   [59] *Ibid.*, pp.159-168.

summarily dismissed. Menger laid down the broad lines of doctrine; the others elaborated, and the elaboration became so subtle in its higher reaches, that one is tempted to concur in the view that the consequent advantage is to be found rather in the intellectual gymnastics performed by these authors than in any new results obtained. Friedrich von Wieser[60] (1851-1926), who followed Menger with his *Ursprung und Hauptgesetze des Wirthschaftlichen Werthes* (1884), provided in his later *Natural Value* (1889) what was doubtless the most characteristic statement of Austrian doctrine. Relying on Gossen's Law of Diminishing Satisfaction, he gives a more precise statement of the doctrine of marginal utility, to which he gave the now accepted name of 'Grenznutzen.' His approach is definitely psychological. Our interest is primarily in our satisfactions; but under certain conditions – primarily the limitation of the supply of goods and the power to modify the extent of that supply – the interest is transferred from the need to the thing which satisfies that need, and which thus becomes invested with value.[61] The most characteristic part of Wieser's contribution to the school lies in his doctrine of *Zurechnung*, which has been acclimatized in this country as 'imputation' or 'attribution.' It has been seen that one of the leading tenets of the school is that value exists primarily and essentially in goods of the first order – goods, that is to say, which, immediately serving the uses of the consumer, obtain a value directly from an estimate of their marginal use. To all goods of higher order, production-goods, value is reflected back. The needle derives its value from the value of the stocking; the plough, ultimately, from the value of the bread, and so

[60] Born 1851; educated at Vienna; for a short time in the Civil Service; then teaching in the Universities of Vienna and Prague, returning to Prague in succession to Menger. Minister of Commerce, 1917, returning later to his Chair. Died 1926.
[61] *Ursprung*, p.81.

on. Here arises the problem of 'imputation.' In a sense the higher goods have no value until a value is 'imputed' or 'attributed' to them; but on what principles is a share of the value to be imputed to goods of a higher order? It is scarcely too much to say that Wieser's whole theory consists in an analysis of the working of the process of imputation. Two points are worthy of notice. Firstly, imputation follows the marginal law; here also it is in the light of the least important product that we must determine what value is to be reflected back or 'imputed.'[62] Secondly, he differs from Menger in his method of determining the value of complementary goods. Menger, it will be remembered, had suggested that the value in such a case would be determined by the loss which would result from the withdrawal of the good from the combination. In a series of chapters[63] Wieser argues, as against Menger, that in the case of a stock of heterogeneous goods, when one is removed, the others are simultaneously deprived of a portion of their effect. Consequently, 'the deciding element is not that portion of the return which is lost through the loss of a good, but that which is secured by its possession.'[64] Wieser's own solution is to determine what he calls the 'productive contribution' by the use of a series of equations, showing the results of using the goods in varying combinations.

Though Wieser furnishes the classical statement of marginalist doctrine, nevertheless he seems to attempt a reconciliation of the Austrian theory of value with the cost-of-production theory. In one passage of his *Ursprung*[65] he speaks of the process of value-formation as being a circular course. It rises from consumption-goods to production-goods;

[62] *Natural Value*, Book III, chap. 8.
[63] *Ibid.*, Book III, in particular chaps. 4-6.
[64] *Ibid.*, p.85 of English translation.
[65] *Ursprung*, p.156.

when determined there, it again descends from production-goods to consumption-goods. The descending branch whereby, in the hard reality of practice, the cost of the production-goods has to be met by the value received from the product, is visible of all men; not so the ascending (and prior) branch, which originally gives the productive goods their value. Once value has been conferred on a good of a higher order, it appears to us as a 'gegebene Thatsache,' a datum in all subsequent transactions. Thus Wieser's view would appear to be that the cost-of-production theory of value is not so much erroneous as incomplete. It is true so far as it goes, and in most cases is so in practice; but it does not push its inquiries far enough to find the source of that value which it accepts as existing in the productive goods.

Böhm-Bawerk

The third of the great Austrians who form the core of the Austrian school is Eugen von Böhm-Bawerk[66] (1851-1914), perhaps the best known in this country, by reason of his theories regarding interest, and his very brilliant assault on the Marxian system. For our immediate purposes, Böhm-Bawerk is the author of two considerable works, both of which have fortunately been translated, one under the title of *Capital and Interest,* and the other as *The Positive Theory of Capital.* The former is an elaborate criticism of all earlier theories of interest, so that the work is in substance a very learned and detailed history of economic doctrine on this one point. This work is wholly destructive and critical, and though it prepares the way for a statement of the author's

---

[66] Born at Brünn, in Moravia, in 1851; studied at Vienna; employed for a time in the Finance Department of the Imperial Government. Returned to academic life, and ultimately became Professor in Vienna. In 1890, Ministerialrath in the Finance Department. Remained in the Government service until 1909; thereafter again Professor in Vienna.

own views, it does not in fact contain such a statement. It is to its companion work, *The Positive Theory of Capital*, that we must turn to get Böhm-Bawerk's contribution to Austrian doctrine.

So far as the main parts of his work were concerned, Böhm-Bawerk rightly recognizes that on the whole, and apart from the discussion of interest, he was able to follow in the footsteps of previous theorists (Menger and Wieser). For our present elementary purposes, it is therefore unnecessary to attempt any survey of Böhm-Bawerk as a whole. There are, however, two points in Böhm-Bawerk's doctrine to which reference is frequently made, and which may therefore be briefly noted here. One is his theory that price is determined by what he calls the 'marginal pairs'; the other is represented by his views on interest, a subject which he describes as the 'heavy part' of his leading work.

The theory of the determination of price by the so-called 'marginal pairs' is to be found in the concluding portions of Böhm-Bawerk's discussion of 'price,'[67] in which up to a point he shrouds obvious truth behind considerable complexity of statement. In the case of isolated exchange[68] the price will be 'determined somewhere between the subjective valuation of the commodity by the buyer as upper limit, and the subjective valuation by the seller as lower limit.' Putting it in everyday language, in the isolated exchange the buyer will not pay more than he thinks the thing is worth, nor will the seller sell for less than he, on his side, thinks it is worth, and the actual price will fall between these two limits. Next he advances to one-sided competition among buyers,[69] and again it is obvious that 'the most capable competitor,' the buyer who is willing to go furthest, will be the purchaser,

[67] *Positive Theory of Capital*, Book IV.
[68] *Ibid.*, Book IV, chap. 2.
[69] *Ibid.*, Book IV, chap. 3.

and it is also obvious that the price will be somewhere
between his valuation (the price to which he is willing to
rise) and the valuation of the 'most capable of the unsuccess-
ful competitors.' In an auction the buyer will be the man
prepared to give most, and he will have to go beyond the
limit set by the bidder, who, next to him, hangs on longest.
All this is truth such as scarcely requires an Austrian for
its unveiling.

It is when Böhm-Bawerk comes to the idea of two-sided
competition[70] that the idea of 'marginal pairs' emerges.
For the sake of clarity it may be as well to take his own
example. Ten people anxious to buy a horse come to market,
where they are confronted by eight people each anxious to
sell a horse, and by a remarkable coincidence no one horse
differs from any of the other seven in any conceivable
respect. The buyers and sellers each come with a different
valuation of what a horse is worth, and in Böhm-Bawerk's
illustration the valuations are as follows:

	Buyers.			Sellers.	
A_1	values a horse at (and will buy at any price under)	£30	B_1	values a horse at (and will sell at any price over)	£10
A_2		28	B_2		11
A_3		26	B_3		15
A_4		24	B_4		17
A_5		22	B_5		20
A_6		21	B_6		21 10
A_7		20	B_7		25
A_8		18	B_8		26
A_9		17			
A_{10}		15			

Under these circumstances what will happen? Clearly A_1,
the most capable buyer, will buy a horse; he is in fact

[70] *Ibid.*, Book IV, chap. 4.

prepared to give a price which would induce any of the eight potential sellers to part with his horse. So likewise B_1 is sure to sell for similar reasons. A_1 and B_1 are in fact sure to do business (though not necessarily with one another). Had they met in isolation, the price arrived at between them might have been anything ranging from just over £10 to something just under £30, depending on which happened to be the better player of poker. But in actual fact the limits within which the price may range will be restricted for them by buyers and sellers with less latitude. So A_2 and B_2 can be relied on to do business, again within limits determined by less 'capable' buyers and sellers. Looking down the table, it is clear that the last people who could do business would be in fact A_5 and B_5; those who just fail to do business are A_6 and B_6. These are the marginal pairs; and while B_1, who is a certain seller, may sell his horse to any of the A's who in fact buy, the price at which the transaction will be carried through will be determined within the limits set by the last ins and the last outs. Waiving refinements, price is determined within the limits set by the subjective valuations of the marginal pairs. The important point in all this lies in the inferences which flow from the doctrine of marginal pairs; for it follows, firstly, that every market price is itself a marginal price; and secondly, that price, despite its apparent objectivity, is the product of subjective valuations.

The other point of fundamental importance in Böhm-Bawerk, that indeed which he made peculiarly his own, is the subject of interest. The point to be explained is why present goods have a higher subjective value than future goods of a like kind and number, why in fact £100 to-day is worth £105 a year hence; in other words, why interest emerges. Of this problem neither Menger nor Wieser had given a wholly satisfactory account. Böhm-Bawerk's explanation is largely psychological, resting on the fact that we systematically discount the future. He advances three main influences operating in this direction.[71] Firstly, in so far as we expect to be better off in the future, a like sum to-day will have a higher marginal value than the same sum in those more affluent times towards which (as we hope and trust) we are steadily moving. This applies to all who, being in embarrassment, expect to escape from their toils; it applies to the vast multitude who hope to be better rewarded in future, when their deserts are more worthily recognized. It does not apply to people on the down-grade, who are moving inexorably towards a pension of 40/80ths, or something worse, but even here present goods are, in the worst case, at least equal in value to future goods, since they can in general be carried forward without loss of value, and moreover they may act in the meantime as a reserve fund for anything that may turn up. Even such people therefore will rate present goods as high as, and perhaps slightly higher than, future goods. This, then, is the first reason for discounting the future, and arises from the fact that the hope which springs eternal in the human breast leads us to anticipate less stringent days ahead.

The second reason is that, just as we tend to over-estimate our means in the future, so we tend to under-estimate our future wants. This likewise is a complex of various influences. Partly it is due to a lack of imagination; we do not realize how many things we shall want next year, how many pleasures will plead to be tasted, how many 'calls,' not to be avoided, are sure to be made upon us. Partly it is lack of will; we are feeble creatures, running through our salary on the day we get it, although we have an intellectual apperception of the fact that there are other thirty days in the month, weakly making promises even when, in making

---

[71] Dealt with successively in *Positive Theory of Capital*, Book v, chaps. 2, 3 and 4.

them, we know we are letting ourselves in for trouble. As a consequence we pit our goods in the future against a body of wants and demands which, when the time comes, will be greater than we have allowed for. The effect of these two errors of optimism, in putting our future resources at a maximum and the future claims against us at a minimum, leads us to think that our money will go further in future, and will therefore have a lower marginal utility than, alas, we shall find to be the case when the time comes. Thus, quite apart from the fact that life is short and uncertain and we may never have a future, 'we look at the marginal utility of future goods diminished, as it were in perspective.'[72]

The third cause advanced by Böhm-Bawerk in explanation of the emergence of interest is of a different character. It relates to the superiority of what he calls 'roundabout methods of production.' More can be produced by a wisely chosen capitalistic process than can be obtained by direct unassisted production. Longer methods of production lead to a greater product, and therefore in comparing present and future goods, present goods are technically preferable in enabling the capitalist to obtain the advantages of roundabout methods of production, and the larger yield in the future. This leads to some of the points round which most discussion has centred; it is sufficient here to note the technical superiority of present goods, viewed from the angle of roundabout processes of production.[73]

Menger, Wieser and Böhm-Bawerk together sufficiently represent for the beginner the core and nucleus of the Austrian school; but perhaps a fourth writer claims, and can hardly be refused, inclusion among the original founders. It is obvious to us to-day that all the essentials of the Austrian theory are applicable not merely to the

[72] *Ibid.*, p.258 (English translation).
[73] See, e.g., pp.82, 268 of the English translation.

economy of the individual, but also to the economy of the State; and in particular that in that most crucial point of contact between the individual and the State, represented by taxation, that which is transferred to the State will also have for the State a marginal utility. The State may take, and apply to less urgent purposes, money which might have been more profitably employed by the tax-payer. This is indeed a rather dowdy old truth, which, however, is clearly capable of being neatly dressed in a chic Viennese confection. A discussion of this aspect of the question was the peculiar contribution of Emil Sax in his *Grundlegung der Theoretischen Staatswirthschaft* (1887). He applied Austrian thought to the economics of the State, and in particular used it to develop a theory of taxation.

CHAPTER XIII

Alfred Marshall

ALFRED MARSHALL (1842-1924) was the descendant of a family of non-conformist businessmen, and his father had been Cashier at the Bank of England. Marshall's heritage was one of commitment to individualism – economic, religious and political. His belief in efficiency was closely linked to his moral belief in the value of discipline, loyalty and self-denial.

He was pre-eminently Victorian in his encyclopædic approach, both to learning and to life: a man could be competent at many things without risking the accusation of dilettante. This confidence in discoursing upon a variety of subjects, and constantly displaying a breadth of knowledge and understanding, was the great gift of the Victorians which leaves their successors a little pallid and uncertain in their shadow.

Marshall never shrank from massive moral judgments, but he combines them with a sophistication and delicacy in historical detail and mathematical theory. To these moral and theoretical insights he added a typically Victorian empiricism: his family background furnished him with a knowledge of the business and industrial life of his time. It is this empiricism which links Marshall to Adam Smith.

Marshall was the first Principal of the University College at Bristol, its Professor of Political Economy, and later a Fellow of Balliol College, Oxford. In 1885 he was elected to the Chair of Political Economy at the University of Cambridge. Like all great university teachers, his influence stretched much further than his written works: the impact of his creative thought and his powerful (and in a Victorian sense, authoritative) personality directed the thoughts and actions of several generations of students. Some of his students, like Keynes, became eminent academics: many others entered the world of politics, the civil service, the city, business and industry.

Marshall's academic achievements were always presented with modesty and understatement. Although in his exposition of the theory of utility he ranks with Jevons, Walras and Menger, he never made excessive claims for the revolutionary impact of these ideas. On the contrary, he emphasized that these innovations should be viewed in the wider context and broader intellectual heritage of economic thought from Adam Smith and Ricardo onwards.

Although Marshall did so much to make marginal utility theory respectable in British academic life, his predominant respect and affection were probably for his earlier classical predecessors. In fact, there is not much acknowledgment of the work of Jevons and the Austrian school. It may be argued that the triumph of Marshall's economics lay precisely in this approach. He quietly took over and modified classical theory, and blended it with the ideas of the new utility school. The eclectic system he devised aroused no passions and controversies, and by appropriating 'foreign' ideas with only the most cautious, and perhaps (in the case of Walras) with inadequate acknowledgment, he could appear as a thoroughly respectable 'British' economist of unchallenged and impeccable descent from Adam Smith himself. Nor does one feel that this was a mere tactic: in his thought, his assumptions and his exposition, Marshall is the most 'British' of all economists. Like Queen Victoria, he also reaped the advantages of longevity: surviving until his 82nd year, he became the honoured elder statesman of

economics, revered by generations of students who successively achieved influence in many spheres of national life.

Marshall inherited the Benthamite view that institutions
and social relationships should be judged by their utility,
rather than by custom and tradition. Men should be free to
determine the nature of the world in which they live: freedom involved choice and the need to choose placed an obligation on individuals to act rationally rather than blindly,
whether it were choice in the market place or choice in the
ballot box. 'Freedom' and 'choice' are words which beg
many questions. But Marshall's Victorian confidence and
optimism never led him backwards into introspection or
logic-chopping: he accepted the postulates and moved
forward with a blend of authority and eloquence which
charmed and excited the best minds of his time at Cambridge, and which is his permanent legacy to the study of
economics.

Marshall was a legatee of the Whig version of history,
and his view is very close to Macaulay's. The history of
Britain demonstrates a progressive growth of freedom and
order. He does not see freedom as anarchy: the more free
mankind becomes, the more it will arrange its affairs in a
rational and orderly manner, developing its institutions, its
political system and its educational opportunities in a manner which cements the alliance of freedom and responsibility.
He is not afraid of competition, provided it takes place
within the context of stable government (which Marshall
equates with British parliamentary democracy). He sees the
dangers of ruthless competition, but he is enough the product of the age of Charles Darwin to see that life is something of a struggle, and if this struggle can be harnessed to
social ends it can be productive of economic welfare. But
competition, in Marshallian thought, does not merely maximize output: it is the arena in which the individual develops

his moral, physical and intellectual qualities. Competition is more than economics: it is the story of civilized Western man, and its fruits are to be found in spheres as remote from economics as those of art, literature, music and learning. It is the basis of civil government, where powerful men compete for the support of the lowly and the underprivileged. It is not an arid economic abstraction: it enters the models of the economists from a larger, truer, more enduring world outside. This belief in competition made Marshall suspicious of the power of monopolies. Monopoly was the enemy at every level: economic, political and human. But his hatred of monopoly is tempered with his basic empiricism. Some kinds of monopoly may be inevitable for natural, economic or technological reasons. If this is so (and Marshall, as we shall see, places the onus of proof heavily on those who say it is so), then he is prepared to consider State intervention as a means of making an honest woman of the wrong-doer.

Marshall's preference for a world of small businesses competing with each other had some objective validity in the Britain of his time, although he perhaps underestimated the tendencies towards large-scale organization which were occurring towards the end of his life. He did not, however, postulate the 'pure' competition of later theorists (i.e., a situation in which individual firms were assumed to be so numerous and small, that each one's decisions and actions would be strictly determined by external market conditions).

The 'pure' competition of later economists assumed away any elements of monopoly power or market power on the part of individual firms. Marshall anticipated these characteristics in his 'partial-equilibrium' analysis, but he never built them into his total system. He was prepared to start with highly simplified assumptions, but was always anxious to move as quickly as possible towards conditions of the real world. His method of ' partial analysis ' (a situation in which he considered two variables, holding everything else under *ceteris paribus*) is a pedagogic starting point. He subsequently introduced into his analysis the difficulties, complexities and ambiguities of reality, and his aim throughout is progressive approximation towards the world in which we live. Unlike his contemporary theorists, particularly in the sphere of utility doctrine, Marshall tried to avoid an extensive use of mathematics in his presentation. He himself was an accomplished mathematician and used mathematics in working towards his conclusions. In communicating his thoughts to the world, however, Marshall played down the mathematical inputs in his work. He once stated ' I had a growing feeling in later years of my work at the subject that a good mathematical theorem dealing with economic hypotheses was very unlikely to be good economics.'[1] He once described his use of mathematical methods as following certain informal rules of his own. These were to use mathematics as a shorthand language rather than as an engine of inquiry, to translate into English, and to illustrate by examples that are important in real life. He believed that once this point had been reached, the mathematics should be discarded. If no illustrations could be found from real life, this implied that the original mathematical exercise would not prove very fruitful, and he observed that it was his experience that this was more often the case than not. Marshall's approach stemmed from two motives: first, a methodological inclination to keep economics firmly rooted in objective data (which involved subordinating his mathematical method to empiricism), and second, a wish to reach as large a public as possible. In this latter motive, Marshall was very much in the spirit of Victorian scholar-

[1] Quoted in Horst C. Recktenfeld, *Political Economy: a historical perspective* (1973), p.279.

ship, with its passion for informing and educating the largest possible number of people. Spencer, Darwin, Macaulay and other great names of the Victorian era had all kept this aim firmly in mind, and Marshall, who had benefited from their teachings, was, in his turn, determined to hold aloft the lamp of learning to his fellow citizens. Marshall's main work is his *Principles of Economics*, first published in 1890 and frequently re-issued. His work is divided into six sections or 'books'. The first two deal with the scope of economics; he gives a definition which is wider than his immediate predecessors of the utility school. To Marshall, economics is not merely the study of weath, but of 'the study of mankind in the ordinary business of life.'[2]

In chap. II he expands his definition by stating that 'economics is a study of men as they live, and move, and think in the ordinary business of life.'[3] This definition sets the tone of Marshall's thought. He sees human life in general – and economic activities in particular – as providing evidence of man's continual progress. Further, he sees economic betterment leading to physical, social and moral development. As men are freed from the degradation of poverty, they become better people. They assume greater responsibilities for their own welfare and actions, and they become fitted for the energetic and responsible pursuit of success. Marshall sees this occurring within the context of responsible and representative government, where the State provides the framework for economic activity, and when necessary, intervenes; but he is equally concerned with the other role of the State, which lies in defending the individual's freedom and property, so that he is not the victim of arbitrary and bureaucratic impositions. Marshall's con-

[2] Alfred Marshall, *Principles of Economics*, Book 1, chap. 1, p.1 (all references are to the 9th Variorum Edition edited by C. W. Guillebaud, 1961).
[3] *Ibid.*, p.14.

cern is with an economic system which will ultimately abolish the hateful poverty he saw in his own life-time, and which will thereby enable everyone to live a fuller, freer life based upon wider choice than the poor had hitherto possessed. The normative strand in Marshall's thinking was recognized by Keynes in his famous comment that 'Marshall was too anxious to do good.'

Economic growth enables the poor to increase their consumption of goods and services, and enrich their experience. His Victorian optimism is marred by two main misgivings: the possibility of increased State control and intervention which will strangle initiative and narrow the range of men's creative possibilities, or, on the other hand, the growth of big businesses and monopolies which will operate in ways not dissimilar to the State, in the bureaucratic tyranny they impose, and in the way they undermine the initiative and efficiency of smaller concerns. In the long run, however, he predicts that large size can be self-defeating, and this could control the growth and power of big enterprises. In a famous passage, he describes how the whole economy – and each of its industries or sectors – would be like a forest, made up at each point of time of many individual firms (trees) of all ages and sizes or positions in their individual life-cycles. The largest and oldest units would be declining toward their death, while in many cases the youth and vigour of the smaller firms would more than off-set the disadvantages of smallness, and these firms would grow and lose those disadvantages, taking the place of the dead and the dying.

Marshall's metaphors set him apart from the more explicitly mathematical of his utility school forebears: he does not hesitate to borrow analogies from biology and botany to convey a sense of growth and to remind the reader of the changing world to which the postulates of economics are as subject as any others.

After the grand design outlined in the first two books, Book III gets down to a more theoretical exposition of wants, consumption, and demands. The utility school had believed that their switch of emphasis to consumption and demand was a great improvement on the doctrines of Adam Smith, and of Ricardo. Marshall shares their view of the need to bring consumption much more into the picture, and his own analysis is painstaking and mathematically neat. But, rather than claim that these new ideas have displaced, or at least over-shadowed, the pre-utility doctrines, Marshall tries to blend them into a larger pattern which takes account of Ricardian economic analysis. This analysis, he argues, must undergo some revision to the light of new ideas on consumption and demand, but it is by no means superseded.

Marshall achieves a high degree of logical order in his presentation. Book III deals with the starting point of our need for goods – i.e., utility and demand; Book IV deals with how these goods are produced; Book V deals with how goods are exchanged; and Book VI examines the distribution of national income. It is true that this sometimes involves an arbitrary separation of theories which are inter-connected, but as an orderly expository treatment it is difficult to fault.

Marshall gives a useful precision to the concept of 'demand' – a word which has been (and still is) frequently used loosely. To the layman 'demand' often means a vague need or want felt by individuals or by social groups. The classical school had seen demand as largely the demand for subsistence goods (which, in the light of their own time, was not an unreasonable assumption) and they had not ventured very far into psychological or motivational speculation about consumer tastes, or about the way in which consumer preferences affected prices in particular markets.

To Marshall 'demand' refers to the relationship between

quantities demanded, and prices. Consumers are usually more willing to buy at lower prices than at higher, and for each commodity a range of price and quantity combinations can be formulated. Marshall's diagram – the curve which represents price on a vertical axis and quantity on a horizontal axis – has, of course, been one of the basic diagrams for economics students ever since. He shows clearly and elegantly how such a curve is derived.[4] First, consumers enter the market to secure satisfaction from their purchases. They are subject to the 'law of diminishing marginal utility' – i.e., after a certain point has been reached in the consumption of a good, the utility derived from successive increments continuously diminishes. The consumer, therefore, is prepared to pay less for the last unit than for the preceding ones, and price must fall if he is to be persuaded to go on buying. This is obviously related to Marshall's general law of demand: 'the greater amount to be sold, the smaller must be the price at which it is offered in order that it may find purchasers; or, in other words, the amount demanded increases with a fall in price and diminishes with a rise in price.' The marginal utility basis for demand suggests a consumer buying successive amounts until marginal utility and price intersect (which is the basis for Marshall's concept of consumer surplus – the difference between what we do pay and what we would be prepared to pay). We must remember, however, that for some consumers the price would have to fall before they bought any units of a commodity, because price would be higher than the marginal utility of the first unit.

The second step in Marshall's exposition is to consolidate the demand curves of individual consumers, and the price relationships which will probably obtain in the whole of the

[4] Marshall's original demand graph can be seen as a footnote on p.104 of *Principles, Ibid.*

market can thus be set forth. For this to be possible, however, *ceteris paribus* must prevail. Money incomes, the tastes of consumers, and the prices of other goods must be deemed to be constant. If they do change, we have to construct a new demand curve. Marshall distinguishes between movement along the same demand curve (an extension or contraction of demand), and an entirely different curve (a rise or fall in demand). This distinction has been a favourite with first-year University examiners in Economics ever since.

Thirdly, Marshall demonstrates that in order to maximize utility from a given income, consumers adjust their expenditure until no gain in satisfaction can be achieved by any other allocation of expenditure (i.e., the last penny spent on any of the goods involved yields the same amount of satisfaction). It is difficult to over-emphasize the importance of this proposition, and it was to become crucial to the development of Neo-classical Economics (with its emphasis on 'economizing' as distinct from some of the older preoccupations of political economy). By setting out the functional relationship between the price of a good and the demand for it, Marshall removes ambiguities which sometimes exist over the difference between movements along the same demand curve and changes involving the construction of a new demand curve (e.g., changes in consumer preferences or changes in income).

Turning to supply, Marshall examines the terms on which sellers are willing to put goods and services into the market (i.e., the costs and sacrifices involved). These costs and sacrifices tend to rise as the quantity offered increases; here, the supply curve moves in the opposite direction from the demand curve, rising from left to right. Allied to this is the concept of 'opportunity costs'. These are costs in the form of income which the supplier is compelled to forgo when committing himself to one activity (in this manner, pre-cluding other options). We are now able to go on to construct a supply curve analogous to our demand curve. Firms nor-mally operate under conditions in which marginal costs (the addition to total costs arising from the production of addi-tional units of output) are rising. This is because increased output involves them in purchasing further inputs of the factors of production at increased cost. Hence higher prices are required to elicit increased supplies. Re-inforcing this tendency is another important law – that the addition to the total output obtainable from adding a unit of one pro-ductive input, while the quantity of the other remained un-changed, is likely to decline. This is, of course, the famous law of diminishing returns.

The shape of the supply curve thus depends on the be-haviour of marginal costs. If there is a change in conditions of supply, then we have a movement of the whole curve, in-stead of an extension or contraction along it.

Marshall then proceeds to aggregate the supply curves of individual firms to arrive at consolidated supply curves of firms producing identical outputs.

Having set forth his analysis of demand and supply, Marshall brings them together to show how the market (or equilibrium) price is determined. This is at the point of in-tersection of the two curves. A price above the equilibrium would mean that the seller would be prepared to offer more than buyers would take, and competition among sellers would force the price down to the level at which the market would be a price below equilibrium, and would lead to competition among buyers which would push price upwards again. To Marshall, these two curves are like a pair of scissors. In a famous phrase, he states:

'we might as reasonably dispute whether it is the upper or

the under blade of a pair of scissors that cuts a piece of paper, as whether value is governed by utility or cost of production.'[5]

Briefly, Marshall believes that demand conditions and their changes play the dominant role in the short run in determining the relative prices of different products. But in the long run, the Ricardian emphasis on supply conditions comes into its own again. Having started by looking at the behaviour of consumers, we have to move on to consider what adjustments the suppliers are making to meet changing demand. We have to examine what sort of supply conditions are in operation: and also to examine the behaviour or variation of the physical variables (ratios of required inputs of labour, time and other resources to resulting outputs of products) involved in the cost–supply functions. In the long run, equilibrium will have taken account of both demand and supply conditions. We should pause here to examine more clearly what Marshall means by different time scales in economics.

Marshall's famous three periods are ingeniously, if perhaps rather arbitrarily, set forth.

The first is a 'market period', i.e., a period too short for the producer to make any adjustment in his output in response to a change in prices. The second is the 'short run', in which output can be adjusted within the context of a given plant. The labour force may be induced to work longer hours, or more workers may be engaged, and additional raw material may be purchased. Thus, in face of increased demand, output would be increased by the measures described above. They would, however, probably involve a situation of rising marginal costs.

In Marshall's third time period, the 'long run', there is an

[5] *Ibid.*, p.348.

opportunity to expand the plant or for new firms to enter the industry. These various consequences, in face of increased demand, operate in the opposite direction if demand is falling. Marshall's treatment of his 'three periods' is a good example of how his clear, expository style can be slightly (if unintentionally) misleading. The unwary reader might assume that Marshall has based his analysis on empirical observation of existing industries and that his analysis could be directly helpful in the formulation of economic and industrial policy. In fact, the distinction made in the three periods is somewhat abstract (if not arbitrary), it has little operational significance, and is not securely grounded upon the facts of economic history. Nevertheless, in opening up the discussion on supply price elasticities, it is important conceptually for students, and appeals to 'common sense' – a quality which Marshall much admired. Knowledge of demand and the elasticity of supply influence the decision of a price-maker on what price to charge, assuming prices are flexible.

The length of the adjustments will vary in the real world from industry to industry. It can be argued that Marshall pays too much attention to the concept of 'industry' (a collection of independent firms all contributing to the aggregate supply of one kind of product) and too little to the individual firm's behaviour. This bias has been corrected in the work of later writers (e.g., in the theory of monopolistic competition) who emphasize the role of the individual firm and its freedom to make, within certain limits, its own price and output decisions. This approach has provided a more detailed and accurate picture than Marshall's broad brushwork, with its somewhat arbitrary portrayal of 'industries' each selling a product. It is in Marshall's distribution theory that we see perhaps the best example of his eclecticism. Whereas the utility school had seen demand as ultimately determining distribution, and Ricardo had emphasized supply conditions, Marshall combines the two.

The pricing of productive services determines income shares, and the marginal productivities of the suppliers of the productive factors are important here. It should be noted that Marshall develops von Thünen's marginal productivity theory.[6] But Marshall also brings in the idea (based on Ricardo) of long-run adjustments of aggregate supplies of productive factors. Unlike Marx, Marshall sees the three factors, labour, capital and land, as in some way entitled to their appropriate share. Wages are the reward for effort, and interest is the reward accruing to owners of capital for ' waiting' (i.e., the sacrifice involved in forgoing present consumption in favour of prospective future gains). Rent is the reward for the use of the factor land.

Not only is capital linked to the concept of ' waiting ' but it makes possible the additional output that can be produced by a longer gestation period (the productivity of capital). Marshall's capitalist is far removed from the parasitic role assigned to him by Marx. Not only does the capitalist make a sacrifice by ' waiting' but the ' productivity ' of capital (in which Marx in no way believed) gives the capitalist something on which to stake a legitimate claim.

Marshall's theory of wages is a combination of two themes: the marginal-productivity doctrine, and a modified Malthusian doctrine of the level of average aggregate wages. Wages tend to equal the net product of labour: its marginal productivity rules the demand price for its use; and, on the other side, wages tend to retain a close, though indirect, and intimate, relation with the cost of rearing, training, and sustaining the energy of efficient labour.

Marshall has misgivings, however, about marginal pro-

[6] See pp.223-231 above.

ductivity determining wages. How do we isolate the marginal net product, and how do we measure it?

To Marshall, the factors of production possess a supply price, and there is a certain rate of return which a factor must receive in order to call a certain quantity into use. This approach gives a unity and clarity to Marshall's system, although critics could argue that the worker's reward for effort stands in a somewhat different category from a capitalist's reward for 'waiting'. And what justifies the reward for the use of land? Marshall accepted that wages alone were not always decisive in determining the choice of jobs. He develops Adam Smith's theory of non-monetary advantages: workers tend to evaluate and balance all the advantages and disadvantages to themselves of different jobs. This involves, in addition to prospective remuneration, the working and living conditions, a wide range of environmental factors including neighbourhood situations and schools for their children. They choose the jobs which they feel offer the greatest 'net advantages'. Thus, the level of wage rates which an employer has to offer may be increased or reduced by some of the non-economic considerations. The emphasis Marshall places on this make his approach more realistic (and more relevant to our conditions to-day) than that of some other economists. In addition to the factors land, labour and capital, Marshall introduces another factor – 'organization'.

Marshall argues that in addition to the yield that businessmen may get as interest on their equity capital, and the wages they receive as a reward for routine management in established business, they have a claim for creating and developing effective organizations. This is a category of special reward for active and successful businessmen. This view reflects Marshall's respect for the distinctive role of the entrepreneur in the economy.

It is not, however, completely integrated into Marshall's system, and his treatment of 'organization' as a factor is diffuse, drawing on biological analogies which we would to-day find methodologically controversial.

Another significant contribution of Marshall was in the sphere of monetary theory. The classical economists, dealing with the quantity theory of money, had thought of the velocity of circulation of money as constant. Marshall did not believe that this was true and switched the emphasis into studying the reasons for the variability of this velocity. He pointed out the importance of people's decisions about the amount of cash-balance they decided to hold. If all members of the community decide to increase their cash balances (or, to put it another way, to reduce spending) they reduce one another's money-income. This leads to a decrease in the aggregate money-income of the community, to a smaller multiple of the existing quantity of money in people's balances. By dealing with the velocity of circulation as a very significant variable rather than as a constant, Marshall paved the way for later theories of 'liquidity preference' which emphasized the importance of examining how people vary the proportions of their liquid and non-liquid assets. One should not, however, exaggerate the degree to which Marshall anticipated Keynes. Marshall is so comprehensive and eclectic that there are dangers, as with Adam Smith, in making him the direct ancestor and only begetter of almost every category of current economic thinking.

In spite of his new ideas, Marshall's main conclusions tend to support the self-correcting and optimistic implications of Say's Law. He treats money largely in its uses for spending and its impact on the general price level. He sees the role of the rate of interest as determining the equilibrium between decisions to save and invest. He accepts the evidence of the world around him that there are booms and slumps in economic activity, but does not consider that these arise from any fundamental weaknesses (or, as Marxists would call them, ' contradictions ') in the Capitalist system. He finds that the cause of these upward and downward swings lies in the psychological attitudes of businessmen, who are liable to moods of pessimism and optimism. Nevertheless, over time (and left free from too much government intervention) the system would adjust itself to a high level of employment.

Alongside Marshall's admiration for the successful Victorian businessman runs a streak of strong reforming purpose. He was concerned that Britain lagged behind Germany in scientific and industrial education, and behind America in the industrial equipment available to workers. ' It is specially incumbent on Britain to strive against the stiffness of the joints that is almost inevitable in each old industry.'

Although Marshall supported the maximum possible freedom for businessmen, he favoured measures for scrutinizing and controlling monopoly, and for the employment of effective teams of investigators to distinguish between the injurious, and the beneficial effects of monopoly. There can be little doubt that Marshall would have supported the current legislation and policy in Britain for the control of monopolies, mergers and restrictive practices – he would, in fact, have been an admirable chairman of the Monopolies Commission.

On the subject of state intervention in the economy and on nationalization, he is prepared to give cautious (but only very cautious!) examination as to the possibility.

Marshall recognized that supply conditions could affect the criteria for choosing between public and private enterprise. He considered that ' natural monopolies ' were a proper subject for public regulation, and he admitted the possibility of re-allocating resources (by the use of taxes and subsidies) from decreasing to increasing-return industries. Since the time of Marshall's cautious observations on the boundaries of public and private enterprise, economists have come to recognize the case for certain kinds of goods and services to be supplied by governments rather than entrepreneurs. The case for government intervention as later developed came to depend (in the view of some economists) on one or another of three considerations: the public character of the good, the existence of major economies of scale, or the existence of significant external effects. But although Marshall laid the foundations for future analysis of public-sector economics, he himself remained highly cautious and sceptical.

His final verdict on the merits of State intervention is not very enthusiastic. He admits that government and local government carry out important tasks, but they are mainly concerned with activities that lend themselves to standard, repetitive and routine administration rather than entrepreneurial activity. They are concerned with such things as transport, water, light and power and the meeting of 'elementary needs ... they make use of plant, the central ideas of which have been worked out by private enterprise and gradually become private property.'

Elsewhere, he writes:

'There is therefore a strong *prima facie* case for fearing that the collective ownership of the means of production would deaden the energies of mankind, and arrest economic progress, unless before its introduction the whole people had acquired a power of unselfish devotion to the public good, which is now relatively rare; and though this matter cannot be entered upon here, it might probably destroy much that is most beautiful and joyful in the private and domestic relations of life.'[7]

[7] Alfred Marshall, *Elements of the Economics of Industry* (1892), p.405, 1913 reprint of 3rd Edition.

Marshall's caution on State control, does not, however, in his own words 'imply acquiescence in the present inequalities of wealth'.[8] Marshall sees these inequalities as a serious flaw in our economic organization. He would not, however, approve of redistributive measures which would 'sap the springs of free initiative and strength of character'. He favours attempts to raise the living standard of the lowest-paid workers, even at the expense of especially well-to-do families.

Marshall's emphasis on price theory was characteristic of his generation of economists. It was helpful, insofar as it provided signposts for later economists (and equally valuably, stimulated them into challenging some of his conclusions) by formulating a more refined theory of prices than the earlier Classical School had devised.

After Marshall, however, there was a switch of emphasis, (particularly in more recent years) away from considering price-determination as the central economic problem. Keynes was to focus attention on the more visible human and social problems of unemployment and the need for practical policy solutions rather than the theoretical niceties of price analysis (although pure price theory, of course, plays a part in the Keynesian system). There are signs, however, that interest is re-awakening in some of the old Marshallian pre-occupations: the need for a system of flexible relative prices that both reflect demand conditions and serve as a guide to efficiency in the deployment of our national resources. The role of prices, while banished from the predominant position it once occupied, is coming once again to be regarded, as Marshall regarded it, as performing an essential contribution to the full and balanced satisfaction of people's needs. The view that economic activity exists to serve human wants was the starting point of Marshall's

[8] *Ibid*, p.406.

'Principles' and although its implications must be studied afresh in every generation, economists should not shrink from continuing to assert its fundamental validity.

In concluding our survey of Marshall, we should perhaps leave the last word with Joan Robinson. Her comment aptly summarizes the combination of idealism and empiricism in the great man's writings.

'Marshall certainly was a great moraliser, but somehow the moral always came out that whatever is, is *very nearly* best.'[9]

[9] Joan Robinson, *Economic Philosophy* (1973), p.72.

CHAPTER XIV

John Maynard Keynes

JOHN MAYNARD KEYNES (1883-1946) was the son of a
Cambridge economist, John Neville Keynes, who was also
a logician of some repute.[1] After a brilliant sojourn at Eton
(where he excelled alike at scholarship and athletics), he
proceeded to King's College, Cambridge, where he took a
First in Mathematics. His university interests were wide,
covering politics (he became President of the University
Liberal Club), philosophy, drama, literature and art (he
formed friendships with Leonard Woolf and Lytton
Strachey which later widened into the famous 'Blooms-
bury' set) and he was elected President of the Union.

After taking his degree in mathematics, he studied economics under Marshall and Pigou and entered the Civil Service, being assigned to the India Office.

Two years later, he returned to Cambridge, subsequently
becoming a Fellow of King's College. His career, however,
was by no means confined to the academic cloisters. As a
result of his book *Indian Currency and Finance* (1913)[2] he
was appointed to a Royal Commission to examine Indian
currency. In 1915 he joined the Treasury, and was given
special responsibility for co-ordinating the foreign exchange
expenditure of Britain and her allies on essential imports.
He accompanied the British delegation to the Paris Peace
Conference, but became rapidly impatient both of what he

[1] He wrote the influential exposition of economic methodology,
The Scope and Method of Political Economy (1890).
[2] Reprinted as Vol. 1 of *The Collected Writings of John Maynard
Keynes* (Royal Economic Society, 1971).

regarded as the duplicity of Lloyd George, and the short-sighted approach of the bankers. In 1919 he resigned his post in protest at what he interpreted as the vindictive treatment of Germany. The consequences of this immoral and im-practicable settlement, he predicted, would be another war with Germany '... which will destroy, whoever is victor, the civilization and the progress of our generation.'[3]

His *Economic Consequences of the Peace* was followed by an attack on the proposed return to the pre-war gold stan-dard – *A Tract on Monetary Reform* (1923),[4] which was followed by *The Economic Consequences of Mr. Churchill* (1925),[5] – a denunciation of the Minister who took the de-cision to return to gold.

In 1932 he published a two-volume *Treatise on Money*,[6] – a widely acclaimed masterpiece, which was, in many re-spects, to develop the ideas which formed the basis of his *magnum opus* – *General Theory* – in 1936.

The Second World War (which Keynes had predicted so long before) brought him back into harness, and in 1940 he became an economic adviser to the Government, concerned with the mobilization of the national economy in support of the war effort. His proposals in *How to Pay for the War*[7] – published in 1940 – made new demands for restraint and for effective and equitable methods of financing the war (in sharp contrast to the practices of the First World War). He developed new methods of national income analysis, (with the aid of Erwin Rothbarth and others) which were to have a lasting effect on government accounting. He assisted in the Beveridge Report on Social Insurance and Allied Services,

[3] John Maynard Keynes, *Economic Consequences of the Peace*, Vol. II, *Collected Writings . . ., Ibid.*, p.170.
[4] *Ibid.*, Vol. IV.
[5] *Ibid.*, Vol. IX.
[6] *Ibid.*, Vols. V and VI.
[7] *Ibid.*, Vol. IX.

and the famous 1944 White Paper on Employment Policy, with its revolutionary declaration that 'the Government accept as one of their primary aims and responsibilities the maintenance of a high and stable level of employment after the war ... total expenditure on goods and services must be prevented from falling to a level where general unemployment appears.'[8]

Having seen so many of his hard-fought battles brought to a victorious conclusion on the domestic front, he turned back to his earlier battlefield – the international scene. He was the senior British negotiator with the U.S.A. over Lend-Lease, and went on to play a significant role in the establishment of the International Monetary Fund, and the International Bank for Reconstruction and Development. He had been raised to the peerage in 1942 and made a number of major contributions to debates in the House of Lords. Married to the famous ballerina, Lydia Lopokova, of the Diaghilev Ballet, Keynes took a lifelong interest in the arts. He played a leading part in the building of the Arts Theatre in Cambridge, and was responsible for the establishment of the Arts Council. These activities did not preclude him from a shrewd and highly productive involvement in financial affairs; he was Chairman of an insurance company, and he invested in a highly profitable manner, both for himself and for his College (of which he was Bursar).

In his earlier days, Keynes had been thought by many to be a dangerous, unpredictable, revolutionary character. His pro-German views in 1919 aroused intense irritation throughout the country – Noël Coward was later to write a satirical song called 'Don't let's be beastly to the Germans' which epitomized British impatience with those who were disposed to forgive Germany. But it was his *General Theory* which

[8] *Employment Policy*, Ministry of Reconstruction, Cmnd 6527, May 1944.

earned him accusations of undermining the capitalist system, ridiculing sacred economic institutions, and pouring scorn upon the traditional economic virtues of thrift, prudence and initiative. In fact, Keynes was no revolutionary. He stated:

' I think that Capitalism wisely managed, can probably be made more efficient for attaining economic ends than any alternative system yet in sight, but that in itself it is in many ways extremely objectionable. Our problem is to work out a social organisation which shall be as efficient as possible without offending our notions of a satisfactory way of life.'[9]

In spite of his prodigious output of work in scholarship, in public affairs, in cultural activities, Keynes was always moving on to new interests. He stated, for instance, that he intended to take up the serious study of economic history when he was 70. We shall never know how serious he was in this intent; he died of a heart attack in April 1946 at the age of 62.

This, then, was Keynes the man – a blend of radical and conservative inclinations; talented in both analysis and exposition, cultivated in all the arts, shrewd and practical in financial management, skilled in the arts of political debate and negotiation, and deeply committed to some of the major social issues of his time. All these divers qualities, achievements, and experiences were brought together in his *General Theory* – a book which, like the *Wealth of Nations*, persuaded its own generation and governed the next. The full title of Keynes' masterpiece is *The General Theory of Employment, Interest and Money*, but it is usually known as his *General Theory*[10] and it is accepted that its main con-

[9] John Maynard Keynes, ' The End of Laissez-Faire ' (1926) in *Essays in Persuasion*, p.294. Vol. IX, Collected Writings . . ., *op. cit.* (1972).
[10] Vol. VII, *op. cit.* (1973); see also Vol. XIII, *The General Theory*

cern is with the first of the trinity of topics in the title, i.e., employment. Keynes, himself, says 'The ultimate objective of our analysis is to discover what determines the volume of employment ...'[11] and all the concepts and relationships subsequently discussed must be assessed in the light of this objective. It was failure to understand this fact which misled some of his contemporary critics. Even the scholarly and humane Professor A. C. Pigou was too harsh in his criticism of Keynes (a fact he later graciously admitted) because he was viewing his work in the light of Marshallian economics, and had not sufficiently realized the extent to which Keynes had changed the rules of the game.

Why had Keynes made the determination of the level of employment his main concern? He was, it must be remembered, writing in the mid-1930s, when unemployment was running at an alarmingly high level, and causing widespread distress and social tension. Whereas in the century before 1914, unemployment in Britain had averaged 3 or 4%, between 1929 and 1939 it average 13%, and in 1932 it rose as far as 22%. The end of the 1920s and the start of the 1930s saw the world in the depths of a slump from which it seemed there was little prospect of emerging. Keynes did not believe that existing economic theory, with its strong *laissez-faire* bias, was capable of providing the remedy for this overwhelming economic and social malaise. The Marxists, he saw, were expressing confidence in their founder's prediction that capitalism was doomed by its inner contradictions, and were expecting its final collapse at any moment. Keynes did not accept this view (it could be argued that his *General*

and After, part 1: 'Preparation', and Vol. xiv, *Ibid.* (1973), part ii: 'Defence and Development'; these provide extensive details of Keynes's early drafts and revisions and correspondence with colleagues during his creative work while writing the *General Theory* and exposition afterwards among the academic community.

[11] *Ibid.*, Vol. vii, p.89.

Theory is aimed as much at disproving Marxism, as disproving the theory of *laissez-faire*) but he recognized that unless a new economic theory could be formulated, which gave hope to thousands of disillusioned citizens, then Marxist ideology might well triumph.

Keynes directed his attack on the body of theory deriving from Say's law. Broadly speaking, this argued that, given time, unemployment would be cured by the normal operation of supply and demand. J. B. Say had argued that general over-production and unemployment cannot persist because supply creates its own demand. People who receive payments for supplying goods, are, in turn, buyers of goods. The supply of products in particular industries may temporarily outrun the demand for the products of those industries, if entrepreneurs misjudge the demand for their goods. But in Say's view, *general* over-production is impossible. Say's Law, re-formulated in various minor ways, was adopted by Ricardo and became part of conventional economic theory. There was only one major dissenter – Malthus. He argued that general unemployment could be caused by deficient demand, and he is quoted approvingly by Keynes:

'Malthus, indeed, had vehemently opposed Ricardo's doctrine that it was impossible for effective demand to be deficient; but vainly. For since Malthus was unable to explain clearly (apart from an appeal to the facts of common observation) how and why effective demand could be deficient or excessive, he failed to furnish an alternative construction; and Ricardo conquered England as completely as the Holy Inquisition conquered Spain. Not only was his theory accepted by the city, by statesmen and by the academic world. But controversy ceased; the other point of view completely disappeared; it ceased to be discussed. The great puzzle of effective demand with which Malthus had wrestled vanished from economic literature...'[12]

[12] *Ibid.*, (1973), p.32.

It was the ' puzzle of effective demand ' which Keynes was to revive and place at the centre of his analysis.

Keynes rejected the idea that full employment is the normal state of affairs, achieved by some self-adjusting mechanism. He believed that the economy might come to rest at a position of *unemployment equilibrium*, i.e., an equilibrium where there were no natural forces operating (as Say had argued) to achieve full employment.

Therefore, the tools of economic analysis should be directed to the fact that the level of employment is determined by certain causal factors. What are these factors? Do they operate in a way which achieves full employment, or do they lead to unemployment?

Keynes divides effective demand into two components – consumption and investment. Employment depends on effective demand – i.e., the sum of expenditure on consumption, and the actual expenditure on investment. The volume of consumption in a country depends on the consumption decisions of individuals in that country. The amount spent by the country as a whole is therefore the total of the sums spent by individuals. Keynes starts by looking at what determines the consumption of the individual. He assumes that consumption shows a definite and fairly stable functional dependence on income. Thus, where, for any single consumer, C =Consumption, and Y =Income, then $C = f(Y)$. This functional relationship (f) between income and consumption is called by Keynes the 'propensity to consume'. The propensity to consume of the individual depends on two sets of forces – his *subjective* attitude to consumption, and certain *objective* conditions. Keynes' treatment of the subjective aspects is, it may be argued, more detailed and realistic than the treatment of consumption by the Classical School. The Classical economists had tended to represent the main choice as between present and future consumption, and laid emphasis on the virtue of thrift.

Keynes said that decisions as to whether to consume or save are more complicated than this; an individual wishing to save money may be motivated by such feelings as pride and avarice, by desire to bequeath a fortune to his heirs or by the need to provide for certain contingencies (e.g., illness or unemployment). These are motives which reduce consumption; on the other side are those which increase it (e.g., ostentation, extravagance and generosity). There are echoes of Veblen in these observations. Similar motives may affect businesses. Some firms will be overcautious in putting funds into reserve, while others will err in the opposite direction. The businessman, motivated by what Keynes called 'animal spirits', operating in a world of uncertainty, governed by ever-changing expectations, is no less affected by the constant ebb and flow of circumstance and opportunity than the consumer. All those motives, operating in their various ways, will affect the propensity to consume of the country as a whole. However, short-run changes in these subjective factors affecting the propensity to consume are unlikely.

Turning to the objective factors: apart from money income, the main objective fact will be prices. However, it is assumed, in order to construct a relatively simple theory, that prices are constant. Changes in consumers' tastes alter demand for goods, but it is thought that in the short run, these changes will not be important. Another objective factor is the rate of interest, but Keynes argued that the direct effect of the rate of interest on the propensity to consume was usually small.

With regard to their decisions to save, individuals were not, according to Keynes, as sensitive as the Classical School had imagined to interest-rate changes. Individuals first sought an acceptable level of consumption and undertook to save only when their income was more than sufficient to cover consumption requirements. In this sense, saving was a residual, varying in amounts with changes in the level of income.

With regard to the propensity to consume, the conclusion which Keynes arrived at was that, with the exception of money income, no change in objective conditions would significantly affect an individual's propensity to consume. Keynes develops a further concept, the *marginal* propensity to consume. This is the proportion of any *additional* income which is spent on consumption. It is reasonable to assume that rich people save a larger proportion of their income than poor people (or put another way, their average propensity to save is higher). There is a limit to the number of yachts, country houses, bottles of gin, and expensive cigars on which the richest man can spend his money. On the other hand, the old age pensioner may well spend his entire weekly income on necessities.

Keynes placed great emphasis on the use of the marginal propensity to consume; he saw that it was the key to the size of the change in National Income that would be required to achieve equilibrium (i.e., to correct a situation in which businessmen wanted to invest more – or less – than people wanted to save). The greater the marginal propensity to consume, the greater will be the change in national income which results from a given change in investment or saving. This is brought about by the operation of a central Keynesian tool (developed from an earlier theory by R. F. Kahn), the multiplier. The multiplier shows the ratio between an increase in income and the increase in investment which has given rise to it. If, in a situation of unemployment, the Government spends £1 million on public works, the workers employed on these projects spend their money on consumer goods. This increases the incomes of workers in consumer-goods industries, who in turn spend their money on more consumer goods. Thus, the country may end up with an increase in income several times the amount of the initial investment in public works. It is of crucial importance to the Keynesian objective to note that the effect of the increase in investment, through the operation of the multiplier, is to increase both income *and employment*.

Keynes starts with a simple proposition: the size of the multiplier (given certain carefully defined conditions) depends on the size of the marginal propensity to consume. If the latter is high (i.e., if people are spending a large proportion of additional income) they will generate further spending throughout the community. Therefore, the multiplier will be correspondingly high.

If their marginal propensity to consume is low (i.e., if they are saving instead of consuming extra income) then they will generate less further spending in the community. This seems a fairly obvious point, based upon common sense. Nevertheless, the great achievement of Keynes is the manner in which he integrates these two concepts – marginal propensity to consume, and the multiplier – into a theoretical model designed to combat unemployment. Three important qualifications must be added to the simple multiplier theory. First, we are dealing with *additional* investment over the previous level of investment. Second, we assumed a 'closed economy' i.e., there are no 'leakages' through spending on imports which might mean that the multiplier effects of increased investment in this country might accrue to foreign workers rather than our own. Third, taxation is a similar leakage, although the Government can, of course, off-set this effect by spending the proceeds of taxation on new investment.

Later developments in multiplier theory have added

many refinements (and aroused fresh controversies), but it enters the history of economic thought as an important new concept, not only theoretically elegant, but of direct relevance to public policy. Say, and many of his Classical successors, had assigned a somewhat subordinate role to money, and had concentrated on the 'real' exchange (for goods, services, etc.) which goes on under the veil of money. They had seen money largely as a medium of exchange, and directed their analysis to the fundamental economic phenomena which lay beneath the monetary system. This approach was by no means misguided and the Classical heritage yielded many important new insights. Nevertheless, Keynes did much to restore the balance between 'real' and 'monetary' analysis.

His early experience and specialization made him admirably (one might almost say uniquely) qualified to achieve this synthesis. Instead of concentrating on money as a medium of exchange, he stressed its importance in the sphere of 'liquidity'. By this, he meant 'command over goods in general'.

Keynes describes 'liquidity preference' (the demand for money) as depending on three motives: the transactions motive (the need to pay for things – whether as consumer or businessman – at short notice); the precautionary motive (as a guard against accidents, unemployment, ill-health and all the uncertainties of life); and the speculative motive (a readiness for profitable opportunities).

It is important to emphasize the special nature of Keynes' synthesis of 'real' and 'monetary' phenomena. The Classical School, in its rejection of Mercantilist thought, had tended to downgrade money and concentrate on 'real' wealth. Keynes helped to restore the Mercantilist view that money possessed an importance in itself. The utility schools had bolstered the older classical viewpoint by arguing that money did not possess utility. Keynes widened the discussion of monetary theory by the use of his concept of liquidity (which, it might be argued, provides money with something analogous to a utility of its own in contrast to the 'medium of exchange' theory, which sees money largely as a lubricant assisting in the production and exchange of real wealth). Marshall, as we have seen, to some extent anticipated Keynes, but he never linked the monetary and the non-monetary economic variables as effectively as Keynes. Keynes demonstrated that the pursuit of liquidity (i.e., the desire for large cash holdings) could cause a reduction in spending and thereby in national income, production, and employment. He uses the idea of liquidity to drive a final nail in the coffin of Say's Law, and demonstrates that it was possible for people to save too much. He goes further, however, in his analysis and demonstrates that the contraction of income, production and employment continues to the point where *realized* saving is only equal to all profitable investment spending.

When the *General Theory* first appeared there was some confusion among readers as to what Keynes meant by the equality of saving and investment. It is obvious that on Keynesian assumptions, what entrepreneurs actually invest will be equal to what families *actually* save. Keynesian analysis reveals, however, that what entrepreneurs want to invest is not necessarily equal to what families *want* to save. If entrepreneurs attempt to invest more than families want to save through the multiplier, they will increase national income and thereby increase the total savings of families; if, on the other hand, they attempt to invest less than families want to save, through the multiplier they reduce national income and thereby reduce total savings. These are two categories of people taking decisions for different reasons. There is no reason why the investment decisions of some tens of thousands of entrepreneurs should match exactly the saving decisions of millions of individuals.

Investors are interested in. acquiring wealth-creating assets. They choose among those that are available on the basis of the prospective yield to them from selling the output that the assets can produce. In this exercise they have to make a judgment. If they judge correctly, they make profits, and if they choose incorrectly, they make losses. The ratio between the prospective yield of an asset's output and the acquisition cost of that asset is what Keynes called the *marginal efficiency of capital.*

The investor is able to compare his estimate of the present value of an asset's future earnings from selling its output against the rate of interest. If investors as a group have expectations regarding the earning capacity of assets which result in the marginal efficiency of capital, in their view, being greater than the rate of interest, they will tend to attempt to acquire assets and order new ones, with the result that employment in asset-producing industries will increase and, through the multiplier, employment in consumer-good industries will increase. The reverse will be true where the rate of interest is greater than subjective estimates of the marginal efficiency of capital.

In describing the behaviour of investors in this way, Keynes was highlighting the necessary condition for the functioning of a profit-stimulated economic system. What investors want to do depends on their subjective estimate of the profit opportunities available from acquiring assets and putting them to work, with labour, to produce output that has yet to be sold. Whether this coincides with what savers want to do will determine whether the economy as a whole is expanding or contracting or remaining in equilibrium. If the latter is the case, the intentions of both groups will be identical, but this state of equilibrium need not be one of full employment. In this manner, Keynes unlocked the door to understanding the workings of the capitalist economic system.

It is important to remember that an important point of departure by Keynes from Classical theory lies in Keynes' insistence that spending and saving are predominantly 'functions' of the level of income. He emphasized that the amount of saving done in the economy is not influenced as much as previously thought by the extent of opportunities for profitable investment (i.e., by the demand for the use of savings in financing production and by the inducement offered to savers in the form of the rate of interest), although of course, these opportunities do play some part. Saving is far more heavily dependent on people's incomes than upon the demand of the entrepreneurs for new capital. Whereas the Classical School had seen the amount of savings as responding to changes in the rate of interest, Keynes argued that it depended mainly on the level of incomes, and that saving does not always respond easily and smoothly to changes in the demand for capital.

According to Keynes, a level of national income is finally established at a point where saving and investment are in equilibrium with each other. A level of national income where saving and investment are not in equilibrium is unstable, and it will change until it is at a level at which the amount which families want to save is equal to what entrepreneurs want to invest. It should be noted however, that this equilibrium level may involve large-scale unemployment. In other words, there is nothing particularly admirable about an equilibrium level of national income. If investment is low, the equilibrium level will involve unemployment and unused resources. The only level of national income which Keynes was prepared to regard as desirable was one near to full employment. We end up with a high level of employment only if investment opportunities match full-employment saving. A deflationary gap arises if they fail to do so, and its size is measured by the deficiency of investment scheduled at full employment, compared with full-employment saving. There are no automatic forces – argued Keynes – which achieve equilibrium at the level of full employment.

It may be necessary for the Government to intervene, either by raising consumption directly (e.g., through tax cuts, social-security payments, pensions, etc.), or by introducing public-investment programmes. The resulting increase in effective demand assisted by the operation of the multiplier will help to achieve the only equilibrium level which Keynes thought was justifiable – the one which achieves full employment.

It would be unfair, however, in defending Keynes, to accuse the Classical School of complacency over a low level of employment and output. They believed, as we have seen, that there were forces working naturally and spontaneously within the economy which would increase the level of employment. These forces depended, however, on the flexibility of wage rates. Classical theory argued that a country can employ a larger labour force if the average real wage is allowed to fall. This theory, it will be remembered, was based upon the law of diminishing returns (which stated that the more men were employed, given a fixed amount of capital equipment, the less each additional man would produce) and the law of marginal productivity (which postulated that the wage of the men employed would be equal to the value of what they produced). Although modern textbooks give varying interpretations of marginal-productivity theory, the theory as stated above is closest to the original meaning.

Keynes does not challenge these two basic laws, but he

argues ingeniously that under his system of aiming at full employment, real wages can be reduced less painfully by rising prices. This would come about as follows – as employment increased, output would increase less than proportionately and costs per unit of output would rise. Rising costs would lead to rising prices and therefore, since money wages would not rise proportionately, to falling real wages. The Classical School had argued that we should cut real wages to secure full employment. Keynes stood this argument on its head, and argued that we should first go for full employment, and this would have the effect of reducing real wages. As Keynes stated – 'it can only be a foolish person who would prefer a flexible wage policy to a flexible money policy, unless he can point to advantages from the former, which are not obtainable from the latter. Moreover, other things being equal, a method which it is comparatively easy to apply should be deemed preferable to a method which is probably so difficult as to be impracticable.'[13]

To sum up, Keynes starts the pump-priming exercise with an active monetary policy to stimulate private investment, assisted, if necessary, by government expenditure and redistributive tax measures. Falling real wages would follow, but they would be disguised and would not present the frightening political confrontation which the Classical School risked by arguing for wage cuts at the beginning, rather than at the end of this process. The increased power and sophistication of trades unions since Keynes wrote the *General Theory* make it much more difficult to argue that workers are confused over the difference between 'real' and 'money' wages. Nevertheless, some residue of the Keynesian argument remains. It could be easier to let real wages decline (while seeming, in money terms, to increase) in a period of inflation, than to aim, in a period of stable or even

[13] *Ibid.*, p.268.

declining prices, at forcing trade unions to accept wages cuts. Keynes was not, however, merely concentrating on the practicability of forcing unions to accept wage cuts; in theoretical terms, he argued that although wage cuts in one industry may increase employment in that particular industry, wage cuts in every industry would not increase employment nationally – a conclusion which is central to Keynesian analysis (falling wages throughout the economy mean falling income, which, in turn, mean falling employment).

We should note here that Keynes is more sanguine about the effectiveness of public investment to restore full employment than the use of reductions in interest rates (although he was also prepared to use the latter method).

Keynes believed that initial deviations from full employment were not necessarily corrected by movement in interest rates (rather were they amplified by movement in incomes).

Although Keynes believed that interest rates should be kept low by the manipulation of such devices as open-market operations, he foresaw that the supply of money at even very low interest rates might be off-set by the increases in the desire for liquidity (once again, he brings this concept into the centre of the picture) and he does not shrink from further measures such as Government investment to revive the economy.

Keynes' message is that almost everything depends on the level of income. Get that right, and most other things come right. The level of income determined the volume of saving (with all the economic consequences which, as we have seen, flow from that). Anything which the Government could do to keep up this level of income – and a high and rising volume of investment is crucial to this goal – leads us towards the twin objectives of economic efficiency (in terms of mobilizing unused resources) and social harmony (in terms of ending the disruptive and self-destroying effects of mass unemployment).

The Classical School would have queried the 'economic efficiency' argument. Their concern for micro-economic analysis implied that the goal of full employment could, in certain circumstances, lead to a mis-allocation of resources, and – it may be argued – contemporary experience lends weight to their doubts and suspicions (although nowadays we would describe this mis-allocation as *over-full* employment).

There is one important innovation in Keynesian analysis which we have not so far discussed. This is the concept of equality. Hitherto, economists with a conscience (of which Marshall was a supreme example) had been uneasily aware that the dynamic of capitalism (the survival of the fittest), which had secured triumphs of technological innovation and rising economic output, had not always fostered economic equality. The goal of increasing equality was a moral objective (as seen by Mill and Marshall) or a political objective (as seen by liberal leaders like Campbell-Bannerman and Lloyd George in Marshall's day) which had to be grafted on to an economic system not entirely compatible with its assumptions. Keynes pointed out that increasing equality was not merely a Christian – moral – political goal belonging to the distant future; it actually worked in the here-and-now. Because the marginal propensity to consume of the poor was higher than that of the rich, transferring purchasing power from the latter to the former, increased consumption (and through the operation of the multiplier) raised the level of national income. Equality was elevated (or should we say demoted?) from a moral aspiration to an economic precept. It is not difficult to see how quickly the Labour Government of 1945 (which, under its first Chancellor of the Exchequer, Dr. Hugh Dalton, was strongly pro-

Keynesian) grasped the significance of Keynes' egalitarian arguments, although it blended them with policies of which Keynes would not necessarily have approved (e.g., large-scale nationalization programmes). Keynes had favoured the creation of a climate in which private enterprise could flourish, and although this might involve significant Government intervention, it stopped short of outright state owner-ship of a large sector of the economy.

To sum up, the achievements of Keynes lie in both theoretical analysis and in recommendations to Govern-ments in the sphere of public policy. In the former, his claim to fame lies in his bringing together of 'monetary' and 'real' phenomena; his emphasis on macro-economics – or state of the economy as a whole – (in opposition to what he regarded as the Classical obsession with micro-economics – individual markets, and individual firms, workers and con-sumers), the pioneer work he did on identifying the 'defla-tionary gap' and the carefully formulated reasons for the possibility of continuing under-employment equilibrium which the Classical School had not fully acknowledged.

In the sphere of public policy, Keynes came to rival (and perhaps even out-strip) Adam Smith in his influence on statesmen and administrators. Keynesian ideas were applied in a tentative manner in the U.S.A. Although it could be argued that his basic ideas on economic management were more systematically enforced by Nazi Germany, President Roosevelt's New Deal programme in the 1930s in some aspects followed Keynesian theory rather than remedies of the Classical School by aiming at a high level of public spending (in excess of what it received in tax revenues) on land reclamation, irrigation, roads, harbours, leisure and recreational projects, public buildings, and a host of other schemes. This was one of the first practical applications of public spending generating successive waves of employment, through the operation of the multiplier. There is still some controversy among economists about the effectiveness of the Roosevelt programmes, and it is true that unemployment rose again towards the late 1930s. Some economists attribute this to a lack of business confidence due to Roosevelt's apparent acceptance of the principle of budget deficits; others believe that the considerable size of idle productive capacity which Roosevelt had inherited made it extremely difficult to achieve a high level of employment.

Nevertheless, American experience did much at the time to secure public acceptance of Keynesian ideas. Rightly or wrongly, it seemed as if, at last, here was a body of abstract economic theory which provided explicit and immediate guidance to those involved in practical policy-making and administration. Keynes was criticized – both during his lifetime, and since – for taking too short-term a view of the economy and neglecting the long-term dynamic factors which cause change and innovation. A contemporary of Keynes, Professor Joseph Schumpeter, for example, emphasized those elements which he thought that Keynes had taken too much for granted – the role of creative entrepreneurship and innovation in explaining business investment and economic growth (a theoretical development of certain aspects of Marshallian analysis). Keynes' famous reply to those of his critics who thought him obsessed with immediate problems – ' in the long run we are all dead ' – was perhaps unfair to those of his fellow-practitioners whose patient scholarship was throwing new light on longer-term problems of economic change. Criticisms of Keynes for being too short-term in his analysis are not confined to the pro-Schumpeter *laissez-faire* school, or to those economists who specialize in economic-growth models. If Marx were alive to-day to answer Keynes he would probably assert that Keynesian analysis failed to distinguish between qualitative and quantitative change. Economic growth, it may be argued, is a process of qualitative change which appears as a response to a situation in which it is no longer possible to make quantitative extensions to the economic system. The Keynesian assumption of a constant relationship between various factor inputs and production, Marx would probably argue, neglects the aspect of technical change. The neat theoretical Keynesian aggregates can be undermined by a flow of productive innovations which are factor-saving. These innovations have social repercussions for which Keynes, in spite of his political insights, did not devise adequate tools to cope.

Finally, it must be repeated that Keynes was not a collectivist; he was essentially an exponent of the mixed economy and he argued that the relative agenda for public and private economic activity was not inflexibly fixed for all time, but could vary from decade to decade, and must take account of people's fears and aspirations, as well as objective economic data.

His attack on the Classical School was admittedly sharply polemic, at times unfair, and occasionally cruel. We must remember, however that there is a good deal of polemic in most of the great economists (Adam Smith's denunciation of the Mercantilists and Marx's repudiation of his classical predecessors often went further than the neutral standards gentlemanly scholarship permitted). Keynes admitted his propensity to rush into battle against the Classical economists – 'I must ask forgiveness if, in the pursuit of sharp distinctions, my controversy is itself too keen. I myself held with conviction for many years the theories which I now attack, and I am not, I think, ignorant of their strong points.'[14]

Keynes believed, however, that if he had written a rather

[14] *Ibid.*, Preface, p.xxi.

more gentlemanly and bland book, paying generous tribute to Classical wisdom, and noting his disagreement in a muted manner, the critics would have missed the radical implications of his central theme, and quoted heavily those sections which supported the views of his predecessors and contemporaries. Towards the end of his life, Keynes felt confident enough to pay tribute to what was best in Classical thinking. He hoped that governments would 'use what we have learnt from modern experience and modern analysis, not to defeat but to implement the wisdom of Adam Smith '.[15]

[15] For an unrelenting critcism of Keynes' work see Harry Hazlitt, *The Failure of the ' New Economics ': an analysis of the Keynesian fallacies* (1959).

CHAPTER XV

Neo-Classical Developments

Knut Wicksell (1851-1926)

ALONGSIDE MARSHALL, the Swedish economist Knut
Wicksell was also refining and developing classical theory,
particularly in the fields of marginal theory and monetary
economics.

Wicksell's work is more explicitly theoretical and mathematical than Marshall's (Wicksell tried unsuccessfully to
persuade Marshall to make greater use of mathematical
exposition in his books). Wicksell was a paradoxical combination of aloofly abstract thought and passionate social
involvement in some of the most controversial issues of his
day. He was opposed to such institutions as marriage and
the monarchy, and was an ardent exponent of birth control
and pacifism. He denounced the religious belief of the Virgin Birth, and went to gaol for blasphemy. This explains
why, in spite of his outstanding ability, he was denied promotion by the authorities. Various reasons were given (e.g.,
that his formal training in economics was inadequate and
that he lacked a Law qualification), but he was eventually
given a Chair, at the age of fifty.

Wicksell's first major work was his essay on *Value, Capital
and Rent in Recent Economic Theory*, in 1893,[1] which was
incorporated and developed later in his *Lectures on*

---

[1] *Über Wert, Kapital und Rente: nach den neueren nationalökono-
mischen Theoren*, Jena (1893); published in translation as *Value,
Capital and Rent* (1954).

Political Economy on the Basis of the Marginal Principle[2] (1901-6). In 1898 he published his *Interest and Prices*.[3] He accepted the doctrine of his predecessors that pure competition can achieve a situation in which the prices of productive factors are equated with the value of their marginal products, and the prices of outputs are equal to the marginal costs of production. He was, however, concerned about inequalities in the distribution of the fruits of production. His criticisms do not drive him into socialist remedies, although he believes that the State should use its taxation powers to secure greater equality. ' You cannot ', he wrote, ' have a just part in an unjust whole.'[4]

He considers that public ownership should operate marginal cost-pricing (indeed, he argues that it can sometimes do this more effectively than private industry) and his elegant theoretical presentation of the arguments foreshadows the long and intense debate on pricing in the nationalized industries which has taken place among economists in Britain since the late 1940s. Wicksell questioned the sharp division made by contemporary economists between monopoly prices and competitive prices. He drew attention to the gap between monopolies as theoretically described by economists and how they actually operate in the real world and he examines and refines the concept of oligopoly.

Wicksell's most interesting (and ultimately influential) break with the Classical School occurs in his treatment of

---

[2] *Forelasninger i Nationalekonomi: forstadelen: Teoretisk Nationalekonomi* (1901), *Andra delen: Om penninger och Kredit* (1906); published in translation as *Lectures in Political Economy* (1935).

[3] *Geldzins und Gunterpreise: eine studie über den Tauschwert des Geldes bestimmenden Uraschen* (Jena, 1898); published in translation as *Interest and Prices* (1936).

[4] *Finanztheoretische Untersuchungen nebst Darstellung und Kritik des Steuersystems Schwedens* (Jena, 1896), p.143; translated in R. Musgrave and A. Peacock, *Classics in the Theory of Public Finance* (1958), pp.72-118.

money. Whereas his predecessors had seen money mainly as a medium of exchange (a criticism Keynes was later to take up in greater depth), Wicksell gives money a more crucial role. He comes close to the later Keynesian idea of the 'income approach' to monetary theory, with its relevance to the concept of aggregate demand (the macro-economic approach which the Classical School had allegedly neglected) and the link between the consumption and savings–investment elements. Wicksell saw that the market rate of interest (i.e., that charged by the banks) did not always coincide with the real rate of interest, or as Marshall called it, the 'normal' rate, (i.e., that which corresponded with the marginal productivity of capital) and to a saving–investment equilibrium.

One of Wicksell's concerns in thus linking monetary theory with value theory was to achieve a rate of interest which kept prices stable. He believed that a stable price-level was the prime object of monetary policy. In this aim, he seems to be activated more by social and moral values (the avoidance of the injustices to which inflation gives rise) than to purely economic considerations, but this does not preclude him from presenting an analysis of considerable complexity and ingenuity. He saw that the movement of interest rates might, instead of achieving aggregate equilibrium, move in the opposite direction and that (unlike the assumptions of some Classical writers) there was nothing necessarily self-correcting in these movements.

Wicksell suffered the fate of some great artists: his work received international recognition and fame only towards the end of his life and after his death (although he had been widely read in his native Sweden and in Germany). With the ferment in economic thinking which occurred in the 1930s, Wicksell was 're-discovered' and economists of various schools found ideas and inspiration in his wide-ranging and highly original works.[5]

Joan Robinson and Edward Chamberlin

It is difficult (and invidious) to choose individual names from the many talented and scholarly economists who were writing in the main neo-Classical tradition between the First and Second World Wars.

Mention must be made, however, of Joan Robinson's *Economics of Imperfect Competition* (1933) and Edward Chamberlin's *Theory of Monopolistic Competition* (1933). Both these writers tried to come to grips with a fundamental weakness in Marshallian economics – the gap between theory and the real world in the treatment of competition and monopoly. This theory had seen the economy consisting mainly of competitive industries and markets with a few exceptional firms possessing monopoly power.

To be fair to Marshall and his contemporaries they were aware that competition in the real world was not as perfect as that which existed in their theories and they recognized that monopoly in reality was not such a tidy and comprehensive economic entity as the model suggested.

It was left to Joan Robinson and Edward Chamberlin, however (although useful pioneer work had been done in an article by Piero Sraffa in the *Economic Journal* in 1926),[6] to show that competition and monopoly were not totally separate and mutually exclusive phenomena. Robinson's

---

[5] See Erik Lindhal (editor), *Knut Wicksell: Selected Papers on Economic Theory* (1958) and Carl G. Uhr, *Economic Doctrines of Knut Wicksell* (1960) which includes an extensive bibliography.

[6] Piero Sraffa, 'The laws of returns under competitive conditions', *Economic Journal*, Vol, xxxvi (1926) pp.535-550; reprinted in George Stigler and Kenneth Boulding (editors), *Readings in Price Theory* (American Economic Association, 1953), pp.180-197.

analysis drew attention to the imperfections of people's knowledge in the operation of the economic system in contradistinction to the presumption of rational behaviour in traditional theory, and to imperfections of mobility and use of resources. People did not, for instance, transfer from declining industries to new industries as easily or as inevitably as had been argued. Imperfections, in Robinson's world, are not transient obstacles which natural economic forces overcome, but are enduring characteristics of the system.

Chamberlin demonstrated that all monopolies are limited by some degree of competition from firms producing different, but in some cases, substitutable, products; similarly, most firms – although ostensibly in industries in which competition prevails, possess some degree of monopoly power. Chamberlin develops the theory of oligopoly (as the situation in which competition exists between a few rival sellers of the same good, each offering a large proportion of the total supply). He also presents a theory of competition among all suppliers of 'differentiated' products. These are different, but easily substitutable (and therefore rival) products, or varieties of one general kind of product.

In this situation, each of the competing sellers is the only seller of his exact product, and his aim is (usually through advertising) to persuade people that his product is superior to that of all his rivals. His objective is to acquire his own special market rather as the monopolist does.

It is important to notice that Chamberlin gives a very wide definition to his concept of 'differentiation' and thereby uses it as a very considerable tool to undermine existing market theory. Differentiation, according to Chamberlin, may be based upon certain characteristics of the product itself, trade marks, peculiarities of package or container, singularity in quality, design, colour or style. It may exist with respect to the conditions surrounding the sale, convenience of the seller's location, the general tone or character of his establishment, his way of doing business, his reputation for fair dealing, courtesy, efficiency and all the personal links which attach his customers either to himself or those employed by him. What Chamberlin is arguing is that nearly all products are differentiated (at least slightly) and that over a wide range of economic activity differentiation is highly important.

Differentiation, as Chamberlin rightly claimed, had received only fragmentary recognition in previous economic literature. It had never been used as a part of the general explanation of prices. The theoretical concept which Chamberlin's work develops is directed more to product differentiation rather than market imperfection (although both ideas are related and are part of the same problem). It will be seen that Robinson and Chamberlin moved away from the classical model (where a large number of suppliers are competing on the basis of price and where they are adjusting ouput to the price prevailing in competitive markets). Although they were working within the broad framework of neo-classical micro-economic theory, they brought a welcome new realism into economics.

In particular, new analytical insight was applied to the role of advertising. This was an activity with which classical economists hitherto had never been entirely happy, recognizing its value in informing the consumer, but suspicious of its capacity to mislead. What had not been previously recognized was the extent to which powerful advertising could blur the boundaries between competition and monopoly, by the creation of inelastic demand: by rendering consumers less sensitive to prices and 'binding' them to a particular supplier who has convinced them of the unique qualities and delights of his own product. It can be argued that the consumer is more rational than he is given credit for by advertisers and that his consciousness of price is never far below the surface. Nevertheless, this analysis of the function of advertising was novel and ingenious and was to be developed by later economists. In terms of public policy, the micro-economic contributions of Robinson and Chamberlin could hardly be expected to have the impact which the Keynesian macro-economic revolution was to have upon politicians and administrators. Nevertheless, their analysis of how firms behave in varying degrees of competitiveness has been invaluable to bodies like the Monopolies and Restrictive Practices Commission in Britain, which have been concerned with what criteria and guidelines should be established to maintain competition or (in certain circumstances) to permit monopoly. Although Robinson and Chamberlin did not supply precise answers for those who formulate government policies, they provided a coherent and accurate analysis from which answers could more effectively be deduced. They carried micro-economic analysis a significant step beyond Marshall. In so far as they demonstrated the limitations of consumer sovereignty (and thereby showed how the consumer might be better protected) they bore aloft the banner of Marshall and carried his colours into new terrain. The master, had he lived another decade, would have been proud of them.

Thorstein Veblen (1857-1929)

The neo-classical tradition was wide enough to encompass those who challenged its assumptions and mobilized their criticisms around its central propositions.

Thorstein Veblen occupied a leading position in the neo-classical controversy over what time period was the proper concern of the economist. To Veblen, the neo-classical school was excessively static and deductive, and neglected the element of change in economic life. In his dynamic approach he was a residuary legatee of Marx, but his academic upbringing (as a pupil of the great American economist J. B. Clark) led him to confine his critical approach mainly to a series of fusillades on classical concepts, and it can be argued that he never developed a comprehensive anti-capitalist critique. Veblen's first major academic project was a dissertation on Kant (he followed the example of Adam Smith in preceding his economic interests by a scholarly incursion into philosophy).

He attacked the concept of marginal analysis for its narrow and arid view of man as a mathematical machine concerned with maximizing pleasure in a *ceteris paribus* situation of given tastes; there was no proper analysis of change and growth. In his *Theory of the Leisure Class: An Economic Study of the Evolution of Institutions* (1899) he argues that conspicuous consumption – the ostentatious demonstration of riches by socially irrational expenditure – e.g., by dressing muscular young men (who possess intrinsic potential productive capacity) in the frills and laces of a footman who produces nothing, is a characteristic of demand in capitalist society. The neo-classical assumption of rational calculating behaviour with thousands of individual choices adding up to present spontaneous schedules of demand, was replaced in Veblen's analysis, with socially determined demand. He saw human behaviour as more instinctive than reflective: and he saw the power of institutions (rather than random choices of individuals) as influencing economic life. He drew attention to the emergence of a leisure class (there are faint echoes of Malthus here), whose function was to dissipate the abundance which ordinary labour toiled to create. Veblen argued ingeniously that consumers could sometimes be induced to buy at higher rather than lower prices (a direct repudiation of Marshallian economics). This was the special case of luxury goods: if commodities are valued as status symbols, demand might fall if their prices fell. We all know that if we are buying our wives a bottle of perfume for our wedding anniversary, we eschew the cheaper brands and buy something ostentatiously expensive, even though we have very little idea of the intrinsic value of the raw materials involved. Sometimes we take our wife or a guest to a restaurant because it is expensive; the utility is not primarily in the food or service, but in the price-tag which is elaborately displayed. These examples, however, occupy a very restricted area of economic behaviour: in most of what Marshall called the ordinary business of life we do not squander our money on ostentatious display. When we go out in search of electric cookers, bed linen, garden tools, carpets and the like, we are carefully balancing price and quality. No doubt there are people who buy cars *because* they are expensive: but it is possible to argue that although a Rolls-Royce is an impressive status symbol, it is also technically a very efficient car, and worth its price in terms of old-fashioned neo-classical utility.

Veblen's originality was to insist upon an institutional approach to the theory of demand (the validity of the narrow pain-versus-pleasure principle governing individual behaviour was already fraying at the edges by Veblen's time).[7] He was also right in seeing that producers might try to influence consumer taste by advertising, in order to dispose of abundant products. He rejected, however, the Marxist view that all the contradictions and irrationalities of the existing system necessarily lead to socialism. Veblen wrote in a witty, lively, iconoclastic manner, and he inspired a coterie of devoted followers (although his influence was mainly in America. His books made little impact in Britain,

[7] See David Seckler, *Thorstein Veblen and the Institutionalists: a study in the social philosophy of economics* (1957).

until near the end of his life).[8] His legacy may, however, have proved to be more in the sphere of academic sociology than economics; there may be more basic common sense (and price consciousness) in the economic behaviour of ordinary people than he perceived, and more than some modern sociologists are prepared to admit.

The Neo-classical Synthesis

Marshall gave Anglo-Saxon economics a determined bias in favour of partial equilibrium analysis which perceived economic problems as manageable in the form of a discussion of the relationships between two variables, all other variables tidied away under the *ceteris paribus* assumption. This enabled Marshall, in Book III of the *Principles*, using simple mathematics and graphs, to explore the elements of demand-and-supply theory as a price–quantity relationship. This became, for thirty years or more, the dominant theory taught in Universities, Colleges and Schools on both sides of the English-speaking North Atlantic. There were, however, other schools of economists working largely on the Continent, whose works and papers were not translated into English, who were not bound by Marshallian partial equilibrium. Among these there was the so-called Lausanne School, associated with the works of Leon Walras (1834-1910) (See Gray and Thompson, p.333-6); and Vilfredo Pareto (1843-1923). The approach of Continental economists was one of general equilibrium which attempted to capture the inter-relationships of many variables rather than just two. The price of one good was influenced by the price of all other goods.

[8] See Joseph Dorfman, *Thorstein Veblen and his America* (1934 reprinted 1961); and Douglas F. David (editor), *Thorstein Veblen: a critical appraisal: lectures and essays commemorating the hundredth anniversary of his birth* (1958).

Leon Walras was the son of the distinguished Auguste Walras, remembered for his exposition of the early principle of value related to scarcity (*rareté*). Leon contributed to the marginal utility revolution in economics using calculus techniques, but found that much of his work had been anticipated by others. It was in the field of general equilibrium that he was to make his mark and main contributions. His *Éléments d'économie politique pure*[9] was published in 1874 and gradually established his reputation in the field of pure economic theory, but it was not until many years after his death that his ideas penetrated into the textbooks and teaching of economics.

Pareto, who followed Walras to the Chair of Political Economy, at Lausanne, published the *Manuel d'économie politique* in 1909,[10] and this incorporated a restatement of general equilibrium theory after Walras, but it is more famous now for its treatment of utility in demand theory.

The connecting link between the continental school and the Marshallians was John (later, Sir John) Hicks, who was awarded the Nobel Prize in 1972. His book, *Value and Capital; an inquiry into some fundamental principles of economic theory*, was published in 1939. It brought to the attention of English-speaking economists the significance of Walrasian general equilibrium and Pareto's theory of value. The book was an instant success, and allowing for the disruption caused by the War, its main elements soon appeared in economics textbooks and teaching all over the world.

Hicks was able to break economic theory from its utility-

[9] Published in translation as William Jaffe (translator), *Leon Walras: Elements of Pure Economics, or, The Theory of Social Wealth* (1954). See also, William Jaffe (editor), *Correspondence of Leon Walras and Related Papers*, 4 vols. (1965).
[10] Published in translation as Ann S. Schweir and Alfred N. Page (editors), *Manual of Political Economy by Vilfredo Pareto* (1971).

theory contraints. Marshall's demand theory was rooted in some form of utility theory which required economists to suspend their disbelief when pressing upon their students the notion of individuals maximizing something called *utility* which was indefinable and elusive to measurement. The principle of equi-marginal allocation of scarce resources across abundant wants had been adapted by Professor Lionel Robbins in his *Essay on the Nature and Significance of Economic Science* (1932) as a definition of what economics as a science was about. Hicks was able to give that definition a scientific edge by bringing together Pareto's exposition of indifference curve technique and Marshall's partial equilibrium demand theory.

Instead of a consumer facing commodities with specific marginal utilities embodied in them we have a consumer facing bundles of commodities, which have one bundle in a unique combination with his means and their relative prices. The consumer does not need to know the marginal utility of the commodities at all. He only needs to know their prices, his income and his preference for the commodities. The relationship between the commodities follows the rate at which one commodity can be substituted for another within an individual's indifference map which states which bundle of commodities he prefers to another, and which bundles he is indifferent between, without having to specify by how much or little one bundle is preferred to another.

It was a step forward of considerable importance for Hicks to integrate Pareto and Walras into Marshallian economics. In doing so, neo-classical economics was synthesized out of the Anglo-Saxon and Continental Schools. The result is seen in every modern textbook of elementary economics.

CHAPTER XVI

Contemporary Economic Controversies

W H E N we pass from a review of the great economists of the past and immediate past, we face certain problems. How effectively can we judge the importance of our contemporaries? Issues which seem important to us may, a hundred years hence, have faded into insignificance. Economists who at present dazzle us with their insight and wit may not pass the final test at the bar of history. Writers who, at present, appear minor and even marginal in their place in the development of economic thought, may a century hence, be seen to have been major and innovative contributors to economic analysis. Not only do we run the risk of misjudging contemporary economic writers, but may make the even greater mistake of incorrectly assessing what are the central economic problems. The importance of an historical approach is that we should not be overwhelmed and engulfed by dramatic short-term issues – yet these are precisely the issues which are sometimes seized upon by economists with the greatest flair for self-advertisement and partisan commitments. This is not to argue that there is anything improper about a concern for the present and the immediate, but that such a concern is not a substitute for scholarly and laborious achievement (which may also sometimes be disagreeable to contemporary politicians who are constantly demanding quick and easily understood answers). Great economists like Adam Smith and Keynes combined contemporary relevance with outstanding scholarship, but this was not immediately apparent to their contemporaries.

There are, therefore, certain risks in embarking upon a

discussion of those economic controversies which seem to be important to the last two decades of the twentieth century; nevertheless, we will embark upon them with a warning to readers that, although this is the last chapter in this book, it will almost certainly not be the last word on the subject, and should be read with suspended belief and numerous reservations.

The controversial issues with which we shall deal fall under four main headings: first, the role of monetarism; second, the theory of relative over-consumption and the limitations of consumer sovereignty; third, the ecological debate; and fourth, Neo-Marxism.

At a time when there is considerable debate within the Marxist camp itself (for example in the controversies over Eurocommunism) there is some danger of over-simplification in speaking of ' a Marxist approach '. Nevertheless, the main corpus of Marxist economic analysis still seems to present a sufficiently coherent and consistent methodology to justify this summary of Marxist views, although it cannot pretend to be exhaustive.

In conclusion, reference will be made to the neo-Marxist approach to a number of these controversial issues.

The Monetarist Debate

Although monetarism has become an issue of considerable importance in the last decade, controversy over the role of money goes back much further in the history of economic thought.

The financing and aftermath of the Napoleonic wars focussed attention on monetary matters, and Ricardo and Malthus, among others, exchanged ideas on the subject.

The long and continuing debate on the Quantity Theory of Money has occupied economists for many decades. Re-

cently, however, this debate has assumed a new significance
and has been joined by some of the most eminent and respected economists in Europe and America.

The controversy over monetarism, it may be argued, is
mainly technical. With the agreed assumptions of a basically
capitalist mixed economy, it is concerned with the question
how rather than *why*. Professor Milton Friedman, the leading monetarist, admits the wide agreement between himself
and the Keynesians on the major goals of economic policy –
high employment, stable prices and rapid growth,[1] although
there is less agreement about the degree of mutual com-
patibility of these goals. There is also considerable disagreement on the role that various instruments should play in
achieving the several goals.

The debate does not challenge those fundamental premises which have occupied the mainstream of economic
thought from Adam Smith onwards – the assumption of
the existence of the factors land, labour and capital, the
need for entrepreneurial initiative and the existence of a
limited public sector. Given all these assumptions, our concern is how to reconcile orderly economic growth with
reasonable price stability. There are, however, other issues
in the Keynesian versus monetarist argument. Milton
Friedman has argued that, in addition to his desire to make
the existing economic system work more effectively in terms
of employment, growth and price stability, he wishes to see
government expenditure decrease in the long term. This
is not an argument against inflation (although it could so
be used), but a somewhat different argument that the indi-

[1] Milton Friedman, ' The Role of Monetary Policy ', *American
Economic Review*, Vol. 59, no. 1 (March 1968), pp.1-17; see also his
Optimum Quantity of Money, and Other Essays (1969) and Franco
Modigliani, ' The monetarist controversy or, should we forsake stabi-
lisation policies ', *American Economic Review*, Vol. 67, no. 2 (March
1977), pp.1-19.

vidual consumer does not get the same value from government spending as he gets from competitive enterprise.
Friedman is here echoing an older classical view on the need
to limit the role of the state, with philosophical and political
implications for the liberty of the individual, and his challenge to the Keynesians is more fundamental than a discussion of the mechanics of money supply. Nevertheless, in
so far as the debate has revolved around the operational
effectiveness of various techniques of economic management,
it is these issues which must be considered. We must bear
in mind, however, the deeper philosophical undertones
which have their ancestry in Adam Smith, and even earlier,
in the physiocratic belief in the superiority of 'natural'
over 'positive' law.

The starting point of monetarist belief is that the authorities should use money supply to support real activity in the
economy, instead of supplying money on demand as a
substitute for real activity in the economy. In other words,
the supply of money should be used to fund business
activity and should respond to the expansion or contraction of business activity. The monetarists believe broadly
that the supply of money should not be an endogenous
variable, i.e., one that attempts to influence changing
economic conditions. In other words, the money supply
should not be the arbitrary decision of the government.
This, however, requires considerable courage and nerve on
the part of the politicians and the authorities; in practice it
means that cries for help from business to maintain production and employment above what Friedman calls a
'natural' level (to which the supporters of the 'endogenous'
theory would have responded) should, if necessary, be ignored. The monetarists are suspicious of the Keynesian use
of fiscal and monetary policies as means by which the public
sector offsets instability in the economy arising from

changes in the private sector. In the opinion of most modern Keynesians, the aim of fiscal policy is to offset unforeseen changes in private expenditure and to maintain expenditures at full employment levels, while the aim of Keynesian monetary policy is to offset undesired changes in interest rates caused by unforeseen changes in investment. Monetary policy is described as restrictive if market rates are permitted to rise, and permissive if market rates are prevented from rising. It is described as co-ordinated if the balance of payments is in deficit and market rates are permitted to rise so as to attract an inflow of short-term capital from foreign sources. It will be observed that monetary policy, on these hypotheses, is operating largely through the medium of interest rates.

Monetarists would, as we have seen, give monetary policy a more comprehensive and controlling function, and direct attention to the importance of long-term effects (and the avoidance of undue emphasis on the effects of initial changes in interest rates, which could give rise to errors of judgment). The monetarist view is that changes in the supply of money directly affect the economy to a greater extent than Keynes seems to have admitted (although it is likely that, had he been alive to-day, he would have acknowledged the force of some of the monetarist arguments, particularly in the light of the considerable empirical research conducted by this school of economists).

Keynes had argued that the demand for money was considerably influenced by liquidity preference. This demand, however, is related to the money level of national income *via* the 'precautionary' and 'transactions' motives for holding it, although at any given level, the demand for money will be determined by the rate of interest. Although Keynes had departed from Classical analysis in the role he ascribes to the rate of interest, it nevertheless continues to play a part in his theory. The monetarists believe that people are accustomed to holding a certain amount of money in relation to their money incomes and it is, therefore, the level of money incomes, operating through this relationship, upon which the demand for money depends.

The rate of interest plays little part in all this. Keynes and his followers had accepted that a change in money supply causes people to substitute money for other financial assets, but the monetarists argue that changes in money supply affect other people's *total* asset structure – the proportions they hold in money, government securities, houses, and consumer goods. Upward and downward movements in money supply, therefore, affect consumption, and national income. Thus, money supply, on this view, is more closely correlated with national income than is investment (which Keynes had emphasized). The monetary multiplier (the relationship between change in the supply of money and change in national income) will therefore be a more stable co-efficient than the Keynesian multiplier.

In the period after the Second World War, Keynesian ideas were dominant in government circles (although there is some argument whether Keynes would have agreed with everything which was done in the name of Keynesianism).[2] Emphasis was laid upon the manipulation of government expenditure, fiscal measures and physical controls, rather than on money supply. Interest rates were kept low to help finance the tasks of reconstruction which faced the nation in the aftermath of war. Running through Keynesian thinking was the belief that if we put the burden of solving unemployment on to money supply, it might just run into a liquidity trap.

Briefly, the monetarists have revived (with considerably more sophistication) the quantity theory of money, where

[2] T. W. Hutchison, *Keynes v. the Keynesians* (1977).

M provides the clue to money national income (without recourse to every aspect of Keynesian analysis and with much less need to invoke fiscal measures in the sphere of policy).

Central to Friedman's analysis is the hypothesis that there is a 'natural' rate of unemployment (which is connected with such long-run trends as capital formation and technological improvement) as well as a market rate. Friedman's concern is to keep natural and market forces in some alignment, although he admits that monetary policy is not a panacea and has its limitations. For this reason he denies that fiscal policy can maintain, except in the very short term, employment above the natural rate and attempts to do so must lead to price inflation and eventually higher unemployment. Each unemployment round will provoke the government to pump greater amounts of money into the system to restore employment above the natural rate and each round of the money-pumping exercise will provoke yet higher unemployment.

In the extreme, Friedman predicts severe and prolonged unemployment levels combined with high rates of price inflation. He does, however, see three main practical goals for monetary policy. First there is the need to prevent money supply from becoming a major source of economic disturbance (he gives the example of early banking panics in the U.S.A.). Second, we must provide a stable background for the economy ('Our economic system will work best', he says, 'when producers and consumers, employers and employees, can proceed with full confidence that the average level of prices will behave in a known way in the future – preferably that it will be highly stable'). Third, it is necessary to hold inflationary changes in check by a slower rate of monetary growth than would otherwise be desirable.

Friedman believes that monetary authorities should avoid sharp swings in policy (their 'propensity to over-react') by achieving a steady rate of growth in a specified monetary total. He argues for a rate of growth of 3–5% per year in currency plus all commercial bank deposits, or a slightly lower rate of growth in currency plus demand deposits only. His Keynesian opponents have described his 3–5% target as the 'fixed throttle' formula, which locks the financial steering gear into place, regardless of the twists and turns in the road ahead. What, to Friedman, is setting a steady, orderly course for the economy is seen by some Keynesians as an invitation to catastrophe. Like most great controversies in the history of economic thought, there are powerful arguments on both sides. It has only been possible here to pick out the main points of what is an extremely complicated and scholarly argument (backed by a large amount of empirical research on each side). It is perhaps fair to say that Keynes, with his Cambridge tradition and his unrivalled experience of monetary affairs, might have yielded a little more to the Friedman school than some of the Keynesian successors (although he would have probably responded sharply to Friedman's more trenchant and polemic attacks on his central propositions – particularly those relating to the efficiency of fiscal policy).

Relative Over-consumption and the Limitations of Consumer Sovereignty

Adam Smith looked confidently forward to rising output and rising living standards, and the Classical School remained faithful to his goal. Subsequent criticisms of the Classical School were not directed so much against their ostensible goal as the adequacy of their analysis and policies for achieving it. Marx looked forward to the revolution to provide higher levels of consumption; Keynes pinned his faith largely in new forms of public expenditure, re-distributive taxation, and the power of compound interest to raise living standards within a generation. There was, however, one important dissentient voice in Classical Theory – that of John Stuart Mill. Although Mill accepted many of the basic classical propositions, he was alarmed that a preoccupation with economic growth could militate against the quality of life and the quality of human relationships. He questioned ' why it should be a matter of congratulation that persons who are already richer than anyone needs to be, should have doubled their means of consuming things which give little or no pleasure, except as representatives of wealth '.[3]

He was concerned that American experience seemed to show that economic growth and abundance did not have the civilizing effects which the earlier Classical School had envisaged and did little to reduce people's selfishness and self-aggrandisement. He looked forward to the day when people would be mature enough to turn their backs upon the unrestrained, debilitating struggle for material progress, and turn to cultural and intellectual interests. Mill envisaged a stationary state in which poverty had been abolished and all men had enough to consume, but not too much (he linked this idea with the need to convert the labouring classes to controlling their birth-rate – an interesting combination of the idealism of Godwin, with the prophetic exhortations of Malthus). Nevertheless, Mill was a lonely voice among Classical writers on the dangers of over-consumption: ' I confess I am not charmed with the ideal of life held out by those who think that the normal state of human beings is

[3] John Stuart Mill, *Principles of Political Economy with some of their applications to social philosophy* (1848), W. T. Ashley edition (1909), Book IV, chap. VI, s.2, p.749.

that of struggling to get on, that the trampling, crushing, elbowing, and treading on each other's heels, which form the existing type of social life are the most desirable lot of human kind, or anything but the disagreeable symptoms of one of the phases of industrial progress . . .[4] the life of one sex is devoted to dollar-hunting and of the other to breeding dollar-hunters.'[5]

To-day, one cannot deny that industrial societies have achieved higher standards of comfort than were common earlier and that they enjoy a wider range of goods. Utility theory, as described in previous chapters, yielded concepts of consumer satisfaction and consumer sovereignty which provided a theoretical validity for the achievements of industrial societies. Not only did utility theory show that consumption assisted us in the pursuit of economic welfare, but also that free choice was valuable in itself. It was held to be a good thing for the individual to have what he prefers and that external restraints on consumer behaviour should, as far as possible, be avoided. Free markets, it was argued, provided an effective mechanism for revealing preferences.

Although Veblen questioned some of the assumptions of consumer sovereignty at the beginning of the century, this critical theme largely vanished in subsequent decades. The overwhelming problem of the 1920s and 1930s was how to raise output and consumption: the 1940s were devoted to world-wide war (where individual personal consumption played little part in the thoughts of either theorists or policy-makers), and from the 1950s onwards, the emphasis was on economic reconstruction and the formulation of new policies to maintain high levels of economic activity. The theories of Joan Robinson and Edward Chamberlin had

[4] *Ibid.*
[5] *Ibid.* (1891 edition, p.496 – this sentence is deleted from the 1909 edition).

subjected the bastion of consumer sovereignty to some penetrating small-arms fire from the flank, but the impact of
their contribution was largely confined to academic circles.

In more recent years a group of writers have emerged who
have taken the battle into the public arena. The leading
exponent of this school is John K. Galbraith, who in three
major books, *The Affluent Society* (1958), *The New Industrial State* (1967), and *Economics and The Public Purpose*
(1975) has challenged the basic assumptions of consumer
sovereignty. Galbraith's work is eclectic and (as he emphasizes) draws heavily upon the research of others, but
the arrangement and emphasis of his material make him
an eloquent (not to say polemical) critic of what he calls 'conventional wisdom'. It has been argued that his contribution
is mainly destructive and excessively vehement, but we must
remember, in fairness, that these charges have, in their
time, been levelled at many famous economists. Galbraith's
approach is unequivocal and explicit: 'I think very little of
the central ideas of economics. But I do think a great deal of
the men who originated these ideas. The shortcomings of
economics are not original error but uncorrected obsolescence.'[6] Why has obsolescence in economic thinking gone
so long uncorrected? According to Galbraith it is partly
because of the vested interest of ideas. Men have a vested
interest in what they have laboriously learned and they
react to criticism of their basic methodology with something
approaching religious passion. Galbraith is not making a
political point against conservatives: he argues that this
touchiness about cherished beliefs applies to most political
groups, from left to right, and to non-political protagonists
as well. Galbraith's starting point is that modern industrial
societies are fixated by economic theories which belong to
the past. 'The ideas by which the people of this favoured

[6] John Kenneth Galbraith, *The Affluent Society* (1958), p.3.

part of the world interpret their existence and in measure guide their behaviour, were not forged in a world of wealth. These ideas were the product of a world in which poverty had always been man's normal lot, and any other state was in degree unimaginable.'[7]

Galbraith argues that our economic attitudes are rooted in the poverty, inequality and economic peril of the past and these attitudes underlie our obsession with continuing economic growth and consumption.

He goes on to argue a further point: that there is an imbalance between public goods (which are under-produced) and private goods. This is because government spending, involving taxes, is seen as 'bad' (an attitude inherited from an era when profligate monarchs frivolously squandered their subjects' wealth) whereas private spending is 'good' (an attitude based on the original utility theorists and their successors). Galbraith is here making a highly controversial statement. It may be argued (and in Britain, a Labour Chancellor of the Exchequer, Roy Jenkins, has argued it) that if the public sector becomes too large, the repercussions must be judged not only in economic terms, but in terms of the possible threat to political freedom and the rights of the individual.

Galbraith also argues that the pressures of mass advertising are biased in favour of private rather than public goods. Advertising operates almost exclusively on behalf of privately produced goods and services. Television commercials nightly assail the eyes and ears of the community on behalf of more beer, but not on behalf of more schools or more cancer research.

In the *New Industrial State*, Galbraith proceeds further with the theory that consumer sovereignty is greatly exaggerated in conventional economic theory and that it is the

[7] *Ibid.*, p.1.

producer rather than the consumer who is the sovereign. Market forces operate much more weakly than is usually admitted; planning by firms has replaced subservience to competitive markets. Technology has also led the firm to liberate itself from the uncertainties of the market. The firm finds it can operate with some degree of certainty only if it controls the prices at which it buys materials, components and talent, and takes steps to ensure the necessary supply at these prices.

Looking forward, it controls the prices at which it sells and it tries to ensure that the public and other producers take the planned quantities at these prices. It may even ensure that the state makes large purchases (and, in the case of expensive and sophisticated technology, it may persuade the state to underwrite costs, including those of research and development, as well as guaranteeing a market). Instead of being controlled by the market, the firm (to the best of its ability) has made the market subordinate to the goals of its planning. Prices, costs, production and resulting revenues are established not by the market but, within certain limits, by the planning decisions of the firm.

Firms may still aim at the greatest possible profit, but the market is no longer specifying and enforcing that goal. There is, therefore, no longer reason to believe that profit maximization will be the goal, and this thesis is supported by the fact that control of firms is more typically carried out by salaried managers rather than by shareholders. Managers may aim at greater autonomy and an assured level of earnings rather than maximum profits in all circumstances. Other goals (some more social than economic) may influence management (e.g., if society sets high store by technological virtuosity and rapid technical advance, management may respond to this challenge).

Galbraith argues that the high level of consumption of

private goods and services in America is not a matter for unqualified self-congratulation. Some of this consumption is frivolous and unnecessary. Furthermore, the large business corporation (often a conglomerate producing different kinds of goods) has, to a great extent, superseded the small firm – a Marxist prophecy which seems to have come true; he also alleges that firms are controlled by management (including technologists) rather than by shareholders, and that a major goal of policy (involving, if necessary, the co-operation of trades unions and the State) is to avoid uncertainty. Advertising assists in the price manipulation required to achieve this aim. Industry continues to foster, however, a growing output of consumer goods, because this is in line with American conventional wisdom (even though America has more of some things than it needs). He argues that firms grow by re-investing earnings; hence they still need profits. They do not, however, necessarily aim at *maximum* profits, although, obviously, they will require to provide a dividend which will give some satisfaction to shareholders. Management will keep a close eye, however, on its own salary structure, pension opportunities and conditions. (It may, for instance, aim at growth rather than profits). It will not necessarily be thinking all the time of its shareholders and it will, in addition, be responsive to certain social goals.

Galbraith's thesis has been challenged by many contemporary economists.[8] One point of dispute is that although firms do not maximize profits in a rigorous and single-minded way, they nevertheless continue to seek profits in a more purposeful and sophisticated manner than Galbraith suggests. Some critics go further and argue that, for certain

[8] See Sir Frank McFadzean, *The Economics of John Kenneth Galbraith: a study in fantasy* (1977), Milton Friedman, *From Galbraith to Economic Freedom* (1977) and Myron E. Sharpe, *John Kenneth Galbraith and the Lower Economics* (1973).

industries, the hypothesis of rough profit-maximization (which Galbraith so summarily dismissed) is still valid. Furthermore, in so far as there still seems to be a tendency for capital to flow to firms where profits are highest, aggressive profit making still seems a worthwhile activity.

Another criticism is that Galbraith is too arbitrary in his condemnation of the aspirations of ordinary Americans to increase their consumption in many different ways. Is not personal consumption, after all, the main vehicle by which the individual can bring comfort and happiness to himself and his family? Is it not one of the ways in which every generation struggles hard (and legitimately) to make life easier and more pleasant than it was for its predecessors? And has not Galbraith attempted to apply normative judgments to the highly abstract, neutral, and impersonal theory of utility, by presuming to judge what other people ought to gain satisfaction from, and how they should spend their money? Galbraith would probably admit this last criticism and reply that there are lots of value judgments, anyway, lurking under the scientific propositions of economic theorists.

What he has done is to make his own value judgments explicit. The allegations of relative over-consumption (or badly allocated consumption) is taken up by another writer, Dr. E. J. Mishan, in *The Costs of Economic Growth* (1967). Like Galbraith, he rejects the economists' conventional preference for privately produced goods as against public goods, but he puts the argument more in terms of strict micro-economic analysis (e.g., by emphasizing such aspects as external diseconomies). Mishan believes that an exposition of formal economic propositions (rather than an emotional and polemic appeal) can provide authoritative arguments to those citizens, politicians and groups who, for instance, are in continual protest against pollution, noise, smoke, and the destruction of wild life and beauty which, according to Mishan, follows in the wake of expanding industry and communications. Mishan's work falls into three main categories: first (like Galbraith) an attack upon the so-called economic sagacity of our times which places too much emphasis on growth at any price; second, an exposition of the theory of external diseconomies, which alerts his readers to the ever-increasing and dangerous spill-over effects of modern industry (and its products) on the amenity of society at large; and third, (following on from the first two) a critical enquiry into the social value of economic growth. Like Galbraith, Mishan makes no apology for appealing over the heads of his contemporaries to a mass audience.

'Ideas that seem, at first, to be doomed to political impotence may strike root in the imagination of ordinary men and women, spreading and growing in strength, until ready to emerge in political form. For what is politically feasible depends, in the last resort, on the active influences on public opinion.'[9]

In his attack upon the concept of consumer sovereignty, Mishan argues that the consumer can still choose only that which is offered to him by the market. A range of physical environments which he might want to have included in his choice – 'quality of life' considerations – are not provided by the market at all. Even when new kinds of goods or new models appear on the market, the other goods and models are not always simultaneously available. They are withdrawn from production at the discretion of the industry. Hence, it is difficult to argue that consumers' wants ultimately control output. Unless consumers' wants exist independently of products created by industrial concerns, it is not correct to speak of the market as acting to adapt the

[9] E. J. Mishan, *The Costs of Economic Growth* (1967), p.xiv.

given resources of the economy to meet the material requirements of society. Not only do producers determine the range
of market goods from which consumers must take their
choice, they must also seek continuously to persuade consumers to choose what is being produced today and not to
choose what was being produced yesterday. In Mishan's
view, the market has become more of a want-creating than
a want-satisfying mechanism. He believes that Britain is
learning the wrong economic lesson from America (like Mill,
he makes generous use of American examples to frighten
us into mending our ways). Our political leaders have been
too impressed by America:

' by the efficient organisation of industry, the high productivity, the extent of automation, the new one-plane, two-
yacht, three-car, four-television-set family. The spreading
suburban wilderness, the near traffic paralysis, the mixture
of pandemonium and desolation of the cities, a sense of
spiritual despair scarcely concealed by the frantic pace of
life – such phenomena not being readily quantifiable and
having no discernible impact on the gold reserves, are obviously not regarded as agenda.'[10]

Both Galbraith and Mishan argue that, on the larger
questions of style of life and urbanization, the market-
mechanism is defective in its operation and government
action is required on a broader front than micro-economic
solutions. (Their opponents would argue that, once we have
spelled out the external diseconomies, more can be done
within the existing system than these two writers admit.)[11]
Mishan argues that while we are offered a bewildering
range of gadgets and new products, the carpet of choice in
our way of life is being rolled up behind our backs. If we are
to secure the proper balance between public and private

[10] *Ibid.*, p.7.
[11] See Wilfred Beckerman, *Defence of Economic Growth* (1974).

consumption, we shall have to devise not only new methods of analysis but also new legal machinery and new institutions. The citizen, for instance, should be given 'amenity rights' (e.g., rights against noise and pollution) analogous to his property rights. These rights, which would necessitate compensation by government in lieu of their relinquishment, would provide cost-benefit analysis with an economic realism that is sometimes lacking in current studies. Real costs rather than notional costs would have to be considered. Mishan gives aircraft noise as an example:

'Admittedly there are difficulties whenever actual compensation payments have to be made, say, to thousands of families disturbed by aircraft noise. Yet once the principle of amenity rights is recognised in law a rough estimate of the magnitude of compensation payments necessary to maintain the welfare of the number of families affected would be entered as a matter of course into the social cost calculus. And, unless these compensatory payments could also be somehow covered by the proceeds of the air service, there would be no *prima facie* case for maintaining the air service.'[12]

This is strong stuff and would certainly (if adopted) have escalated the costs of 'Concorde' aircraft beyond even their present level. Older utility theorists would have been unhappy with the concept of 'noise' as a dis-utility. People vary greatly in their reaction to noise (some, particularly the young, seem to find it positively invigorating), and to give it an arbitrary objective compensatory value brings us into the old arguments about the difficulty of interpersonal comparisons of utility and of dis-utility. Mishan, however, never shirks from value judgments.

'The upward movement in the indicators of social disintegration – divorce, suicide, delinquency, petty theft, drug-

[12] Mishan, *op. cit.*, p.72.

taking, sexual deviance, crime and violence and the un-
checked erosion of standards of taste and propriety is reflected in the resigned acceptance by the quality press of
obscene language and allusion, and in the diffusion of porno-
erotic literature, display and entertainment...'[13]

Nevertheless, Mishan's policy prescription (arising out of a
detailed and sophisticated micro-economic analysis which
we have not the space to pursue here) is simple and categorical enough; we should tilt the law (and the working of
our institutions) more in favour of the 'victims' of industrial growth.

Galbraith and Mishan have been chosen as examples of
what I have called rather loosely the relative 'over-con-
sumptionist' school, because they reflect an American and
British viewpoint respectively. Although many of their
points are similar, the differences are also interesting. Not
least is the cultural difference; for all his vehement denunciation of contemporary economic theory and practice,
Galbraith remains triumphantly American – bright, breezy
and basically optimistic about the future. Mishan is almost
Malthusian in his gloom and pessimism, although he admits that there are some things which we can do to 'make
modern living more bearable than it is today'. Beckerman's
reply to this would be 'bearable to which class – Mishan's
middle class or the vast majority of people whose lives,
without mass consumption, would be as unbearable as
that of their grandparents and the generations before
them?'

In dealing with economists who have recently enjoyed
popularity with a wide public, far beyond the ranks of
their professional colleagues, reference should also be made
to Ernest Schumacher (1904-77).

[13] E. J. Mishan, *The Economic Growth Debate: an assessment*
(1977), p.10.

Schumacher belonged to a school of Central European philosophers (of whom Karl Popper is an outstanding example) whose thought was influenced by the horrors of totalitarian government in their own countries between the wars. His main works are *The Roots of Economic Growth* (1963); *Small is Beautiful* (1973) and *A Guide for the Perplexed* (published posthumously in 1978). Schumacher's experience left him with a distrust of 'big' government and of the motives and ambitions of political leaders. This, it may be argued, is common to all the leading classical economists from Adam Smith onwards (it was, after all, Smith who had commented on 'that insidious and crafty animal vulgarly called a statesman or politician'). What, however, gives new force and urgency to Schumacher's message is the recognition that political tyranny in our day is strengthened by the scale and efficiency of modern technology. The tyranny of political and economic organizations combine in the worship of size and efficiency and (following from this) the need to plan and control the destinies of the ordinary citizen on an ever-increasing scale. Schumacher challenges the idea that bigness (whether in the nation state, or the size of business enterprise) is always a desirable aim. He believes that the aims of the state must be small and limited, because man himself is small and limited. In business there are obvious gains from the economies of scale, but there are also disadvantages. Adam Smith had warned of those disadvantages in his chapter on the division of labour – the dulling of sensibility and intellect in the pursuit of routine tasks and the declining capacity for the fullest possible enjoyment of life. However, whereas Smith seems to argue that this is a price which must be paid for economic growth, Schumacher would rather sacrifice the uninhibited pursuit of growth.

He draws attention to the sharp contrast between the aims

of production and consumption in modern society. The eminent politician, the business leader, the manager and the technocrat will devote his working day to devising systems of regulation, control, and the efficient exploitation of man and resources: when he retires home after work, he will turn to the cultivation of his own interests and personality, the enrichment of his life, within a context of harmony and repose. Do not these men recognize the contradiction between the way they organize the lives of others and what they demand for themselves as consumers?

Schumacher believes that we can satisfy our economic needs without the pursuit of aggressive inhuman and violent technologies. The purely economic problems of our society are less urgent, but the moral problems are immediate and overwhelming. Schumacher writes with the experience of a man who already in his lifetime has seen civilization destroyed and believes that it can easily happen again. Hence his anxiety to devolve the conduct of government and business to smaller units: at almost any cost we must take power away from the centre. We cannot here deal with the political implications (although his ideas have aroused considerable interest in countries like Scotland, where methods of devolution are still a continuing subject for debate).

The economic aspects of his argument are difficult to prove or refute. Once he had discarded efficiency as a goal, and admitted willingness to accept the implications of that decision, he has – to some extent – passed beyond the boundaries of theoretical economic argument. What he has done is to revive the old utilitarian debate – the pursuit of the greatest happiness of the greatest number – in a modern context. Like Bentham, his arguments lie more in the realms of politics and philosophy, but as with Bentham, no good economist can afford to ignore the implications of his views for their own science – particularly for their definition of what constitutes economic welfare.

The Ecological Debate

The debate about ecology and economic growth overlaps with the three writers with whom we have just dealt. Nevertheless, it has enough distinctive features to deserve separate treatment. This particular debate[14] is perhaps less specifically economic: the ecological approach is an inter-disciplinary one, and for this reason has earned the criticism of being weak (if not downright misleading) on economic theory. Its inclusion here is based perhaps less on the force and originality of its economic analysis as on the fact that it has aroused passionate and widespread concern through-out the world, and is seen by some as one of the most funda-mental issues facing contemporary society.

Economists who take an ecological approach stress the need to study a system of organisms in relation to their environment, to themselves and their neighbours, and to examine such considerations as the balance of harm and good. The basic proposition of the ecological school is that our industrial way of life, with its goal of continued expan-sion, is just not sustainable. Present increases in human numbers and *per capita* consumption, by depleting resources and disrupting ecosystems, are undermining the very foundations of survival. Sooner or later our industrial world will come to an end in one of two ways: either against our will in a succession of famines, epidemics, social crises and wars (shades of Malthus!), or by rational, humane pre-paration in which we can plan for a society which will not impose chaos and hardship upon our descendants.

On these arguments, we are threatened on the one hand by

[14] See particularly *A Blueprint for Survival* (1972).

increasing population (with annual growth rates of between
0.5 and 1% in industrial countries, and, more alarmingly,
by rates between 2 and 3% in developing countries) and
rising *per capita* use of energy and raw materials. This
combination of rising population and consumption has a
considerable impact upon the environment, in terms both
of the resources we take from it, and the pollutants we impose upon it.

In the time taken for world population to double (one
estimate gives this as around the year 2000) ecological demand (which is defined as a summation of all man's demands
on the environment, such as the extraction of resources and
the return of wastes) will have increased six times. The
world cannot accommodate this continued increase in
ecological demand: indefinite growth cannot be sustained
by finite resources. We depend for our survival on the pre-
dictability of ecological processes; if they were at all arbitrary we would not know when to reap or sow. Fortunately,
we can formulate ecological laws (e.g., that all ecosystems
tend to stability and that the more diverse and complex the
ecosystem, the more stable it is). By stability is meant
the ability to return to an equilibrium position after any
change.

It is argued, however, that we have been too obsessed with
economic laws rather than ecological laws and we have
treated our environment with scant regard. Hence we have
disrupted our ecosystems, moved along the road to food
shortages, if not famine; we are exhausting our resources,
and by precipitating distress and social chaos we may be
moving towards a collapse of society. What are the remedies
for this deplorable state of affairs? One solution is to reduce
environmental disruption by technical means, e.g., pollution control, re-cycling of materials, etc. Another is to convert from 'flow' to 'stock' economics by effective resource

management and social accounting. We should introduce a raw material tax to penalize resource-intensive industries, and favour employment-intensive ones, and an amortization tax to penalize short-lived products. This tax would also encourage craftsmanship and employment-intensive industries. Social accounting would take more account of disamenity (or more positively, the enhancing of amenity, reinforced by disamenity legislation). These accounting procedures must be used not just to weigh up the merits of alternative development proposals, but whether or not society actually wants such development. We must avoid the imposition on poor neighbourhoods or sparsely inhabited countryside of such things as nuclear power stations and motorways. Social costs of development should be paid by those who propose to perpetrate it – i.e., the polluter must pay. Then there is the neo-Malthusian argument that we must stabilize the population by such methods as education in birth control, the provision of free contraception and sterilization, and abortions on demand. The Schumacher argument is also invoked to create a new social system by decentralization. ' Small is beautiful ' is the principle here; e.g., small farms rather than prairie-type crop-growing or factory-type livestock rearing. Small farms can become productive suppliers of eggs, fruit and vegetables to neighbourhoods. A more diversified urban mix will then become possible. Reduction in transport costs and the return of domestic sewage to the land will thus be facilitated. Small communities are desirable because they reduce human impact on the environment. For example, the urban superstructure required per inhabitant rises rapidly as the size of a town increases beyond a certain point (the *per capita* cost of high-rise flats is much greater than that of ordinary houses, and the cost of roads increases with the number of vehicles carried). Politically, decision-making should, when possible (and admittedly it will not always be possible) be at the community level, and there must be a sensitive and efficient method of communications between all communities.

The ecological debate has been greatly enlivened (and given increased economic precision) by the intervention of Professor Kenneth Boulding in a series of articles and lectures during the 1970s. He brings in the twin concepts of reservoirs of raw materials (the beginning of the economic process) and reservoirs of pollution (the end). He demonstrates that the success of a country's economy is at present measured by the amount of throughput derived in part from the reservoirs of raw materials, processed by factors of production, and passed on in part as output to the pollution reservoirs. Gross National Product roughly measures this output. However, both the reservoirs of raw materials and the reservoirs of pollution are finite and limited, so that ultimately the throughput from the one to the other must be detrimental to our well-being and must therefore not only be minimized but regarded as a cost rather than a benefit. We should reduce our obsession with income-flow concepts and look more at capital-stock concepts. The more effectively technology can show us how to maintain stock with less throughput (i.e., a reduction in production and consumption) the better it will be.

In a provocative and lively manner, Professor Boulding stands a number of basic economic propositions on their heads, and re-defines welfare in a novel way. An important new goal is added to our objectives – the overwhelming need to re-cycle our waste products in order to keep our resource base replenished. An armoury of fiscal measures and new forms of social accounting (on this view) should be devised to secure this aim – measures which may run counter to Keynesian thinking.

One problem of basing taxation and expenditure policies

on long-term ecological estimates is that the economist has to rely upon outside experts who are by no means agreed among themselves. As we saw in the debate in monetarism, serious difficulties arise from the fact that economists themselves are not in agreement on a number of initial issues; how much more difficult if we have to call in experts from other fields who also fail to agree on such issues as future world production possibilities in food or energy. Long-term population forecasts are subject to similar disagreements among the experts. Even if we admit the consequences of exponential growth on finite resources, it may be argued that the classic operation of the laws of demand and supply upon price will provide the incentives for us to substitute resources that are plentiful for those which are running out. However, the solution provided by the market mechanism may be limited by a possible gap, for instance, between the exhaustion of fossil fuels and the discovery of an effective fusion power system (scientists do not seem to be agreed on how much time we have before such a system is operative, and a crisis situation could develop in any interlude which might occur).

Against this, there is some ground for optimism, in the fact that the rate at which human beings can discover substitutes is increasing as the rate of technological change is increasing. Government and industry will be stimulated to conduct research and development to bring about necessary transfers of production and consumption. As world consumption increases, it is admittedly possible that people will attach less importance to the frantic accumulation of new consumer goods; but it may be argued that we have a long way to go before the world reaches this stage. To 'freeze' economic growth prematurely would involve us in the danger of freezing present inequalities of income, particularly on an international scale. Some economists admit the strength of the ecological diagnosis, but are wary of the remedies proposed: sudden crisis action to halt growth could bring about the very social chaos which the ecologists wish to avoid. A consensus economic reply to the ecology school would probably be to say thank you for the warnings, particularly the need for better planetary resource management: but a more empirical and gradual approach (e.g., perhaps some cautious experiments with fiscal measures) is preferable to dramatic, arbitrary action here and now.

The Neo-Marxist Approach

The three issues which we have discussed – monetarism, consumer sovereignty and ecology – do not, of course, exhaust the economic controversies of the present day. Alongside these debates, there is a wealth of literature from the pens of Marxist economists, challenging contemporary economic thought and policy, and frequently re-formulating and re-assessing Marxist economic ideas. Some of these Marxist contributions have been concerned with similar problems to those raised by such writers as Galbraith and Mishan who see the problem of ' relative over-consumption ' as one in which the political process has not been able to achieve optimum allocation (i.e., a position in conformity with the dominating preferences in society between private consumption, public consumption and the quality of the environment). The quality of life is said to be sacrificed by too much concentration on the output of commodities and the level of private consumption, with the consequent neglect of the externalities of production and consumption. Marxist analysis is, of course, more concerned with what it believes to be the fundamental contradictions in the system, and these cannot be corrected by tinkering with the balance between public and private consumption. It is also agreed that the blame for the misallocation of resources lies not so much in this imbalance as in the short-term objectives of technology in a capitalist system (a view which is arrived at by a different route by the ecologists). These lead to a readiness to sacrifice the future for the present and to achieve short-lived successes at the cost of future crises. Thus, a scientific and technological system which claims to be rational is, in fact, irrational, because its definition of rationality is too narrow. This criticism challenges the neutrality of scientific and technological processes, although it accepts that the isolation of partial phenomena from their wider context can be intellectually useful. However, it believes that this isolation obscures their relationship to the capitalist context as a whole. Thus, capitalism has discovered that this partial philosophy enables it to ignore the side-effects and consequences of technological activity and to pursue the exploitation of man and nature under the guise of a scientific and technological neutrality. This results in the misallocation, not only of material resources, but also of human resources. Under capitalism, industry produces an increasing number of technical miracles which few people want, while the vast majority of human beings develop only a small fraction of their capacities. While the ecologists see the coming crisis as largely due to the exploitation of nature by man, the Marxist criticism directs more attention to the exploitation of man by his fellow man. The universality of the ecological criticism (which could apply to both communist and non-communist societies) is in contrast to the Marxist view which sees the problem as specifically created by the capitalist system.

Two distinguished American scholars who have developed Marxist analysis to include more recent trends (e.g., in the growth of monopoly) are Paul M. Sweezy, *Theory of Capitalist Development* (1952),[15] and Paul Baran and Paul M. Sweezy, *Monopoly Capitalism* (1966). They have kept alive a specifically Marxist critique of the changes which are chronicled (from a different critical stance) by writers like Galbraith and Schumacher.

Like Galbraith and Schumacher, they are sceptical of the concept of consumer sovereignty and turn their attention to the forces governing supply rather than demand. They focus attention on the power of monopolies in the present era of capitalism. Marx had seen monopolies in two ways: first as remnants of the feudalist and mercantilist past, and second, as an aspect of the trend towards the concentration and centralization of capital inherent in a competitive economy.

There is, however, no coherent economic theory of monopoly in Marx's original analysis. Baran and Sweezy try to remedy this omission by using Marxist tools to bring the theory up to date. They continue the use of Marx's method of isolating 'contradictions' in the system, and they see monopoly capitalism as a major contradiction. It generates increasing surplus, but fails to provide consumption and investment outlets required to absorb surplus at this level. Because surplus which cannot be absorbed will not be produced, the normal state of monopoly capitalism will be stagnation. Human and material resources are, therefore, under-utilized. What happens is that the system must operate at a point low enough on its profitability schedule not to generate more surplus than can be absorbed. As the profitability schedule is always moving upward, there is a corresponding downdrift of the 'equilibrium' operating rate. The ability of monopoly capitalism to absorb as much

[15] For an interesting Marxist commentary on Keynesian economics, see also Paul M. Sweezy in Robert Lekachman (editor), *Keynes General Theory: report of three decades* (1964).

surplus as it is capable of producing leads to unemployment, to agricultural surpluses, and to the constant dilemma of entrepreneurs who find that sales are falling short of what could profitably be produced. This production of 'too much rather than too little' is not a micro-economic problem which can be corrected by market forces, but it is a pervasive problem affecting everyone at all times. Nor is it possible to stimulate demand through price reduction: this, according to Baran and Sweezy, is impossible within the framework of monopoly capitalism. There is the further problem that the giant corporation withdraws large segments of economic activity from the sphere of the market, and subjects this to scientifically designed administration. This change represents a continuous increase in the rationality of the whole – the monopoly interest, on the contrary, lies in maintaining scarcity in the midst of potential plenty. Human and material resources remain idle because there is in the market no *quid* to exchange against the *quo* of their potential output.

We are forced to witness the spectacle of large pockets of poverty in advanced industrial countries, while millions suffer from disease and starvation in the developing countries. According to Baran and Sweezy, this is because there is no mechanism for effecting an exchange of what they produce for what they so desperately need. Insistence on the inviolability of equivalent exchange is not, in these circumstances, rational. We witness the additional absurdity of strictly economizing human and material resources when a large proportion of them goes to waste.

These economists are sceptical of the use of the words 'free enterprise system'. In America, it could perhaps have been argued, at one time, that competitive capitalism was relatively freer than the restriction involved in the mercantilist state, or the old guild system; but to describe the exercise of power by large corporations as 'free enterprise' is, it is argued, a shibboleth devoid of all explanatory or descriptive validity. To sum up, the contradiction of monopoly capitalism lies in the contrast between the increasing rationality of society's methods of production and organization on the one hand, and the irrationality in the functioning (and in the traditional economist's perception) of the system as a whole.

Although there is a new Marxist diagnosis in the Baran–Sweezy approach, their remedy remains fundamentally that of the master himself: the overthrow of bourgeois ideology (in all spheres) and the replacement of capitalism by a communist system. They would certainly not be satisfied by the piecemeal reforms of a Galbraith or a Mishan, or the idealistic exhortations of a Schumacher.

A dissident Marxist view was presented by Eugene Varga in *Changes in the Economy of Capitalism Resulting from World War II* (1947). He questioned the assumption of the inevitable downfall of capitalism as postulated by Marx (and by Lenin, who had widened the assumptions of a closed economy to take account of international exchange and investment, but whose prediction of capitalist doom was as categorical as Marx's). Varga agreed that capitalism was becoming more stable, largely through the techniques of state intervention, and planning (which had been strengthened by wartime experience). The speed with which former colonial possessions achieved national independence in the aftermath of the war also seemed to weaken Lenin's prophecies of doom, based on the instability and contradictions of the relationships between capitalist countries and their colonies. Varga came close to admitting that capitalist societies were capable of orderly internal change. This viewpoint dealt a severe blow to Marxist revolutionary theory, and it is scarcely surprising that Varga was denounced by the Soviet Academy of Science, and suffered victimization at the hands of the Soviet authorities.

Although as we have seen, there are areas where Marxism and the ecological school overlap, there is one area of sharp division. This is in population theory. Whereas the ecologists are shrouded in Malthusian gloom, Marxists steadfastly refuse to admit the economic advantages of restraints on population growth. Orthodox Marxist theory remains a separate and self-contained minority viewpoint within the corpus of Western economic thought, and has probably less in common with contemporary economics than it had with its classical predecessors. Another development in Marxist economic thought, while retaining some ideas in common with the writers discussed above, pursues a sufficiently differentiated approach to justify separate consideration. This is the so-called ' New Left '. In the New Left, economic ideas are linked to activism; ideas are used both as an explanation of events and a spur to activity. This makes discussion of the economic doctrines of the New Left more than normally controversial because criticism of the economic ideas is often taken as a criticism of the particular issues that are the centre of protest, when in fact the critic may be out of sympathy with the former while in sympathy with the latter.

For the purposes of this book, we will try to concentrate only on the economic content of the New Left and avoid, as far as possible, being drawn into the political content of their activism.

Economic Doctrines of the New Left

The first thing to note about the New Left is that it is heterogeneous. There are, literally, dozens of schools of thought within the Marxist tradition and many authorities for its modern interpretations. We can only give a summary of concepts and ideas which in their natural setting involve subtle and sometimes convoluted complexities and which, for those readers looking beyond graduation, promise plenty of scope for research degrees and treatises. The second thing to note about the New Left is that its economics are largely a critique of non-Marxist economic theory and contemporary economic arrangements, rather than a coherent exposition of an alternative theory or an alternative society. This results in a dialogue of the deaf between Marxists and non-Marxists each addressing themselves to different aspects of the same problem from entirely different premises. At the risk of over-simplification, we can highlight a number of crucial differences between the New Left and modern consensus economics. These include the antithesis between such concepts as markets and bureaucracy, co-operation and competition, material and moral incentives, private and public ownership. On a wider canvas they raise controversies over such issues as the economic basis of imperialism and domination, and the economic basis of war and peace. This summary should give a flavour of the economics of the New Left, and hopefully, encourage the reader to embark on further study of the writers of various points of view.[16]

One thing that unites most of the disparate tendencies that make up the New Left is a firm hostility to markets which are seen as the centre-piece of all capitalist systems for the allocation of goods and services. One radical economics text summed up the differences between supporters and critics of the market mechanism by noting that 'one's view of the desirability of the market system depends on whether one is more impressed with the efficacy and impersonality

[16] See particularly Assar Lindbeck, *The Political Economy of the New Left: an outsider's view* (1977), for a critique of new left economics.

of this allocation mechanism or with its lop-sided results.'[17] Another critic has stated that a 'market is also a financial slaughter-house, where the strong chop up the weak.'[18] Basically, these are powerful criticisms not of markets *per se*, but of the distribution of income, wealth or power among citizens in the economy. It can be argued that decisions as to what are the right distributions of relative market or political power in a society are not necessarily the same as decisions as to the right allocative mechanism for a society's goods and services among the citizens. A major argument in favour of a market mechanism is that, in allocative terms, it is probably more efficient compared with likely alternatives.

Critics of markets as an allocative mechanism must supply an alternative. There has been no shortage of alternatives offered from the wildly utopian (everybody doing what they want to do) to the extremely centralist (everybody doing what they are told to do). The experience of the planned economy in Stalin's Russia divides the New Left from the Old Left. In the latter, criticism of capitalism was to a large extent discredited by association with the alleged totalitarian excesses of the Communist Party in power. In the former, an attempt has been made to distance their criticism of capitalism from association with the patently unattractive features of bureaucratic socialism. Hence, one finds in New Left literature criticism of the Russian, but rarely criticism of Chinese, experience of non-market socialism. All societies must find a way to collect information on resource availability, consumer or social preferences and technological possibilities. Information-collecting is only one part of the task. Information has to be translated

---

[17] E. K. Hunt and Howard Sherman, *Economics: an introduction to traditional and radical views* (2nd edition, 1975), p.207.
[18] D. T. Bazelon, *The Paper Economy* (1963), p.52.

CONTEMPORARY ECONOMIC CONTROVERSIES

in some way into productive organization. This will require some form of incentive for millions of people to co-ordinate their activities in such a way that what people want is made available in sufficient quantities at acceptable standards of quality at approximately the right place and time. The more complex or developed the society the more complex the information and co-ordinating problem. Writers like Professor A. J. Hayek are eloquent exponents of the achievements of capitalism in solving this problem.

In the absence of markets the task falls on bureaucracies. They have to plan everything that is to happen in the economy, which involves millions of decisions, most of them interlinked – if, for instance, steel production fails to meet planned targets then outputs which use steel as an input will fall below their targets. There is no question that some sort of planning on such a gigantic scale is possible (as the experience of the USSR demonstrates). The development of powerful computers will assist the allocative mechanisms of the planned economy. But the central question that remains as yet unanswered is whether bureaucratic planning can avoid a non-democratic environment and be as efficient as a market system. If the inequities of the market are a disadvantage of non-socialist economies it is also plausible that the inequities of bureaucratic socialism are a disadvantage of non-capitalist economies.

Some would agree that the totalitarian consequences of bureaucracy are inevitably the result of abandoning markets for allocating resources. Where there are shortages in a market, prices will rise to eliminate customers who must do without or secure money to make a purchase. Where there are shortages in a bureaucratic system the bureaucrats can supply their loyal supporters; ration the goods, with the attendant escalation of bureaucracy to administer the rationing system; or supply the first in the queue only. To keep order in the queues police are necessary; to control dissent, it must be punished. The cycle of shortage and control follows from the nature of the allocative mechanism. This leaves the New Left critic of capitalist-type markets in a quandary. To be against markets *and* against bureaucracy exhausts experience of available allocative mechanisms. The critic is forced back to a pre-1917 position which ignores the events of the past 60 years. This is all the more ironical in that a frequent criticism of orthodox economics is that it is *ahistorical*, or outside the experience of the real world. Competition is a frequent target for New Left critics of capitalism and there is no doubt that long lists of wasteful expenditures can be drawn up. Baran and Sweezy calculated that the difference between what society produced and what it cost to produce, which they defined as the surplus available to that society 'for whatever goals it may set itself '[19] reached about 56% of 1963 U.S. GNP. They further calculated that well over half of that surplus was accounted for by waste in distribution and corporate advertising expenditures, or in other words the 'process of selling the output of the business' which includes advertising, market research, expense-account entertaining, the maintenance of excessive numbers of sales outlets and the salaries and bonuses of salesmen.[20] To this catalogue of waste is added a heavy moralizing tone that in some way competition between people, or groups of people in firms, is unethical. It is far better, ethically, for people to co-operate with each other, to seek to help each other, to be more human in their relationships and to offer a friendly hand to those in need or distress.

Although ethics is thought to be outside the scope of

[19] Paul A. Baran and Paul M. Sweezy, *Monopoly Capital: an essay on the American economic and social order* (1966), pp.9 and 389.
[20] *Ibid.*, pp.379-380.

economics, most readers would accept the moral require-
ment to help others. In terms of individual moral standards
it is doubtful whether people are less co-operative and helpful in capitalist societies than they are in socialist societies
or that co-operation and help has declined or increased historically. Given that most religions in the world preach the
spirit of neighbourly love, it is an audacious person who
claims any particular society or economic system engenders
more of it than another. Nor is competition always a natural
feature of capitalism. Adam Smith warned two centuries
ago of the monopolizing spirit of 'merchants and manufacturers' and how these capitalists would conspire against
the public at the first opportunity if given the chance. Experience shows how capitalist firms grow to absorb their
rivals which, in effect, limits and curtails the competitive
market – they expand to eliminate competition rather than
enforce it. It takes a most determined anti-monopoly government to enforce competitive rules in capitalist markets. A
capitalist, in his individual capacity, appears as willing to
forsake the market as a socialist is to criticize it. Competition
forces change by challenging accepted ways of producing or
supplying goods and services and it does this relentlessly
through innovation and efficiency-seeking activity. The
urge for the 'quiet life' with protected profits is probably as
strong among capitalists as a quiet life with high wages is
among employees. The real problem is that the quiet life
could leave things as they are at any particular moment,
with incomes and means for millions of people in the world
well below the level that makes the quiet life for a minority
tolerable. Without some mechanism of cost-cutting and
some way of responding to what people want – which is
essentially what the objective of competition is about, whatever the social basis of society – the result is stagnation and
competition of another kind through political, nepotistic

or racial means. A not inappropriate example of non-market competition is to be found in the sometimes violent and abusive competition between the various groups and parties of the New Left for the hearts and minds of students. Hunt and Sherman, quoted earlier, present the role of profit in a capitalist economy in the following clear way:

'Capitalists, or their hired managers, are motivated primarily by their drive to maximise profits. They go to market to hire labour and buy raw materials, which they combine with the factories, machinery and tools they own in order to produce an output ... they then sell their output in the market. Their objective is to maximise the difference between their sales proceeds and their money expenses incurred in buying raw materials, hiring labour, and replacing used-up capital. This difference is, of course, profits. They constantly search for commodities that can be produced and sold profitably. The capitalists' cost of production represent income to labourers and the owners of raw materials. Profit is the income that accrues to the capitalist. The recipients of these incomes spend them in the market for the goods produced by the capitalists' business firms. Thus money circulates from the business firms to the general public in the form of incomes generated in the production process. The money then returns to the business firms when the public purchases the goods and services these firms sell in the market.'[21]

The incentive to find efficient means of producing goods and services is the profit motive – if it is not profitable, capitalists will move out of that particular line of production and into one that is; they do not require to be told to do so by a bureaucracy. Life, of course, is always more complex than simple illustrations. But Marx was among those who was prepared to give credit where it is due; he saw the capitalist system in both its productive and counter-productive lights. 'The bourgeoisie,' he noted in 1849, 'during its role of scarce

[21] Hunt and Sherman, *op. cit.*, p.206.

one hundred years, has created more massive and more colossal productive forces than have all the preceding generations together.'[22] The supreme governing motive of the capitalist in Marx's time and ours is that of profit. Adam Smith called such motivation (in another context) an 'invisible hand' and so, in a sense, it is. It ensures that somebody puts together the necessary means, sometimes at great personal risk and effort, to produce an output for which other people are prepared to pay.

As Bastiat pointed out long ago, while Paris sleeps, thousands of people are working to bring to it all the food it can consume and clothes it can wear, not because they know or care about the welfare of the inhabitants, nor because they are conscripted by a government to do so, but because their own livelihood depends on it.

So powerful is this motivation when utilized by an economy, that the central planners of Russia, Hungary, Czechoslovakia and Poland have experimented with profit-based incentive systems as an alternative to their own incentive systems devised within strict non-profit rules. In their criticism of profit making, the New Left is not dissimiliar from the Old Left; the goal is to produce for need rather than for profit. This, once again, has a powerful emotive appeal, provided we can agree on what is meant by need and in what circumstances this conflicts with profit. It is easy to think of examples of obvious needs conflicting with profits. Hunt and Sherman note that a profit system can place ' more importance on psychiatric care for the neurotic pets of the wealthy than it does on the providing of minimal health services for the children of the poor '.[23] High living is not, however, an exclusive preserve of capi-

[22] Karl Marx and Frederick Engels, *The Communist Manifesto* (1849).
[23] Hunt and Sherman, *op. cit.*, p.206.

talism; one of the many criticisms of Madame Mao in the recent Chinese purge was her alleged life style in expensive villas, and her proclivity for private showings of western-world films, and a frequent criticism of the Soviet Union by the Trotskyist wing of the New Left is the privileged life-style of the bureaucracy.

The search for New Proletarian Man (whose productive energies are unleashed under new socialist freedoms) permeates much of the New Left's writings and speeches. It is by no means cynical, and as a standard of conduct towards which people might be encouraged to conform it has its merits. After all, the message of Christianity, in its many forms, set standards of conduct probably beyond the abilities of all but a few to meet, but this is not an argument for abandoning Christianity. However, it is doubtful if the introduction of economic systems based on the assumption that such highly motivated people already exist is likely to score dramatic production and consumption levels comparable to the levels we know today, or have seen in the more distant past. Experience – alas! a brutal school for idealists – suggests that abandoning material incentives – be it a profit-based production system, or a differential incentive wages system – leads to significant and substantial inefficiences. Where moral man fails, coercive man intervenes, and the history of most socialist societies of the communist model has been one of the use of coercion as a substitute for incentive. The connection is unlikely to be accidental.

This might explain why some campus (and just off-campus) radicals favour a scrapping of the entire industrial system as we know it as the only way to create a society in which people can be human and moral towards each other. No economist could prove that such communes are worse than what we have got inside our industrial systems, but the costs of reverting to such a life deserve attention.

There is no economic proof of the superiority or inferiority of commune life styles. The practical point is that millions of people in the world are unlikely to opt for them while they have knowledge of the alternatives available.

On the relative merits of private and public ownership ideological debate comes closer to economic analysis. In the standard textbook presentation of the circular flow of income,[24] the owners of the factors of production – land, labour and capital – receive incomes from the sale of those factor services to business units which use the factor units to produce outputs for sale in markets to final consumers, who buy what is for sale according to their ‘dollar votes’. The New Left (e.g., Linder) attack this presentation because it cloaks the reality of the imbalance in factor ownership in capitalist societies.

It could be argued that the New Left have some substance in their criticisms. Factor ownership is maldistributed to the extent that most people do not own anything other than their abilities to work as employees for those who own capital assets (business firms). The individual employee confronts the employer in an unequal relationship by virtue of owning nothing other than a capacity to work; without work, the employee will earn no income and without some other form of subsistence the employee will simply starve. Put this way, which is extreme (because it ignores the ability of employees to correct the imbalance through collective unionization and also the existence of social-security programmes in most modern societies), the imbalance can be seen to be veiled by presentations that simply lump all factor owners together as if they were equal in bargaining power. There is widespread consensus, certainly among social-democratic countries, that the naked imbalance of

[24] Paul A. Samuelson, *Economics* (10th edition, 1976), p.46.

power in a purely capitalist society has many drawbacks and unfortunate consequences. There is also a long record of legislative measures and extra-parliamentary pressures to create what Galbraith called 'counter-vailing powers' in these societies. The existence of the welfare state and independent trade-union movements are two manifestations of this counter-vailing power. However, there is still room for debate as to the effectiveness and the consequences of counter-vailing power of this kind.

For the present we will concentrate on the alternatives proposed by the New Left. They propose, in one form or another, to take into public or common ownership the means of production. This will eliminate private ownership of capital assets and, necessarily, private incomes from that ownership. The question that is raised here, then, is what effect will such a change have on the distribution of factor incomes in society? It is not obvious that it will have much effect. A small minority who were very rich from their capital ownership may suffer, but for the vast majority of income earners who would remain as employees, nothing will change, except that in name they will now be owners of the capital assets through 'public ownership'.

It can be argued that public ownership could actually worsen the imbalance of power in society against the majority of the population. There are two lines of evidence available for this belief; firstly, there is the experience of state nationalization in capitalist societies; and secondly, there is the experience of total public ownership in the communist countries. In mixed capitalist–public ownership societies, such as Britain, the power relationship inside the capitalist firms does not appear to be markedly different from the power relationship in the nationalized firms. It could be argued that in nationalized firms which have a monopoly of a product or industry, the power relationship is more unequal, because the individual is confronting a single – the only – employer of his services and loss of a job through a management decision or withdrawal of trade-union membership means total removal from employment in that industry. One of the arguments used at the time of the introduction of commercial television into Great Britain was that the BBC monopoly placed broadcasting staffs too much at the mercy of a single employer. In centralized public-ownership economies, such as Russia, the problem of power imbalance could be greater; loss of position by an individual could mean severe economic hardship, quite apart from the political hazards of offending the state bureaucracy. While the New Left is critical of Samuelson-type circular-flow models, the circular-flow model of a public ownership society is equally, if not more so, open to criticism because it can mask the nature of the maldistribution of power in such societies. Much more debate and discussion has to take place before a workable system of running a complex society can be devised which meets both the egalitarian ideals of the New Left, and the output standards of the mixed capitalist economies of the West.

Imperialism and Domination

An interesting feature of New Left economic thinking is its reassessment of Lenin's theories. The 'classical' exposition of Marxist-based theories of Imperialism go back to Lenin's time, and in particular, his book *Imperialism: the Highest Stage of Capitalism* (1917). The classical theories attempted to explain the scramble for overseas possessions by the European powers at the end of the 19th century. The Leninist theory was unsatisfactory, in that it did not fit all the facts, although it provided a partial explanation. He had argued that imperialism was necessary for capitalist economies which faced excessive productive capacity in the home markets and a declining rate of profit (as home investment soaked up profitable opportunities). This led to a net out-flow of capital, and the acquisition of colonies was one way of securing investment outlets. This could only be achieved, however, at the expense of intense national rivalry with other European capitalist economies. The result was war; the objective of these wars was a re-division of the 'spoils'. One possible objection to this theory was the fact that the bulk of British capital exports went to North America and Australasia and South Africa, while the territorial expansion occurred elsewhere in Africa and Asia. In other words, capital flowed mainly to already existing developed capitalist economies, while spasmodic warfare was waged in expeditions to the underdeveloped economies. If imperialism, as Lenin knew it, was the 'highest stage of capitalism', subsequent developments since 1917 suggest it might have been the highest stage but one. In economic terms, striking differences have taken place; the real incomes of the workers in western capitalist-type economies have grown enormously since Lenin wrote: the share of GNP accruing to the State in western economies has risen dramatically (to over 50% in Britain) to create an increased internal demand for goods and services in health, education, welfare and military defence. Political independence has been attained in all but a few island colonies since 1945. New situations demand new theories and this is where the contribution of the New Left has focussed on new issues for economic debate. Among these new theories of imperialism, mention should be made of Magdoff[25] which relates it to the need to secure supplies of raw materials for capitalist economies, Moran's theory which relates imperialism to a response to barriers to trade,[26]

[25] Harry Magdoff, *The Age of Imperialism* (1969).
[26] T. Moran: 'Foreign Expansion as an Institutional Necessity for US Corporate Capitalism: the search for a radical model', *World Politics* (April, 1973).

and Galtung's theory of imperialism as the relationship between the centre (the ' top-dogs ') of the centre nations, and
the centre of the peripheral nations which combine to exploit
the Third World economies for raw material essential to the
economies of the industrialized nations. There is also
Emmanuel's theory of imperialism based on the ' development of under-development' through the transfer of resources from low-wage Third-World countries, to high-
produce-price industrialized countries.[27] This is basically a
terms-of-trade theory in which the rich countries (through
the domination of the world economy) worsen the terms-of-
trade of the poor countries in an ' unequal exchange ' of
products between them. Wage rises in the rich countries
push up prices which lowers international profit rates in rich
and poor countries. In the poor countries, prices must fall –
wages are already low – to maintain the volume of exports to
the rich countries. Thus, underdevelopment worsens and
the gap between rich and poor widens.

The economic theory of imperialism does not fully explain why countries go to a lot of trouble to acquire land
space where the economic potential is nearly zero, if not
negative. The period ranging from the scramble for Africa
in the 1870s to America's involvement in Vietnam in the
1960s cannot easily be explained by a simple economic
theory of imperialism on these lines.

There is also the problem of whether Communist countries can be equally as guilty of economic imperialism as
capitalist ones. Does this require a reformulation of the
economic theory of imperialism? In the case of Russian involvement in Eastern Europe (which involves economic as
well as political arrangements between the Russians and

[27] J. Galtung, ' A structural theory of imperialism ', *Journal of Peace Research*, no. 2 (1971); A. Emmanuel, *Unequal Exchange* (1972).

their allies) it can be argued that some economic benefits accrue to the Russian economy, possibly at the expense of Eastern Europeans. If socialist economies can engage in socialist imperialism and economic exploitation, this phenomena must be properly analysed by the economic imperialism school of thought.

In this last section we will take up briefly two representative, if opposed views from the New Left on the issues of war and peace and the contribution to both of capitalist economies.

First, the views of Ernest Mandel, one of the European leaders of the New Left. In his book *Marxist Economic Theory* (1968) he presented the relationship between defence expenditures and capitalism in the following way: ' The ever greater – and stable – share of armament expenditure in the national income of all capitalist nations is the chief factor determining the growth of public expenditure in the national budget; the development of the social services plays only a secondary role in this connection – a role which is often, moreover, indirectly linked with the arms economy.'[28]

The analysis runs into difficulties at the level of empirical evidence. Firstly, military expenditures do not represent an ever greater, or even stable, share of national income in ' all capitalist nations '. Since Mandel's book appeared, the share of defence in GNP in NATO countries (all of them mixed-capitalist economies) has been declining and it has been declining fastest as a share of government expenditure.[29] If ' armament expenditure ' is declining as a share of both GNP and the state budget, it can hardly be a chief cause of the growth of public expenditure. Indeed, Mandel's asser-

[28] Ernest Mandel, *Marxist Economic Theory*, 2 Vols. (1968), Vol. 2, p.254.
[29] Gavin Kennedy, *The Economics of Defence* (1975).

tion that social services play 'only a secondary role' in the expansion of the public budget is contradicted by experience in Britain, where the central problem of government appears in the form of how to contain the ever greater demands of the social services.

Mandel's critics argue that it was a mistake to take a short-term trend in military expenditures and link them to a political criticism of the Cold War and to a political belief in the 'crisis of capitalism'. On this view, Mandel undervalued the impact of the social democratic programmes of welfare expenditures prevalent in most European countries and overstated the importance of war preparations in an international atmosphere of severe distrust between the communist and capitalist nations.

Turning to another New Left writer, Michael Kidron, we find an exposition of the alleged relationship between capitalism and war in his book *Western Capitalism Since the War* (1970). In this version of the relationship we find a similar analytical framework to that of Lenin's regarding imperialism – over-production and excess capital flows – being applied to defence expenditures. Kidron writes:

'In so far as capital is taxed to sustain expenditures on arms, it is deprived of a resource that might otherwise go towards further investment; in so far as expenditure on arms is expenditure on a fast wasting end product, it constitutes a net addition to the market for 'end goods.' ... Were capital left alone to divest its entire pre-tax profit, the state creating demand as and when necessary, growth rates would be very much higher ... once adopted, if only by chance, an arms economy becomes necessary.'[30]

Armaments expenditure is about half of defence expendi-

[30] Michael Kidron, *Western Capitalism Since the War* (1970), chap. 3.

ture, the rest being paid out in pay and allowances for uniformed and civilian personnel. With defence expenditure in Britain at 5% of the GNP, this means that Kidron is postulating a key role in the counter-recessionary measures of the State for armaments expenditures at about 2·5% of the GNP. In the case of other capitalist economies, with total defence expenditures at under 4%, and therefore armament expenditures of under 2%, the use of defence spending as a counter-recessionary measure should not be exaggerated.

Kidron notes the declining ratio of defence to GNP in capitalist states, and predicts a 'freer play for recessionary tendencies' as a result. Yet public expenditures in all capitalist economies have risen more than defence has fallen and in some cases the fall in defence expenditures has been proportional rather than absolute – higher personnel costs and high capital costs of weapon systems force up the defence budget, but growth in the GNP reduces the ratio of defence to GNP.

Mandel and Kidron have in common a view that all capitalist states engage in military preparations in order to seek opportunities to engage in war. Indeed, some writers in the New Left have had grave suspicions that the defence industry in a capitalist economy can actually dominate the political system and secure for itself large and expanding orders for weapons systems. Furthermore, it can encourage a foreign policy that will lead to increasing demands for new supplies of armaments. In the extreme, these authors see America as a 'Warfare State', an 'Economy of Death', as 'Pentagon Capitalism' or as a 'Garrison State' in which the 'military industrial complex' decides defence budgets, foreign policy, and local wars. Once again, more empirical evidence is needed to support these views. Also, from a theoretical and general point of view such explanations must take account of the one economy in the world where defence expenditures are a secularly increasing proportion of GNP, namely the Soviet Union. Here, we have a profound contradiction as yet unexplained: what is the nature of the military industrial complex in Russia? Is it a prop to the economy of a socialist country? What economic role does rising military expenditure have in a planned economy? The economic doctrines of the New Left present significant insights into the nature of the economies of the capitalist type countries which are often omitted from conventional economics text-books, but they are liable to exaggeration of particular relationships, or to incline to excessively sweeping generalizations. Also they do not take sufficient account of certain similarities between relationships inside existing socialist economies and some of the features for which capitalist economies are criticized. This can lead to statements which are confused and contradictory, relying more on aspirations than experience. However, in the history of economic doctrine, such deficiencies are by no means a monopoly of the New Left.

It should also be noted that the best of the New Left exposition is marked by an eloquence and wit which are in the highest traditions of economic writings past and present.

The mood of 'consensus economics' today is one of cautious optimism. It is a little more sceptical of rapid economic growth than perhaps it was two decades ago, and it is not indifferent to the warnings of the ecology school. Economics retains its belief, however, in the importance of material progress. Its definition of 'wealth' may have changed over the last two hundred years, its analysis of the distribution of wealth has become increasingly sophisticated and it provides a more distinctive role for the public sector. Nevertheless, its main preoccupations and its theoretical achievements would still be recognized and appreciated by the author of The Wealth of Nations.

Notes for Further Reading

T H E purpose of these notes is not to provide anything which claims to be regarded as an adequate bibliography, but merely to furnish some suggestions for further reading. The list is therefore restricted to books which are likely to be readily available in a good University or College library, or to be obtainable as new books, or in the second-hand market.

The main problem facing anybody compiling notes on books in this topic is the sheer extent of the titles available. A bibliography in 1964 listed 100 books in the history of economic thought published since 1824, and many dozens more have appeared in the past decade. The subject has attracted enough interest to produce a specialist journal, *History of Political Economy*, and other economics journals, such as the *Scottish Journal of Political Economy*, regularly carry articles on the history of economic ideas.

Many of the books originally recommended by Professor Gray are now unobtainable, being long out of print. Others implied a reading knowledge of foreign languages, probably beyond the reach of many modern students, although perhaps the integrationist forces of the EEC will remedy this during the 1980s. Among the books still available which he recommended is the French classic, *A History of Economic Doctrines* (1948) by G. Gide and C. Rist, in an English translation, and published as recently as 1960. It is still worth consulting.

One of the liveliest outlines is by Robert L. Heilbroner, *The Wordly Philosophers: the lives, times and ideas of the great economic thinkers*, published in 1961. He brings to life the major economists alongside an outline of their ideas. W. E. Kuhn's *The Evolution of Economic Thought* gives good biographical notes on the leading economists of the past at the end of each chapter. A similar format can be found in Horst C. Recktenwald (ed.), *Political Economy: a historical perspective* (1973).

Vincent Bladen, in *From Adam Smith to Maynard Keynes: the heritage of political economy* (1974), provides comprehensive extracts from the major works of Smith, Malthus, Ricardo, Marx, Mill, Jevons, Marshall and Keynes. The extracts are extensive but selective, and are a good start for the new student who wants to read the masters himself, but may shy away from the task of toiling through hundreds of pages. Marc Blaug tackles this in a different way. In his *Economic Theory in Retrospect* (3rd edn., 1979) he analyses the contributions of the major economists from the point of view of modern analysis. For example, he puts Adam Smith's ideas into modern terminology and uses modern textbook diagrams to discuss Smith's strengths and weaknesses. He also provides ' Reader's guides ' to most of the main classics, and detailed notes on further reading. Students hoping to specialize in economics will find Blaug particularly useful, although a knowledge of economics is essential if any benefit is to be gained.

Joseph Schumpeter's *History of Economic Analysis* (1954) (1260 pages) and possibly only for the specialist, is an encylopædic survey of the subject. Those readers hoping to teach economics after graduation should acquire a copy now while it is still in print, as it is unlikely to be surpassed.

At a comparable level of scholarly and comprehensive coverage is O. H. Taylor's 'A History of Economic Thought' (1960).

Joan Robinson's *Economic Philosophy* (1962, and regularly revised) is a *tour de force*, if somewhat controversial. It gives a succinct critique of neo-classical economics and the use of metaphysical and ideological propositions in economic theory. She expresses what is known as the relativist view of economic theory – that economic ideas cannot be divorced from the society in which they originate or find application. Additional material can be found for the relativist position in her *Freedom and Necessity: an introduction to the study of society* (1970): (compare this with John Hicks, *A theory of Economic History* (1969) and Everett J.

Burt, *Social Perspectives in the History of Economic Theory*). Another classic is Karl Polyani's *The Great Transformation* (1964) which is also useful for its contextual discussion of the emergence and meaning of markets.

Guy Routh's *The Origin of Economic Ideas* (1975) can be read with profit by anybody who has completed this book, and readers will find his non-sequential tracing of specific ideas a stimulating support to the way this book has tackled the subject. Sir Eric Roll's *A History of Economic Thought* (1973) remains an outstanding book in this field and students will note several differences in interpretation and approach between it and this book. In this genre, W. J. Barber's *A History of Economic Thought* (1967) is also excellent, relating, as it does, past ideas to the present.

Special

Apart from the foregoing works, which are general and comprehensive in their character, it may be convenient to add a few references to some of the chapters for special reference.

CHAPTER I Schumpeter (1954) Part II, Chapter I, ' Graeco-Roman Economics '.

CHAPTER II R. H. Tawney, *Religion and the Rise of Captitalism; a historical study* (1922) (1964 in paperback).

CHAPTER III Thomas Mun's *England's Treasure* (1664) can be found in J. R. McCullock (ed.), *Early English Tracts on Commerce* (1952); Adam Smith's classic critique of mercantilism will be found in his *Wealth of Nations* (1776) in Book IV, Chapters 1–8. Schumpeter's survey of ' Mercantalist Literature ' will be found in Part II, Chapter 7 (op. cit. 1954) – it is masterly. A full-length study of the subject, originally published in Sweden in 1931, is Eli Heckscher, *Mercantilism* (2 vols, 1955 and 1962), translated by M. Shapiro. It has extensive source notes.

CHAPTER IV A difficult but excellent selection of Quesnay's writings is available in R. L. Meek, *The Economics of Physiocracy; essays and translation* (1962). His main work was published as Marguerite Kuczynski and Ronald L. Meek (eds.), *Quesnay's Tableau Economique* (1972).

CHAPTER V *The Wealth of Nations*, edited by Andrew Skinner, is available in paperback (1970) and in hardcover as Adam Smith, *An Inquiry into the Nature and Causes of the Wealth of Nations* (1776); R. H. Campbell, A. S. Skinner and W. B. Todd (eds.), *Glasgow Edition of the Works and Correspondence of Adam Smith* (1976). This and several other related books were published to mark the bicentenary of the *Wealth of Nations*. Among these the student will find much of interest in Thomas Wilson and A. S. Skinner (eds.), *The Market and the State; papers in honour of Adam Smith* (1977); E. C. Mossner and I. S. Ross (eds.), *The Correspondence of Adam Smith,* and A. S. Skinner and Thomas Wilson (eds.), *Essays on Adam Smith* (1975). In the last volume the essays by A. W. Coats, ' Adam Smith and the Mercantile System '; and A. T. Peacock, 'The Treatment of the principles of Public Finance in the Wealth of Nations ' are particularly valuable.

John Viner's essay ' Adam Smith and Laissez-Faire ' (1927) is reproduced in H. C. Recktenwald (1973) mentioned earlier and is well worth attention, along with the relevant essays in R. L. Meek's *Smith, Marx and After* (1977). A brilliant new study of Smith in the context of the 18th Century is available in Donald Winch, *Adam Smith's Politics, an essay in historiographic revision* (1978). This can be compared with Lionel Robbins, *The Theory of Economic Policy in English Classical Political Economy* (1952).

CHAPTER VI Students will enjoy reading the essay by John Maynard Keynes, ' Thomas Robert Malthus ' (1922) in his *Essays in Biography*, Vol. X, *Collected Writings* (1972). His *Essay on the Principle of Population* (1798) is in paperback (1970) edited by A. Flew.

David Ricardo, *On the Principles of Political Economy and Taxation* (1817) is also in paperback (1971) edited by R. M. Hartnell. A modern hardback edition of this work, edited by P. Sraffa and M. Dobb, was published in 1953, as Vol. 1 of his *Works* (10 vols.). Sraffa's introduction to this volume is particularly interesting.

CHAPTER VIII F. List's *The National System of Political Economy* (1885) was reprinted in 1966. Von Thünen's wages theory can be seen in B. W. Dempsey, *The Frontier Wage* (1960) and his major work in P. Hall (ed.), *Von Thünen's Isolated State* (1966), translated by C. M. Wartenberg.

CHAPTER IX Frederic Bastiat's *Harmonies of Political Economy* (1850) was first published in Edinburgh in 1860. Since then it has become a very rare work in translation; however, his influence runs on in at least one text, though unacknowledged. Paul A. Samuelson's *Economics* (1948) in its 10th edition (1977) still carries a 'paraphrase of a famous economic example' from its first edition, namely, how millions of people can sleep in New York without fear of starving because the market will ensure that what they will need will be provided. This is only one of the many gems from Bastiat which make his *Harmonies* such lively and educative reading.

CHAPTER X Say's *A Treatise on Political Economy, or the Production, Distribution and Consumption of Wealth* (1821) has been reprinted (1964). So has Nassau Senior's *An Outline of the Science of Political Economy* (1836) (1938).

On Mill the literature is extensive. His *Autobiography* (1873), is fascinating for the insight into his ideas. It was reprinted in 1943. M. St. J. Packe's biography, *The Life of John Stuart Mill* (1954) is very good, and should be read with John Plamenatz's *The English Utilitarians* (1958). Pedro Schwartz, *The New Political Economy of John Stuart Mill* (1972) analyses his economics from his philosophical policy prescriptions which is probably the best way to understand his contribution. He also gives a twenty-six page bibliography.

CHAPTER XI The enormous volume of works on Marx makes it difficult to present a balanced selection of manageable proportions. The Pelican *Marx Library* is probably the most accessible. Also useful is Ernest Fischer, *Marx in his own words* (1973), and Robert Freedman (ed.), *Marx on Economics* (1962). A useful outline is Ben Fine's *Marx's Capital* (1975) and, more critically, Joan Robinson's *An Essay on Marxian Economics* (1967). The chapter 'Marx

the Economist' in Joseph Schumpeter's *Capitalism, Socialism and Democracy* (1942) is worth consulting. Boehm-
Bawerk's *Karl Marx and the Close of his System* (1898) was
reprinted with a reply by H. Hilferding ('Boehm-Bawerk's
Criticism of Marx') in 1959, edited by Paul Sweezy. This
is an important criticism of Marx on the contradiction between Vol. I and Vol. III of *Das Capital*, in the treatment of
the labour theory of value.

CHAPTER XII   Three essays in R. D. Collison Black, A. W.
Coats and C. D. W. Goodwin (eds.), *The Marginal Revolution in Economics: interpretation and evaluation* (1973) are
particularly useful to support this chapter; Marc Blaug,
'Was there a marginal revolution'; N. B. de Marchi, 'Mills
and Cairnes and the emergence of marginalism in England'
and V. J. Tarascio 'Vilfredo Pareto and marginalism'. See
also George J. Stigler: 'The development of utility theory'
in his *Essays in the History of Economics* (1951) and T. W.
Hutchinson's scholarly and comprehensive work, *A Review
of Economic Doctrines 1870–1929* (1953), chaps. 8 and 9.

CHAPTER XIII   Good copies of Marshall's *Principles* (1890)
still turn up in second-hand bookshops. The Variorum
edition (2 vols.), is still in print as *Marshall's Principles of
Economics*, edited by C. W. Guillebaud (1961). The key
readings are Books III and V.

John Maynard Keynes wrote a perceptive biographical
essay on his former professor (1924) which is published in
his *Essays in Biography* in Vol. X of his *Collected Writings*
(1972), along with a biographical essay on Marshall's wife,
Mary Paley Marshall, an economist in her own right.

See also A. C. Pigou (ed.), *Memorials of Alfred Marshall*
(1925), reprinted 1956, and his *Alfred Marshall and Current
Thought* (1953).

G. F. Shove's 'The Place of Marshall's *Principles* in the
Development of Economic Theory' (*Economic Journal*,
1942) is reproduced in J. J. Spengler and W. R. Allen (eds.),
Essays in Economic Theory (1960). See also J. Schumpeter,
Ten Great Economists from Marx to Keynes (1951), and
Chapter 4 of T. W. Hutchinson, *Review of Economic Doc-
trines* (1953).

CHAPTER XIV T. Gordlund, *The Life of Knut Wicksell* (1956) and C. G. Uhr, 'Knut Wicksell – a centennial evaluation' in *American Economic Review*, Vol. 41, 1951 are excellent commentaries.

On Joan Robinson see her 'Imperfect Competition revisited' in *Economic Journal*, September, 1953, and her preface to the second edition of *The Economics of Imperfect Competition* (1933), 1969, for her comments on the use made by textbooks of her work in this field. In like spirit, see the symposium 'The Theory of Monopolistic Competition after Thirty Years' in the *American Economic Review*, Vol. 54, 1964.

Chamberlin's own bibliography in successive editions of his book reached one thousand titles – enough to keep the most diligent student busy for a year or more. For a good summary, see J. Bain, 'Chamberlin's impact on microeconomic theory' reprinted in Harry Townsend (ed.), *Price Theory* (1971), and 'Edward Chamberlin – the wastes of competition' in W. Beit and R. L. Ranson, *The Academic Scribblers*.

R. L. N. Heilbroner, in his *The Worldly Philosophers* (op. cit 1961) has a fascinating account of the life and work of Veblen: 'The savage world of Thorstein Veblen.'

CHAPTER XV The various volumes of Keynes *Collected Writings* are specially rewarding, especially Vol. IX, *Essays in Persuasion* (see particularly 'The End of Laissez-Faire,' (1926), and 'Economic Possibilities for our Grandchildren' (1930); also Vol. X, *Essays in Biography*, which has already been cited above.

The most detailed biography of Keynes is R. F. Harrod, *The Life of John Maynard Keynes* (1951), and in paperback (1972). The best short one is Donald Moggridge, *Keynes* (1976). Moggridge is one of the editors of the *Collected Writings* and displays considerable knowledge of the man and his work, in a few pages.

See also Michael Stewart, *Keynes and After* (1967) and R. Lekackman, *The Age of Keynes* (1969) for concise accounts of his theories. For help with *General Theory* (1936) these can be supplemented with Alvin H. Hansen,

A Guide to Keynes (1953). The great work itself is published as Vol. VII of the *Collected Writings*, and in paperback from Macmillan.

CHAPTER XVI For the monetarist debate, with a clear summary of the position for and against, plus a possible synthesis, the best introduction is J. A. Trevithick, *Inflation: a guide to the crisis in economics* (1977). A slightly more difficult book for beginners is A. D. Bain. *The Control of the Money Supply* (1976, 2nd edition). Students will find J. K. Galbraith's *Money: whence it came, where it went* (1977) very lively and provocative.

For Galbraith's economics there are his own writings mentioned in the text: *American Capitalism* (1958), *The Affluent Society* (1958) and *The New Industrial State* (1967). His most recent summary and partial revision is *Economics and the Public Purpose* (1975). There is a lively interchange between Galbraith and Robert M. Solow in *Public Interest* No. 9, Fall, 1967, which is also reproduced in Richard T. Gill, *Economics* 1978, 3rd edn., pp. 584-601. Students should consult Milton Friedman's *From Galbraith to Economic Freedom* (1977) for a criticism of Galbraith.

On the ecological debate a wide choice is available. Among them is Edwin G. Dolan, *TANSTAAFL: The economic strategy for environmental crisis* (1971); (TANSTAAFL means ' there ain't no such thing as a free lunch ').

For a trenchant criticism of some of the more extreme ideas of Dr. Mishan, students must read Wilfred Beckerman, *In Defence of Economic Growth* (1974). This book relates environmental concern to economics; if pollution is to be cleared up this must be recognized as a cost, as well as a benefit, and as a cost it will mean a reduction in either investment or consumption, or both.

The new Left criticism of conventional economics overlaps with a great deal of work from other sources and students would find it best to read widely in this area and refrain from taking any particular work as representative.

Among the general criticisms, Benjamin Ward's *What's wrong with economics* (1972) is a good place to start from. More difficult is Joan Robinson, *Economic Heresies; some old-fashioned questions in Economic Theory* (1971), which could be read alongside her *Economic Philosophy* (1962), followed by Martin Hollis and Edward Nell, *Rational Economic Man: a philosophical critique of neo-classical economics* (1975) and J. A. Kregel, *The Reconstruction of Political Economy; an introduction to post-Keynesian economics* (1973). These express the academic criticism of mainstream economics. They are powerfully challenged in a devastating critique of the new Cambridge School by Marc Blaug: *The Cambridge Revolution: success or failure* (1974).

The shift-over to the New Left criticism can be accomplished by a look through Robin Blackburn (ed.), *Ideology in Social Science: readings in critical social theory* (1972) and thence on to Marc Linder, *Anti-Samuelson*, 1974, 2 vols., which is a blow by blow, almost line by line, critique of one of the world's most popular standard textbooks, Samuelson's *Economics* (1948). Assar Linbeck's *The Political Economy of the New Left: an outsider's view* (1977, 2nd edn.), cited in the text, is an outstanding contribution to the subject. As this is a current debate, still strongly contested on all sides, students are unlikely to be bored by the many aspects of the arguments. In this respect, see Mary Kaldor's *The Disintegrating West* (1979), and Benjamin J. Cohen, *The Question of Imperialism: the political economy of dominance and dependence* (1974), the latter of which both summarizes and criticizes some New Left conceptions and the former of which moves on to new ground.

Some empirical tests of competing theories of imperialism will be found in Steven J. Rosen and James R. Kurth (eds.), *Testing Theories of Economic Imperialism* (1974). The ideas of the New Left on defence are challenged in Gavin Kennedy, *The Economics of Defence* (1975), S. Rosen (ed.), *Testing the Theory of the Military-Industrial Complex* (1973) and Sam C. Sarkesian (ed.), *The Military Industrial Complex; a re-assessment* (1972). They are defended in Labour Party Defence Study Group, *Sense About Defence* (1977), Michael Kidron's *Western Capitalism Since the War* (1970), and R. P. Smith 'Military expenditure and capitalism,' *Cambridge Journal of Economics*, Vol. I, No. 1, 1977. This debate, although somewhat specialized, forms an essential part of any comprehensive treatment of the history of economic ideas.

Two recent expositions of Marxist economics are well worth reading. The first, and most demanding, is: M. C. Howard and J. E. King, *The Political Economy of Marx* (1975). Written by two Marxists it thoroughly develops his analysis and examines it critically. The second is: Angus Walker, *Marx: his theory and its context* (1978). This is a good general introduction to Marx and could usefully be read as an introduction to Howard and King.

A book which examines the attitudes of leading contemporary economists to some of the major political and social issues of the future is Leonard Silk's ' The Economists ' (1976).

Index

INDEX

467

Communist Manifesto, 281,
284, 286–9 and n.¹, 292
Summary of doctrines of, 282–
3
Materialistic conception of
history, 282–3, 286–91, 310
Class struggle, 282–3, 285,
286–7, 288, 291–2, 308; the
bourgeoisie and the pro-
letarians, 287–8, 292, 360,
438–9
Labour theory of value, 161,
162n., 174, 283, 285–6, 287,
293–305 *passim*, 310; notion of surplus value, 283,
289, 298 *et seq.*, 310;
method of exclusion, 294–
5; element of utility, 293,
295; skilled and unskilled
labour, 296–7; constant
capital and variable
capital, 299–301, 303–5,
306–7; discussion of in-
terest, 301–2; managerial
functions, 302
Industrial Reserve Army,
173, 283, 305–6, 307, 308,
309
Law of Capitalistic Accu-
mulation, 283, 305, 307,
308–9
Exploitation, 287–8, 292, 299
Estimation of the prophecies
of, 309–13; defence of, 310–
11
Otherwise mentioned, 21, 157,
158, 161, 387, 408–9
Mazzini, *quoted*, 312
Mediaeval asceticism and accumulation of wealth, 60
Mediaeval economic doctrine.
See Middle Ages.
Menger, Karl, 323, 329–37, 345,

358; *Grundsätze*, 325, 329;
theory of the order of ' goods,'
330–1; economic and non-economic ' goods,' 331–3; theory of
value, 332–7, 339; exchange,
337; Mentioned, 341, 343, 348
Mercantilism, 53 *et seq.*, 73, 77–
8, 109, 112; general outline,
61 *et seq.*; one-sided character,
81; rooted in practice, 61, 67;
fundamentals in, 62–3; and
state making, 56–7; and
balance of trade, 63, 64, 112;
and governmental activity, 64–
6; population, 65; bullionist
aspect, 62–3, 72; appreciation
and criticism, 66–7, 109; four
typical mercantilists, 67 *et seq.*;
divergence from, 77–8; reaction against, 88
Middle Ages, the, 29; economic
teaching of, 29 *et seq.*; feudal
system, 30–1; status, 30–1, 38;
trade, 31; dearth of money,
31; the Church, 31–2, 34–5;
non-national atmosphere, 31–
2, 53, 55; dominant influences,
32–4; economic questions in,
35; just price, 35, 39–41, 48;
usury, 35, 42–8; idea of justice,
35, 41; division of labour, 48–
9; transition period, 53 *et seq.*,
60; fundamental idea, 41;
wages, 41–2; attitude towards
trade, 48–9. *See also* Aquinas
and Oresme.
Mill, James, 261n., 263
Mill, John Stuart, 177, 261 *et
seq.*; position of, in the development of Political Economy,
261–3; the *Principles of Political Economy*, 261, 262, 263;
association of principles with